RAPE INVESTIGATION
HANDBOOK

RAPE INVESTIGATION HANDBOOK

Editors
John O. Savino
Brent E. Turvey, MS

Contributors
Det. John J. Baeza, NYPD, MSVS (ret.)
John Butler, PhD
Terilynne W. Butler
Linda E. Ledray, RN, PhD, SANE-A, FAAN
Michael McGrath, MD
Stephen M. Pittel, PhD
Alan Sandomir
John O. Savino
Laila Spina, PsyD
Brent E. Turvey, MS

ELSEVIER
ACADEMIC
PRESS

Amsterdam • Boston • Heidelberg • London • New York • Oxford
Paris • San Diego • San Francisco • Singapore • Sydney • Tokyo

Acquisition Editor: Mark Listewnik
Project Manager: Sarah Hajduk
Associate Acquisitions Editor: Jennifer Soucy
Developmental Editor: Pamela Chester
Marketing Manager: Christian Nolin
Cover Design: Monty Lewis
Interior Design: Kenneth Burnley
Composition: SNP Best-set Typesetter Ltd., Hong Kong
Printer: The Maple-Vail Book Manufacturing Group
Cover Printer: Phoenix Color

Elsevier Academic Press
30 Corporate Drive, Suite 400, Burlington, MA 01803, USA
525 B Street, Suite 1900, San Diego, California 92101-4495, USA
84 Theobald's Road, London WC1X 8RR, UK

This book is printed on acid-free paper. ∞

Library of Congress Cataloging-in-Publication Data

Rape investigation handbook / by editors, John O. Savino, Brent E. Turvey; contributors, John J. Baeza . . . [et al.].
    p. cm.
  Includes bibliographical references and index.
  ISBN 0-12-072832-X (alk. paper)
  1. Rape–Investigation–United States.   2. Rape–United States.   I. Savino, John O.
II. Turvey, Brent E.   III. Baeza, John J.

  HV8079.R35.R36 2004
  363.25′9532′0973–dc22   2004047096

British Library Cataloguing-in-Publication Data

A catalogue record for this book is available from the British Library

ISBN: 0-12-072832-X

For all information on all Academic Press publications
visit our Web site at www.books.elsevier.com/forensics

Printed in the United States of America
04   05   06   07   08   8   7   6   5   4   3   2   1

"Nothing is more wretched than a man who traverses everything in around, and pries into the things beneath the earth, as the poet says, and seeks by conjecture what is in the minds of his neighbors, without perceiving that it is sufficient to attend to the daemon within him, and to reverence it sincerely."

—Marcus Aurelius, *Meditations, II: 13*

CONTENTS

FOREWORD

Three months after I became Police Commissioner of the City of Philadelphia in March 1998, a young female graduate student was sexually assaulted and murdered by an unknown intruder. I suspected that this was not the first time that this perpetrator had struck and so I directed our detectives to go back over old cases to see whether they could find any evidence of previous attacks by the same person. After spending months searching through old files and sending large numbers of DNA samples to the laboratory for analysis, our investigators reported to me that they believed that he had struck almost exactly one year earlier. In fact, they were now pretty sure that during the summer of 1997 he had sexually assaulted four women under similar circumstances: undetected intrusion into the victims' apartments during the early morning hours while the victims were asleep in their beds.

There were two reasons why the Philadelphia Police Department had failed to detect a serial rapist while he was on the rampage. First, the investigators in our Sexual Battery Unit did not have a case management system that looked for emerging serial patterns. Similar assaults in the same geographic area could be assigned to different investigators depending on when these crimes had occurred and which detective was "catching." There was no system in place to ensure that investigators talked to each other or compared notes about the incidents on which they were working. For this reason, patterns of crime could easily go unnoticed.

Second, and more important, was the Department's procedure for DNA testing of crime scene material. The policy in Philadelphia, as in other police departments across the country, was that DNA tests were conducted in only very limited circumstances: for example, when the local Assistant District Attorney had a person under arrest and facing trial or when a sharp investigator suspected he had a serial rapist on the loose and could persuade his bosses that that DNA might be able to prove his hunch. As a result, the vast majority of DNA samples remained untested in our police lab and property locker just as they did in police departments all across the United States. The problem was a lack of personnel, money, training, and imagination. In addition, there is the tendency of police departments to become overwhelmed by the sheer size of the problem; thousands of cases to be tested and very limited resources leads to almost nothing getting done while everyone sits around complaining about the situation.

But as far as rapes are concerned, the problem is not as large as many believe. The immediate purpose of DNA testing is to identify an offender. But we know that 75 percent of rapes are committed by "known doers": for example, date rapes, incest, neighbors, etc. The question that is usually at issue in these cases is whether the sex was consensual. This is a matter to be determined by a judge and jury. There is no need for DNA testing in these cases. DNA analysis, which is expensive, should be reserved for those rapes committed by "strangers". These are the ones that may include the activities of a serial offender. But these stranger rapes account for only 22 to 25 percent of all rapes reported each year.

For this reason, I directed the Philadelphia Police Department laboratory to do a DNA test on all "stranger" rape kits collected during the last five years, the longest that we could go back and still make an arrest. I also instructed them to do a DNA test on all stranger rapes reported to the Department from now on. Interestingly, while conducting the DNA tests on the old cases, the scientists discovered another serial rapist who had struck three times in another part of the city. Without DNA tests, this person would never have been identified because of the size of the geographic area in which he had struck and the conflicting identifications provided by the victims; one described him as black while another said, correctly, that he was white.

Five months after I had become Chief of the Miami Police Department in January 2003, a serial rapist attacked three young girls over a period of two weeks. While our sexual battery detectives knew that they had a serial rapist on their hands and our DNA tests of material taken from the victims confirmed this, I was not convinced that this was the first time that this particular rapist had been active in our city. I therefore directed our detectives to review all our old cases and focus on "stranger" rapes, just as I had done in Philadelphia. As I suspected, the rapist had struck before, almost a year earlier. But he had struck numerous times and his pattern was not typical. Over the course of a year, he had committed ten sexual assaults. These had involved girls as young as 11 and women as old as their late 70s. Without DNA testing, most of these cases would not have been connected.

Both the Philadelphia and Miami serial rapist were caught because of a combination of modern DNA analysis and old-fashioned detective work. The main lesson for me, however, was the importance of giving detectives much better training in case management and the use of science and technology. It is not an exaggeration to say that science has outpaced training in most police agencies—but it would be unfair to blame police officers and detectives for this situation. It is the responsibility of top management to provide appropriate training for all officers. While the lack of money and resources are real issues, they can never be offered as an excuse. Police departments must do better!

I can think of no better place to start this improvement in training than with this handbook. It is a comprehensive review of the best policies and practices from the moment the first officer arrives on the scene of a crime right up to the trial of the offender. Science and case law are interwoven easily so that even a rookie right out of the police academy will find it comprehensible and useful. I suspect that defense counsel will also use it to brush up their knowledge of science and best practices. Police officers, detectives, laboratory technicians, and state attorneys will all find it invaluable. At a minimum, this book should be available in every precinct, district, and detective squad room for ready reference. Ideally, it should be used by police training academies and colleges to teach students how these investigations should be conducted.

John Timoney
July 2004

PREFACE
THE ROLE OF THE
SEX-CRIMES INVESTIGATOR

From 1981 to 1999, the Sex Crimes Unit in the Philadelphia, Pennsylvania, Police Department dismissed one third of victim complaints without investigation, deliberately mislabeled one fourth of victim complaints to manipulate crime data and make the city appear safer, and managed to maintain one of the worst solve rates in the country (McCoy, 2003). In one record-breaking 3-year period, the number of sex crimes that went uninvestigated exceeded 2000. According to Fazlollah, McCoy, and Moran (2000):

> The sex-crimes unit, founded in 1981, buried nearly a third of its caseload over the next 17 years. Rapes, attempted rapes and other reported acts were given administrative labels such as "investigation of person" or were rejected as unfounded. Either way, they did not show up in crime statistics. The victims were never told their complaints had been shelved.
>
> Current and former investigators said they dumped cases to cope with an overwhelming workload and pressure from commanders to generate favorable statistics.

The supervisors and detectives of that unit betrayed their victims for political gain with apathy, allowed an untold number of offenders to stay on the streets, and ultimately failed to protect the community they were sworn to serve. In short, it was one of the most publicly documented examples of how not to run a major sex-crimes unit in the United States.

After being confronted with these problems in the press, the Philadelphia Police Department came clean and admitted their wrongdoing. Then Police Commissioner John Timoney (shown in Figure FM-1) ordered a review of thousands of unsolved, dead-end cases. To relieve the pressure, he added dozens of new detectives to the unit and assigned some of them solely to that task. And, finally, he invited a handful of legal experts and victim advocates to examine some of those cases and make recommendations about how they might be

Figure FM-1

John Timoney, former Commissioner of the Philadelphia Police Department.

brought back to life. More than dramatic, this combination of reforms was unprecedented.

Four years later, with the benefit of those reforms, the Philadelphia Police Department Sex Crimes Unit experienced marked improvement (McCoy, 2003):

> A squad that was once among the nation's worst now makes more rape arrests than such larger cities as Los Angeles and Houston. Its rate of solving rapes is the best among America's largest cities.
>
> As the squad prepares to move into its new $2 million headquarters next month, it is a third larger; its investigators are better-trained and more motivated.

At the heart of this unit's success was openly admitting the problem, asking for outside advice, and providing the resources to ensure that cases were appropriately investigated. A commitment to integrity, tenacity, and innovation defines the successful sex crimes investigator.

Success in the East is blunted by findings up North, however. In 2001, the state of Alaska had the highest rape rate in the United States; from 1982 to 2001, the rate of rape per 100,000 people in Anchorage, for example, was on average 122% higher than the overall U.S. rate; it ranked fifth when compared to other U.S. metropolitan cities. Between 1999 and 2001, the rape rate increased by 27% in Anchorage; it decreased by 3% nationwide during that same time period (Langworthy and Rosay, 2003).

But the real tragedy in Alaska hasn't been the numbers. It has been the law enforcement response, or rather, lack of response, to the problem of rape and sexual assault. Unbelievably, almost a quarter of the sexual assaults reported are not assigned to a detective. According to published reports, which confirm the experiences of this author (Brant, 2003):

> An internal report released in late October showed that 23 percent of sexual assaults reported to APD are not assigned to a detective, primarily because of staffing shortages.
>
> . . .
>
> Police Chief Walt Monegan could not be reached Friday, but he said in a recent interview that the "solvability" of a case is a major factor when deciding whether to assign it to a detective.
>
> Any case that looks like it can be solved is assigned, Monegan said. "It is the policy of the department, that if we can make an arrest on the case, either with a warrant or an arrest, we will do so," he said.
>
> The difficulty comes when you've got a case that is missing key elements—evidence, a suspect's name, a cooperative victim—and you think maybe you could solve it, but it's going to be very time-consuming, Monegan said. Sometimes those cases have to be set on the back burner so detectives can work the more promising ones.
>
> "Those few cases in the gray area can stockpile," Monegan said. "If we had additional people, we might be able to work those gray areas."

What is happening in Anchorage, and elsewhere in Alaska, is that cases are not being responded to. There isn't even the pretense of an investigation. A patrol officer responds, takes a statement, writes a report, and if a suspect is not named and apprehended by the end of the officer's shift the case typically goes no further. According to official reports in Anchorage, the problem is one of poor leadership and poor communication (Coyne, 2003):

> A mayoral transition team report released July 8 found all sorts of problems with the department: low morale, low diversity, a lack of communication between police Chief Walt Monegan and his staff. But a major problem is staffing, and an undefined recruiting policy.

As of this writing, these problems with sexual assault in Alaska remain.

Sex crimes must be investigated. Otherwise, the sworn protectors are essentially abandoning the citizenry—a citizenry that by law cannot police itself against these dangers. For any law enforcement leadership to fail to assign any sexual assault case to at least one detective as contact for the victim is ignorant, identifying a clear training need. As they learned in Philadelphia, there is simply no better way to build resentment with your victims, let alone your community.

THE ESSENTIAL QUALITIES

Dr. Hans Gross (as shown in Figure FM-2), the Austrian jurist whose seminal works help provide the foundation for modern-day criminal investigation, agreed in regard to the importance of integrity and tenacity. He wrote of "Certain Qualities Essential to an Investigating Officer," arguing that investigators require (compiled from Gross, 1934, pp. 14–33):

Figure FM-2
Hans Gross.

1. Indefatigable (tireless) energy and zeal

2. Self denial

3. Perseverance

4. Swiftness in reading men

5. A thorough knowledge of human nature

6. Education

7. An agreeable manner

8. An iron constitution

9. Encyclopedic knowledge

10. Orientation—complete knowledge of their department and jurisdiction

11. The renouncement of expeditiousness

12. Absolute accuracy and precision in details

Putting tirelessness at the top of this list was not arbitrary. Dr. Gross witnessed much investigative apathy in his career, and made note of it as a major contributor to unresolved cases. According to Gross (1934, p. 14):

> First and above all an Investigating Officer must possess an abundant store of energy; nothing is more deplorable than a crawling, lazy, and sleepy Investigating Officer. . . . He who recognizes that he is wanting in energy can but turn to something else for he will never make a good Investigator. Again the Investigating Officer must be energetic not only in special circumstances, as when, for example, he finds himself face to face with a witness or an accused person who is hot-headed, refractory, and aggressive, or when the work takes him away from his office and he proceeds to record a deposition or make an arrest without having his staff or office bell to aid him; but energy must always be displayed when he tackles a difficult, complicated, or obscure case. It is truly painful to examine a report which shows that the Investigating Officer has only fallen to his work with timidity, hesitation, and nervousness, just touching it, so to speak with the tips of his fingers; but there is satisfaction in observing a case that has been attacked energetically and grasped with animation and vigour. The want of special cleverness and long practice can often be compensated by getting a good grip of the case, but want of energy can be compensated by nothing.

As we have discussed, apathy remains a significant problem in the investigative community, along with poor training, poor leadership, and diminished resources (such as funding for extra manpower and overtime). In the words of Jack Maples, former Deputy Commissioner of the New York Police Department, discussing recruits fresh out of police academies and how crime-solving knowledge fails to find its way to those who need it (Maples, 1999, p. 39):

> Recruits are taught how to take reports, a skills set passed on at precincts by training officers who are usually young and inexperienced themselves. They, in turn, are supervised by inexperienced and under-trained sergeants. In essence, we have kids who know very little training kids who know even less training kids who know nothing.

The authors of this work have seen their share of barely worked cases from overworked, undertrained, or apathetic investigators, scratching only the surface of events and writing final reports that span only a few poorly written paragraphs.

WORKING CASES

The role of the sex-crimes investigator is gatherer and assembler of facts and evidence pertinent to justly clearing assigned cases. This includes helping locate evidence and witnesses, documenting each, and figuring out how they can best be used to move a case forward. When criminal charges result, it will also include sworn testimony about everything the investigator has done on a case and why. Investigators are not politicians and they are not advocates for the victim or the accused. What should be asked of them is only that they work their cases with integrity and with keen attention to detail, until every lead uncovered is an exhausted possibility. This must be without sanction, pressure, or prejudice from their peers or superiors.

Working and solving cases should be the first and only role of the sex-crimes investigator. That means investigators' time should be spent on evidence, witnesses, suspects, or learning how to understand these more completely. Less time or resources spent on any of these is not better.

Any deviation from this role working to clear cases, whether it comes from themselves or others, can corrupt a case effort and hamper, distort, or prohibit its just resolution.

It is with these kinds of problems in mind that we have prepared this text, to help those who are tirelessly motivated work their cases without prejudice by providing real tools and real solutions.

REFERENCES

Brant, T. Rape records broken down: GRIM: Review reveals typical crime locations, times and victims. *Anchorage Daily News*, November 29, 2003.

Coyne, A. The safety dance—What would it take to protect women on city trails? *Anchorage Press*, Vol. 12, Ed. 29, July 17–July 23, 2003.

Fazlollah, M., McCoy, C., and Moran, R. Timoney to allow sex-case oversight. *Philadelphia Inquirer*, March 21, 2000.

Gross, H. (1934) *Criminal Investigation*. 3rd ed. London: Sweet & Maxwell.

Langworthy, R., and Rosay, A. (2003) Descriptive analysis of sexual assaults in Anchorage, Alaska. Alaska Justice Statistical Analysis Center, Justice Center, University of Alaska Anchorage, JC 0107, October.

Maples, J. (1999) *The Crime Fighter*. New York: Doubleday.

McCoy, C. Rape unit reborn out of disgrace. *Philadelphia Inquirer*, June 22, 2003.

ACKNOWLEDGMENTS

The Editors extend their deep personal and professional appreciation to the following friends and colleagues for their support, encouragement, and guidance:

To our families—For their tireless support, and for putting up with our long hours late into the night.

To all of the contributors—For their love of the work, their professionalism, and their integrity. This book would not have been possible without their help, guidance, and support. To each of them we owe special thanks and appreciation.

Jerry Chisum, Criminalist—For his friendship, for his acute mind, and for his dedication to excellence in forensic science and crime reconstruction. His case-work provides a standard for the field of crime reconstruction.

Dr. Robert E. Gaensslen, Criminalist—Under whom Mr. Turvey studied at the University of New Haven. His efforts to shape Mr. Turvey's thinking were not wasted.

Dr. Henry Lee, Criminalist—Under whom Mr. Turvey studied at the University of New Haven. For his enthusiasm, for his tirelessness, and for teaching Mr. Turvey to read the language of crime scenes.

Mark Listewnik, Editor—Our fearless editor at Academic Press. For his belief in the project and his patience. Without him, this work would never have gotten off the ground.

Dr. John Thornton, Criminalist—For his friendship, for his professional advice, for taking the time to explain things slowly, and for being a valuable sounding board. Though not the reason Mr. Turvey became a forensic scientist, he is one of the reasons Mr. Turvey remains one. His casework and publications are beacons in the dark sea of the incomprehensible.

We also extend our professional gratitude for the excellent quality of work and reason found within the published works of:

- Dr. Katherine Baker
- Dr. Hans Gross
- Dr. A. Nicholas Groth
- Jack Maples, the "crimefighter"
- Dr. Richard Saferstein
- Dr. John I. Thornton

They have taught us, guided us, and inspired us. Through their example we have bettered ourselves. And, we hope, our readers as well.

AUTHOR'S NOTE[1]

Brent E. Turvey, M.S.

Students, clients, colleagues, and new friends . . . each finds their own way to ask me the same question: "What made you decide to choose this work?" It is an incredibly important question to ask. It tends to surface when the conversation runs over ground that is particularly painful for them, as they begin to reflect on themselves and their relationship to those who commit violent crime.

How do people do these terrible things? How can they be stopped? Why am I drawn to understand them? Am I more like them than not? Am I responsible for them? How could anyone do something like this to someone else? What makes the work important enough to you, that you would take on the burden of knowledge, and risk finding out things that are still difficult to speak of openly?

Before I unpack my emotional bags and give my answers, I think about who they are and what they may need. I try to measure my response out accordingly. The question that I'm trying to answer for myself before I give them both barrels is whether or not they really want to hear the response that I am about to give.

The truth is I didn't choose this work. It chose me. Or put a different way, what didn't kill me defined me.

Now, bear with me here, as I am going to leave a lot of the details associated with this part of my life out. Not necessarily for my sake, but for the sake of the person involved, and for the sake of brevity. Suffice it to say that as much as I've related here, it's not even the half of it. It's much worse.

It began in March of 1987. I was almost 17 years old, and still a high school student in Tigard, Oregon (a small, semiaffluent suburb of Portland). A friend of mine named Tom invited me to go with him to a supervised youth sleepover at the local YMCA where he volunteered his time.

---

[1] This note was originally published at the beginning of the first edition of *Criminal Profiling: An Introduction to Behavioral Evidence Analysis*, published by Academic Press in 1999.

At the time, I was painfully depressed over life in general, felt that I had a right to be miserable, and genuinely wanted nothing more than to be left completely alone. But my friends were pretty faithful, and we spent a lot of time talking about life, late into many nights. What happened today, what would we do tomorrow, and what did we miss about yesterday? My friends even put up with my ridiculously self-serving misery poetry, and encouraged my dangerous flirtation with marathon-length music binges consisting almost exclusively of Pink Floyd and post-Genesis Peter Gabriel.

So, back to the YMCA: I was actually staying with my best friend, Ben, because my parents and I had been arguing and we needed some distance from each other. Tom and I packed our bags for the night (it was Friday), left Ben's, and headed out for the YMCA. When we met up with the youth group, we decided to spend our social time lifting weights (an interest that Ben did not share, and that I have all but successfully disabused myself of).

While we were lifting and talking about lifting and how much more we should be lifting, two girls from the group came over to speak with us. They both knew Tom. One of them was Kelly (not her real name). Kelly was a little more than a year younger than Tom and I, attended St. Mary's Academy in Portland, volunteered some of her afternoons at the YMCA, and was very attractive (and incredibly intelligent, I would later learn and fail to fully appreciate). Naturally, I was completely uninterested in her, being the self-absorbed idiot that I'd become by that time. Undeterred by my idiocy, she followed Tom and me around for the rest of the evening. Looking back, she was probably trying to cheer me up. But I had learned the fine art of being disconsolate, so her work was not easy.

We wound up having a conversation together that took us well past midnight. I came to the conclusion that she was very intelligent, very presumptuous, and very persistent. I don't recall the exact conversation anymore, but I'm sure that I managed to make everything we spoke about relate to my own pain and misery, and the injustice of being 16 and without my own car or something insipid like that. Regardless, she found a way to make a big impression on me by simply being herself, and by listening to me complain.

With the omission of a few slightly embarrassing, mostly innocent, and only semi-important details that established her in my mind as unabashed and curious, that one-night sleepover concluded and I found myself wondering who this girl was and whether or not I would ever see her again.

By that Sunday I was back at my friend Ben's house, where I was still staying. Kelly was Tom's acquaintance, and we were waiting for Tom to come over so that he could give us her telephone number. I was thinking about calling her, but hadn't really come up with a plan regarding what I would say if she were actually on the other end of the phone. While we were waiting, Kelly called asking for Ben because she was looking for *my* telephone number.

I became very nervous very quickly. The phone found its way into my hand. She did most of the talking. And to my shock, she asked me out. I had never been out on a date, let alone asked anyone out on a date, let alone been asked out on a date by anyone. I was excited and horrified.

On our first date, I picked her up from the YMCA in Portland sometime in the evening and took her home to a house near the farming community of Wilsonville. It's about an hour's drive if you don't take the Interstate. We stopped at a little park in the city of Metzger, where I used to go with my sisters, when I was 5 or 6, before my father died of cancer. We talked a lot. It seemed to go very well.

Over the next month or so, I inflicted on her my narcissistic, self-deprecating love poetry, as well as full courses of Pink Floyd and Peter Gabriel played as loud as the stereo in my mother's station wagon could manage. To her credit, she listened attentively and really seemed to care about what I had to say. Again, this was a completely new experience for me; a beautiful, intelligent, and attentive human was interested in who I was and how I felt.

I was truly devoted to my friend Ben, and felt like I was less when I wasn't with him. Before long I was able to manage it so that Ben, Kelly, and I were doing things together. Movies, dinner, long drives. I was very close to Ben. He was the most important person in the world to me at that time and for many years after. It was important for me to include him, because he was an important part of who I was.

For a little while, a month or so, it seemed as though I had the world figured out. My problems seemed less heavy when distributed evenly between the three of us, I never had to be alone (always a huge issue with me), and Ben and Kelly really got along well (her unabashedness was the perfect antidote for his constant fear of public humiliation). We were having a lot of fun together. I forgot how miserable I was through these two people, their friendship, and Kelly's great affection.

It was sometime in May when Kelly disclosed to me. Disclosure in this instance meant that she told me about her history of sexual abuse. Of course I didn't know what it meant to be disclosed to. And I certainly didn't know that disclosure was the type of thing that happened often enough for it to have a name.

But sure enough, there we were in my 1973 Toyota Corolla (my parents paid $350 for it), listening to the end of "Mama," by Genesis. It was one of my favorites at the time. And Kelly said to me, something along the lines of, "This makes me think about someone who is going to rape someone, and hurt them. Did I ever tell you that I was sexually molested?" The words materialized that easily.

Now keep in mind that my experiences with life were very limited, and my experiences with dating and the opposite sex were very much in their infancy.

Still, with a stepfather who was an attorney and a mother who was a RN, you'd think I would have been able to handle it a little better. But ultimately I didn't.

That night in the car, she detailed to me the full extent of her past abuse. As I remember it, she told me that from the time she was 9 or 10 until the time she was 12, her older brother (8 or so years older) had sexually molested her on a regular basis. As I recall, it ended when she invited a friend over to spend the night and her brother attempted to have sex with the friend.

Kelly intervened on the friend's behalf, and Kelly was struck. She then went to her parents and told them what had been going on. The police were called, but ultimately the police and Kelly's parents worked to convince her that keeping her brother's behavior a secret was the best thing for everyone. So they did, and it was never spoken of.

A year or so later, her family had moved to Tampa Bay, Florida (her father was a salesman and they moved around a great deal). An older man named "Joe" soon befriended a now very depressed and emotionally ashamed Kelly. He watched her ride through the park every day on her bike. She loved to ride (or more accurately, she loved any activity that kept her out of her home). So Joe watched and waited and when he was ready, when he had learned enough, he approached her. Joe began to invite her over to his trailer after school. He was nice to her; bought her gifts, flowers, and made her feel special and important and above all, desirable. He also introduced her to alcohol and pornographic films. He would get her a little drunk, turn on his pornographic films, and have her perform sex acts on him. In time, he was also performing sex acts on her. In exchange for this, she was given gifts, treated like an adult, and made to feel needed.

I'm not sure how that relationship ended. But it did end when her family moved out of Florida to Oregon, and she began attending St. Mary's Academy in downtown Portland. Keep in mind that St. Mary's Academy is no joke. They put out some brilliant girls there. And Kelly quickly proved herself to be one of them.

About this time her ongoing self-esteem problems intensified, and she wanted to talk about her past abuse. She approached a school counselor at St. Mary's and tried to disclose the sexual abuse involving her brother. According to Kelly, the female counselor told her to "stop making up stories" and gave her a litany of consequences that she could suffer for telling such terrible lies.

So she buried it inside of herself again, telling maybe one or two friends and swearing them to secrecy.

A year or so after that, Kelly told me, she got into a relationship with a really nice college guy who attended Portland State University (only a block away from St. Mary's Academy). This guy met her at the YMCA where he was a part-time counselor. He was, by all appearances, a good Christian boy who bought her

Ziggy paraphernalia and told her that she was special. The week before she met me for the first time at the YMCA, he had taken her to his grandmother's house in Lake Oswego, gotten her really drunk, and forced her to have sex with him on the kitchen floor.

It appeared to my limited senses that Kelly was very ashamed of what had happened. She seemed to feel that these were things that she had brought on herself. That she had encouraged them and that she could have prevented them from happening. Kelly appeared to believe that she was to blame for these things. And she secretly believed that perhaps she even deserved them. She had resolved to keep them a secret so that others wouldn't think she was a bad person. But she needed to tell me. She wanted my acceptance, and needed me not to judge her. She needed a true friend.

Keep in mind that the only person I had ever loved outside of myself by that time was Ben. And he could take care of himself (6′4″, 250 lbs, very strong, very intimidating when he wanted to be). So it was really the first time that I'd ever felt someone I truly loved was in real pain and needed protecting. I began to feel these strong protective desires swell up and over me. Thanks to my stepfather, I felt that I knew what to do with these feelings in general. My stepfather, the attorney, had imbued in me, since the age of 7, a potent and unswerving sense of justice and how it can be lawfully achieved. He also taught me that the only way to handle bad things was to tear them down to their essential truths, and throw a lot of light on them so that everyone could see just how erroneous or harmful those truths were.

Now, incest and sexual molestation can only exist for any length of time in an environment of mutually agreed-upon secrecy. Both the victim and the offender have a great deal to lose if the truth comes out. Ultimately victims cannot fully heal and move forward unless the truth is reconciled in them, and the perpetrators of the abuse are made accountable. If the victim is made to be accountable for the abuse, while the offender escapes all responsibility, the victim's shame and guilt and confusion increase dramatically.

Knowing this (a little knowledge making me incredibly dangerous), and knowing that the brother, and now in my view the parents, had never been held accountable for Kelly's sexual abuse, I decided it was my duty to hold them accountable. This was arrogant presumption. Especially given her evident pain and my growing inability to deal with that pain directly. But before I could do much more than take a few steps backward and regroup and try to figure out who I was in this completely new world, things took an unexpected turn.

Kelly's father accepted a sales position with his company in Columbus, Georgia. This was a huge deal because they were not supposed to ever move again. He had promised the family stability, and even purchased a beautiful new home with some land. It was no small decision. Kelly became more depressed. She needed my support, and I was too busy making her pain my own to be there for her in the way that she needed. And her family did not want her discussing their past with me at all. So she found a very powerful way to let us all know just how fragile, alone, and confused she was.

What happened next changed me in a way that I'll probably never fully understand. And it taught me that most people, no matter how well intentioned, can't step outside of their own assumptions about life and others unless someone whacks them on the head with a very big sledgehammer. (Notice that I just made the whole thing about me again. You think you've made progress, grown a little, but then there it is.)

I remember that school had not yet let out, but that it was warm. So that puts it somewhere in May. The end of May, maybe. I know that it was before my 17th birthday. It's gross to me that I cannot remember the exact day. And telling.

Ben and I were at his place. I had long since moved back home by then, but Ben and I still spent a lot of time together. He lived only a mile or so down the road into town from Kelly. Whenever I dropped her off I would go immediately to post-mortem the day with him.

That day Kelly and I had been out sailing with my family and friends from church. I was brooding and inattentive. She played with some toddlers who were along for the ride. I dropped her off that evening and headed directly for Ben's to whine—she was just not getting through to me.

Before dark the phone rang in Ben's room and it was Kelly. I immediately recognized an unusual sluggishness in her voice, like she was drunk. I asked her where she was calling from, and she said that she was calling from her bedroom. Then she said that she couldn't feel her legs, and that she wanted to go to sleep because she was very tired.

She had taken almost a full bottle of over-the-counter rubbing alcohol, which I'm told is a potentially fatal amount.

This was my fault, I kept thinking. My arrogance. If I had just listened and heard her, really heard her, then she wouldn't have needed to do this to herself. If she dies, it will be because I was not strong enough to see past my own self-interest to the hand that was reaching out to grab mine.

While I kept her on the phone, Ben ran around to the neighbors' homes begging them to let him in so that he could use their phone to call the poison control center. This took almost a full 15 minutes, because Indian Woods, the community that Ben lived in, was particularly paranoid about giving help to strangers or those who look strange. Eventually poison control began monitoring the call, and an emergency unit was dispatched to Kelly's home. They broke down the fence that enclosed the property, they smashed through the front door, bypassing her parents, and followed my instructions right into her bedroom.

Then her father picked up the phone on the other end of the line and said, "Who the hell is this?" When I told him what was going on, he slammed the phone down while shouting, "Kelly, what in the hell have you done?"

He was very angry about the cost of the doors, the fence, and the ambulance ride. And they told her so while she was recovering that night in the hospital.

The next day, Kelly was released from the hospital and I spent the day at her house with her. I sat on this very comfortable couch and she slept with her head on my chest, leaving a big pool of drool. The smell of her perfume was on everything ("Beautiful," by Estée Lauder), and I just kept running my right hand over and over her face, and through her hair. The quiet after the storm. What a moment of pure exhaustion, and pure relief that must have been for her. For me, it was a moment of honesty. Of realization and resolution.

I think that was probably the first time that I realized that people outside of myself could be hurt, and that their pain mattered. This is something that is supposed to become evident in one's moral development by the time one is 8 or 9. But I've always been a little slow, emotionally.

Her mother came in once or twice to speak with me. "She kept asking for you at the hospital. Did she tell you why she did this? Do you know why she did this?" her mother asked, and I could tell that she was really concerned, even a bit confused.

But it was not a conversation that I was able to have with Kelly's mother. All that I could think of then was that Kelly could have died. And that she did not deserve to be marginalized or ignored. I knew what a suicide attempt was. She needed me to hold on, and not let go. I resolved from that point forward to hear her before I heard anything else. And it was that day that I surrendered whatever good judgement I had left.

Kelly went into weekly family therapy that consisted of her and her mother. Her father did not wish to participate, and her oldest brother, the abuser, was married and living in Florida. In therapy, she talked about her brother sexually abusing her for so many years. She also disclosed the relationship with Joe, from Tampa Bay, and the more recent rape at the hands of her Christian boyfriend. Both parents were in disbelief—but maintained stringent denial. They even told both Kelly and the therapist that they thought her brother had only tried to have sex with her the one time, that it had been an isolated incident.

Needless to say, both parents came to focus on me as the cause of their family's current pain. I had stirred embers that had been left to die down, they believed. After all, from their point of view, Kelly was the current problem and not the improprieties of their son so many years ago. That was evident from all of the things that Kelly had let happen since then. That was where the focus needed to be.

The therapist agreed.

Kelly was scheduled to move away with her family to Georgia in August. She did not want to go. First because we had grown very close. And second because her older brother, who lived in Florida, was really looking forward to her return, and had stated a number of times how mature she was looking lately.

When the time came she refused to get on the plane. She was taken over to juvenile hall and told that she could either get on the plane willingly or be handcuffed and thrown on the plane as a prisoner. We later learned that this would not have been legal, as she was still a legal resident of Oregon, but she didn't know it at the time and complied in fear.

Within a week of being in Georgia she ran away.

The four days that she was missing were the longest of my life. The opening lines from *The Inferno* come to mind: "Midway in our life's journey, I went astray from the straight road and woke to find myself alone in a dark wood. . . . Its very memory gives a shape to fear." Every person I encountered, from my parents, to law enforcement, to counselors, told me that her chances of survival on her own were very low. She was very likely dead, they told me. I was told the horror stories of hitchhikers who had accepted rides from the wrong people, and the survival rates of runaways. I was shown pictures that fed my fears.

Looking back on that time now, I cannot believe the misguided and horribly ignorant information that law enforcement and counselors were giving me.

On the evening of the fourth day Kelly called me from Louisville, Kentucky. The relief I felt was overwhelming. She told me that she'd hitched a ride with a trucker headed cross-country and intended to go either to California, to be with friends there, or to Oregon. Either way, she was determined not to go back.

I went to the bank, emptied out my college fund, and bought her a plane ticket to Sea-Tac Airport in Washington state. I picked her up the next day and we spent the next 2 months hiding out, calling her parents to negotiate some sort of peaceful end, and waiting for December to roll around so that Kelly could turn 16 and declare herself an emancipated minor.

I was particularly concerned because her parents, while she was missing, had already arranged for Kelly to become a full-time resident of the Bradley Center. This is a private, secure mental hospital in Columbus, Georgia. Her parents explained how this was just what she needed, and how it would help her to forget the past. When I told Kelly about her parents' plans, it took away any doubts that she was doing the right thing.

We knew that things could not continue the way they were, however. We tried to keep our lives from being completely on hold until she turned 16. She got an apartment in Salem, Oregon. She got a job as a waitress. And she enrolled in the local community college. I commuted back and forth from Salem to Tigard almost daily, starting my senior year in high school just in time.

At the end of October, she was picked up by local law enforcement and flown back to Georgia. They immediately placed her into the Bradley Center where she stayed until she was of legal age. They held her against her will, and they medicated her against her will. They told her that I was the problem in her life, that I had caused all of her troubles, that she in turn had caused her parents great suffering, and that she owed it to them to "grow up" and "accept responsibility for her actions like an adult."

When this did not work right away, they told her that I had married an Asian woman and moved to Korea. The therapist and the family agreed that this lie was essential to breaking down her will. That and the medication.

Ultimately, they achieved their objective with her. They got her to accept responsibility for the sexual abuse, they were able to have her fixate on me as the source of all of her troubles with her parents, and she was released as an outpatient just before her 17th birthday. Though she was not told this, they could not have held her past her 17th birthday. So placing her on outpatient status and letting her believe that this was a reward for good behavior was a very clever tactic.

Needless to say, I was not allowed to see her or make contact with her, though I tried everything that I could think of. I tried harder than one could imagine. But in the end I was unsuccessful on every level.

The experience, and the events that it precipitated, left in me a very pointed understanding of how inadequate the judicial system is, how ignorant the law can be in application, and how ignorant and unethical the mental health community can be. I also came to understand that people under an arbitrary age are really without constitutional rights. And that they are really no more than property and can be treated as such even when the environments that they live in by all standards are criminal.

So as I proceeded into my undergraduate work I began to study sex offenders. I wanted to know why they did what they did. I wanted to understand how they chose their victims, what they wanted from them, and how they avoided the attention of law enforcement. But I didn't want to go into sex offender treatment. I was doing all of this for one single reason—to learn as much as I could so that I could help investigate sex offenders and stop them.

After a number of years doing undergraduate research with the published literature, I came to the conclusion that offender interviews were in order. It was time to confront offenders in prison and ask them the tough questions.

The published works of people like Robert Hazelwood and the late Bruce Danto had inspired me, and I wanted to duplicate their efforts.

It was after my first interview with the incarcerated serial murderer Jerome H. Brudos that I realized how truly naïve my understanding of sex offenders was. I spent 5 hours with him, and he lied to me almost the entire time. He lied about almost everything he had ever done (or rather, he claimed, everything that he hadn't done). The only reason that I was not completely taken in by his charming personality and generous, affable nature was the fact that I had reviewed the investigative file. Before the interview, I had gone to the Marion County Sheriff's Office in Salem, Oregon. I had read autopsy reports on all the victims, looked at the crime-scene photos, and read the investigators' reports. I had even seen some of the photos that Jerry had taken of himself posing with his victims.

I learned an important lesson through that experience. The lesson was that offenders lie. The only way to get an objective record of the behavior that occurs in a crime scene between a victim and the offender is through the documentation and subsequent reconstruction of forensic evidence. It's a lesson that I took to heart.

I decided then and there that what I needed to complement my undergraduate study in psychology was graduate-level education in the forensic sciences. Finding back issues of the *Journal of Forensic Sciences*, I searched for graduate programs in the forensic sciences all over the country.

Ultimately I applied to and was accepted in the Graduate Forensic Science Program at the University of New Haven in West Haven, Connecticut. There I found instructors of the highest caliber and was able to learn some of the most important lessons of my academic career. These lessons were important because they actually carried over into my professional career.

The career that I've chosen, the methods of forensic investigation and criminal profiling that I employ, and this work that you are about to read, all stem from those events that began late one night at the YMCA on Barbur Boulevard in Portland, Oregon, when I met a girl named Kelly. She was a single victim with multiple offenders over time, who was pathologically ignored and ultimately revictimized by a mental health and legal community that was and remains inadequate to the task of understanding and competently investigating crimes of a sexual nature. With this work, and others, I am fulfilling a deeply personal promise that I made as the result of those early experiences with Kelly. It has been and remains my determination to learn as much as I can from those who are my betters, to share as much I can with those colleagues who surround me, and teach as much as I have learned to those who are following the path behind me. Education, after all, is a process and not a result.

It is my deepest honor to be working on this project with the help of so many talented and brilliant colleagues. And it is my greatest hope that readers will take things from this work that they did not understand or appreciate before, that they will share things they take from this work with their colleagues, and that they will teach the things they take from this work to their students.

Brent Turvey

ABOUT THE AUTHORS

DETECTIVE JOHN J. BAEZA, NYPD (RET.)

John Baeza started his career in law enforcement as a New York State Correction Officer working at the Sing-Sing and Otisville correctional facilities. He was employed by the New York City Police Department for nearly 12 years. He began his police career in Harlem's 32nd Precinct as a patrol officer. He was then assigned to the Manhattan North Tactical Narcotics Team where he performed undercover work for 3 years. He was promoted to Detective during his Narcotics assignment. From 1994 to 2000, he was assigned to the Manhattan Special Victims Squad where he personally investigated more than 2000 sex crimes and child abuse cases.

DR. JOHN M. BUTLER

Dr. John M. Butler is Project Leader of the Human Identity Team within the Biotechnology Division at the National Institute of Standards and Technology in Gaithersburg, MD. He holds a BS in chemistry from Brigham Young University and a PhD in analytical chemistry from the University of Virginia. While a graduate student working in the FBI Laboratory, he pioneered development of the techniques now widely used for short tandem repeat forensic DNA typing. Dr. Butler serves on the FBI's Scientific Working Group on DNA Analysis Methods (SWGDAM), and is author of *Forensic DNA Typing: Biology and Technology behind STR Markers* (2001). He is also widely published in the area of DNA technology, research, and application.

TERILYNNE W. BUTLER

Terilynne Butler holds a bachelor's degree in exercise science from Brigham Young University. She began her writing career in 1994 and has contributed to newspapers and magazines. A member of a long-standing writer's group in

California, she is currently preparing two self-help manuscripts. She has broad experience editing and enjoys trying to make her husband's writing understandable to the general public. Working from home, she is the mother of four small children, all of whom her husband has proven to be theirs through DNA testing.

LINDA E. LEDRAY, RN, SANE-A, PhD, FAAN

Dr. Linda E. Ledray is the founder and director of the Minneapolis, Minnesota–based Sexual Assault Resource Service (SARS), one of the first Sexual Assault Nurse Examiner (SANE-SART) programs, which she developed in 1977. Dr. Ledray is also an adjunct faculty member at the University of Minnesota. She has taught nationally and internationally on the topic of victim assistance, SANE-SART program development, and program evaluation. Dr. Ledray is a retired U.S. Army colonel. She was stationed at the 2nd General Hospital in Landstuhl, Germany, and was mobilized in support of Operation Desert Storm. Dr. Ledray has published many articles and books including *Recovering from Rape* (1994) and the *Sexual Assault Nurse Examiner Development and Operation Guide* (1999).

MICHAEL McGRATH, MD

Michael McGrath, MD, is a Clinical Associate Professor, Department of Psychiatry, at the University of Rochester Medical Center in Rochester, NY. He is also Associate Chair for Ambulatory Services, Department of Psychiatry and Behavioral Health, at Unity Health System, in Rochester, NY.

Dr. McGrath divides his time among clinical, administrative, teaching, and research activities. His areas of special expertise include forensic psychiatry and criminal profiling. He has lectured on three continents and is a founding member of the Academy of Behavioral Profiling.

STEPHEN M. PITTEL, PhD

Dr. Stephen M. Pittel holds a BA from Rutgers University in Newark, NJ, and a PhD from the University of California at Berkeley. He has been a professor of psychology at The Wright Institute since 1970, and a director of research at Center Point Programs since 1991.

Dr. Pittel has more than 30 years of experience in the field of substance abuse research and treatment. He is the author of more than 100 articles, monographs, and reports on drug and alcohol abuse and treatment, and has qualified as an expert on the effects of drugs and alcohol in Superior Courts throughout California and in federal district and military courts.

He may be contacted through his private consulting firm, SMP Associates, in Berkeley, CA (office: 510-486-1888; email: drugshrink@comcast.net).

DETECTIVE ALAN SANDOMIR, NYPD

Detective Alan Sandomir was born and raised in New York City. He attended Cortland College in upstate New York where he received a dual bachelor's degree in both anthropology and political science. After college, Detective Sandomir spent 4 years in the United States Army, where he was involved in a classified intelligence collection operation in Eastern Europe during the height of the Cold War. After his military service, Detective Sandomir joined the ranks of the New York City Police Department in 1984 and began his career walking a beat in the housing projects along Manhattan's Lower East Side. His stint as a Lower East Side cop included a 4-year assignment in a plainclothes street crime unit that targeted guns, shootings, robberies, and burglaries in and around those housing projects. Following that, he began an assignment in an undercover narcotics unit that targeted lower Manhattan. His experiences there led him to a position in the highly acclaimed Organized Crime Control Bureau's Manhattan North Tactical Narcotics Team (TNT), where he was involved in undercover investigations against the organized drug gangs that battled for upper Manhattan. By 1992 he had been decorated 19 times and was transferred to the Detective Bureau. Detective Sandomir was then sent to the South Bronx where he investigated everything from harassment to homicide. In 1995 he requested a transfer to the Manhattan Special Victims Squad where he began specializing in investigating violent sex crimes. In 2001 he created and initiated a program that allowed him to specialize in and investigate the trickle of incoming DNA-based cases that was correctly forecasted to soon turn into an avalanche. As the DNA databanks began to churn out DNA cases, Detective Sandomir and his partner, Detective Edward Tacchi, became the first DNA Detectives in the NYPD, where they led both New York City and New York State in DNA arrests and indictments while working out of their Manhattan office.

During his tenure at the Manhattan Special Victims Squad Detective Sandomir became immortalized as fictional Special Victims Squad Detective Al Vandomir in mystery writer Linda Fairstein's "Alex Cooper" murder/mystery series. Detective Sandomir continued to hone his investigative, interrogation, and interview skills while working on thousands of sex crime cases over the years and becoming an in-house lecturer and DNA consultant. He was soon promoted to the highly vaunted rank of Detective 2nd Grade, where he continued to be involved in some of the most publicized, notorious, and serious sex crime cases that the City of New York encountered.

DETECTIVE JOHN O. SAVINO, NYPD

John Savino has been a member of the New York City Police Department since 1982. His career has spanned all aspects of law enforcement, beginning with a short assignment as a uniformed police officer and quick advancement to the Narcotics Division. His investigative skills began developing while he was assigned to the Manhattan North Narcotics Division. This assignment also helped develop his ability to talk with people from all walks of life, as he worked in an "undercover" capacity buying narcotics in Manhattan.

For the past 15 years he has been assigned to the Manhattan Special Victims Squad, where he investigates reports of child abuse and any sexual assault occurring in the Borough of Manhattan. While assigned to the Special Victims Squad, he has risen to the prestigious rank of 1st Grade Detective. Detective Savino has been involved in thousands of investigations of rape and sexual assault and has been the lead investigator in many successful serial rape and pattern investigations.

LAILA SPINA, PsyD

Dr. Spina completed her undergraduate studies in criminology and psychology at the University of South Africa and her doctoral degree in clinical psychology at the Wright Institute in Berkeley, California. She completed her clinical psychology internship at the University of Miami. Dr. Spina has worked extensively as a crisis counselor for sexual assault survivors.

She is currently completing a postdoctoral fellowship in neuropsychology at the Mt. Sinai Medical Center in New York City.

BRENT E. TURVEY, MS

Brent E. Turvey spent his first years in college on a pre-med track studying biology and chemistry, only to change his course of study when his true interests took hold. He received a bachelor of science degree from Portland State University in psychology, and an additional bachelor of science degree in history. He went on to receive his master of science in forensic science after studying at the University of New Haven, in West Haven, Connecticut.

Since graduating in 1996, Brent has consulted with many agencies, attorneys, and police departments in the United States, Australia, China, Canada, and Korea on a range of rapes, homicides, and multiple death cases, as a forensic scientist and criminal profiler with Knowledge Solutions, LLC. He has consulted with law enforcement serial rape and serial homicide task forces in California and New York. He is the author of *Criminal Profiling: An Introduction to Behavioral Evidence Analysis*, currently in its second edition. In August 2002, he was invited by the Chinese People's Police Security University in Beijing, ROC, to lecture there, and before groups of detectives at the Beijing, Wuhan, Hanjou, and Shanghai police bureaus. He is also a founding member of the Academy of Behavioral Profiling, where he currently serves as a board member. He has been qualified as an expert in the areas of criminal profiling, forensic science, staged crime scenes, and crime reconstruction in courts throughout the United States.

He can be reached through the Knowledge Solutions Web site at http://www.corpus-delicti.com (office: 907-747-5121; email at: bturvey@profiling.org).

DEFINING RAPE AND SEXUAL ASSAULT

John O. Savino and Brent E. Turvey, MS

Myths which are believed in tend to become true.
George Orwell, *The English People* **(1944)**

Mythos: (3) The pattern of basic values and attitudes of a people,
characteristically transmitted through myths and the arts.
The American Heritage Dictionary of the English Language, 4th ed. (2000)

As subordinates of the justice system, the authors are inclined in that direction
when it comes to terms and definitions. We define sexual attacks in terms of
the nature of any physical contact and the amount of force or coercion. That
is to say, rape and sexual assault tend to be defined by tangibles that can be
investigated, and then either supported or refuted by witness or victim statements, and further corroborated by forensic evidence. We investigate the facts
and examine them, and the penal codes guide the nature of any subsequent
arrests or charges.

In this work we will not use the term rape interchangeably with the generic
term sexual assault. *Rape* will be defined as nonconsensual sexual penetration.
Sexual assault will be defined as nonconsensual sexual contact. There are other
definitions worth examining, however, without which ours are perhaps
misleading.

DEFINITIONS

A review of the myriad rape-related laws, publications, and research reveals
definitions and thresholds unique to each. Whenever rape is considered it is
redefined, often becoming more and more vague and complex. This is because
rape means different things to different groups of people, each with their own
goals, biases, and assumptions. Subsequently, definitions of rape are determined largely by the divergent roles and agendas of those who need the word
defined.

There are, primarily, four types of definitions to contend with:

1. Legal
2. Clinical
3. Moral
4. Political

We will briefly discuss each.

LEGAL DEFINITIONS

For most investigators, rape is a legal term defined by a penal code with the assistance of the court. Each state defines the crime of rape or sexual assault differently. Some criteria are short and general; others are lengthy and specific. A review of these laws is at best trying, if not ultimately confusing and frustrating.[1]

Penal codes tend to define rape in unemotional, functional language for the purpose of successful criminal prosecutions. Or at least they should. As discussed in Tredoux (1997):

> By the common law definition, rape is sex without consent. Rape is thus sexual robbery, sexual burglary being unknown, and this sort of definition has been employed in all major legal systems.

Legal statutes tend to distinguish between degrees of rape and other forms of sexual assault. However, a few antiquated sex-crimes-related laws do remain on the books entrenched with intensely moral and ultimately judgmental language, sometimes providing arguably inappropriate and even bizarre exemptions.[2]

---

[1] Illinois, for example, passed a new rape law in 2003 to clarify the issue of consent by emphasizing that people can change their mind while having sex. According to Wills (2003):

> Under the law, if someone says "no" at any time the other person must stop or it becomes rape. . . .

> Lyn Schollett, general counsel for the Illinois Coalition Against Sexual Assault, said the law was important to make it clear to victims, offenders, prosecutors and juries that people have the right to halt sexual activity at any time.

Some call the law empowering to prosecutors and victims. Others call it demeaning to existing laws and common sense.

[2] The law has often treated men and women differently. For example: Until the 1970s, husbands were immune from rape charges in most states (Lithwick, 2003). North Carolina law still provides that it is illegal for a man to peep through a window at a woman, but it is not illegal for anyone to peep into a room occupied by a man (NCGA General Statutes, Chapter 14, Criminal Law, Sub-

Consider these examples of legal definitions.

According to Article 130 of the *New York State Consolidated Laws*, "Sexual intercourse" is required for the crime of *rape* to occur, and the term "has its ordinary meaning and occurs upon any penetration, however slight." Furthermore, rape is broken down into three levels of severity with the following criteria:

Section 130.25 Rape in the third degree.

A person is guilty of rape in the third degree when:

1. He or she engages in sexual intercourse with another person who is incapable of consent by reason of some factor other than being less than seventeen years old;
2. Being twenty-one years old or more, he or she engages in sexual intercourse with another person less than seventeen years old; or
3. He or she engages in sexual intercourse with another person without such person's consent where such lack of consent is by reason of some factor other than incapacity to consent.

Rape in the third degree is a class E felony.

Section 130.30 Rape in the second degree.

A person is guilty of rape in the second degree when:

1. being eighteen years old or more, he or she engages in sexual intercourse with another person less than fifteen years old; or
2. he or she engages in sexual intercourse with another person who is incapable of consent by reason of being mentally disabled or mentally incapacitated.

It shall be an affirmative defense to the crime of rape in the second degree as defined in subdivision one of this section that the defendant was less than four years older than the victim at the time of the act.

Rape in the second degree is a class D felony.

chapter I, General Provisions, Article 1, Felonies and Misdemeanors, § 14–202. Secretly peeping into room occupied by female person).

Also, much written law is infected with subjective and personally intrusive morality, often reflecting religious origins. For example: Michigan law provides that it is a felony for anyone to engage in acts of "gross indecency," including masturbation and fellatio, whether public or private (The Michigan Penal Code, Act 328 of 1931, 750.338 Gross indecency; between male persons; 750.338a Gross indecency; female persons). And Michigan law is not alone in referring to sodomy (oral and/or anal penetration) as an "abominable and detestable crime against nature" (The Michigan Penal Code, 750.158 Crime against nature or sodomy; penalty). However, on June 26, 2003, the U.S. Supreme Court ruled 6–3 that all sodomy laws are unconstitutional (*Lawrence v. Texas*).

S 130.35 Rape in the first degree.

A person is guilty of rape in the first degree when he or she engages in sexual intercourse with another person:

1. By forcible compulsion; or
2. Who is incapable of consent by reason of being physically helpless; or
3. Who is less than eleven years old; or
4. Who is less than thirteen years old and the actor is eighteen years old or more.

Rape in the first degree is a class B felony.

In Texas, the criterion for the crime of *sexual assault* is quite detailed and specific, with the additional crime of aggravated *sexual assault*. As provided in Title 5 of Chapter 22 of the Texas Penal Codes regarding "Assaultive Offenses":

§ 22.011. Sexual Assault

(a) A person commits an offense if the person:

   (1) intentionally or knowingly:

   (A) causes the penetration of the anus or female sexual organ of another person by any means, without that person's consent;

   (B) causes the penetration of the mouth of another person by the sexual organ of the actor, without that person's consent; or

   (C) causes the sexual organ of another person, without that person's consent, to contact or penetrate the mouth, anus, or sexual organ of another person, including the actor; or

   (2) intentionally or knowingly:

   (A) causes the penetration of the anus or female sexual organ of a child by any means;

   (B) causes the penetration of the mouth of a child by the sexual organ of the actor;

   (C) causes the sexual organ of a child to contact or penetrate the mouth, anus, or sexual organ of another person, including the actor;

   (D) causes the anus of a child to contact the mouth, anus, or sexual organ of another person, including the actor; or

   (E) causes the mouth of a child to contact the anus or sexual organ of another person, including the actor.

(b) A sexual assault under Subsection (a)(1) is without the consent of the other person if:

(1) the actor compels the other person to submit or participate by the use of physical force or violence;

(2) the actor compels the other person to submit or participate by threatening to use force or violence against the other person, and the other person believes that the actor has the present ability to execute the threat;

(3) the other person has not consented and the actor knows the other person is unconscious or physically unable to resist;

(4) the actor knows that as a result of mental disease or defect the other person is at the time of the sexual assault incapable either of appraising the nature of the act or of resisting it;

(5) the other person has not consented and the actor knows the other person is unaware that the sexual assault is occurring;

(6) the actor has intentionally impaired the other person's power to appraise or control the other person's conduct by administering any substance without the other person's knowledge;

(7) the actor compels the other person to submit or participate by threatening to use force or violence against any person, and the other person believes that the actor has the ability to execute the threat;

(8) the actor is a public servant who coerces the other person to submit or participate;

(9) the actor is a mental health services provider or a health care services provider who causes the other person, who is a patient or former patient of the actor, to submit or participate by exploiting the other person's emotional dependency on the actor; or

(10) the actor is a clergyman who causes the other person to submit or participate by exploiting the other person's emotional dependency on the clergyman in the clergyman's professional character as spiritual adviser.

§ 22.021. Aggravated Sexual Assault

(a) A person commits an offense:

(1) if the person:

(A) intentionally or knowingly:

(i) causes the penetration of the anus or female sexual organ of another person by any means, without that person's consent;

(ii) causes the penetration of the mouth of another person by the sexual organ of the actor, without that person's consent; or

(iii) causes the sexual organ of another person, without that person's consent, to contact or penetrate the mouth, anus, or sexual organ of another person, including the actor; or

    (B) intentionally or knowingly:

        (i) causes the penetration of the anus or female sexual organ of a child by any means;

        (ii) causes the penetration of the mouth of a child by the sexual organ of the actor;

        (iii) causes the sexual organ of a child to contact or penetrate the mouth, anus, or sexual organ of another person, including the actor;

        (iv) causes the anus of a child to contact the mouth, anus, or sexual organ of another person, including the actor; or

        (v) causes the mouth of a child to contact the anus or sexual organ of another person, including the actor; and

(2) if:

    (A) the person:

        (i) causes serious bodily injury or attempts to cause the death of the victim or another person in the course of the same criminal episode;

        (ii) by acts or words places the victim in fear that death, serious bodily injury, or kidnapping will be imminently inflicted on any person;

        (iii) by acts or words occurring in the presence of the victim threatens to cause the death, serious bodily injury, or kidnapping of any person;

        (iv) uses or exhibits a deadly weapon in the course of the same criminal episode;

        (v) acts in concert with another who engages in conduct described by Subdivision (1) directed toward the same victim and occurring during the course of the same criminal episode; or

        (vi) administers or provides flunitrazepam, otherwise known as rohypnol, gamma hydroxybutyrate, or ketamine to the victim of the offense with the intent of facilitating the commission of the offense;

    (B) the victim is younger than 14 years of age; or

    (C) the victim is 65 years of age or older.

(b) In this section, "child" has the meaning assigned that term by Section 22.011(c).

(c) An aggravated sexual assault under this section is without the consent of the other person if the aggravated sexual assault occurs under the same circumstances listed in Section 22.011(b).

(d) The defense provided by Section 22.011(d) applies to this section.

(e) An offense under this section is a felony of the first degree.

In Georgia, the rape statute is short and very specific, covering only penile–vaginal penetration. However, it does specifically address the issue of marriage. According to the Criminal Code of Georgia, Chapter 16, Section 6-1:

16-6-1

(a) A person commits the offense of rape when he has carnal knowledge of:

(1) A female forcibly and against her will; or

(2) A female who is less than ten years of age.

Carnal knowledge in rape occurs when there is any penetration of the female sex organ by the male sex organ. The fact that the person allegedly raped is the wife of the defendant shall not be a defense to a charge of rape.

If a sexual attack does not involve penile–vaginal penetration but rather "the sex organs of one person and the mouth or anus of another", the Criminal Code of Georgia provides that it be prosecuted as *aggravated sodomy* (Criminal Code of Georgia, Chapter 16, Section 6-2).

CLINICAL DEFINITIONS

Clinicians and therapists define rape in treatment-oriented terms, helpful to the purpose of understanding the pathology of an offender, or seeing a victim through personal and emotional crisis.

According to Groth (1979, p. 3) a treatment-oriented definition should focus on the perceptions of the victim and the impact of offense behavior, rather than the intent of the offender:

. . . from a clinical rather than a legal point of view, it makes more sense to regard rape as any form of forcible sexual assault, whether the assailant intends to effect intercourse or some other type of sexual act. . . . The defining element in rape is lack of consent.

This definition is related to understanding and helping victims overcome the impact of their trauma.

Groth and Hobson (1983, p. 159) present rape as "a form of sexual aggression" that is not sexually motivated. They define it by explaining that rape is (p. 160):

> . . . any type of sexual activity imposed on a person against will and without consent. It refers, then, to any form of sexual assault. In every act of rape, sexuality and aggression are involved but we conceptualize rape as the sexual expression of aggression rather than the aggressive expression of sexuality. Rape, then, is a pseudo-sexual act, complexly determined, but serving primarily non-sexual purposes. . . .

This definition is wrought with an eye to understanding, classifying, and treating sex offenders.

According to Palmer and Thornhill (2000, p. 1):

> Rape is copulation resisted to the best of the victim's ability unless such resistance would probably result in death or serious injury to the victim or injury to individuals the victim commonly protects. Other sexual assaults, including oral and anal penetration of a man or woman under the same conditions, also may be called rape under some circumstances,

This definition was fashioned to serve the purpose of researching the biological origins of rape with an eye to treatment of both the victim and the offender.

POLITICAL DEFINITIONS

Political definitions of rape are based on or motivated by partisan or self-serving objectives. Rather than assisting justice or clinical treatment, they seek to advance the agenda of a particular group. This includes the varied agendas of offender or victim advocates, political parties and movements, and religious institutions.

In a class on rape investigation taught by one of the authors (Turvey), a female student defined rape as *any* sexual conduct between a male and female, including consensual partners. This, she argued, because it is not possible for females to engage in consensual sexual activity in any context with a male. She seemed to argue that the power structure of society has eliminated the ability of a woman to choose whether or not to have sex, because of the economic dependence of many women on men, and their greater physical and political power. Men and women cannot be considered equally leveraged, she argued, and subsequently women cannot not give their consent. Sex under such circumstances is necessarily pressured at best, and therefore must be considered a form of rape.

Robin Morgan, the poet, writer and editor of *Ms.* magazine, argues that (Lewis, 2003) "rape exists any time sexual intercourse occurs when it has not been initiated by the woman, out of her own genuine affection and desire." This definition suggests that women who did not initiate sexual intercourse must have been coerced to engage in it.

MORAL DEFINITIONS

Moral definitions of rape are a particular kind of political definition. They are judgmental, emphasizing the goodness, badness, rightness, or wrongness of offenders or their actions. Often inflammatory, they are a vehicle for anger, a desire for retribution and even revenge. Moral definitions tend to come from victims, their advocates, and the media. They are easy to discern, including subjective and emotional terms like "loser," "coward," "vicious," "perverse," "evil," "monster," "heinous," and "animal."

There are those, however, who do provide moral definitions and descriptions of rape in favor of the offender. In a highly publicized incident, Seiichi Ota (shown in Figure 1-1), a Liberal Democratic Party politician from Tokyo, Japan, stated during a debate on population growth organized by a kindergarten association that ("Fury . . .", 2003):

> Gang rape shows the people who do it are still vigorous, and that is OK. I think that might make them close to normal. . . .

According to other reports regarding the statements of Mr. Ota (Simkin, 2003):

> The senior lawmaker declared that, "those who gang rape are fine as they are in good spirits," and suggested such people are "close to normal" compared with spineless men.

Mr. Ota later apologized for the statements, saying ("Fury . . .", 2003):

Figure 1-1

Seiichi Ota, Liberal Democratic Party lawmaker, Tokyo, Japan.

> If you only took what I said, well of course it would be regarded as extremely careless remark. I wanted to add that rape is a serious crime that should be punished severely, but the topic had changed and I wasn't given the chance to speak any further.
>
> I think the fact that such comments were reported made victims . . . and many women feel unpleasant, so I want to reconsider and express my apologies. . . .

In response, Japanese Prime Minister Junichiro Koizu levied his own opinion of Mr. Ota and of the crime of rape ("Fury . . .", 2003):

> He deserves to be criticised. Rape is an atrocious act of cowardice and has nothing to do with virile qualities.
>
> . . .
>
> Yasuyuki Takai, vice chairman of the Japan Federation of Bar Association's committee on victim support, said Mr Ota's remarks were indicative of Japanese society's passive attitude to rape, which often goes unreported.

The role of investigative and forensic personnel is to examine and describe sex-crime-related behavior in the most objective manner possible. Political and moral definitions of rape should be of little interest, detracting from the task at hand. Such terminology certainly should not find its way into investigative or forensic reports. The use of moral definitions or inflammatory descriptions of rape in such contexts telegraphs bias and ignorance and identifies a training need.

PRECONCEIVED THEORIES AND INVESTIGATIVE BIAS

Even when we follow the more objective legal-style definitions as our guide to rape investigation, there are still dangers with the application of those definitions to actual casework. Specifically, no matter how we try, it is impossible to remove the observer from the observed. Each of us sees events through our own lens of experience and accumulated prejudice. The result is a haze of a priori investigative bias, or preconceived theories, which clouds objective reasoning.

As discussed in Turvey (2002, pp. 54–57) *a priori investigative bias* is a phenomenon that occurs when investigators, detectives, crime-scene personnel, or others somehow involved with an investigation develop theories uninformed by the facts. These theories, which are most often based on subjective life experience, cultural bias, and prejudice, can influence whether or not investigators recognize and collect certain kinds of physical evidence at the scene. A priori investigative bias can also influence whether or not certain theories about a case are ever considered.

Similarly, in *Criminal Investigation*, Dr. Hans Gross has explained the concept of *preconceived theories*. The discussion is so valuable, and the volume so difficult to obtain, that it is best presented here in nearly its entirety. Despite being over a century old, his writings are still terribly relevant (Gross, 1924, pp. 10–12):

Section iv.—Preconceived Theories.

The method of proceeding just described, that namely, in which parallel investigations are instituted, which to a certain extent mutually control each other, is the best, and one is tempted to say the only, way of avoiding the great dangers of a "preconceived theory"—the most deadly enemy of all inquiries. Preconceived theories are so much the more dangerous as it is precisely the most zealous Investigating Officer, the officer most interested in his work, who is the most exposed to them. The indifferent investigator who makes a routine of his work has as a rule no opinion at all and leaves the case to develop itself. When one delves into the case with enthusiasm one can easily find a point to rely on; but one may interpret it badly or attach an exaggerated importance to it. An opinion is formed which cannot be got rid of. In carefully examining our own minds (we can scarcely observe phenomena or a purely psychical character in others), we shall have many opportunities of studying how preconceived theories take root: we shall often be astonished to see how accidental statements of almost no significance and often purely hypothetical have been able to give birth to a theory of which we can no longer rid ourselves without difficulty, although we have for a long time recognized the rottenness of its foundation.

Nothing can be known if nothing has happened; and yet, while still awaiting the discovery of the criminal, while yet only on the way to the locality of the crime, one comes unconsciously to formulate a theory doubtless not quite void of foundation but having only a superficial connection with the reality; you have already heard a similar story, perhaps you have formerly seen an analogous case; you have had an idea for a long time that things would turn out in such and such a way. This is enough: the details of the case are no longer studied with entire freedom of mind. Or a chance suggestion thrown out by another, a countenance which strikes one, a thousand other fortuitous incidents, above all losing sight of the association of ideas end in a preconceived theory, which neither rests upon juridical reasoning nor is justified by actual facts.

Nor is this all: often a definite line is taken up, as for instance by postulating, "If circumstances M. and N. are verified then the affair must certainly be understood in such and such a way." This reasoning may be all very well, but meanwhile, for some cause or other, the proof of M. and N. is long in coming; still the same idea remains in the head and is fixed there so firmly that it sticks even after the verification of M. and N. has failed, and although the conditions laid down as necessary to its adoption as true have not been realized.

It also often happens that a preconceived theory is formed because the matter is examined from a false point of view. Optically, objects may appear quite different from what they really are, according to the point of view from which they are looked at. Morally, the same phenomenon happens, the matter is seen from a false point of view which the observer refuses at all costs to change; and so he clings to his preconceived theory. In this situation the most insignificant ideas, if inexact, can prove very dangerous. Suppose a case of arson had been reported from a distant locality, immediately in spite of oneself the scene is imagined; for example, one pictures the house, which one has never seen, as being on the left-hand side of the road. As the information is received at head quarters the idea formed about the scene becomes precise and fixed. In imagination the whole scene and its secondary details are presented, but everything is always placed on the left of the road; this idea ends by taking such a hold on the mind that one is convinced that the house is on the left, and all questions are asked as if one had seen the house in that position. But suppose the house to be really on the right of the road and that by chance the error is never rectified; suppose further that the situation of the house has some importance for the bringing out of the facts or in forming a theory of the crime, then this false idea may, in spite of its apparent insignificance, considerably confuse the investigation.

All this really proceeds from psychical imperfection to which every man is subject. Much more fatal are delusions resulting from efforts to draw from a case more than it can yield. Granted that no Investigating Officer would wish by the aid of the smallest fraud to attach to a case a character different from or more important than that which it really possesses, yet it is only in conformity with human nature to stop the more willingly at what is more interesting than at what belongs to everyday life. We like to discover romantic features where they do not exist and we even prefer the recital of monstrosities and horrors to that of common every day facts. This is implanted in the nature of everyone, and though in some to a greater, in some to a lesser, extent, still there it is. A hundred proofs, exemplified by what we read most, by what we listen to most willingly, by what sort of news spreads the fastest, show that the majority of men have received at birth a tendency to exaggeration. In itself this is no great evil; the penchant for exaggeration is often the penchant for beautifying our surroundings; and if there were no exaggeration we should lack the notions of beauty and poetry. But in the profession of the criminal expert everything bearing the least trace of exaggeration must be removed in the most energetic and conscientious manner; otherwise, the Investigating Officer will become an expert unworthy of his service and even dangerous to humanity. We cannot but insist that he should not let himself slip into exaggerations, that he should constantly with this object criticize his own work and that of others; and that he should examine it with extra care if he fail to find traces of exaggeration. These creep in in spite of us, and when they exist no one knows where they will stop. The only remedy is to watch oneself most carefully, always work with reflection, and prune out everything having the least suspicion of exaggeration. It is precisely because a certain hardihood and prompt initiative are demanded of Investigating Officers that one finds in the best of them a slight leaning towards the fictitious: one will perceive it in careful observation of oneself and get rid of it by submission to serene discipline.

The challenge for all concerned is to develop strategies for focusing on the facts despite our walls of habit and belief, and despite our personal interests.

The first line of defense against any kind of bias is a strict adherence to the physical evidence, without embellishment or exaggeration. Offenders, victims, and witnesses can lie or be entirely mistaken, but the evidence won't. As provided by the court in *Philippines v. Aguinaldo* (1999):

> When physical evidence runs counter to testimonial evidence, conclusions as to physical evidence must prevail. Physical evidence is that mute but eloquent manifestation of truth which rate high in our hierarchy of trustworthy evidence.

Physical evidence is the only objective record of events when a crime of any kind has been committed. All statements, including confessions, should be contrasted with the known forensic evidence. This guideline will resound throughout all of the chapters in this work.

The second line of defense is full knowledge and appreciation of the true nature and extent of rape, its perpetrators, and its victims. As provided in Palmer and Thornhill (2000, p. 2): "Most people don't know much about why humans have the desires, emotions, and values that they have, including those that cause rape."

Developing this and other related knowledge is a goal of this work. Before we can do that, however, we must tear down some of the prevalent stereotypes and thinking that persist.

OFFENDER MYTHS

One of the most pervasive myths about rape is that it is committed to satisfy an offender's sexual desires, as though they become overwhelmed with sexual excitement and commit rape because they cannot control themselves. The stereotypical rapist is described by Groth (1979, p. 2) as:

> . . . a lusty male who is the victim of a proactive and vindictive woman, or he is seen as a sexually frustrated man reacting under the pressure of pent up needs, or he is thought to be a demented sex fiend harboring insatiable and perverted desires.

Additional stereotypical elements include the ignorant notion that rapists tend to be strangers or loners. The loners are characterized as single "losers," fixated on pornography, who live alone or, as suggested above, with overbearing women. These elements too often find themselves in what are offered as professional reports assessing rape behavior and offender characteristics ("An FBI . . .", 2000; "East End . . .", 2001; Giguiere, 2003; Ross, 1998; Shearer, 1996).[3]

These stereotypes are not just false, but potentially misleading to the inexperienced investigator.

THE MYTH OF THE STRANGER

There are still those who consider rape a crime that can and does only happen between strangers. This conjures up images of shadowy figures lurking in dark alleys in undesirable parts of town. This myth is particularly dangerous because it suggests that there is perfect safety being out in the daylight, being in your own home, in your own car, or being with people that you know. Potential

---

[3] It is possible for a rapist to be a "loner" (whatever that may mean) or to possess some or all of the stereotypical characteristics described. However, the frequent boilerplate manner in which such assessments have been offered, as well as the use of subjective and judgmental terminology (i.e., "loser"), is a hazard for investigators to avoid. They speak to an overreliance on the perception of average offender types, forgoing in-depth case analysis in favor of expediency, and the desire to appeal to the masses. Neither is of interest to rape investigators.

On the issue of pornography, Murrin and Laws (1990, p. 89) explain that their research suggests:

> it is not pornography *per se* that has an influence upon the incidence of sexual crime, but rather the nature of the person being exposed and the existing cultural milieu in which that exposure occurs.

This was conceptualized earlier by Groth (1979, p. 9), who argued as follows:

> Although a rapist, like anyone else, might find some pornography stimulating, it is not sexual arousal but the arousal of anger and fear that leads to rape. Pornography does not cause rape; banning it will not stop rape. In fact, some studies have shown that rapists are generally exposed to less pornography than normal males.

Subsequently, those who suggest a causal or even correlational link between pornography and crimes do so most frequently with a political or moral agenda. They are essentially pandering, betting on the inflammability and ignorance of their audience.

victims are at risk from without and from within, in public and private, at home and away, in familiar surroundings and strange ones, at all times day and night, as shown in Figures 1-2 and 1-3.

Kilpatrick (2000) has compiled data from a number of studies to refute the stranger myth:

Relationship of the Victim to the Offender

The NWS [National Women's Study] dispelled the common myth that most women are raped by strangers. For example:

- Only 22% of rape victims were assaulted by someone they had never seen before or did not know well.
- Nine percent of victims were raped by husbands or ex-husbands.
- Eleven percent by fathers or stepfathers.
- Ten percent by boyfriends or ex-boyfriends.
- Sixteen percent by other relatives.
- Twenty-nine percent by other non-relatives, such as friends and neighbors.

In addition to the data just presented, the NWS gathered information about new cases that happened to adult women during the two-year follow up period. This information on the 41 such cases provides excellent information about the breakdown for new rapes experienced by adult women (Kilpatrick, Resnick, Saunders, & Best, 1998) (Dohrenwend book chapter).

- 24.4% of offenders were strangers.
- 21.9% were husbands.
- 19.5% were boyfriends.
- 9.8% were other relatives.

Figure 1-2

From the author's case files— a jogging path around Delaware Park, centrally located in downtown Buffalo, NY. This very open, public location has been a hunting ground of choice for at least one unapprehended serial rapist who prefers to attack some of his victims in the morning while they are jogging or walking.

Figure 1-3

From the author's case files—the vehicle of a 16-year-old victim of abduction–rape–homicide. She was taken by force from the church where she volunteered her time cleaning, and her white Maverick was found backed into the trees off the road a few miles away. All the doors were locked. Her body was inside of the vehicle situated in the driver's seat, redressed after a brutal attack, with her keys on the floor next to her feet. The author's examination revealed that the primary suspect was someone that she knew.

- 9.8% were friends.
- 14.6% were other nonrelatives.

The NVAW [National Violence Against Women] survey used different categories for victim–perpetrator relationships but reported similar findings with respect to the types of perpetrators most prevalent in rape cases occurring after age of 18.

- 76% of perpetrators were intimate partners (i.e., current and former spouses, cohabiting partners, dates, and boyfriends/girlfriends).
- 16.8% were acquaintances.
- 14.1% were strangers.
- 8.6% were relatives other than spouses.

The NSA [National Survey of Adolescents] provides a different perspective because it provides data on cases during childhood and adolescence (Kilpatrick and Saunders, 1996).

- 32.5% of perpetrators were identified as friends.
- 23.2% were strangers.
- 22.1% were relatives (fathers, stepfathers, brothers, sisters, grandparents, others).
- 18.1% were other nonrelatives known well by the victim.

THE MYTH OF UNCONTROLLABLE AROUSAL

This myth has its origins in some facts that are easily confused by those with an agenda or a less than perfect understanding of human biology, chemistry, and psychology. It is true that visual and auditory stimuli play a major role in human sexuality. Put more simply, seeing things and hearing things can cause sexual arousal. However, a male's erection, one primary indicator of sexual arousal, occurs as a result of harmony achieved among nerves, hormones, blood vessels, and psychological factors. Each of these elements is aroused and dampened differently in different individuals. Everyone's brain chemistry is different; everyone's psychological pleasure and pain associations are different. In the case of the rapist who successfully achieves an erection and penetrates their victim, more often than not it is not just arousal that is at work, but arousal associated with the circumstances of a particular kind of rape. Ejaculation is the same; everything has to be working harmoniously or it simply won't happen.

The first clue to the fallacy of the argument that rape is the result of sexual arousal gone awry is the fact that many people experience extreme levels of sexual arousal every day without thinking about, let alone committing, the crime of rape.

More specifically, and perhaps lesser known to the general public, there are rapists who experience varying degrees of sexual dysfunction during the commission of their crimes. That is to say, they may experience the inability to achieve an erection, maintain an erection, or ejaculate. Some rapists experience sexual dysfunction infrequently; some rapists experience it during many if not all of their crimes. Certainly, for serial rapists who fall into this category, personal sexual arousal and sexual gratification are not a primary concern, although anger over the condition may well be.

Moreover, as discussed in Baker (1997):

> Seventy percent of rape victims report no physical injury and another twenty-four percent report only minor physical injury. Most rape victims are not victims of angry, sadistic rapists. This does not mean that most rape victims are not raped; it does not mean that rape victims fabricate their stories; and it does not mean that what happens to them is okay. It does belie the common belief that rapists are crazy men whose sadistic hunger for sex or hatred of women compels them to rape.

There is wide agreement in the literature that rape is not committed to satisfy sexual arousal gone unchecked. Rather, rape is currently believed to be committed to satisfy the offender's need for power (Groth, 1979; Marshall, Laws, and Barbaree, 1990; Schlesinger and Revitch, 1983). Darke (1990, p. 58) provides a very useful definition of power as the ability to control. Power also includes the feelings and perceptions (i.e., strength, authority, acceptance, reassurance) that may come from achieving that control.

Rape is subsequently best described as a pseudosexual act ("pseudo" meaning "false"). That is to say, rape involves sex, and it can involve sexual arousal, but that's not what it's all about. Sexual penetration, sexual contact, and sexual control are only means to achieving the rapist's goals, not the goals themselves.

THE MYTH OF THE "LONER"

For some reason, there are a number of experts who believe, and a general public eager to accept, that rapists are largely disenfranchised social outcasts who are not able to have normal sexual relations and must therefore resort to rape. This is perhaps because it fits nicely with images of an undersexed male whose social isolation and sexual inactivity result in uncontrollable sexual arousal that must lead to rape. This was not the case with Mark Rathbun, shown in Figure 1-4, and David Alan Shuey, shown in Figure 1-5.

Groth (1979, p. 5) dispels the myth of the predominance of "loner" or socially outcast rapists by explaining that

> one third of the offenders that we worked with were married and sexually active with their wives at the time of their assaults. . . . Of those offenders who were not married

Figure 1-4

Alleged serial rapist 32-year-old Mark Rathbun. He was stopped by police riding his bicycle three blocks from the most recent attack in Long Beach, CA. After police received a report of a break-in and attempted sexual assault, they immediately activated a perimeter around the location where the crime had occurred. Rathbun was questioned by police, had an injury to his finger in the location where the victim said she had bitten her attacker, and was taken into custody for allegedly possessing a crack cocaine pipe. After voluntarily giving police a DNA sample, he was released on bail until his DNA results came back positive, linking him to 13 rapes since 1997. According to reports, he would enter his victim's homes, typically in the middle of the night; they were single women, from 30 to 77 years old, who lived alone. He would also cover his face during the attacks to conceal his features. Rathbun was by accounts friendly, sociable, and lived with various friends over the years; they even trusted him enough to let him housesit while they were away.

Figure 1-5

Alleged serial rapist, 30-year-old David Alan Shuey, faces a total of six charges of rape or attempted rape from police agencies in Pennsylvania, Connecticut, and Florida. In a number of the attacks, he allegedly gained the victims' trust and access to their homes by posing as a maintenance worker. In the early 1990s, he enrolled in hotel management school at Penn State. He played rugby with the school's club and graduated with a bachelor of science degree in hotel, restaurant and institutional management in 1996. He has no criminal record, and his arrest came as a complete shock to friends and family.

(that is, single, separated, or divorced), the majority were actively involved in a variety of consenting sexual relationships with other persons at the time of their offenses.

Furthermore, Groth and Hobson (1983, p. 161), who studied 1000 offenders over a 16-year period, found the following:

All of the offenders we have seen were sexually active males involved in consensual relationships at the time of their offense. No one raped because he had no other outlet for his sexual needs.

The literature goes on to describe rape as a symptom of psychological disturbance that tends to manifest itself during times of stress or tension. However, the rapist is not necessarily crazy or intellectually diminished. They are in a state of desperation and turmoil (Groth, 1979, p. 6).

VICTIM MYTHS

The view that rape is about sex and unchecked sexual arousal can lead to the false conclusion that victims may be in some way responsible for arousing the rapist or failing to fully dissuade them. Even to this day the authors hear comments from professionals regarding victim culpability, suggesting that they were dressed too seductively, or acting in a provocative manner. This includes statements regarding the victim's clothing if they are wearing a skirt that is too short, heels that are too high, an outfit that is too tight or revealing, or failing to wear a bra and/or underpants. The inference is that the victim's conduct was essentially encouraging the rapist, and the victim is therefore less deserving of sympathy and the benefit of a complete and thorough investigation. The further inference being that perhaps their crime falls into a gray area that isn't actual rape.

As explained by Groth (1979, p. 7):

> Issues of provocation really are ridiculous when one realizes that the victims of rapists include males as well as females and occupy all age categories from infancy to old age. . . . There is no place, season, or time of day in which rape has never occurred, nor any specific type of person to whom it has never happened.

Sadly, the more competent serial offenders count on this reaction from investigators and target those victim populations they perceive as being less likely to be investigated thoroughly, or less likely to be believed. As argued in Maples (1999, p. 38): "In short, they are attracted to vulnerability. Wherever and whenever their victims are available and vulnerable, that's where they'll be." He further places the responsibility right back on leaderless, untrained, and inexperienced law enforcement (Maples, 1999, p. 57):

> Years of uncreative policing must have taught the crooks to overestimate how much they could get away with, because despite our notoriety, our unit enjoyed a front-row view of the predatory instinct at work.

These vulnerable victim populations include drug addicts, the homeless, those under the influence of drugs or alcohol, runaways, and prostitutes. Although it is true that such populations do take more risks with their personal safety and have more contact with crime, it should not be true that crimes committed against them have less meaning. It is certainly not true that they are responsible for the sexual offenses committed against them. Serial offenders hunt them because they perceive investigators are less likely to give such cases their full attention and skill; they are a lower risk than someone whose tragedy will catch the sympathetic eye of an investigator or a news camera.

Nobody ever desires actual rape be committed against them, by the very nature of rape itself. Nor should the way that a person walks or dresses or simply lives be interpreted as any kind of invitation or entitlement to rape. Investigators must accept this and attend the details of every case not as though it was committed against some undeserving stranger, but as though the victim is someone's mother, wife, sister, or daughter. Because they are.

It helps to recall the words of Alice Vachss, former chief of the Special Victims Bureau of the Queens District Attorney's office (Vachss, 1993): "Sexual assaults flourish in a climate of 'gray areas.' So long as the myth of 'real' rape survives, rapists will thrive."

REFERENCES

An FBI profile of a rapist. *Philadelphia Inquirer*, May 24, 2000.

Baker, K. (1997) Once a rapist? Motivational evidence and relevancy in rape law. *Harvard Law Review*, January.

Darke, J. (1990) Sexual aggression: Achieving power through humiliation, in Marshall, W. L., Laws, D., and Barbaree, H. (eds.), *Handbook of Sexual Assault: Issues, Theories, and Treatment of the Offender*. New York: Plenum Press.

East End rape suspect's profile refined. *The Pittsburgh Channel*, June 9, 2001.

Fury over Japan rape gaffe. *BBC News*, June 27, 2003.

Giguiere, J. (2003) FBI: Pornography linked to sex crimes. *Brigham Young University*, February 25.

Gross, H. (1924) *Criminal Investigation*. London: Sweet & Maxwell.

Groth, A. N. (1979) *Men Who Rape: The Psychology of the Offender*. New York: Plenum Press.

Groth, A. N., and Hobson, W. (1983) The dynamics of sexual assault, in Schlesinger, L., and Revitch, E. (eds.), *Sexual Dynamics of Anti-Social Behavior*. Springfield, IL: Charles C. Thomas.

Kilpatrick, D. (2000) Rape and sexual assault. National Violence Against Women Prevention Research Center, Medical University of South Carolina.

Kilpatrick, D. G., Resnick, H. S., Saunders, B. E., and Best, C. L. (1998) Rape, other violence against women, and posttraumatic stress disorder: Critical issues in assessing the adversity–stress–psychopathology relationship, in B. P. Dohrenwend (ed.), *Adversity, Stress, and Psychopathology*, pp. 161–176. New York: Oxford University Press.

Kilpatrick, D. G., and Saunders, B. E. (1996) *Prevalence and Consequences of Child Victimization: Results from the National Survey of Adolescents*. U.S. Department of Justice, Office of Justice Programs, National Institute of Justice, Grant No. 93-IJ-CX-0023.

Lewis, J. J. (2003) Robin Morgan quotes. *About Women's History*, URL: http://womenshistory.about.com/library/qu/blqumorg.htm, retrieved August 15.

Lithwick, D. (2003) She said, he said? Our mixed-up rape laws have created a system that's bad for both sides. *Slate* (slate.msn.com), July 30.

Maples, J. (1999) *The Crime Fighter.* New York: Doubleday.

Marshall, W. L., Laws, D., and Barbaree, H. (eds.) (1990) *Handbook of Sexual Assault: Issues, Theories, and Treatment of the Offender.* New York: Plenum Press.

Murrin, M., and Laws, D. (1990) The influence of pornography, in Marshall, W. L., Laws, D., and Barbaree, H. (eds.) *Handbook of Sexual Assault: Issues, Theories, and Treatment of the Offender.* New York: Plenum Press.

Palmer, C., and Thornhill, R. (2000) *A Natural History of Rape: Biological Basis of Sexual Coercion.* London: The MIT Press.

Philippines v. Rodrigo Loteyro Aguinaldo, GR No. 130784, Oct. 13, 1999.

Ross, B. (1998) He sees rapes as "dates": E. Side rapist a "loser"—FBI. *New York Daily News*, April 27.

Schlesinger, L., and Revitch, E. (eds.) (1983) *Sexual Dynamics of Anti-Social Behavior.* Springfield, IL: Charles C. Thomas.

Shearer, L. (1996) Five Points rapist' search going beyond A-C area. *Onlineathens.com*, November 1.

Simkin, M. (2003) Japanese politician apologises for rape remark, *ABC Radio Australia News*, June 28.

Tredoux, G. (1997) Rape mythology. *Politically Incorrect*, Vol. 1, No. 2, April.

Turvey, B. (2002) Criminal Profiling: An Introduction to Behavioral Evidence Analysis. London: Academic Press.

Vachss, A. (1993) All rape is "real" rape. *The New York Times*, Op-ed, August 11.

Wills, C. (2003) Illinois' new rape law clarifies that consent can be withdrawn during sex. Associated Press, July 29.

CHAPTER 2

THE FIRST INVESTIGATIVE RESPONSE

John O. Savino and Brent E. Turvey, MS

Never esteem anything as of advantage to you that will make you break your word or lose your self-respect.

Marcus Aurelius Antoninus, *Meditations* **(121–180 AD)**

The study of crime begins with the knowledge of oneself. All that you despise, all that you loathe, all that you reject, all that you condemn and seek to convert by punishment springs from you.

Henry Miller "The Soul of Anaesthesia," in *The Air-Conditioned Nightmare* **(1945)**

The purpose of this chapter is to help investigators prepare for that very real moment when they are first notified that a sex crime has been reported, and their assistance is required. The knowledge, capabilities, confidence, and decisions in the initial response will dictate the depth and competence of the work that follows. They will have a tremendous influence over the outcome of the case. Investigators must therefore be prepared and have a plan of action. Less knowledge, less skill, and less preparedness are not better. Though nothing is guaranteed, a thousand mistakes of every kind can be avoided by following the suggestions in this chapter.

KNOW YOUR LAW

Every state has its own laws relating to rape and sexual assault. Investigators should be familiar with the laws of their region, and able to cite them verbatim. Or at least have the pocket version with them for quick reference. In this way they will know whether or not the circumstances described in a notification involve the potential violation of criminal statutes, and which, if any, may apply.

This sounds basic, and it is. However, the authors are routinely confronted by inexperienced or poorly trained investigators with an embarrassingly limited grasp of the laws they are sworn to enforce,[1] to say nothing of their own agency's policies and procedures. For such investigators, ignorance is a vice that must be overcome before irrevocable harm is done. Knowing the law of the land is a start in that direction.

KNOW YOUR PEOPLE

Every investigative agency, law enforcement or otherwise, has its own uniquely trained and uniquely capable personnel. Investigators should know those in their jurisdiction as best they can, on a first-name basis when possible. As time and casework continue, they should take note of the strengths and weaknesses of each.

For law enforcement, this means developing particular knowledge of patrol officers and their routes; these are the eyes and ears to everything happening on the street. Patrol is also, more often than not, the first responder to any crime scene. A partnership must exist or be forged between investigators and patrol, so that one understands the purpose of the other, communication is enhanced, and rivalry is minimized. Everybody is working toward the same goal, and everybody is an important part of the team with a job to do.

DUTIES OF THE FIRST RESPONDER

To ensure that patrol understands the importance of their role in an investigation, and how they can help, Lee (1994, pp. 12–13) and Svensson and Wendel (1965, pp. 10–11) provide complementary lists of duties, even guidelines, for the officer that has responded to a crime scene and is waiting for investigators to arrive. The following has been adapted from both sources:

1. Assist the victim and render aid as necessary.
2. Notify the appropriate agencies per departmental guidelines.
3. Make certain the crime scene is safe and free of danger.
4. Secure the crime scene to define restricted areas per departmental guidelines. Assign at least one officer to maintain a log of persons entering and exiting the scene; restrict access to authorized personnel only.

---

[1] One of the authors (Turvey) participated in the investigation of an alleged sexual assault that turned out to be a false report in a rural police department. When it was learned that the false reporter was not to be arrested, the author asked why. The investigating officer responded confidently that there was no need, as the false reporter had broken no laws. The author and his then partner took it on themselves to locate the governing statute relating to false reports, photocopy it, and place it in the investigating officer's mail box. To this day that same department does not make a practice of arresting false reporters of rape and sexual assault.

5. Write down the names of persons at the scene when the first responder arrived.
6. Write down the make, model, color, and plate number of every vehicle parked in or leaving the general vicinity of the crime scene. These should be photographed if time allows.
7. Write down the names of witnesses and other persons who are known to have entered the scene. Note their clothing and footwear.
8. Establish the basic known facts, but avoid any lengthy or detailed interviews or interrogations.
9. Keep suspects and witnesses separated whenever possible.
10. Instruct witnesses not to discuss events with each other.
11. Do not discuss the crime with witnesses or bystanders.
12. Listen attentively but not obtrusively to ambient conversation.
13. Protect evidence that is in danger of being destroyed by time, the elements, or other dynamic circumstances.
14. Provide all information gathered to investigators.

The purpose of these first responder guidelines is to help document and maintain the integrity of the crime scene, as well as the integrity of witness, victim, and suspect statements. By adhering to these guidelines, patrol officers and investigators can help establish and shore up the links among the crime scene, the victim, and any suspects (Lee, 1994, p. 11). Every investigative effort that follows will be shaped by their initial decisions.

ATTITUDE AND CONFIDENCE

Knowing what to do is the first part of successfully implementing these guidelines. The second part, equally important, is a combination of the right attitude with confidence enough to do the job under any circumstance (Svensson and Wendel, 1965, pp. 10–11)[2]:

> The rules of conduct for the first officer on the scene are also largely applicable to the crime scene investigator. He should not approach his task with preconceived ideas, nor should he draw hasty conclusions. He should have his eyes open for details. He should always suspect the worst and rather do too much than too little . . . He must clearly understand that *mistakes made during the investigation cannot be rectified.*

[2] Here Svensson and Wendel (1965) are highly reminiscent of the lessons originally urged in Gross (1924). The advancement of this mindset and attitude was an encouraging trend that has since dried up in recent criminal investigation texts.

The crime scene investigator should not allow a nervous superior or a doctor who has been called in a death case to influence his calm deliberation on the case before he undertakes the actual examination. Nor should he speed up the investigation on their account. They will have to wait, *because the investigator is personally responsible for the mistakes, and therefore he has the right to determine his own actions at the scene.*

Lead investigators must carry themselves confidently and behave in a manner that dictates respect and is at the same time respectful. There should be no doubts about who is in charge at the crime scene.

LEADERSHIP

All of the guidelines in the world are meaningless unless they are backed up by the integrity of strong leadership. First, supervisors must give their officers and investigators the authority they need to do their job. If officers and investigators feel as though they are not supported or appreciated by supervisors, they will be less likely to perform. They will emulate the apathy that they experience. Second, supervisors must assign duties based on "attitude, aptitude, training, and experience" (Wade, 1999). Supervisors must not give assignments based on political considerations. This practice telegraphs a disinterest in competence and results, both of which will diminish if not rewarded.

Personnel respond to the pull and integrity of good leadership, so long as they know it will be there to back them up when the tough decisions must be made. Otherwise, they learn to fear and resent it. A department without good leadership will become a lawless place, inhabited by demoralized and apathetic personnel. It is then unavoidably marked by its low solve rate.

KNOW YOUR CRIME LAB

The crime lab is where physical evidence is sent to be examined by forensic scientists known as *criminalists*. There are somewhere around 320 public crime labs operating within federal, state, and municipal government agencies, the majority of them functioning as part of a police department or under the direction of a prosecutorial office (Saferstein, 2001, p. 6). Each is differently organized with its own limitations in terms of mandate, budget, equipment, evidence storage facilities, and the number and type of trained forensic personnel.

The investigator should appreciate the capabilities of the forensic labs that may be involved in their cases, as they are not equal. Additionally, there seem to be those in law enforcement who believe that submitting evidence to their public crime lab will cost them money. This is currently not the case. Only the use of private lab services will cost law enforcement agencies money, and in extreme cases this may be a viable option. Barring that rare circumstance, the citizens of the region have already provided for the wages of public crime lab personnel and the cost of any evidence testing on behalf of law enforcement when they paid their taxes.[3]

FORENSIC PERSONNEL

There are many different kinds of forensic evidence, and there are forensic personnel trained to deal with each. The following definitions of forensic personnel and their roles are applied rather than theoretical, based on work that is performed and not the job descriptions that may be assigned by a particular agency. They are intended to be a starting point only.

An *evidence technician* is trained to recognize, document, collect, and preserve physical evidence. A full-time evidence technician is typically not a forensic scientist and is not necessarily qualified to examine evidence and interpret its meaning. Evidence technicians may be attached to the police department, the crime lab, or the medical examiner's office. They are not necessarily sworn police officers, though they can be. In many jurisdictions, police officers do this work themselves with little or no forensic training. It is common for technicians not to have attended a 4-year degree program at a college or university.

A *forensic scientist* examines physical evidence and then testifies about the results of this examination in court. Forensic scientists are defined by the expectation that they may give expert testimony about their examinations and further provide interpretations or opinions. They may work in a crime lab or in private practice. There are many different kinds of physical evidence, and subsequently there are many different kinds of forensic scientists, all variously educated and trained. As discussed in Thornton (1997):

> The single feature that distinguishes forensic scientists from any other scientist is the certain expectation that they will appear in court and testify to their findings and offer an opinion as to the significance of those findings. The forensic scientist will testify not only to what things are, but to what things mean. Forensic science is science exercised on behalf of the law in the just resolution of conflict.

[3] One of the authors (Turvey) was advised by a sex crimes detective in a rural area that his agency did not submit any forensic evidence to the state crime lab because it would cost too much money. This was after the author had advised that a sexual device recovered in a child sexual assault and molestation case be submitted for DNA testing to link it with the victim. It was this law enforcement agency's general practice to collect physical evidence and store it, untested, until trial.

A *criminalist* is a particular kind of forensic scientist who, according to the American Board of Criminalists (ABC), specializes in one or more of the following areas:

- Forensic Biology (serology and DNA)
- Drug Analysis
- Fire Debris Analysis
- Trace Evidence (hairs, fibers, paints, and polymers)

A criminalist may or may not be board certified by the ABC. Criminalists may also be trained in crime reconstruction related to their areas of specialized knowledge, though this is not always the case. Most criminalists will have a 4-year degree of some kind, likely in a hard science such as chemistry or biology. However, there are exceptions.

A *forensic generalist* is a particular kind of forensic scientist who is broadly trained in a variety of forensic specialties. Forensic generalists are big-picture people who can help reconstruct a crime from work performed with the assistance of other forensic scientists, and then direct investigators to forensic specialists as needed. They can also make for good crime lab administrators or directors. According to DeForest, Gaensslen, and Lee (1983, p. 17):

> Because of the depth and complexity of criminalistics, the need for specialists in inescapable. There can be serious problems, however, with overspecialization. Persons who have a working knowledge of a broad range of criminalistics problems and techniques are also necessary. These people are called generalists. The value of generalists lies in their ability to look at all of the aspects of a complex case and decide what needs to be done, which specialists should be involved, and in which order to carry out the required examinations.

The generalist typically has broad education and training in the major forensic sciences and will often have a master's- or doctorate-level education.

A *forensic pathologist* is a medical examiner or coroner responsible for determining the cause and manner of death (manner or *mode* of death includes only the following possibilities: homicide, suicide, accident, natural, or undetermined). To reach this determination, forensic pathologists are "charged with answering several basic questions: Who is the victim? What injuries are present? When did the injuries occur? Why and how were the injuries produced?" (Saferstein, 2001, p. 17) There is a great deal of difference between medical examiners and coroners. A medical examiner is appointed to the position, must have a medical degree, and must also be board certified in forensic pathology. A coroner is an elected official who in some jurisdictions need only be of voting age with a high school diploma and complete a few weeks of training a year. Abilities vary widely in this field.

A *forensic anthropologist* is responsible for the exhumation and identification of human skeletal remains. Based on such an examination the origin, sex, approximate age, race, and the nature of any skeletal injuries may be determined.

A *forensic entomologist* specializes in the study of insects and their relationship to crime. The primary role of forensic entomologists tends to be the estimation of the time of death when it cannot otherwise be reliably established. However, they are also quite useful in determining the potential existence, nature, and location of other scenes associated with the crime using the entomological transfer evidence recovered. A forensic entomologist will typically have a master's- or doctorate-level education.

A *forensic odontologist* specializes in the identification of human teeth and human bite marks. Forensic odontologists typically have a full-time dentistry practice and conduct forensic work on the side. They will subsequently have that requisite education and training.

A *forensic toxicologist* specializes in detecting the presence of drugs, chemical substances, and their traces in human fluids and tissues. Forensic toxicologists assist in evaluating what role toxicology may have had in the cause and manner of death. They also evaluate the potential role of toxicology in modifying human performance and behavior. They will typically have a master's- or doctorate-level education.

A given crime lab may have some or all of these forensic personnel available for investigative consultation. Investigators should learn this. They should also develop and maintain a list of private forensic experts they can call for consultation on various subjects related to their regular casework, as the need arises. There is nothing wrong with getting an outside opinion.

RESPONSE PROCEDURES

Investigators should know and anticipate the nature and frequency of the assistance they can expect from their crime lab. Not every crime lab has a crime-scene unit or evidence technicians who will be dispatched to the scene. However, they may be willing to send out criminalists to assist investigators in major cases. In some cases, sex-crime investigators may have all the assistance and cooperation they need. In other cases, they may have to do everything short of physically examining the victim themselves.

If investigators foresee an absence of forensic assistance, it would be best to get some training in the area of evidence recognition and collection and make a habit of using that training every chance they get. An investigator who cannot collect his or her own evidence is a particularly useless creature, having no legitimate business inside the crime-scene tape. If this seems harsh, it is meant to. Those who have not been properly trained in the importance of physical evidence, evidence recognition, and evidence collection often show little respect for it and are a liability to their own cases. There is no gain in letting them inside the tape for a look when all they can hope to accomplish is to step on or otherwise obliterate something that may be of value to those trying to conduct the forensic investigation. Better to leave them outside the tape and let them look at the photographs and crime-scene video later.

To avoid this shortcoming, it is advised that crime-lab personnel and investigators get together and devise a joint strategy for responding to rape and sexual assault scenes. This will ideally take the form of crime lab personnel providing on-site training to investigators, and investigators visiting the crime lab to better appreciate just what is involved when they submit their bags of evidence. The desired result is a set of mutually agreeable response procedures that play to the strengths and budgets of each agency involved.

Collection Procedures

Each crime lab, having its own facilities and capabilities, should be able to provide the investigator with written protocols for the proper collection and packaging of every kind of physical evidence they are able to examine. If they cannot provide these written protocols, it is an indication that the services of the lab should be discontinued, and another lab should be sought out. If they can't develop written protocols for evidence collection, imagine what they might do with evidence that is actually submitted for forensic analysis.

Generally, this should not be a problem. The investigator should create and maintain a binder of written evidence-collection protocols in their vehicle. These can be referenced at the scene of any crime should the circumstances require it, or should a question be raised. If, after reading the written protocol, the investigator is still uncertain about how to effect a particular collection, then a training need has been identified.

HISTORY

It is important for investigators to educate themselves regarding the weaknesses and limitations of their crime labs. In just the past few years, a host of public crime labs have been found to be rife with fraud, bias, and error. It is not a foreign or rare occurrence.

Consider the following examples:

In 2000, Dr. John Brown, a forensic DNA analyst for the Washington State Patrol Crime Lab for 16 years and one of the founding members of the DNA section, committed perjury to conceal his errors. According to Burkitt (2001):

> Dr. John Brown had tested swabs of semen taken from a rape victim to determine whether the DNA pattern matched anyone in the lab's databank. His first tests in November 1997 came up negative, but after a colleague reviewed his work and said it was flawed, Brown retested the samples and found a match with Craig Barfield. On May 31, 2000, Barfield became the first person in Washington convicted by a jury on the basis of his genetic profile alone. It was Barfield's third felony, which comes with a mandatory life sentence under the state's "three strikes" law.
>
> Brown initially told defense attorneys there had been no earlier report eliminating Barfield, but then admitted on the witness stand he had lied to cover up his mistake.

This admission calls into question every single case that Dr. Brown has examined, and will be used by defense attorneys nationwide as evidence of the pervasiveness of forensic fraud.

In 2002, Kathleen Lundy (shown in Figure 2-1), a ballistics expert with the FBI Crime Lab, testified that forensic metallurgical tests suggested the bullet removed from a victim's head came from the same batch or lot as the bullets found in the defendant's home. She admitted later that this was false testimony.

According to Taylor (2002):

> An FBI scientist's admission that she lied during a hearing in the murder case against Shane Ragland has prompted one of the agency's attorneys to suggest the expert's testimony in as many as 80 other cases nationwide be reviewed.
>
> . . .
>
> Lundy, suspended from courtroom and FBI case work after she revealed her lie in April, is one of two scientists who do comparative bullet-lead analysis for the agency.

Figure 2-1

Kathleen Lundy, former FBI forensic scientist, testifies at a criminal trial.

The tests, designed to show whether bullets came from the same batch of manufacturing lead, are controversial and dismissed by some experts as unproven and invalid.

In Ragland's case, Lundy testified that tests suggested that the bullet removed from DiGiuro's head came from the same batch as bullets found at Ragland's house.

Lundy pleaded guilty to false swearing in Fayette County District Court and was given the maximum sentence, a 90-day suspended sentence (meaning she will serve no jail time) and a $250 fine (Pitsch, 2003).

Also in 2002, Arnold Melnikoff, the former director of the Montana State crime lab, was found to have overstated and misrepresented findings related to forensic hair analysis. He testified that there was less than a 1 in 10,000 chance that hairs found in a victim's bedroom came from someone other than the defendant. Such an opinion has no basis in fact. Two defendants have been exonerated so far. According to Bohrer (2003):

A former state crime lab manager whose testimony helped convict two men who were later exonerated may have given questionable testimony against at least five other defendants—including one sitting on death row, Montana's attorney general said Thursday.

Presenting his audit of the lab manager's work, Attorney General Mike McGrath said a more thorough examination may be warranted—possibly looking at as many as 300 reports that Arnold Melnikoff prepared in criminal cases.

. . .

Melnikoff, a crime lab manager in Montana until 1989, came under fire last October, when Jimmy Ray Bromgard was freed after 15 years in prison when DNA analysis proved he did not rape an 8-year-old girl.

In a rare move by fellow forensic scientists, a peer review of Melnikoff's work in the Bromgard case was conducted and the results published. The panel of experts who reviewed his work came to the following conclusions:

1. The witness's testimony on pages 237–238 contains egregious misstatements not only of the science of forensic hair examinations but also of genetics and statistics. These statements reveal a fundamental lack of understanding of what can be said about human hair comparisons and about the difference between casework and empirical research. His testimony is completely contrary to generally accepted scientific principles.

2. The witness's use of probabilities is contrary to the fact that there is not—and never was—a well established probability theory for hair comparison.

3. The witness's testimony is contrary to the consensus practice B as it existed in 1987 B for forensic hair comparisons and testimony regarding such comparisons.

4. In the Bromgard case, Mr. Melnikoff matched both head and pubic hairs of the accused to questioned hairs from the crime scene. Based on the postconviction DNA testing carried out in this case, we now know that none of the questioned hairs could have come from Mr. Bromgard. While an experienced hair examiner might erroneously associate a single head or pubic hair, it is highly unlikely that a competent hair examiner would incorrectly associate both head and pubic hairs.

5. If this witness has evaluated hair in over 700 cases as he claims in his testimony, then it is reasonable to assume that he has made many other misattributions.

As of this writing, Arnold Melnikoff is a forensic scientist for the Washington State Patrol Crime Laboratory charged with testing drug evidence, but is on administrative leave. In September of 2003, an internal review by the Washington State Patrol determined that he was incompetent and should be fired.

Objective investigators are not interested in deficient or biased forensic examinations. They seek to understand the facts as provided by the objective forensic evidence. They seek the just resolution of their cases. They know that fraud, deception, and exaggeration are the enemies of a respectable career.

But even the smallest unintentional error can have a dramatic impact on a case, as was learned by investigators in Kansas (Laviana, 2003):

> The Kansas Bureau of Investigation's admission that it made a mistake that allowed a rape suspect to go unprosecuted may send some ripples through Sedgwick County's legal community, but it will have little impact, if any, on local court cases, lawyers said Friday.
>
> . . .
>
> KBI Director Larry Welch said Thursday that the mislabeling of a blood sample in October 1991 eliminated Douglas Belt as a suspect in a rape in McPherson County. When the sample was later retested, it linked Belt to the crime.
>
> Belt has since been charged with a series of rapes and the June 2002 murder of Lucille Gallegos of Wichita. Had the error not been made, Welch said, Belt perhaps would have been convicted of the 1991 rape, and perhaps would have been behind bars when the subsequent crimes were committed.

It is duty of investigators to be aware of any such troubles in their local crime lab, past and present. In this way they will understand any potential implications for their current and future casework. Each one of these situations presents a lesson to the investigator that should be studied and learned, as someone else has already paid the price for it. It is not necessary to make the mistake to learn the lesson.

BACKLOGS

It has come to light that some police agencies and crime labs are experiencing significant evidence backlogs, especially when it comes to processing sexual assault kits. The constraints include time and the funding for both lab equipment and trained personnel to operate it. According to Moore (2002), the problem is nationwide:

> The head of the State Police Crime Lab said Tuesday that the agency has gotten about 500 requests for DNA analysis—and finished about half of them—since it started performing the tests about 18 months ago.
>
> Untested evidence from physical exams on rape victims has become a national issue after the discovery of 16,000 untested packages in storage in the New York Police Department and after the Los Angeles Police Department admitted this summer the department had destroyed about 1,000 of the packages, called "rape kits."
>
> In some agencies, DNA analysis is not done on the items in the rape kit unless police have a suspect to whom to try to match the results.
>
> The kit includes samples from areas the rapist is likely to have deposited DNA during the attack.

Ryan (2003) agrees that the problem is national and attributes it to the investigative mindset that existed prior to the advent of nationwide or regional DNA databases:

> . . . rape kits . . . contain semen, hairs, blood or other biological material left behind by a rapist. But in hundreds of thousands of instances, this DNA evidence is never analyzed by a forensic lab and remains in police basements and coroner's backrooms.
>
> "These are not numbers, these are lives," said Debbie Smith, a Virginia woman whose rape kit languished for six years before being tested. "It's so unfair to put a victim through the evidence collection—at best a very invasive process—and then not to do anything with it."

The reason for this inaction is money. Lab analysis of the kits, which are gathered in emergency rooms soon after victims report a rape, can cost $1,000. An estimated 350,000 kits await testing around the country.

. . .

"To me, that kit held my life. I couldn't go forward with my life until my case was solved and I knew that the best chance of solving my case was in that kit," said Smith.

Until recently in many areas, priority in testing kits was given to "suspect cases," or cases in which the police investigation focused on one person. In those cases, investigators asked lab technicians to compare the DNA in the rape kit with the genetic profile of the suspect. Departments saw little reason to test rape kits of "non-suspect" rapes because there was no alleged assailant to match to the DNA in the kit.

That changed with the advent of state DNA databases, as well as CODIS, the national computer database of convict DNA. Now, labs can determine the rapist's DNA from the kit and then run that profile through CODIS to see if it matches any of the 1.4 million offenders in the database. DNA from rape kits alone can also reveal the existence of a serial rapist even if his identity remains a mystery.

Referring specifically to New York, Ryan (2003) writes:

New York City is one locality that has succeeded in reducing its testing backlog. In October 2000, the police department had more than 16,000 untested rape kits sitting in its Queens warehouse, each representing an unsolved rape. The city decided to reduce the backlog by spending $12 million to send the kits to outside contractors. Nearly two-thirds of the kits have been tested so far.

Referring specifically to Louisiana, Hill (2003) writes:

Publicity surrounding the Baton Rouge serial killer caused the Legislature to put up $650,000 and the state to obtain a $2.4 million federal grant to wipe out the backlog of about 3100 rape kits—instances where there was DNA evidence collected but never scanned—but not to increase operating expenses.

. . .

Louisiana has DNA samples collected in rape cases that date back to 1987, Wickenheiser said. The backlog should be wiped out by Dec. 31, he said, predicting many cases will be solved. A DNA sequencer computer costs about $150,000, he said.

"The equipment is a critical part," he said.

While equipment helps, Barnhill said there is a critical need for more personnel.

Referring specifically to Florida, Kidwell (2003) writes:

> Miami police sent only nine of 40 rape kits to the county crime lab this year for critical DNA analysis—a lapse top commanders are scrambling to correct.
>
> Rape investigators began this week sending dozens of the untested rape kits from their property room to the Miami-Dade police lab.
>
> The department recently has been criticized for shelving DNA samples that could have confirmed months earlier that a serial rapist was stalking several southwest Miami neighborhoods.
>
> . . . since Christmas Eve, Miami investigators did not send 31 rape kits—fluids and physical evidence recovered from the victim—to the crime lab, according to records obtained by The Herald. That number includes more than a half-dozen additional cases from the same area where a serial rapist has attacked three school girls and four women. It could not be determined Thursday how many of the 31 untested kits involved cases in which the attacker was unknown.
>
> A Miami officer, who spoke on condition of anonymity, said many rape allegations often result from tumultuous relationships and domestic violence cases.
>
> "There are a lot of reasons why a rape investigator might not send a rape kit to the lab," the source said.
>
> "Sometimes the victim changes her story. Sometimes the suspect is so obvious you don't need a DNA confirmation. Sometimes these things happen under circumstances that you know are not going to lead to a prosecution."

As suggested in Kidwell (2003), leadership, investigator attitude, and ignorance have played a role in creating and maintaining this rape evidence backlog. (See Figure 2-2.) There may be confusion between the crime lab and police investigators regarding when sexual assault kits may be submitted for testing. Some crime labs will not accept kits for testing unless investigators have a strong suspect. Alternatively, some investigators won't submit kits because they believe this to be the lab policy when in fact it is not. And sometimes, everyone acts confused until the media runs a story that shines a bright light on the hundreds or thousands of untested sexual assault kits sitting in police evidence rooms collecting dust. When it is explained that potential DNA information from untested kits cannot be entered into the DNA databases that taxpayers have paid a great deal to develop and maintain, everyone has some explaining to do.

Figure 2-2

A backlog of some 50 rape kits sit untested, shelved in a police evidence room. Note the obvious disarray and careless stacking of paper evidence bags in and around other evidence from other cases.

By understanding and appreciating these aspects of their particular crime lab, investigators can more effectively navigate and communicate their forensic needs and concerns in a given case. They can also get the most out of the resources that their lab has to offer. It will educate collection habits, increase investigator confidence, and streamline the utilization of forensic evidence in their casework. Less information is not better.

INVESTIGATOR'S KIT

At all times investigators should keep a kit in their vehicle that holds at least the following:

1. Business cards with name, agency, and contact information
2. Pens—lots of pens (you can never have too many pens)
3. A small notebook
4. A flashlight
5. Paper evidence bags of various sizes
6. Paper evidence envelopes of various sizes
7. Evidence labels
8. Evidence tape
9. Crime scene tape
10. Permanent marker, fine point
11. Rubber gloves
12. Camera and film
13. Tape recorder and blank cassettes
14. Spare batteries for everything

15. Q-Tips or similar applicator for buccal (oral) swabs or other collections
16. A pair of tweezers for collecting hairs and fibers and other fine material
17. A binder containing copies of local sex crimes statutes
18. Proper evidence collection and packaging procedures
19. Blank consent forms for taking suspect or exclusionary samples of hair and other biological material (i.e., blood, oral swab, hair, etc.)

This kit should be examined and refreshed at the beginning of each shift or tour. It is the investigator's lifeline to a complete and thorough investigation, and to getting it right the first time.

PRE-SCENE CHECKLIST

Before leaving for the crime scene or location of the victim, investigators should get as much information about the case as possible. They should make written notes of the following:

1. The name of the person reporting the case, whether it is a patrol officer, hospital worker, or citizen. Always attempt to speak directly with the reporter so that miscommunications are minimized.
2. The telephone number of the reporter as well as the name and telephone number of the facility (i.e., hospital, clinic, etc.) where the victim is being examined and treated.
3. The victim's name, date of birth, and address.
4. Witness names, dates of birth, and addresses.
5. The name, date of birth, and address of the alleged offender, if known.
6. The circumstances of the allegation.
7. If the scene of the crime is known, are patrol officers protecting it? Has it been secured?
8. Has the crime scene unit been notified? If so, get the names of personnel notified.

Without this information, investigators are walking into a new and potentially deceptive situation without the information necessary for asking the right questions of the witnesses, suspects, and evidence. It is not an exaggeration to suggest that they will not have a clear idea where to begin when they get there.

It is easy to forget these things in the rush to get to the action. Remember this—they must wait; there is no action until the investigator gets there. If anyone has a problem waiting, address this issue in private. It doesn't matter how fast investigators can get to the scene if they can't do a good job when they get there.

THE PRE-SCENE INTERVIEW

After checking to be certain the kit is in order and completing the pre-scene checklist, the investigator should respond to the location of the victim. Depending on the timing of the initial notification, this may be the crime scene, the hospital, the victim's residence, or the residence of a friend or relative. If a crime scene is being secured, the investigator should advise the crime-scene unit personnel to hold off their processing until initial interviews have been completed. The reason for this delay is so that the investigator can obtain (if possible) the following information from the victim, other family members, and/or witnesses. This information is crucial for effectively processing the scene and squeezing everything of value from it the first time:

1. Exact location of the alleged assault.
2. Circumstances of the alleged assault: This includes a description of the activities of the victim—i.e., walking home from school; jogging in a park; sleeping in their apartment; etc.
3. Time of occurrence: This will assist when canvassing neighbors and nearby businesses as may be appropriate.
4. Victim injuries: Crime-scene unit personnel should photograph all injuries, no matter how minor. If they refuse, investigators should take their own photos.
5. Items used during the attack by victim and offender: i.e., weapons, ligatures, sexual items and materials, etc.
6. Items touched by the offender: These should be examined for trace evidence to corroborate the victim's story and help establish the identity of the offender if necessary.
7. Possible location of bodily fluids: i.e., blood, semen, saliva, etc.
8. Point of entry to the crime scene, if applicable.
9. Detailed description of the suspect: This includes the suspect's physical characteristics, clothing and smells such as alcohol, cigarette smoke, perfume, or cologne. This information should be distributed to area patrol units immediately.

All of the information gathered should be relayed to crime-scene unit personnel to educate their search for, and subsequent examination of, the physical evidence associated with the attack.

If investigators follow the guidelines presented in this chapter, they will be well prepared to start their investigation into the reported crime.

REFERENCES

Bisbing, R., Deadman, H., Houck, M., Palenek, S., and Rowe, W. Peer review report: *Montana v. Jimmy Ray Bromgard.* URL: http://www. innocenceproject.org/causes/Bromgard_print_version.html, retrieved August 23, 2003.

Bohrer, B. "More cases questioned in crime lab case," Associated Press, May 29, 2003.

Burkitt, J. "Drug use tainted evidence in state crime lab," *Seattle Times,* July 11, 2001.

Deforest, P., Gaensslen, R., and Lee, H. (1983) *Forensic Science: An Introduction to Criminalistics.* New York: McGraw-Hill.

Gross, H. (1924) *Criminal Investigation,* 3rd ed. London: Sweet and Maxwell.

Hill, J. State's crime lab directors push for more money. *Shreveport Times,* August 12, 2003.

Kidwell, D. Evidence in 31 rapes untested for months. *The Miami Herald,* June 20, 2003.

Laviana, H. KBI error a "wake-up call" to lawyers. *The Wichita Eagle,* June 7, 2003.

Lee, H. (1994) *Crime Scene Investigation.* Taoyan, Taiwan: Central Police University.

Moore, M. Lab processing backlog of DNA kits, official says. *The Baton Rouge Advocate,* October 9, 2002.

Pitsch, M. Ex-FBI scientist pleads guilty: She admits false testimony in Ragland case, is fined $250. *Courier-Journal,* June 18, 2003.

Ryan, H. Ending rape kit wait puts price on justice. *CourtTV.com,* April 24, 2003.

Saferstein, R. (2001) *Criminalistics: An Introduction to Forensic Science,* 7th ed. Upper Saddle River, NJ: Prentice Hall.

Svensson, A., and Wendel, O. (1965) *Crime Scene Investigation,* 2nd ed. New York: American Elsevier.

Taylor, L. Ragland case lie sparks call for FBI review; expert admitted to perjury about bullet-lead tests. *Lexington Herald-Leader,* July 20, 2002.

Thornton, J. I. (1997) "The General Assumptions and Rationale of Forensic Identification," in Faigman, D., Kaye, D., Saks, M., and Sanders, J. (Eds.) Modern Scientific Evidence, Vol. 2, St. Paul, MN: West Publishing Co.

Wade, C. (ed.) (1999) *Handbook of Forensic Services.* U.S. Department of Justice, Federal Bureau of Investigation.

CHAPTER 3

INVESTIGATIVE CRIME SCENE MANAGEMENT

John O. Savino and Brent E. Turvey, MS

Vivacity, leadership, must be had, and we are not allowed to be nice in choosing.
We must fetch the pump with dirty water, if clean cannot be had.
Ralph Waldo Emerson "Power," in *The Conduct of Life* **(1860)**

In every investigative effort, from the initial response to the crime scene, and from the evidence to the interviews, somebody has to be in charge. One person must lead and make decisions, having the very last word on every aspect of the case. This person must be confident, qualified, and know enough about criminal investigation and forensic evidence "to run the whole show" (Maples, 1999, p. 67). Such a person is generally referred to as the *lead investigator.*

Generally, a lead investigator's capacity to govern, route, and manage is first put to the test at the crime scene. Every crime scene is different, not just because of the location involved but because of those who may be reacting within it, according to role, character, culpability, and mood. As a consequence, there is always some level of intensity, some degree of excitement, and a great deal of confusion.

The purpose of this chapter is to help lead investigators with the often overwhelming and thankless task of running their case once they have arrived at the crime scene. It is not easy to run a case, and not everyone has the ability to do it. Subsequently, not everyone should.

For starters, there are two inflexible rules for the lead investigator to communicate and enforce at all times:

1. "The first concern of the trained observer is to exclude everyone from the immediate area *who does not have some duty to perform in carrying out the investigation.*" (Snyder, 1944, p. 12)
2. "Never touch, change or alter anything until identified, measured and photographed." (Snyder, 1944, p. 17)

This is accomplished by command and example. If these sound like rules for the scene of a homicide, it is because they are meant to. Every rape and sexual assault should be investigated with that same attention to detail.

At some point in the history of criminal investigation, somebody decided that the investigation of rape and sexual assault was less important than the investigation of homicide. They felt that less attention should be given to evidence at rape crime scenes, less training was required for rape investigators, and that less overall work should or could be done on those cases. They reasoned that fewer or no photographs should be taken, that little or no evidence needed collecting at the scene, and that no crime-scene sketch was necessary. They considered a search of the area around the crime scene for evidence a waste of time, and canvassing the area for witnesses a waste of manpower. They decided that victim statements need not be written out, or otherwise memorialized. They decided that a paragraph describing the offense on a complaint form, from their estimation of events, was enough.

This person must have had a lengthy career and risen to a position of rank and authority, because they seem to have trained a lot of people to think the way that they apparently did. And those people in turn have trained many others. Such investigative disinterest is no way to run a homicide investigation, a sex crimes investigation, or any kind of investigation. By truncating or eliminating the ingredients mentioned, whoever started the trend decided that rape and sexual assault did not really need to be investigated at all.

A recent case investigated by one of the authors (John Savino) provides a good example:

Example: Stranger rape/apartment lobby

A young woman unlocked the lobby door of her apartment building at approximately 0430 hours, and an unknown male followed her inside. The male grabbed her around the neck and began to choke her. During a violent struggle, he repeatedly told her "YOU DESERVE THIS". He forced her further inside the building, knocking her to the floor.

The victim's last memory, prior to losing consciousness, was the male struggling to remove her pants. When she woke, he was gone along with her purse. She believed that her clothes had not been removed.

911 was called and uniformed personnel responded. Officers arrived at scene and interviewed the 911 caller. The caller stated that she had heard the victim's screaming and crying, and found her lying on the floor with her pants down.

The victim told the officers that she did not think she had been sexually assaulted. The victim based this on the fact that her clothing appeared intact, and that she felt she would have remembered if she was sexually assaulted.

A summary look for the offender proved negative.

The victim was brought to a hospital for treatment of her injuries.

John Savino later became involved with this investigation. After interviewing the victim, he went to the crime scene. During a walk through the scene and what he believed would be the offender's most logical escape route, Savino located a woman who had found a purse in the rear alley of the building just a few hours earlier. The purse had been found after the initial officer's response to the scene.

Along with the contents of the purse was a cellular phone. Savino established that the offender had not taken the victim's phone along with her purse. The phone in the purse most likely belonged to the offender. A search warrant was obtained for the phone and the identity of the offender was learned.

The male offender that was subsequently arrested had a long criminal record. After being interviewed, he confessed to the crime and was charged with Robbery/Assault/Attempted Rape.

Although this case ended successfully it could have gone unsolved because the incident was originally treated as if it was not very serious. The first officers did not establish and secure the crime scene, a search of the rear alley was not done at the time of their initial response, and the cellular phone dropped by the offender was left for anyone to find. The right mindset was absent, basic steps were not taken, and crucial evidence was almost overlooked.

There is a very real threshold for investigative competency. It starts with the right mindset, which is that every crime should be treated with the same attention to detail as a homicide. Why? Because it could be that your burglary or sex crime is part of a series or a "pattern crime." Or it could be that your rapist has killed before, or that he will kill in the future, intentionally or not. Good investigators know what they don't know, and what they can't do, which is go back and get things from the crime scene that were missed the first time through because nobody thought they would be important. If an investigator is assigned to a complaint and fails to perform certain basic tasks, starting with the crime scene, then they have not really done their job. Good investigators practice a very simple investigative philosophy: every scene done right, every time, in every crime.

It is the lead investigator's job to get everyone on board with this philosophy and conduct the investigation accordingly. If this proves too difficult or even impossible, then the lead investigator may need to learn to do some things without any help. Depending on the support that the lead investigator suffers from supervisors, and the people they are meant to depend on at the crime scene, this may or may not be preferable.

What we intend with this chapter are straightforward discussions of a lead investigator's major considerations at the crime scene, and how to direct action amid the excitement and chaos.

Guides to the specifics of evidence recognition, documentation, collection, and preservation, including the sexual assault examination of the victim, are provided in the chapters that follow.

NIJ GUIDELINES

The National Institute of Justice's Technical Working Group on Crime Scene Investigation recommends that lead investigators should do at least the following when taking charge of any crime scene (Rau, 2000, p. 19):

1. Converse with the first responder(s) regarding observations/activities.
2. Evaluate safety issues that may affect all personnel entering the scene(s) (e.g., blood borne pathogens, hazards).
3. Evaluate search and seizure issues to determine the necessity of obtaining consent to search and/or obtaining a search warrant.
4. Evaluate and establish a path of entry/exit to the scene to be utilized by authorized personnel.
5. Evaluate initial scene boundaries.
6. Determine the number/size of scene(s) and prioritize.
7. Establish a secure area within close proximity to the scene(s) for the purpose of consultation and equipment staging.
8. If multiple scenes exist, establish and maintain communication with personnel at those locations.
9. Establish a secure area for temporary evidence storage in accordance with rules of evidence/chain of custody.

The authors agree that taking these steps is a good starting point for the lead investigator.

GO TO THE SCENE

The authors cannot overemphasize the importance of attending the crime scene. If the investigator catches the case near the time of the attack and arrives at the crime scene in a timely fashion, only that one visit may be necessary. If they do not, catching it or arriving after the passage of some time, then the scene should be visited (or revisited as the case may be) at the same time of day and week as the attack. Make no mistake: this is a threshold requirement. Investigators who have not visited and examined the crime scene in person cannot legitimately say that they have completed a thorough investigation. As discussed in O'Connell and Soderman (1936, pp. 1–2):

> Modern criminal investigation in a broader sense also has several phases. The first is the requirement of a thorough examination and inquiry into the method and technique used by the criminal in his approach to the commission of the crime. So it is absolutely vital that a policeman or detective, in order to investigate a crime, should visit the scene of it. This he must do in order to act intelligently, logically, and to avoid any preconceived notions or theories.

The following is just some of the information to be learned from the crime scene:

1. Investigators can experience the sights, smells, and sounds of the crime scene, as the victim and the offender perceived them.
2. Investigators can experience the spatial relationships within the scene.
3. Investigators can experience how open or secluded the scene is, suggesting possible witnesses.
4. Investigators can experience how accessible or hidden the scene is to those not from the area, suggesting possible suspect populations.
5. Investigators can learn what kind of traffic (vehicle and pedestrian), residences, or businesses are nearby, suggesting possible witnesses and suspect populations.
6. Investigators can experience transfer evidence firsthand. Vegetation, soil, glass, fibers, and any other material that may have transferred on to the victim or offender may transfer on to them, providing examples of what to look for on suspect clothing or in suspect vehicles.
7. Investigators can walk victim and offender routes themselves, seeing the sights firsthand, in order to discover additional witnesses and suspect populations. These witnesses can include businesses with active surveillance cameras that may have recorded some or all of the crime.
8. The attentive investigator may discover items of evidence previously thought lost or previously unknown.

This information is vital to the following ends:

- Witness and suspect development
- Corroborating or disputing witness and suspect interviews

- Developing investigative leads
- Crime reconstruction

Investigators may find it valuable to walk through the scene quietly, after familiarizing themselves with the facts of the case. If possible, investigators should later walk through the scene with the assistance of the victim. This must not be done until after the victim has been afforded a forensic examination, medical examination, and any necessary treatment.

Consider the following example, which demonstrates that investigators can never be certain what or who they may find at the crime scene, even days after an attack:

Example: Tony Anthony Deese **(shown in Figure 3-1)**

In June of 2003, a 12-year-old girl was walking near Brookhaven Trailer Park in Monroe, North Carolina, when a man attacked her and pulled her into the woods. According to reports (Gilchrist, 2003, and Hovanec, 2003), the victim told police that the man had tied her hands together with rope, put a knife to her throat, and raped her. He then stole $21 from her. He also threatened to kill her if she told the police.

Afterward, the victim walked back to her residence in a mobile home park, and the rapist followed. He knocked on her door and told her to let him in. After the victim told him that her mother was asleep in the house, he left.

Figure 3-1

Tony A. Deese, 6'2", 275 lbs.; registered sex offender under South Carolina law.

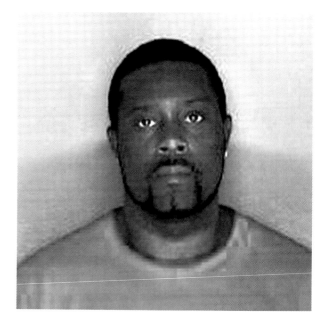

Two days later, when police arrived to investigate the attack, they had the victim walk them through the crime and searched for evidence. According to reports, that's when they found the girl's attacker. According to Gilchrist (2003):

> ... officers were escorting the girl back to the scene Monday to gather evidence when she pointed out a man who she said had attacked her, said Police Chief Bobby Haulk.
>
> "The victim screamed, 'That's him, that's him,'" Haulk said. "And then he took off running."

The suspect, Tony A. Deese, 34, of Pageland, SC, was a registered sex offender in South Carolina. He had been convicted of first-degree criminal sexual misconduct in 1997 in a Pageland in a case involving a 13-year-old girl. He was sentenced to 5 years in prison for that crime. He was apprehended after a short chase and charged with first-degree rape, first-degree sexual offense, kidnapping, armed robbery and resisting arrest.

If the lead investigator fails to visit the crime scene and study what is there, it is not a good sign. At the very least, it identifies a clear training need. There is no excuse for an investigator's failure to visit the scene of the crime. It is a habit born out of a combination of ignorance and laziness. Supervisors charged with reviewing the work of investigators should make note of this. If investigators are not interested in visiting crime scenes, then they are not fully working their cases and must certainly be failing at the task of making vital connections within and across casework.

THE VICTIM AT THE SCENE

In cases involving traumatic or life-threatening injuries, an ambulance must be called and the victim given treatment. All other considerations are secondary. It is the lead investigator's responsibility to make certain that EMS personnel are made aware of the need to follow any set sexual assault protocols.

The victim should be sent to the hospital or clinic where the investigating agency has their prearranged agreement to conduct sexual assault examinations. This will be discussed further in Chapter 6 regarding sexual assault nurse examiners (SANEs).

When appropriate, the lead investigator should assign someone to stay with the victim while they are still at the scene. If at all possible, it should be the lead investigator's partner or at least someone from their unit. Their job is to comfort the victim, and at the same time ensure that victims don't destroy valuable evidence while waiting to be transported off-site for forensic and medical examinations. Victims must not be allowed to wash their hands, discard their clothes, take a shower, or bathe. The specific issue of victim clothing is covered in Chapter 4, "Processing the Rape Crime Scene." Also, the victim must be kept away from the location of the attack. This must be done to prevent evidence cross-contamination and destruction, as well as to remain sensitive to victim's emotional state. The victim is a real person who has survived a terrible event, ideally with few physical injuries. If victims feel marginalized or ignored, they may be less likely to cooperate and be forthcoming with information that might help the investigation. The person assigned to the victim should be a good listener and someone who is comfortable enough with the circumstances to develop a rapport.

The initial response interview should be limited to gathering information that establishes whether a crime was committed and establishing the elements of that crime. It should also include the gathering of information necessary to process the crime scene for evidence and help identify the offender. All victim statements need to be audio recorded in some fashion for purposes of integrity; investigators should never rely on the tenuousness of memory. At the scene, turn the tape recorder on, listen to the victim's statement, and turn the tape off. Do not judge, interrogate, or otherwise question what they have said; it is impossible to know anything for certain until the walk-through of the crime scene or a thorough interview has been completed, and all of the evidence evaluated.

To assist with the investigation of the crime scene and the search for transfer evidence, investigators should, at some point before releasing the scene, get the following information from the victim:

- Where precisely the attack(s) occurred within the crime scene
- Whether or not a weapon was involved
- Whether or not restraints were involved
- What items the offender touched in the scene (dresser drawers, doors, toilet seat, TV, VCR, personal items, etc.)
- Where on the victim's body the offender had physical contact, and with what

It is the responsibility of the lead investigator to make certain that these items are searched out and collected for forensic examination if recovered. Anything that the offender touched or interacted with may hold a trace, such as biological fluids or fingerprints. Not just important to establish the identity of the offender, such evidence is also necessary to establish the elements of the crime. Once the scene is released, this evidence may be lost, discarded, or obliterated.

Investigators should take a full and complete statement later on, after the victim has undergone both forensic and medical examinations, and after the investigator has had the chance to prepare for the interview. This will be discussed further in Chapter 5, "Interviewing Suspects and Victims."

COMMUNICATION

In order to make the constant and critical decisions required in a dynamic investigative environment such as a crime scene, the lead investigator must be able to receive information, integrate it into the investigative strategy, and relay it immediately to those who need it. As explained in Maples (1999, p. 99):

> One thing we quickly discovered was that the timely communication of intelligence did not come easily for many people in the organization. At complex shooting scenes, for example, the detective in charge of the case generally had to work the scene without having any idea what kind of intel other detectives were already developing from interviews at the hospitals or interrogations at the station house.
>
> The simple solution? The squads needed mobile phones.
>
> In policing, even the smallest communication breakdowns could have fatal consequences.

The authors have found this to be true in their own casework.

Example: stranger rape + burglary
An investigation involving a 23 year-old woman who was returning to her apartment after a day's work and an evening workout. The victim lived with two other female roommates.

Approximately a week earlier, the victim's apartment had been broken into. There were no valuables taken by the offender, there were signs that he had gone into the victim's dresser where her under garments were kept and evidence of photographs being moved.

The victim had an uneasy feeling since the burglary, and this was the first time she had returned home without her roommates there.

As she entered the apartment, she went to the kitchen area and picked up a broom as a means of protecting herself, "just in case". She walked around the apartment turning lights on to make sure it was safe. When she got to her bedroom, the light would not go on.

The offender appeared out of a darkened closet wearing a stocking mask and threatening her with a weapon. The offender forced her into a bathroom where he bound her hands with coat hangers and gagged her mouth with a scarf. He sexually assaulted the victim and then fled out the front door.

By the time investigators were notified the victim had been brought to a hospital. There was a slight delay with the initial interview due to the fact the victim needed immediate medical attention. A Crime Scene Unit was already at the victim's apartment processing it for evidence. During this interview, investigators learned of the prior burglary, and in that case the offender had entered via a bathroom window.

After the interview with the victim, investigators responded back to the crime scene just in time to catch the Crime Scene Unit packing up to leave. The investigator went immediately into the bathroom and observed that the window was shut but unlocked. He also realized that it had not been processed for fingerprints.

After interviewing the first officers at the scene and other personel who responded, no one was certain if the window was open or shut when they first arrived. However, one officer thought it was open and he may have closed it, but was not sure.

After carefully opening the window, investigators were able to observe fingerprints on the outside of the window; he also discovered footprints where the offender climbed a pipe to gain access to the window, and located the window screen that was supposed to be in the window. The window screen had been removed and was sitting in the alley under the window. A broom handle was found that was thought to have been used by the offender to determine if the window was open before he would have to climb up to it.

None of these areas were originally processed for evidence and would not have been examined if the investigator had not gone back to the scene to relay the information to the Crime Scene Unit. In this incident, they were able to fingerprint the edges of the window screen thought to have been removed by the offender, the broom handle and some empty beer cans that were also in the alley. They were also able to print the window itself.

This offender struck again approximately 7 months later using a similar M.O. However, in that case a witness had observed him sitting on the victim's fire escape during a heavy rainstorm a week earlier.

CRIME SCENE DOS AND DON'TS

Locard's exchange principle is very simple: every contact results in a transfer of evidence (Saferstein, 2001, pp. 4–5). Contact between items in a crime scene has the potential not only to add new evidence, but also to move it around and obliterate it. The investigator needs to be in the crime scene and have some contact with the evidence, as do forensic personnel. However, reasonable steps can be taken to minimize how much evidence is added, moved, and obliterated. Consider the following guidelines:

1. Do not enter the crime scene until you have signed in on the crime scene security log. If there isn't a security log, start one. The security log should contain name, agency, function, time in and out, and clothing description for later exclusionary purposes. One person should be assigned to maintain the log.

2. Make certain that someone is assigned to photograph the crime scene and surrounding areas. Part of this assignment involves maintaining a log of each roll of film and each item/location photographed.

3. Make certain that someone is assigned to sketch the crime scene. A rough sketch should be prepared at the scene showing measurements between items of evidence and spatial relationships within the scene. A final or "smooth" sketch is prepared later, based on notes, photos, and other information gathered from the scene (Lee, p. 72).

4. Make certain that someone is assigned to maintain an evidence log.

5. Do not collect multiple items of evidence in one bag, or under one evidence number. This provides for potential cross-contamination.

6. Wear disposable latex gloves at all times. This will help prevent the transfer of fingerprints, sweat, and other material from your bare hands into the scene.

7. Change gloves every time you touch a new item in the scene. This will help prevent cross-contamination between items at the scene that you have touched.

8. Do not dispose of your gloves by carelessly discarding them in the scene. They could wind up in a crime-scene photo obscuring evidence, or worse, somebody might collect them as evidence and run lab tests to determine their origin.

9. Do not touch everything in sight. When you touch an object, you may move it from its original position or obliterate any evidence that may have been transferred to its surface during the crime, such as fingerprints or biological fluids containing valuable DNA.

10. Keep your hands in your pockets until they are needed. This will help with item 5.

11. Do not wander aimlessly through the crime scene. This will also help with item 5.

12. Do not touch, move, or otherwise alter items of evidence before documenting them (photographs, measurements, etc.).

13. Do not stage collection efforts from furniture involved in the crime. Set up your equipment elsewhere, away from areas of potential evidence transfer.

14. Do not use the telephone in the scene. The offender may have used the phone. This is evidence that should be seized and processed for fingerprints and other potential transfer evidence. Also, phone records should be checked for all incoming and outgoing local and long distance calls, as far back as possible.

15. Do not use the television/VCR at the scene. The offender may have used them. Examine buttons for latent prints. Also, cable TV records should be checked. Both authors have worked cases where the offender has watched TV and/or ordered pornographic movies while waiting for the victim to return home.

16. Do not use the bathroom. The offender may have used the bathroom and may have lifted the toilet seat. The toilet should be seized and processed for fingerprints and other potential transfer evidence.

17. Do not smoke. Smoking changes the smell of the air and results in hot ashes that have the potential to contaminate, melt, or even burn/ignite potential evidence. It also results in discarded cigarette butts that may be confused as evidence.

18. Do not spit. Spitting results in the transfer of your biological material into a crime scene.

19. Do not eat. This is a distraction and will result in refuse that could find its way into the crime scene and get collected as evidence. Also, dropped food could contaminate or obliterate potential evidence.

20. Do not drink. This is a distraction and will result in refuse that could find its way into the crime scene and get collected as evidence. Also, spilled liquids could contaminate or obliterate potential evidence.

21. Do not bring civilians to a crime scene. This kind of thing shows a lack of respect and professionalism, as well as introducing more potential transfer evidence into the scene, and increasing the possibility that evidence may be carelessly contaminated or obliterated.

22. Do not allow your superiors or colleagues to bring civilians to a crime scene. See item 21.

23. Leave sealed containers sealed. Do not open sealed containers and sniff inside to determine the contents by odor. They may contain a hazardous or toxic material such as anhydrous ammonia, a necessary ingredient in the manufacture of methamphetamine. Contact with body tissue—especially the eyes, skin, and respiratory tract—will cause dehydration, cell destruction, and severe chemical burns.

24. Do not touch pools of liquid in the crime scene. This is TV and movie behavior done for dramatic effect to sell a scene; it has no place in real forensic work. If you do not know what something is and you think it is important, follow the appropriate documentation and collection procedures and submit it to the lab for analysis.

25. Do not taste anything in the crime scene. This is also TV and movie behavior done for dramatic effect to sell a scene; it has no place in real forensic work.

26. Do not interview the victim in the place where the attack occurred. This is extremely insensitive and may erode the trust between the victim and the investigator, to say nothing of potentially retraumatizing the victim.

27. Do not leave the crime scene to get something to eat, play lotto, go back to the office, or work on something else, until you are done.

28. Make written notes of everyone in the crime scene and each person's role. That way you will know whom to call later if you need something.

29. Take written note of everything in the crime scene that gets your attention, because "[n]othing is insignificant to record if it catches one's attention" (Wade, 1999).

30. Do not lead a victim's family members from the crime scene through the area where the attack occurred unless there is no other way.

Supervisors charged with reviewing the work of an investigative unit would do well to note these issues during performance reviews. They should also take measures to ensure that once these kinds of mistakes are discovered they are not repeated. This can be accomplished by training and by the example set by seasoned investigators.

Ignorance of physical evidence and proper crime scene protocols usually starts at the top, with those in charge, and finds its way down through the ranks. This reinforces the need to lead by example. Consider the following examples of negligent crime scene behavior from the authors' case files, none of which could have occurred under the supervision of an alert and knowledgeable lead investigator:

Example: The West Memphis case
On May 6, 1993, the nude bodies of 8-year-old Christopher Byers, Michael Moore, and Steve Branch were found, bound wrist to ankle with shoe laces, in the water of a drainage ditch, in a heavily wooded area called the Robin Hood Hills, behind the Blue Beacon Truck Wash in West Memphis, Arkansas. The three 8-year-

old boys had been murdered and, in the case of Christopher Byers, sexually mutilated.

With around two homicides per year, the West Memphis police have little experience investigating homicides. Their inexperience provided for the crime scene in this case to be compromised repeatedly. For example, the shaky and inadequate 4-minute crime scene video that the West Memphis Police did manage to shoot shows that they allowed third parties to wander through the crime scene unchecked, and that an unknown person was allowed in the crime scene to take pictures amid investigative personnel. The lead investigator, Gary Gitchell, was videotaped smoking as he watched over the recovery of the bodies a few feet away and openly discussed possible suspects for all to hear. They also returned to the scene several weeks after releasing it to recover potential evidence that they had initially not found or left behind.

*Example: The murder of Yvonne Layne (**shown in Figure 3-2**); Ohio v. David Thorne*
On April 1, 1999, Tawnia Layne, the victim's mother, went to Yvonne Layne's home in Alliance, Ohio, to take one of her grandchildren to school. When she arrived, Tawnia found her daughter's body in the living room. Yvonne's throat had been cut, and her body was lying in a pool of blood. Yvonne's five young children were found awake in the house. Tawnia Layne called the police.

Upon taking control of the crime scene, the Alliance Police Department made numerous overt blunders from the chief on down the line. These included the following:

- Chief Lawrence Dordea, a 25-year police veteran and graduate of the FBI National Academy, brought his date, Beth Newman, to the crime scene. She was allowed inside the yellow tape to walk around and view the body of the victim. In police reports, she was referred to as a civilian observer.
- The Alliance Police took the victim's children out of the crime scene by having them go past the living room and her body, both of which were covered with blood. This was unnecessarily insensitive, as there was an alternative method of entering and exiting the scene.
- The Alliance Police attempted to cover the victim's body with a blanket from the house, and then later removed it. They did this to conceal the victim's body from the children as they left the home. All they need have done is hold it up as a barrier, or use the back entrance to the home as the exit. This negligent act transferred unknown material from the blanket on to the body, potentially fouling any future examination for trace evidence.
- The Alliance Police allowed suspects and family members into the crime scene to mourn and/or get clothing for children while it was being processed.

Figure 3-2

From the author's case files. The body of Yvonne Layne was found in her narrow living room, between the couch and the dresser that had been pulled over on top of her.

Only authorized personnel should be inside the tape once the scene has been secured.

Example: Suspected meth lab; Alaska v. Wilhelm & Sylvester

On August 28, 2002, the Sitka Police served warrants on what they had been told were two potential clandestine methamphetamine labs, one on board a fishing vessel, and one in a trailer community. Both locations involved the same two suspects. After a careful review of the case by the defense, law enforcement officers admitted the following under oath in a public hearing:

- None of the officers at either scene wore any protective gear to prevent injury from chemicals commonly found at clandestine meth labs.
- A sergeant with the Alaska State Troopers, the most experienced investigator at the scene in terms of clandestine meth labs, searched for anhydrous ammonia by opening sealed containers and sniffing the contents. This is dangerous because anhydrous ammonia is caustic and causes severe chemical burns. Body tissues that contain a high amount of water, such as the eyes, skin, and respiratory tract, are very easily burned.
- Potentially exculpatory evidence in the form of glassware was collected and intentionally destroyed as hazardous material by the Sitka Police before state crime lab personnel could examine it.

- In many instances, Sitka Police detectives, providing for potential cross-contamination and internal evidentiary confusion, bagged multiple items of evidence together in a single bag, under a single evidence number.
- The items seized from both locations were opened and examined in the same location (displayed on the same tarp) by the same individual in the same short space of time, providing for potential cross-contamination.
- Each item was visually inspected and handled without a change of garment or gloves between examinations. This practice allows for cross-contamination of evidence.
- The items seized from both locations, including potentially hazardous, flammable, and volatile chemicals, were opened and examined in the designated smoking area behind the Alaska State Trooper's Public Safety Academy. Such a practice presents an obvious safety hazard.

Figure 3-3 shows a suspected methamphetamine lab.

Of specific interest is the belligerent ignorance of prosecutors regarding the physical evidence found at the crime scene. A motion to dismiss filed by Attorney Jude Pate, dated November 20, 2002, provides that law enforcement collected, photographed, and then destroyed items of evidence that comprised the components of the alleged lab that had been seized from the fishing vessel *Tillicum*. The motion explains that:

> Police reports and evidence sheets indicate that items of evidence A24, A25, A26, A27 and A29 (the thermos allegedly containing ammonia, the ammonia cleaning compound, the jug of muriatic acid, the bottle of drain cleaner, and the can of starter fluid) were destroyed by police. Sergeant Birt's testimony before the grand jury implies that although samples were taken from the four canning jars as items of evidence A20, A21, A22 and A23, the canning jars themselves were destroyed or disposed of by the police. A conversation between legal counsel for Mrs. Sylvester and the Sitka Police Department evidence custodian on November 20, 2002, confirmed that the four canning jars had been destroyed or disposed of by the police.

According to a legal memorandum filed with the court by Asst. District Attorney Natasha Norris dated December 20, 2002, in reference to the evidence that was destroyed prior to examination for latent prints:

> The defendants argue that the bottles may have had fingerprints on them. The defendants' hypothetical is just that, a hypothetical. Not only is it patently ridiculous to suggest that third parties planted evidence of a clandestine meth lab on a boat that the defendants had been sleeping in when the search warrant was served and

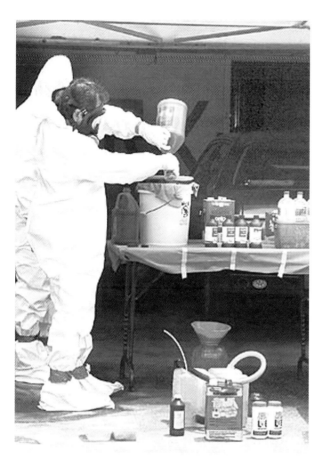

Figure 3-3
Law enforcement officers with the vice squad must wear full protective gear when collecting samples from containers found at a suspected methamphetamine lab.

executed, it is unlikely that any crime lab would do fingerprint testing on mason jars containing potentially dangerous chemicals.

It should be noted that fingerprints are commonly collected and preserved from items of evidence, including all manner of glassware, even those containing potentially dangerous chemicals and unknown substances. Specifically, fingerprints are commonly collected from such evidence found at potential clandestine meth labs. To suggest otherwise is misinformed and irresponsible, telegraphing a training need for inexperienced law enforcement and prosecutors.

THE MEDIA

Media coverage provides a powerful informational link between investigating agencies, criminal cases, and the community. The nature of media coverage varies widely from case to case, but never without the power to rapidly define the public face of an investigative effort. As provided in Gross (1924, p. 199) media reports:

> induce the public to form a definite opinion upon the case itself and upon the culpability of the author of the crime, so that the verdict is often pronounced by the public long before the competent authorities have delivered their judgment.

Media attention to a particular criminal case is a function of sensationalism and public interest. As discussed in Gross (1924, p. 199); "The experienced and expert journalist would rather give up every other article in his paper rather than the first report of a criminal case."

Sustained interest, and the perception of interest perpetuated by intense media coverage and competition, is influenced by a host of genuinely subjective elements. Investigators cannot predict these elements, nor can they really control them.

Media coverage is more instant and penetrating today than ever before. It must be accepted, and even anticipated, that the media can arrive at a crime scene well ahead of investigators, having monitored the call on a scanner or having been tipped off by someone involved in the case (i.e., friends, relatives, witnesses, police officers, EMS personnel, etc.). With the existence of global news services and the Internet, investigators can expect that a crime-related story that generates public interest may be reported locally today, and all over the English-speaking world tonight. Beyond just the facts of the case, coverage can include or focus on any aspect of the investigation, from bizarre to the mundane, from public safety issues to investigative or forensic blunders. Subsequently, it must be accepted as part of the work that whatever an investigator does or says may be subject to media scrutiny, and media criticism.

The lesson here is that the attention of the media to crime-related stories is potentially instant, global, sensational, critical, unpredictable, and uncontrollable. Investigators should conduct themselves accordingly.

MEDIA COOPERATION

The cooperation of the media at the right moment can move a case forward, and the scorn of the media at the wrong moment can set a case back. Investigators ignore this reality at their own peril.

The media today are invasive and persistent, bent on getting the story out, sometimes sacrificing accuracy for expediency. Because of this, the media are also a vast and useful information distributor and resource. Investigators should work to foster consistent and professional relationships with the media whenever feasible. This means working with them as fellow professionals rather than demanding or expecting that they will comply with authoritative demands. The media do not have to help and can punish investigators with negative press if they feel threatened or intimidated.

The media can be extremely helpful in the following ways:

1. Providing investigators with copies of photos or video shot with their cameras.
2. Providing investigators with tips and information received from the public, regarding witnesses, victims, and suspects.
3. Providing investigators with information regarding other similar crimes or patterns, locally and nationally.
4. Leading additional victims to come forward.
5. Disseminating suspect and/or suspect vehicle information to the public.
6. Disseminating requests for public response to specific case-related information, including witnesses who may have seen something at a particular time and place.

These are legitimate investigative uses of the media because they move an investigation forward. Investigators should cultivate their cooperative efforts accordingly—that is to say, be forthcoming to the point of public safety concerns, but withhold as much as possible.

When investigators are dealing with the press, Svensson and Wendel (1965, p. 12) wisely advise:

> Officers at the scene should under no circumstances give information to reporters.
> . . . In dealing with reporters the officer should be firm but not curt or nonchalant,
> even when the newspapermen are persistent. He should remember that newspapers
> often give invaluable help in the investigation of major crimes.

Consider the following additional guidelines when communicating with the press, both at the crime scene and elsewhere:

1. Do release general information about the crime, such as the type of victim attacked, the general time of the attack, and the area where it occurred. This to provide for public awareness and to help investigators in other jurisdictions who may have a serial crime that is similar. The media are still a powerful case linkage resource.
2. Do not release specific details about what the offender did or how he did it. Withholding this information allows for its use in screening those who might

falsely confess to the crime, or falsely implicate someone else. Releasing this kind of information only satisfies prurient curiosity.

3. Do not release specific details about the victim, such as a name or other personal information (home address, place of work, etc.). In many states, releasing this kind of identifying information is a crime. The media are generally pretty good about this, for fear of liability.

4. Do not divulge tactical information about the case. Nobody outside of the investigation needs to know just what is being done, what experts are being utilized, or why. Releasing such information is about public relations, to make the public believe that something is being done about the crimes and to put a good face on the investigation. However, this also serves to educate the criminal. For example, releasing tactical information about specific forensic tests being conducted may cause the criminal to dispose of potentially incriminating evidence.

5. If there is a series of connected crimes, announce it, but avoid providing details regarding how investigators have connected them unless the public can help. Serial criminals can and do alter their behavior based on what they read in the paper or see on TV. For example, if investigators announce that they have linked several unsolved rape cases with DNA evidence from sperm, this may make them appear to be both skilled and modern in the media. It will be short-lived, however, as the criminal learns this and starts wearing a condom to prevent the transfer of this valuable evidence. This will be discussed in greater detail in Chapter 13, "Serial Rape: Investigative Issues."

6. Do not announce who may or may not be a suspect. If asked to comment in general or in specific, be truthful. Explain that everyone is a suspect until the evidence has eliminated them. To suggest otherwise is either naïve or dishonest.

7. Do maintain a record of the media coverage, to establish what information was released by whom, and when.

Press conferences should be avoided. When necessary, prepare written press releases to avoid miscommunications. If a press conference is necessary, have succinct talking points ready. Be certain that they are brief and to the point. Do not take questions; there is no gain in it. The majority of questions asked by the media cannot and should not be answered. Also, avoid emotional displays of any kind. The face of the investigation should be thoughtful, sincere, informed, and professional. If something does not stand to help move the case forward or address a public safety issue, then it should probably not be communicated to the press.

PUBLIC IMAGE

Investigators cannot be concerned with public image. As explained in Gross (1924, p. 202), "The Investigating Officer must not allow himself to be persuaded into allowing general publicity by persons who really want such publicity for its own sake. . . ." This is a vain distraction. The first and only concern of the investigator should be working to establish the facts of the case in order to seek a just resolution.

The media feed on controversy and will find voices of criticism and dissent no matter what the circumstance. If investigators announce their thoughts, intentions, or impressions, an opposing voice will rise. Consequently, anyone working to satisfy or resolve a media-generated image or issue runs the risk of responding to a vocal minority as opposed to issues and criticisms of legitimate concern. It is impossible to satisfy everyone, and responding to a vocal minority gives it undeserved attention, which is what it was after in the first place.

Investigations should be run by virtue of informed skill and ability, not by a desire for good press or the fear of bad press.

SHUTTING DOWN THE MEDIA

The best way to quell media attention surrounding a case is to do so from the very beginning. No press allowed at or near the scene, no press releases, and no response to media inquiries of any kind. However, by doing this, investigators run the risk of alienating their media contacts and discouraging them from helping when their help is much needed. This is not advisable, because there will come a time in certain investigations when the media can help. There is simply no question of it. Investigators should strive to have a good, though entirely professional, relationship with the media.

If there has been intense media coverage of a case, and it has been decided that media attention is no longer desirable, there is one possibility for ending it. The media are a living creature. It lives on information. This means that it can be starved. If investigators desire to tone down or eliminate media coverage of a case, a complete and immediate media withdrawal is the only known solution: no press conferences, no press releases, and no interviews with, or comments from, anyone involved with the case. This requires a great deal of control and restraint, and in some instances may prove impossible (especially in larger departments).

Be forewarned that by cutting off legitimate sources of accurate information, investigators force the media to do one of two things: seek alternate sources of information that are less legitimate and less accurate, or fabricate information.

Both are common occurrences, and both may occur regardless of any calculated media blackout. This has been an issue for investigators as long as news has been reported, as discussed in Gross (1924, p. 199):

> The reporters in every case fall upon the watchmen, the witnesses and their relations, the jailors of the prison, the man who has driven the Investigating Officer to the scene of the crime, the people of the house and all other persons who may have some knowledge of the matter—and then compose their "story," "adding (like Poo-Bah) a touch of verisimilitude to an otherwise bald and unconvincing narrative." Further, they follow the Investigating Officer and his subordinates about, harass him with questions and cause him much waste of time. . . . In this way are those sensational descriptions which overflow our newspapers, fabricated.

Investigators must weigh the potential consequence of poor or false information in the media against their case strategy, and determine whether or not it is of any consequence. It may not matter at all, or it may matter a great deal. This should be understood and appreciated before cutting the media out of the information loop. As explained in Gross (1924, pp. 201–202):

> There are cases where it is quite obvious that general publicity must be resorted to. There are others where it is quite obvious that silence must be kept. The Investigating Officer will only find difficulty in making up his mind as to the course to be taken in those cases where on the one hand there are advantages to be gained, and on the other risks to be run.

The key is recognizing the pros and cons of giving out information, weighing them against each other, and deciding where the greatest risk of harm to a given investigation can be found. When information is released, it should be carefully measured, calculated, and recorded. Only in this way may potential harm to the investigation be mitigated and understood.

REFERENCES

Gilchrist, P. Police nab rape suspect at crime scene: Man accused of girl's rape arrested during search for evidence. *The Charlotte Observer*, July 2, 2003.

Gross, H. (1924) *Criminal Investigation*, 3rd ed. London: Sweet and Maxwell.

Hovanec, P. Man charged with rape of 12-year-old. *The Monroe Enquirer Journal*, September 7, 2003.

Lee, H. (1994) *Crime Scene Investigation*. Taoyan, Taiwan: Central Police University.

Maples, J. (1999) *The Crime Fighter*. New York: Doubleday.

O'Connell, J., and Soderman, H. (1936) *Modern Criminal Investigation.* New York: Funk & Wagnalls.

Rau, R. (2000) Crime scene investigation: A guide for law enforcement. National Institute of Justice, Technical Working Group on Crime Scene Investigation, NCJ 178280, January.

Saferstein, R. (2001) *Criminalistics: An Introduction to Forensic Science,* 7th ed. Upper Saddle River, NJ: Prentice Hall.

Snyder, L. (1944) *Homicide Investigation.* Illinois: Charles C. Thomas.

Svensson, A., and Wendel, O. (1965) *Crime Scene Investigation,* 2nd ed., New York: American Elsevier.

Wade, C. (ed.) (1999) *Handbook of Forensic Services.* U.S. Department of Justice, Federal Bureau of Investigation.

CHAPTER 4

PROCESSING THE RAPE CRIME SCENE

By John O. Savino and Brent E. Turvey, MS

Truth uncompromisingly told will always have its ragged edges.

Herman Melville, *Billy Budd, Sailor* **(c. 1889), Ch. 28**

Truth is always in harmony with herself, and is not concerned chiefly to reveal the justice that may consist with wrong-doing.

Henry David Thoreau, *Resistance to Civil Government* **(1849)**

Processing a crime scene is the task of examining, recognizing, preserving, documenting, and collecting physical evidence from a crime scene for identification, comparison, individualization, and reconstruction at a later time. Depending on the jurisdictional location of the scene, differing agencies with differing policies, procedures, and personnel will be involved. In some jurisdictions, highly trained criminalists sent from the crime lab may process a crime scene. In other jurisdictions with fewer resources, responding officers will process their own crime scenes. Between these two extremes are variably trained evidence technicians who exist only to respond to crime scenes and collect evidence, working for law enforcement in sworn and unsworn capacities. As a result of this diversity, the nature, extent, and quality of crime-scene processing efforts vary widely between jurisdictions.

Regardless of who processes the scene, the goals are the same; protect, document, preserve, and collect. Those charged with processing a crime scene should strive to preserve it from contamination and destruction when possible, and document everything that bears the least trace of meaning. A crime scene cannot be overprotected or overdocumented. Only when these efforts are exhausted should collection procedures begin.

A number of published works have been dedicated to the subject of crime scenes and (Deforest, Gaensslen, and Lee, 1983; DiMaio and DiMaio, 1993; Gross, 1924; Lee, 1994; O'Connell and Soderman, 1936; O'Hara, 1970; Rau, 2000; Saferstein, 2001; Svensson and Wendel, 1965; Wade, 1999). However, only a few have given specific attention to processing evidence at a rape crime scene. Building on their collective work, with the collective training and experience

Figure 4-1

From the author's case files—A filing cabinet in the scene of a rape-robbery in an office building. This particular offender would wait until the end of the day, force entry into often locked professional offices with people inside, bind his victims with available materials, rape the female employees, and sometimes force the male employees to participate at gunpoint. He would then search the victims and the offices for valuables. The offender left the filing cabinet pictured open; subsequently it was processed for latent prints, some of which can be seen. In fact, this photo was taken with the lift tape in place.

of the authors, this chapter will focus on that subject. It will also provide specific guidelines for collecting the two most useful forms of evidence found at a rape crime scene, in terms of available law enforcement databases: fingerprints and biological material containing DNA.

WHAT IS A CRIME SCENE?

A *crime scene* is defined as an area where a criminal act has taken place (Lee, 1994, p. 1). It can also be an area where evidence pertinent to the investigation may be found. Any criminal offense can take place in not just one but several locations. This may create a situation where an investigator is confronted by multiple crime scenes that are related together within a single offense. Perhaps this will be readily evident at the outset of a case, and perhaps not. The best way to determine whether this is the case is by breaking down the scene by virtue of what appears to have happened and where.

In sex crime cases, the victims' bodies, along with their clothing, are part of that scene. It is subsequently important to consider that they may leave the location where the attack occurred, go home, shower, and change their clothes before authorities become involved. This common victim behavior must be anticipated, as it alters and expands the crime scenes in a given sex crime.

The *point of contact* is the precise location where the rapist first approached or acquired the victim(s). This is a neutral term because it includes locations where a victim was encountered under some ruse devised by the rapist, as well as locations where an offender may have forcibly abducted them from to some other preselected *primary* or *secondary scene*.

The *primary scene* is the location where the rapist engaged in the majority of his attack on the victim(s). This is the location where the most time was spent, and where the most physical evidence was deposited during the attack. It is possible for there to be one primary scene per victim, if attacks on separate victims within a single offense occur in separate locations. It is possible for the primary scene to also be the disposal site. It is also possible for the victim to be attacked at multiple locations.

A *secondary scene* is the location where some of the victim–rapist interaction occurred, but not the majority of it. If it is the location where the victim was found, a secondary scene is also the *disposal site*. There can also be several secondary scenes associated with a single crime.

Essentially, the term *secondary scene* encompasses any place where there may be evidence of criminal activity outside of the primary scene.

An *intermediate scene* is any crime scene between the *primary scene* and a *disposal site*, where there may be transfer evidence. This includes vehicles used to transport a victim and locations where the victim may have been held prior to final disposal. *Intermediate crime scenes* are a type of *secondary crime scene*.

Disposal site is a rough term used to describe a crime scene where a body or a victim is ultimately found. More often than not, the use of this term implies that the victim was attacked somewhere else and then transported to this location. That one has located a disposal site only is a dangerous investigative assumption to make. A disposal site may also be the primary scene; this possibility must not be excluded by virtue of an investigator's subjective experience. As already discussed, one crime can have many crime scenes.

LOCATING CRIME SCENES

The key to the search and examination of any crime scene is first locating it, and all of its satellites as just described. As already mentioned, the crime scene may not be completely evident. The investigator may have to look for it. In the case of a rape or sexual assault, understand that the following interactions can occur, and not necessarily in the same location:

1. The offender will have approached the victim.
2. The offender will have attacked the victim.

Figure 4-2

From the author's case files—
The contents of a sexual
assault victim's wallet are
found outdoors at a nearby
secondary scene, disposed of
by the offender. They include
a phone name and phone
number, a business call, and
a bill. This information can
be useful in determining the
route taken by the offender
when leaving the scene,
assisting in the search for
evidence he may have left
behind such as footwear
impressions in the soil or
fingerprints on the items
removed from the wallet.

3. The offender may have moved the victim to a secluded location for privacy during the attack.
4. The offender may have moved the victim to a secluded location for storage before or after the attack.
5. The offender may have moved the victim to a secluded or public location for disposal.
6. The offender may have transported the victim in a vehicle.
7. The offender will have departed from the scene.

Each of these events may represent a different crime scene that the offender must enter and exit. In locating all points of entry, all the points of exit, and the routes between each, the investigator may find evidence of the victim or offender's passing. This may come in the form of patterns or traces left behind as either one came in to contact with objects in each scene. Or it may come in the form of items that either one discarded or dropped incidentally (or purposely) along the way.

LAW ENFORCEMENT CRIME-SCENE SEARCHES

The United States Constitution was written in part to protect individuals from the government and its agents, including unreasonable searches and seizures by law enforcement officers. The Fourth Amendment provides:

> The right of people to be secure in their persons, houses, papers, and effects, against unreasonable searches and seizures, shall not be violated, and no Warrants shall issue, but upon probable cause, supported by Oath or affirmation, and particularly describing the place to be searched, and the persons or things to be seized.

The Supreme Court has held that there is no "crime scene exception" to the warrant requirement.

The investigator must evaluate the need for a search warrant before entry and processing begin. In cases where a suspect has a reasonable expectation of privacy, a warrant should be obtained. There are, however, certain instances when a warrantless entry or search related to a crime scene is permitted:

1. *Exigent circumstances*, or the need to engage in a search or seizure immediately because of an emergency situation where life and/or safety is at risk including:

    - Entry for purposes of finding dead or injured victims and rendering first aid.
    - Entry to preserve and safeguard evidence in a scene while a warrant is being secured.
    - Entry to photograph evidence that cannot be preserved until a warrant has been secured.
    - Entry to find a perpetrator that may still be in the scene.

2. *Consent* when the police have a reasonable assumption that the party granting consent has lawful authority to do so and the consent is voluntary.

3. The *plain view/plain feel exception*, which allows the seizure of evidence when an item is spotted in plain view or is within "plain feel," and there is probable cause to believe the item is evidence.

4. *Search incident to a lawful arrest* to locate and seize weapons and protect the arresting officer and prevent the destruction of evidence.

5. The *automobile exception* to seize and search an automobile based upon the exigency present due to the mobility of a vehicle before a warrant can be lawfully obtained.

6. The *container exception* to search a container in an automobile based upon the same exigency present with the automobile exception. If the container is not in an automobile, the police may seize, but may not search, the container.

Inherent in all of these exceptions is the understanding that a reasonable, articulable suspicion of criminal activity exists, as would be the case in a crime scene.

In most cases, the emergency exception for warrantless crime scene entry is used. In order to enter a crime scene under this exception, a police officer must have a reasonable belief that unless immediate entry is made, a person will be endangered, evidence will be destroyed, or an offender may escape.

Consent searches are also used. This involves someone allowing police officers to conduct a search for evidence on their property or person. Caution is advised in these situations, as anyone can later deny that they gave voluntary consent. To alleviate this issue, secure a signature on a voluntary consent form, and/or audiotape the willingness to consent to be searched. Be warned that in some states [i.e., *Minnesota v. Mustafaa Naji Fort*, No. C2-01-1732, May 1, 2003; *New Jersey v. SJ Carty*, March 4, 2002 (332 N.J. Super. 200, App. Div. 2000)] consent searches without a reasonable, articulable suspicion of criminal activity have been deemed inadmissible.

Law enforcement agencies, and individual officers, are admonished to have search and seizure polices and guidelines in place and know them well. This will provide officers old and new with the ability to better discern what is permissible and what is not without a warrant. They should work closely with their district attorneys in preparing these, as a failure to do so can result in questionable searches, unlawful searches, and civil liability.

EXAMINING THE CRIME SCENE

A competent reconstruction of the crime is not possible until all of the physical evidence from the scene has been collected, examined, and identified. However, a great deal of vital information can be established at the scene through careful observations. This includes the general nature of events and their potential sequence. According to Kirk (1974, p. 34), the most important things to observe at the scene are:

(1) Displaced objects, or objects in unusual locations or attitudes.
(2) Distribution, indications of direction, and character of all blood traces, whether they be spots, stains, pools or smears.
(3) Presence of objects which appear foreign to the environment, e.g., weapons as well as objects, traces, or materials not suitable as weapons but apparently involved with the criminal activity.

Each of these occurrences must be documented with photos and sketches in order to preserve them for later interpretation in the light of other facts revealed during the investigation.

The key is a thorough, planned, practiced execution of duties. That is to say, it is not a good idea to walk into a new scene and start collecting evidence as it is found, jumping from one place to the next as someone shouts "Over here! Look what I found!" Investigators are better served by a deliberate, patient, and systematic approach that is repeated in the same general fashion every time they process a crime scene.

It is also important to avoid becoming entrenched in preconceived theories about the case at any time prior to completing processing efforts. Preconceived theories may not only be inaccurate, they may provide for further inaccuracy by compelling the investigator toward or away from the collection of particular kinds of evidence. As described in O'Hara (1970, p. 49):

> The investigator must initially restrain himself from taking physical action. The natural inclination is to form a quick opinion of what happened and endeavor to verify it by physically examining various articles.

Preconceived theories are just that—theories. The utility of any theory rests in the repeated attempts that investigators should make to falsify it. In failing to falsify it through further investigation, they strengthen their belief in it.

TYPES OF EVIDENCE

Physical evidence is any object, material, or substance found in connection with an investigation that helps establish the identity of the offender, the circumstances of the crime, or any other fact determined to be important to the case. As explained in Lee (1994, p. 21), "It may be as small as a pollen grain or as large as an airplane. It may be a gas, liquid or a solid."

O'Hara (1970, p. 67) explains that physical evidence can be placed into one of three categories: corpus delicti evidence, associative evidence, and tracing evidence. *Corpus delicti evidence* is defined as objects or substances that (p. 67) "are an essential part of the body of the crime." In the crime of rape this involves evidence of force and evidence of penetration. Examples include:

- A condom with the offender's sperm on the inside and the victim's vaginal epithelial cells on the outside.
- Finger-shaped bruising on the victim's arms or neck.
- Vaginal or anal lacerations.
- Ligatures (tape, ropes, belts, coat hangers, telephone cord, etc.) and any resulting ligature pattern injuries on the victim's neck, arms, or legs.
- Sperm or semen found in the victim's mouth, vagina, or anus.

Associative evidence (pp. 67–68) "links the suspect to the crime scene or the offense." In the crime of rape, this involves anything that shows contact between the victim, the offender, and the crime scene. Examples include:

- A condom that has the offender's sperm on the inside, and the victim's vaginal epithelial cells on the outside.
- An offender's pubic hairs recovered from the victim's rectal area.
- Synthetic fibers from the offender's vehicle on the victim's clothing.
- An offender's fingerprints on tape used to cover the victim's eyes or bind the victim's wrists.
- An offender's footwear impression in the soil at the crime scene.
- An offender's fingerprints on the toilet seat in a victim's residence.

Tracing evidence (p. 68) assists the investigator in locating the suspect. In the crime of rape, this includes the following examples:

- An offender's wallet or identification dropped inadvertently at the crime scene.
- An offender's cell phone dropped inadvertently at the crime scene.
- Surveillance video and photographs from businesses at or near the crime scene that capture an offender's physical features, vehicle, direction traveled, and vehicle plate numbers.

Lee (1994, pp. 21–35) suggests that evidence can be broken into four general categories: transient evidence, transfer evidence, pattern evidence, and conditional evidence. *Transient evidence* (pp. 21–22) is defined as evidence that is by its nature temporary, in that it can be changed or lost with the passage of time. Transient evidence commonly includes the following:

- Odor
- Temperature
- Imprints and indentations in temporary or easily disturbed surfaces such as water, ice, snow, sand, and food
- Melting ice cream
- Burning candles/incense

Transfer evidence (p. 35) is defined as evidence that is produced by physical contact between persons and or objects. It may be traced back to its source by examining its physical, chemical, morphological, or biological properties. It includes the following:

- Fingerprints and palm prints
- Tool marks
- Tracks and impressions
- Glass

- Plastic
- Rubber
- Paint
- Clothing
- Wood
- Dust
- Pollen
- Cigarettes
- Ash
- Matches
- Soil
- Hairs
- Fibers
- Tools
- Weapons
- Oil and grease
- Metal
- Bodily fluids

Pattern evidence (pp. 22–31) is apparently defined as evidence produced by physical contact between persons and/or objects involving distinctive or telling features. It is a particular kind of transfer evidence that may be traced back to its source by examining physical and morphological properties alone. Pattern evidence can include the following:

- Fingerprint and palm-print patterns
- Footwear patterns
- Footprints
- Blood spatter patterns
- Glass fracture patterns
- Fire burn patterns
- Furniture position patterns (i.e., displaced, overturned, or broken)
- Projectile trajectory patterns
- Powder residue patterns
- Track-trail patterns
- Clothing or article patterns (i.e., tearing or ransacking)
- Tire or skid-mark patterns
- Injury patterns
- Modus operandi patterns (behavioral evidence established by physical evidence)

Figure 4-3

From the author's case files—Plaster casts of suspect footprints found in the mud in association with a rape crime scene. This kind of evidence associates the suspect with the location, and also reveals that he was not wearing shoes or socks at the time.

Conditional evidence (pp. 31–35) is defined as evidence that is produced by an event or action. That is to say, its existence is direct evidence that an event or action did or did not take place in a particular location. Conditional evidence can include the following:

- Light from a light switch being turned on in a room or from a vehicle
- Smoke from a fire
- Fire color, temperature, and duration
- Location of an item such as a weapon, biological fluids, or discarded clothing
- Locks, in terms of whether and how they are engaged (latch, keys, etc.)
- Windows, in terms of whether and how they are open
- Undisturbed dust on a windowsill, indicating that it was not a point of entry

CHAIN OF CUSTODY/CHAIN OF EVIDENCE

Each item of evidence discovered at a crime scene will go through some or all of the following steps:

1. Recognition or discovery (that it is evidence)
2. Protection (from the environment and those in it)
3. Documentation
4. Collection/preservation
5. Transportation (to forensic lab)
6. Identification (as a general kind of evidence based on its properties)

7. Comparison (to knowns, unknowns, and controls)
8. Individualization (as a unique piece of evidence)
9. Reconstruction (combining it with other evidence from the case)
10. Disposition (storage, destruction, or loss)

The *chain of custody*[1] is the record of everyone who has controlled, taken custody of, or had contact with a particular item of evidence from the beginning of this process to the current day's activities.

In some cases, a chain of custody may not be known or established for a particular piece of evidence prior to its recognition. Investigators may have to work hard in order to establish how it got where it was found. In other cases, the chain of custody prior to recognition may be readily evident and undisputed. Accepting these limitations of the evidence, and working within them when interpreting the scene, is part of the normal investigative and forensic process.

The official chain of custody typically begins with the person who first collected the item of evidence.[2] In this way, potential evidence transfer, evidence contamination, and evidence loss are tracked. The fewer people handling the evidence the better. As described in O'Hara (1970, p. 69):

> The number of persons who handle evidence between the time of commission of the
> alleged offense and the ultimate disposition of the case should be kept at a
> minimum. Each transfer of the evidence should be receipted. It is the responsibility
> of each transferee to insure that the evidence is accounted for during the time that it
> is in his possession, that it is properly protected, and that there is a record of the
> names of the persons from whom he received it and to whom he delivered it,
> together with the time and date of such receipt and delivery.

Kirk (1974, p. 36) provides more specific instructions regarding the chain of custody for those collecting evidence:

> Every article collected for examination must carry an identifying mark, placed on the
> object itself or on its wrapper. If it is the wrapper that is marked, at the crime scene,
> at a later time, and before any chance mixing of wrappers can occur, a permanent
> mark should be placed on the object itself. . . . The mark should include the date,
> place of origin, and the name or initials of the person who collected the evidence.

---

[1] Sometimes referred to as the "chain of evidence," or the "chain of evidence custody."
[2] If at all possible, a note should exist somewhere as to who actually recognized or discovered the evidence. This information may prove important to the investigation of suspects and to the final reconstruction of events.

Photographs and measurements of the evidence that provide its condition and location in the crime scene are also an important and often-overlooked part of the chain of custody. Those looking for doubt can, in some cases, legitimately cast doubt on a chain of custody that does not have this level of documentation.

PRELIMINARY SCENE EXAMINATION

Conducting a preliminary survey of the crime scene informs every investigative and forensic effort that follows. It helps determine the nature of the crime being investigated, and the steps necessary to handle the particulars of rape evidence as it may be found in that location (Rau, 2000, p. 19). Not just a preliminary search for evidence and its boundaries, it is a time for deciding how that evidence may be documented given the environment.

The first part of the preliminary survey is making sure that the crime scene is actually secure, and that someone has been assigned to the following duties by the lead investigator:

1. Photographer
2. Videographer
3. Sketcher
4. Measurer
5. Evidence protection
6. Evidence collection and logging

The second part involves a preliminary walk-through to provide an overview of the entire scene, identify any threats to the scene's integrity, and ensure the protection of physical evidence (Rau, 2000, p. 20). At this time physical evidence and potential witnesses may be observed or identified. Subsequently, initial observations may be made regarding the best way to preserve, document, and collect.

GENERAL DOCUMENTATION

Once an item of evidence has been recognized, and before collection efforts begin, its location in the crime scene must be thoroughly documented. The purpose of documenting an item of evidence prior to collection is to assist with establishing a chain of custody, as well as its relationship to other objects taken from and remaining in the scene. To be useful, documentation methods should provide anyone with the ability to return to the crime scene and place the item in the same location and position that it was originally discovered.

The following methods have proven most successful: photography, videography, and sketching.

CRIME-SCENE PHOTOGRAPHS

Photographs are one of the best ways to quickly and accurately document evidence. Ideally, this would be the duty of personnel trained in the techniques of forensic photography. Unfortunately, trained personnel may not always be available or willing to work a rape crime scene. Investigators should therefore consider carrying a disposable camera at all times; even without training or skill, a disposable camera may be used effectively to provide a competent record.[3]

Consider the following basic guidelines, consistent with, but not limited to, Rau (2000, pp. 24–26):

1. Start each roll of film (or digital photo series) with a written placard that provides date, time, location, agency, case number, and the name of the photographer.
2. Be certain to take overall shots of the scene and associated areas; put the crime scene in a context.
3. Take photographs of any crowds, victims, witnesses, or suspects for later identification purposes.
4. Take photographs of any associated parking areas for vehicle identification purposes. Try to get discernible plate numbers.
5. Photograph the perspective of any witness, from their height and angle.
6. Take long-, medium-, and close-range photographs of each item of evidence.
7. Work with the evidence measurer and the crime scene sketcher. Get additional shots after a scale and evidence number have been placed with an item, prior to its collection.
8. Use side lighting to bring out texture, damage, tool marks, and any other irregularities on a surface.
9. Too many pictures is better than too few.

There is a particular limitation to photographs that is all too often ignored by those examining them, especially when pattern evidence is involved. Photographs provide only a two-dimensional likeness. This limitation is important to remember because a photograph is a flattened representation of evidence

---

[3] A high-quality digital camera is actually preferable and is cost effective given the high costs often associated with bulk film development. In a few cases a digital camera would likely pay for itself. Digital photographs are more easily transferable, viewable, and portable given a laptop or desktop computer. They also generally have a preview feature that allows investigators to know the quality of their shots before the release of the scene.

on sometimes uneven, curved, or even jagged surfaces. As a surface changes, so does the pattern that was left behind. Two-dimensional photographs may also misrepresent spatial relationships; they can distort objects and make them appear closer or farther apart than they actually are. Taking photos from multiple angles, employing detailed sketches, and video documentation may work to alleviate this particular limitation.

The media may also be at or around the areas associated with the crime scene, taking photographs at different locations from different angles. If this is the case, look in to the possibility of obtaining copies of their still photographs. Diplomacy may be required.

It bears repeating that using crime-scene photographs, it should be possible for anyone to return to the crime scene and place the item in the same position that it was originally discovered.

UV Light and Photography

In some cases, the victim will claim to have been injured by the offender but show no visible skin damage. This can include restraint applied to limbs, manual or ligature strangulation, and bite marks. Under these circumstances, ultraviolet (UV) photography may be of use. As provided in Pex (2003):

> Penetration and reflection of light on the skin is a function of wavelength. Shorter wavelengths such as UV do not penetrate the skin very far before it is reflected back to the camera. Therefore a high resolution picture of the skin surface is possible. This works well for bite marks, cuts, scratches and scars. This is not a good technique to apply to bruises unless the blood accumulation is very close to the skin surface.

> UV Photography can be accomplished with an ordinary 35 mm SLR if the lens is capable of transmitting light somewhere between 300 nm to 400 nm. The easiest way to make that determination is to place the lens in a spectrophotometer and test it. Most clinical, university or forensic laboratories have one available. Manufacturers coat most lenses to prevent excess UV penetration. Excess UV will unbalance a color photograph with excess blue. There isn't a common lens manufacturer that can be recommended. Some lenses will allow UV light transmission down to the 350 nm range and some will not. A simple test in the absence of a spectrophotometer is to photograph someone with freckles. The appearance of freckles in UV light is considerably enhanced compared to standard visible range light photography. No focus correction is necessary. Success in UV photography is also a function of light intensity (I) in the absence of the other wavelengths. To handhold photograph a living object requires a high intensity source such as an Omnichrome 1000 or Omnichrome FLS 5000 and a dark room. Photography with small handheld UV

sources is possible, but standardization of source-to-target and lens-to-target distance are critical. The following features are a good starting point for UV photography:

1. 35 mm SLR with f1.4 or 1.8 normal lens
2. 3200 ASA Black and White film
3. UV source
4. Room without windows to turn out the room lights
5. Measuring scale-to-place near injuries

UV photography has also proven successful for illuminating latent fingerprints on multicolored surfaces (when first dusted with fluorescent powder or ninhydrin), or illuminating body secretions such as urine, semen, and perspiration, which often glows when illuminated by ultraviolet light.

CRIME-SCENE VIDEO

Video is a good way to document the crime scene and get an overall perspective of the spatial relationships between objects. It can be used to supplement still photographs and provide a general sense geography and orientation within the scene. It also provides a means of showing the relationship to, and nature of, other areas associated with or adjacent to the scene (geographical features, buildings, streets, parking lots, etc.).

Video documentation can begin immediately upon arrival at the scene and may take place before, during, and after collection efforts have begun.

Consider the following basic guidelines:

1. Do not use the audio feature of a video recording device. Disable it if possible. This avoids the recording of comments and observations that may be less than professional in nature.
2. Start each video with a written placard that provides date, time, location, agency, case number, and the name of the photographer.
3. Move slowly and smoothly while shooting the video; avoid quick movements or unnecessary zooming.
4. Take reference shots that establish the location of the scene, such as street signs, address numbers or apartment numbers next to doorways, or major geographical landmarks such as rivers or bridges.
5. Accompany the lead investigator on their walk-through of the scene.
6. Zoom in slowly on obvious items of evidence. Establish their context.
7. Coordinate with the photographer to determine items of evidence that may need particular attention and multiple angles.

The media may also be at or around the areas associated with the crime scene, videotaping from different angles. If this is the case, look in to the possibility of obtaining copies of their video. Diplomacy may again be required.

Further still, canvass local area business associated with the crime scene and along possible routes to and from the scene. Many businesses have surveillance video that can be retrieved for use in the investigation. These include gas stations, convenience stores, state or government buildings, and bank automated teller machines (ATMs).

CRIME-SCENE SKETCHES

The purpose of a crime-scene sketch is to produce a written and visual record of the crime scene that provides the location and distance between primary features and all of the numbered items of evidence that were collected.

At the scene, investigators should work to prepare what may be referred to as a rough sketch with notes as to measurements and approximate spatial relationships and scaling. Later, the rough sketch should be used to produce what may be referred to as a smooth sketch that contains precise spatial relationships, and scaling. According to Wade (1999):

> The sketch should include
>
> - Case identifier;
> - Date, time, and location;
> - Weather and lighting conditions;
> - Identity and assignments of personnel;
> - Dimensions of rooms, furniture, doors, and windows;
> - Distances between objects, persons, bodies, entrances, and exits;
> - Measurements showing the location of evidence. Each object should be located by two measurements from nonmovable items such as doors or walls; and
> - Key, legend, compass orientation, scale, scale disclaimer, or a combination of these features.

Using a competently prepared and accurate sketch, it should be possible for anyone to return to the crime scene and place the item in the same location that it was originally discovered.

RECOGNITION OF BIOLOGICAL MATERIAL

Biological materials commonly left behind in sex crimes include blood, sweat, semen, sperm, hair, saliva, urine, and excrement. Biological material may be found on any surface that the victim or offender has had any contact with. Every object and surface in a crime scene, or suspected crime scene, is a potential site of biological transfer evidence until the investigation demonstrates otherwise through reason, science, or both.

At the crime scene there are no methods for absolutely confirming that biological material is present on an item, on a surface, or in a stain. What can be accomplished is the presumptive identification of stains, smudges, or smears that may potentially contain biological material. This can be done visually, with presumptive chemical tests, or through the use of alternative light sources such as UV, as previously discussed.

In some cases, investigators may examine an item or surface and fail to visualize biological material, and fail to get a positive UV response, yet desire further proof. One option when looking for blood is luminol, a commonly used presumptive or screening test for human blood that fluoresces when it reacts with the iron in hemoglobin. It is a compound that reacts with copper, iron peroxides, and cyanide. Luminol is sensitive enough to pick up minute traces of blood even when attempts have been made to wash it away. The reaction is fast and requires complete darkness for photographic documentation.

However, luminol has its limitations. First, the alcohol in some luminol preparations may destroy red blood cells, preventing further serological analysis, such as DNA testing. Second, a positive result does not confirm the presence of human blood. The following is a short list of common household substances that produce chemiluminescence intensities comparable with that of hemoglobin (Creamer, Quickenden, Apanah, Kerr, and Robertson, 2003):

- Turnips
- Parsnips
- Horseradishes
- Commercial bleach (NaClO)
- Copper metal
- Some furniture polishes
- Some enamel paints
- Some interior fabrics in motor vehicles

Subsequently, a positive luminol result means that human blood may be present and further testing is required for confirmation. In the case of trails, drag marks, footwear patterns, fingerprints, and spatters, the potential blood patterns revealed may be valuable in terms of helping to establish offender identity, and may even lead investigators to other items of evidence.

Aside from the victim's body, transfer of biological evidence most commonly occurs on victim and offender clothing, particularly on their undergarments

(Kirk, 1974, p. 208). A more robust list of items and surfaces to collect or inspect includes, but is by no means limited to:

- All victim and offender clothing
- Victim purse and wallet
- Jewelry boxes and jewelry
- Safes and lock boxes
- File cabinets
- Drawers
- Computer hardware
- Pillows, sheets, blankets, and other bedding
- Condoms and condom wrappers
- Cigarette butts
- Discarded chewing gum
- Weapons
- Ligatures
- Chairs, seats, couches, and other surfaces designed for sitting
- Light switches
- Personal correspondence
- Toilet seats and lids
- Telephones
- Cellular phones
- Televisions
- VCRs/DVD players
- Remote controls
- Eyeglasses[4]
- Bath towels
- Hand towels
- Paper towels
- Tissues
- Rags
- Gloves, interior and exterior
- Doorknobs
- Vehicle door handles
- Vehicle pedals
- Steering wheels
- Rearview mirrors
- All floors, tabletops, and countertops associated with the crime

---

[4] In Jerusalem, a rape case was prosecuted with DNA evidence collected from a lollipop and a pair of glasses (Oz, Levi, Novoselski, Volkov, and Motro, 1999).

- All ceilings associated with the crime (house, apartment, vehicle, etc.)
- All surfaces at the point of entry and point of exit

The value of biological material is its ability to help establish the identity of the individual who left it behind. This is not the whole story, however. Determining the precise conditions of the transfer of biological material may require further investigation, analysis, and reconstruction. Investigators are admonished to accept this limitation and appreciate that understanding who left biological material where may be only part of the story. The investigator may be required to establish the facts and circumstances that put the biological evidence where it was ultimately found.

COLLECTION OF BIOLOGICAL MATERIAL

Victims and suspects alike should be examined in a hospital or a physician's office using standardized sexual assault evidence collection protocols. The specific protocols are provided in Chapter 6, Appendix I, and Appendix II of this text. However, a crime scene may contain suspected biological transfer evidence that requires an investigator's attention apart from that kind of examination.

Items of suspected biological transfer evidence should be collected and packaged individually while the investigator is wearing disposable latex gloves. These items should not be collected as an aggregate and thrown into a single bag. Change gloves before collecting each item of evidence. If more or different packaging material or gloves are needed, get them. This will help prevent cross-contamination between items of evidence.

Also, be certain to collect not just the potential biological material, but also an undisturbed or unstained sample of the surface where it landed. This is necessary for crime lab personnel seeking to resolve unknown or unclear results, and identify potential contaminants. This is why it is best to collect entire objects when possible. As discussed in Spear (2003, p. 1):

> The standard recommendation for collecting biological evidence is *not* to remove the stain from an object but rather to collect the object with the stain. The advantages of this strategy are that the entire stain is obtained, it is not necessary to collect an "unstained control" sample and there are no further manipulations required that might negatively impact the sample. If the stain is on a smooth, non-porous surface (i.e. it can be easily "flaked" off), it will be necessary to protect the stain from contact with other objects.

When collecting wet or only partially dry items, roll or wrap them first in clean paper. Then use paper bags, not plastic, for packaging as they allow the evidence to breathe. Plastic enclosures will cause condensation of moisture and promote bacterial and fungal growth. Items of evidence not completely dry should be allowed to air dry in a well-ventilated room prior to packaging when possible.

When collecting dry items containing potential biological evidence, wrap the item in clean paper first, and then place inside of a paper bag. In the case of biological stains on pliable surfaces (cloth, rubber, paper, etc.), it may be necessary to fold the item in some way for packaging purposes. Do not fold through visible stains, as this may damage existing biological material and hamper DNA testing efforts. In the case of solid objects with potential biological transfer, cover the stained area with clean paper and seal the edges down with tape to prevent loss or contamination.

In the case of immovable items or surfaces, there are three approaches: cutting, swabbing, and scraping. As discussed in Spear (2003, p. 1), cutting is preferable:

> Some samples will need to be collected in the field. If the entire object cannot be collected then *the next best way to collect biological evidence is to remove the stain by cutting it out (e.g. from a piece of carpet).* Remember to use clean scissors and to cut out an "unstained" control. Scissors or tweezers can be cleaned by rinsing with clean water and then drying with tissue. Repeat this cleaning process twice prior to each sampling.

Cutting is especially important when dealing with pattern evidence, such as bloody fingerprints or bloody footwear impressions. It is preferable to preserve the entire pattern, as it was found, whenever possible.

Sometimes it is not possible to collect a stain by cutting it from an item or surface. This can include biological transfer onto items of great strength or mass, and certain types of walls, floors, or supporting structures. This leaves the remaining options of swabbing and scraping. When swabbing or scraping, it will be necessary to take unstained control samples and package them separately (Spear, 2003, p. 2). It will also be necessary to thoroughly document the stain with photos and sketch work, as either process will destroy it and any evident patterns.

A dampened cotton swab is preferable when swabbing biological material (Spear, 2003, p. 2):

> *The best method for swabbing a stain is to use a minimum amount of distilled water to dampen an appropriate, clean substrate (e.g. cotton swab or cotton gauze) and then absorb the stain onto the slightly dampened substrate.* An unstained control is taken in the same manner

as the stain and is taken from an unstained area as close as possible to the biological evidence sample.

Cotton swabs have traditionally been used to collect biological samples. They are readily available in sterile packages and they are very absorbent. Do *not* use "calcium alginate" swabs for sample collection since these swabs interfere with many of the DNA extraction procedures. Cotton gauze, which does not have any additive (e.g. fabric sizing), is also an acceptable substrate.

Once a stain is collected, the next consideration is drying the swabbed sample. Drying biological samples is critical to preserving these samples because water is necessary in most of the biochemical reactions that result in degradation. Try to dry this sample as fast as possible to minimize degradation of the sample.

Scraping is used to remove dried, crusted stains from smooth, nonporous surfaces. Scrape the dried stain onto a clean piece of paper that may be folded and placed into an evidence envelope. Do not scrape dried biological material directly into an evidence envelope. Do not mix dried stains from different spots in the same envelope. As discussed in Spear (2003, p. 2), scraping is the least preferable because of the potential for cross-contamination:

The most significant problem encountered while scraping stains is that samples tend to "powder" when scraped and it may be difficult to control the retrieval of the entire sample. The "powdered" stain, which is not retrieved, may contaminate adjacent stains. Given these considerations, most samples will not lend themselves to the scraping technique and will need to be collected by swabbing.

Use a freshly washed and dried edge such as a razor, knife, or similar tool. Wash the tool in distilled water and dry with a clean cloth before each use and between each scraping. Do not use bleach to clean any collection tools, as it may destroy biological evidence.

RECOGNITION AND COLLECTION OF FINGERPRINTS

According to both Lee (1995, p. 160) and Saferstein (1998, p. 450), there are at least three different kinds of fingerprints. These include:

Visible prints: Ridge impressions caused by the transfer of a colored medium such as paint, grease, blood, or ink.
Plastic prints: Ridge impressions left on a soft material such as putty, wax, or clay.
Latent (invisible) prints: Ridge impressions that are deposited by the transfer of

natural body secretions to the surface of objects. A true latent print is not visible to the naked eye.

As stated in Saferstein (1998, p. 450):

> Locating latent or invisible prints is obviously a much more difficult task and does require the utilization of techniques that will visualize the print. Although the investigator is presented with a number of alternate methods for visualizing a latent print, the method of choice will depend on the type of surface that is being examined.

> Hard and nonabsorbent surfaces (e.g., glass, mirror, tile, and painted wood) require different development procedures from surfaces that are soft and porous (e.g., papers, cardboard, and cloth). Prints on the former are preferably developed by the application of a powder, whereas prints on the latter generally require treatment with a chemical.

Fingerprint dusting is simple to learn and execute. When fingers come into contact with a surface, the friction releases oil from between the fingerprint ridges. When powder is applied to that surface, it adheres to the oil and brings out the pattern. Powder should be poured on to a temporary palette from its container, such as paper, and discarded after use. Do not apply powder directly from the primary container or reuse powder as this may result in cross-contamination. Powder comes in many shades and colors; use powder colored in contrast to the surface being examined. Brush strokes should be circular to correspond with the general circular pattern of fingerprints. Visualized prints should be lifted using transparent fingerprint tape and mounted on fingerprint card of contrasting color to the powder. Each print should be individually labeled and numbered.

Alternative methods of processing items for latent fingerprints in wide use include the following:

Iodine fuming: Iodine crystals give off vapors that absorb physically to the oily substances of a fingerprint. The brown-colored prints that are developed with iodine are not permanent unless fixed with an additional chemical. The iodine fuming technique can be used on both porous and nonporous surfaces. It works best on fresh prints. Iodine fumes are toxic and corrosive. This technique is nondestructive, and other techniques may be used afterward. This technique works on porous surfaces.

Ninhydrin: Ninhydrin is an amino acid developing reagent that is applied by dipping, brushing, or spraying. Development is catalyzed by the addition of heat and atmospheric water through the use of a humidity chamber. It may also be used to enhance bloodstains. This technique works well on porous and nonporous surfaces.

Cyanoacrylate: Also known as the "superglue" method. An item for processing is placed within an enclosed chamber. Fumes from the active ingredient of cyanoacrylate ester polymerize on the components of the impression's residue, creating a white impression. This technique works on nonporous surfaces such as metal and glossy paper.

ALS (alternate light source): Also referred to as a forensic light or a laser, this technique is used to enhance friction ridge detail or fluoresce biological material. There are several models of ALS available, most of which work on a wavelength range from 350 nm to 600 nm. It may be used in combination with colored goggles, colored filters, fingerprint powders, fluorescent dyes, and chemical reagents. It may also be used all by itself. It is nondestructive and works well on porous and nonporous surfaces. ALSs are not in widespread use, however, because of the cost associated. As costs drop, use will undoubtedly increase.

Vacuum metal deposition: This technique is used on smooth, nonporous surfaces such as milk cartons, garbage bags, and metal containers. It may also be used after other techniques have failed. According to Clede (1997):

> Evidence is placed in a sealed chamber. The chamber is brought to a vacuum. A few milligrams of gold and zinc are evaporated in the chamber. These metals condense on the evidence material rendering any latent prints, more usable images with more detail. System operation is mostly automated, making it easy to use and ensuring high quality results.

There are only a very few working vacuum metal deposition machines in the world.

> *Case example: Abduction–rape–robbery in a hotel*
> Twenty-two-year-old Deadrick Rockett was convicted of forcible rape, forcible sodomy, first-degree burglary, second-degree robbery, kidnapping, and sexual abuse for his involvement, with his partner, Stacey Shelton, in the June 16, 1999, rape of 48-year-old V.F. Mr. Shelton and Mr. Rockett were on release from prison at the time and were staying at the same halfway house. Mr. Rockett had been released to the halfway house after serving 5 years for involuntary manslaughter. Mr. Shelton had been released after serving 12 years of a 20-year robbery sentence.
>
> On the day of the attack, V.F. was a guest at the Marriott Hotel in Kansas City, Missouri, while she was in town to attend the National Athletic Trainers Association annual conference. At 9 P.M., an emergency alarm sounded in the hotel and all of

the occupants vacated their rooms, including V.F. Minutes later, when the hotel guests were allowed to return, V.F. was followed to her room by two black males of medium height. When she reached her door and opened it, the two men tackled her and dragged her inside. According to *Missouri v. Deadrick Rockett* (2002):

> Once inside the room, the men blindfolded V.F., gagged her, and bound her hands and feet with torn-up bed sheets. The men asked V.F. how much money she had, and she told them that she had about $200.00 in her purse. The men untied V.F.'s hands to get the backpack-style purse she was wearing off of her back and then retied her hands.
>
> After taking the purse and dividing the money, one of the men turned V.F. over on her back and dragged her across the room while the other man untied her legs and took off her jeans. The two men then discussed the fact that they only had one "rubber," and the first man told the second man to look for something plastic in the bathroom to use. The first man then vaginally penetrated V.F. with his penis and began raping her.
>
> The first man then rolled V.F. over and attempted to penetrate her anally with his penis but experienced some difficulty. The first man asked V.F. if she had any Vaseline, and she said no. At that point, the second man told the first man to "spit on the bitch." In response, the first man spit on V.F.'s anus and licked it. He then successfully penetrated V.F.
>
> While the first man was sodomizing V.F., the second man knelt by her head and started stroking her hair. When V.F. started praying, the second man hit her and told her to "stop it." Subsequently, whenever she made any noise, one of the men would hit V.F.
>
> After the first man finished sodomizing V.F., the two men dragged her onto the bed, and the second man then penetrated V.F.'s anus with his penis and began sodomizing her.
>
> Subsequently, the two men moved V.F. across the room and bent her over the desk. At that point, one of the men again penetrated her anally.
>
> Eventually, the men put V.F. on the ground, bound her legs, and tightened all of her other bindings. They then obtained a wet washcloth or towel and attempted to clean V.F.'s vagina and anus. One of the men then tried to take V.F.'s wedding ring off but was unsuccessful.
>
> One of the men then stated that they had been there too long and needed to leave. The men placed V.F. next to the bed and pulled the mattress on top of her. One of the men told V.F. that he was seventeen and had already killed two

people. He told her not to move and that he would be back in five minutes to kill her if she had done so.

V.F. then heard the door click. After lying still for a while, she heard the door click again.

Eventually, V.F. managed to free herself and ran to lock the door. V.F. then noticed that the phones had been pulled out of the walls. After putting on her jeans, at approximately 9:45 p.m., V.F. knocked on the door to a neighboring room, and the people inside let her in and called hotel security.

Sex crimes detectives arrived at the scene and began processing it for evidence. They discovered blood spots on the wall and on V.F.'s purse, torn bed sheets containing a piece of used chewing gum, and three pieces of a condom package. They also recovered a used condom found floating in the toilet.

V.F. was taken to the hospital by ambulance for a sexual assault examination. According to *Missouri v. Deadrick Rockett* (2002):

During that examination, rectal and vaginal swabs were taken, and hair samples were collected. The exam revealed that V.F. had sustained multiple bruises and abrasions all over her body. The bruising, swelling and lacerations in her pelvic and rectal areas were so severe that they required examination and treatment by a doctor.

After being examined at the hospital, V.F. was taken back to the hotel to collect her belongings.

During this process, V.F. discovered that a diamond ring, a camera, a small clock, and her cellular phone were missing. During the search for these items, the bedspread was moved, and detectives found a wet towel, a T.V. Guide and a condom wrapper concealed beneath it.

Detectives used phone records to trace V.F.'s cellular phone to a man named Byron Green. He was not considered a suspect because he was 6 feet, 5 inches tall. Mr. Green told the detectives that Stacey Shelton had given him the phone when they had both been inmates at the Kansas City Community Release Center. Forensic testing determined that Mr. Shelton was the source of DNA found in seminal fluid obtained through the rectal swab and on the piece of gum. Later, a tip came in regarding Mr. Rockett's involvement; his right index finger was ultimately identified as the source of the fingerprint found on the used condom wrapper, and forensic DNA analysis identified him as the source of the sperm in the used condom found in the toilet.

In this case, the physical evidence put both of the suspects in the victim's hotel room. It also associated them with her restraint, and with specific forms of sexual contact. The arrest was a result of detectives recognizing and following up on investigative leads, and close attention to the forensic evidence.

DNA FROM FINGERPRINTS

Recently, research scientist Maria Viaznikova of the Ottawa University Heart Institute in Canada released findings that a method pioneered by she and her colleagues could harvest enough DNA from a single fingerprint to perform forensic DNA analysis. According to reports, the method can extract DNA in about 15 minutes, even if a print has been stored for a year, and will cost about half as much as traditional techniques (Chois, 2003). Faster extraction techniques mean quicker DNA results in all areas of DNA analysis—instead of waiting days or weeks for DNA results, investigators may soon only need to wait hours.

Sex-crimes investigators need to keep up with these kinds of advances in the forensic sciences. This can be accomplished on some levels by building and maintaining a good working relationship with their crime lab. But they must also be willing to look beyond the abilities of their lab to other scientists in other places.

REFERENCES

Chois, C. (2003) DNA extractable from fingerprints. *UPI Science News*, July 31.

Clede, B. (1997) New technology solves old cases. *Law and Order*, January.

Creamer, J. I., Quickenden, T. I., Apanah, M. V., Kerr, K. A., and Robertson, P. (2003) A comprehensive experimental study of industrial, domestic and environmental interferences with the forensic luminol test for blood. *Luminescence*, Vol. 18, No. 4, pp. 193–198.

Deforest, P., Gaensslen, R., and Lee, H. (1983) *Forensic Science: An Introduction to Criminalistics*, New York: McGraw-Hill.

DiMaio, D., and DiMaio, V. (1993) *Forensic Pathology*, Boca Raton, FL: CRC Press.

Flaherty, M. (1989) Admissibility, in prosecution for sex-related offense, of results of tests on semen or seminal fluids. *American Law Reports* Alr. 4th, The Lawyers Co-Operative Publishing Company.

Gross, H. (1924) *Criminal Investigation*, 3rd ed. London: Sweet and Maxwell.

Kirk, P. (1974) *Crime Investigation*, 2nd ed. New York: John Wiley & Sons.

Lee, H. (1994) *Crime Scene Investigation*. Taoyan, Taiwan: Central Police University.

Lee, H. (1995) *Physical Evidence*. Enfield, CT: Magnani & McCormick.

Missouri v. Deadrick Rockett, No. WD 59975, Oct. 29, 2002 (87 SW 3d 33398).

O'Connell, J., and Soderman, H. (1936) *Modern Criminal Investigation.* New York: Funk & Wagnalls.

O'Hara, C. (1970) *Fundamentals of Criminal Investigation*, 2nd ed. Springfield, IL: Charles C. Thomas.

Oz, C., Levi, J. A., Novoselski, Y., Volkov, N., and Motro, U. (1999) Forensic identification of a rapist using unusual evidence. *Journal of Forensic Sciences*, Vol. 44, No. 4, pp. 860–862.

Pex, J. (2003) Domestic violence photography. Oregon State Police, Coos Bay Forensic Laboratory, URL: http://www.crime-scene-investigator.net/dv-photo.html, retrieved September 1.

Rau, R. (2000) Crime scene investigation: A guide for law enforcement. National Institute of Justice, Technical Working Group on Crime Scene Investigation, NCJ 178280, January.

Saferstein, R. (1998) *Criminalistics: An Introduction to Forensic Science*, 6th ed. Upper Saddle River, NJ: Prentice Hall.

Saferstein, R. (2001) *Criminalistics: An Introduction to Forensic Science*, 7th ed. Upper Saddle River, NJ: Prentice Hall.

Spear, T. (2003) Sample handling considerations for biological evidence and DNA extracts. California Department of Justice, California Criminalistics Institute, June 16.

Svensson, A., and Wendel, O. (1965) *Crime Scene Investigation*, 2nd ed. New York: American Elsevier.

Wade, C. (ed.) (1999) *Handbook of Forensic Services.* U.S. Department of Justice, Federal Bureau of Investigation.

CHAPTER 5

INTERVIEWING SUSPECTS AND VICTIMS

John O. Savino and Brent E. Turvey, MS

> Lies are never innocent. And yours makes beings and things important.
> That is what I cannot forgive you.
> **Albert Camus, "Caligula," act 1, sc. 10;** *Gallimard* **(1958)**

Whether interviewing suspects or victims, precisely the same skill set is required: the ability to talk with people on their level (without condescension), to listen carefully to what they are saying, and to simultaneously collate and compare what is being said with information that has already been gathered during the investigation. This in concert with an attitude of ability, confidence, and trustworthiness projected from the interviewer.

Suspect and victim interviews are also conducted with the same goals in mind: establish the facts surrounding the crime (who, what, where, when, and how), address inconsistencies between known and emerging facts, and elicit confessions when the interviewee has committed a crime.

This approach to interviewing is useful for the simple reason that until the facts of the case have been investigated, and all of the interviews are complete, it is not always possible to know for certain whether the person being interviewed is a witness, suspect, or victim. Given the proliferation of false reporting as discussed in other sections of this work, this approach is the most reasonable. Every complaint must be investigated, and the role of any of those involved (witnesses, victims, and suspects) must not be assumed; roles must be investigated and established by the facts.

When interviewing victims, it is particularly important to bear in mind that each one responds differently. Victims have their own unique backgrounds, personalities, and circumstances of assault. Investigators are advised to refrain from judging the information obtained from the victim or applying their own sense of morality; keep an open mind, regardless of "gut" feelings.

PREINTERVIEW CONSIDERATIONS

Before any formal interview can be conducted, the investigator must be prepared. In other words, when it comes to planning—do some. This involves gathering background information, establishing the time and location of the interview, deciding on key issues to cover, and deciding how the interview should be documented.

It is important for the investigator to learn as much as possible about the victim, not just for the investigation but also for future considerations. In all sexual assault Investigations, for example, it is important for victims to understand that their background and lifestyle will likely be questioned in court. The investigator needs to grasp this whole picture in order to explain its potential impact on the case to the victim.

BACKGROUND INFORMATION

Only the most seasoned interviewers can expect to go into an interview room with a person they know nothing about and question them intelligently regarding a crime that they have not studied. That is to say, in preparation for the interview, the investigator should have facility with the following:

- The location of the crime
- The nature and extent of the investigation to date
- The known facts of the case
- Evidence that has been collected
- The results of any forensic testing
- The background of the victim
- The background of the accused, if any

Specific interviewee background information that should be gathered by the investigator prior to an interview includes the following:

- Residence history (previous cities and states of residence)
- Educational background
- Employment information and history
- Criminal history (complaints, arrests, convictions, etc.)
- Probation records and parole status, when applicable
- Information from other investigators who know or have previously investigated the interviewee
- Mental health reports
- Information from and relating to family members, friends, neighbors, co-workers, etc.

- Relationships between any of those involved (friends, family members, neighbors, coworkers, strangers, etc.)

Some of this information may exist in public or law enforcement databases, and some may need to be gathered through other interviews.

A lot of this information may not be available at the time investigators are called to the scene of a sexual assault. When conducting interviews with victims, the most important information to be armed with is the victim's prior complaint history:

- Has the victim reported other crimes and if so, what was the outcome of those investigations?
- Has the victim been the subject of Police Medical Aid (many departments keep records of emotionally disturbed individuals who need help from police; these records are not kept with crime reports)?
- How many times has the victim been arrested; and if so, what for?

This information has helped the authors in judging the truthfulness of complainants in some instances. If investigators know that the alleged victim has been arrested numerous times, and the victim fails to mention this during the course of their initial contacts, then the alleged victim is not being truthful.

Collectively, the authors have investigated many cases where prostitutes have been the victim of a serial rapist, or where drug addicts have been sexually assaulted in drug houses. It is important to remember that people with questionable backgrounds can and will be victims of crimes. They can also be perfectly acceptable witnesses as long as investigators establish questionable circumstances up front in order to determine whether or not they bear on the case.

Case Example

In 1999 a 19-year-old woman reported that a stranger on the rooftop of a building had raped her. The original investigating detectives checked her criminal records and learned that she had a few arrests for prostitution and narcotics. They confronted her about the arrests, and she became uncooperative as a result of their attitude. The case languished.

In 2002, an individual was arrested for a string of rapes involving prostitutes. Once in custody, a DNA match was developed to the 1999 rape. Investigators who were assigned the other cases were able to locate the victim from 1999; she was incarcerated at the time. After meeting with her in the jail, she was still able to identify the individual who raped her three years earlier.

She was surprised that someone actually believed she was the victim of a crime, as the original investigators did not think she was being truthful about the rape. Relieved that someone believed her, she admitted making a deal with the suspect. He instead produced a weapon, threatened to throw her off the roof, and then sexually assaulted her. She was completely cooperative from that point forward.

TIME AND LOCATION OF THE INTERVIEW

For the purposes of preserving the freshness of what is already tenuous human memory, it is best to interview any of those involved as soon after the crime or complaint as possible. However, this is not always feasible. There may be circumstances that make it desirable or necessary to postpone the primary interview a day or two. The following factors may be taken into consideration when considering the timing of the primary interview:

- Interviewee health, injury or discomfort
- Desire for privacy
- Prior commitments (school, work, court appearances, etc.)

If the primary interview is postponed for any reason, an initial interview may still be conducted at the scene or hospital to gather information pertinent to processing the crime scene, as discussed in previous chapters.

Not infrequently, there can be a lot of pressure placed on investigators by superior officers who are sometimes standing by awaiting the results of a victim's interview. This often depends on whether or not it is a high-profile case. No matter what the circumstances, it is important for investigators to take their time during their interviews so that they can get what they need.

During the initial interview only minimal information is needed, but remember that there are no time limits. Investigators must gather enough to establish the elements of the crime, identify suspects and witnesses, and process the crime scene competently. That is to say, this is not the interview in which investigators should confront the victim about the veracity or truthfulness of their statements, as it often takes place in a hospital emergency room. Aside from the fact that investigators will not have gathered enough information to broach this kind of doubt (the crime scene itself awaits), such locations are not the place for any kind of confrontation.

The first choice for the location of an interview should be a prearranged interview room, within a police facility. This gives investigators an environmental advantage; they are in a building full of police officers where they are comfortable, familiar, and in control of the environment. From the interviewees' point of view, they are more likely to feel the opposite; uncomfortable, unfamiliar, and without controls. These feelings may so overwhelm interviewees that they may prefer not to be interviewed at the police department. If this is the case, meet their terms as fully as possible. The interviewer can create sufficient advantage through attitude, questioning, and demeanor absent a perfect or controlled environment.

DOCUMENTING THE INTERVIEW

The purpose of documenting any interview is to assist with creating a reliable record of the facts of the case, and show that any statements obtained are reliable and believable. That is to say, document the victim's statement; do not sanitize it. Document observations, including the physical and emotional condition of the victim. Be specific—accurately describe the behavior of the victim. For example, say that the victim was "tearful and trembling"; describe what you observe. If the victim is upset, she may be crying and trembling, her hair may be messy, and her clothing in a state of disarray. Document this. These descriptive words become powerful tools in a courtroom.

As already stated above, *memory* is at times tenuous and unreliable. It is not the best way to document an interview. In fact, it does not actually document the interview in any tangible way. The use of memory alone to recall an interview is almost negligent.

Note-taking is a bit more reliable for refreshing memory, but facts and circumstances may be ignored, filtered, or altogether changed by the note-taker. Subsequently, note-taking is often of little value in regard to creating an objective investigative record for third-party examination unless studious attention to detail is given. It does not document the interview so much as it provides a record of what the note-taker felt was important at the time of the interview.

Some agencies prefer to have investigators record witness, victim, and suspect statements with the rendering of a virtual statement based on the investigator's notes. Others prefer that investigators record statements in longhand, and then interviewees be allowed to sign off on those statements. Neither circumstance represents a verbatim account, which is what is required to create a thorough and reliable investigative record.

Some investigators will ask victims to document their attack in their own writing in place of an interview. This is an incomplete record. In most cases, victims only detail what they think is important and may leave out information vital to the investigation. More importantly, this practice does not lend itself to clarification or confrontation regarding unclear, inconsistent, or inaccurate statements.

In jurisdictions where audio recording of victim and suspect statements is allowed, investigators should carry recording equipment whenever they go out.

Interviews that have been recorded protect both the interviewer and the interviewee from miscommunication and any potential liability that may result. Recording creates a record of what was said, how it was said, and how long it took to say it. It preserves something of the flavor of the interview that is lost in even a verbatim transcript. It can be done discreetly and with the interviewee's permission, with investigators explaining that it is for the protection of all concerned. Most interviewees understand and appreciate this; once the interview begins they may forget that they are being recorded if the recording device is placed out of sight.

There is no evidence to support the position that the presence of audio recording equipment alone inhibits witness, victim, or suspect statements under such conditions. It is the experience of the authors that any resistance to making statements, recorded or not, is largely predetermined, or may even be overcome by the right investigator attitude and demeanor. There is, subsequently, no legitimate reason for the failure to audio record an interview conducted in the course of a rape investigation.

Ironically, while some law enforcement agencies do not require that victim, witness, or suspect interviews be audio recorded, many require that internal affairs investigations be recorded for the protection of all parties concerned. This practice is inconsistent and may be used to suggest bias by those interested in finding it.

Video recording an interview should be done whenever feasible. There is simply no better or more complete way of documenting the statements, appearance, demeanor, and circumstances in any given interview. According to Sgt. L. D. Martin of the San Diego police homicide unit, which has videotaped interviews for more than a decade (Christoff and Zeman, 2001):

> . . . suspects soon forget the tape is rolling and the practice cuts down on defense challenges at trial.

> "It's really difficult for someone to claim you did something to them during the interview if it is videotaped," he said.

In the absence of video capability, an audio recording will do. Notes regarding visual information should be used to supplement.

DETECTING DECEPTION

At some point, investigators may wish that they had a means of determining whether or not an interviewee is being truthful on a particular issue. And they do: physical evidence and continued investigation. Unsatisfied with the obvious work and patience that this path requires, some investigators still choose to spend valuable investigative time and resources looking for a magic box or method for determining deception. Two common investigative shortcuts include the polygraph and statement analysis.

THE POLYGRAPH

A polygraph, or "lie detector," as it is inaccurately referred to, measures breathing, blood pressure, pulse rate, upper body movement, and galvanic skin response (the amount of moisture secreted by the skin). These indicators are recorded and examined based on the theory that when a person is being deceptive, their body will respond or react in a manner inconsistent with their established "normal" responses from nervousness or fear of detection. There are some problems with this theory that keep the polygraph, and the subsequent interpretations of the polygraph examiner, from being reliable:

- The polygraph requires a subjective and artful interpretation of the indicators by the polygraph examiner. That the results are open to this kind of interpretation begins to suggest their inherent unreliability.
- There is no established polygraph "profile" of a deceptive reaction, or a lie. Each person reacts differently to the emotions they feel, and each has their own particular set of biological reactions to any one specific emotion.
- What the polygraph examiner actually purports to detect is stress induced by lying, and not deception. Stress and deception are not the same. Deception does not necessarily induce stress, and many things, not just deception, can induce stress.
- Even if a polygraph can detect the biological responses associated with fear, it is accepted that other emotions can appear the same on a polygraph. Nervousness, excitement, anger, anxiety, and fear unrelated to deceptiveness— all could result in a set of biological indicators that may be interpreted as deception.
- Psychopathic individuals may easily defeat the polygraph examiner, as they have no remorse and operate on a completely alternative form of morality. Thus there may be no biological response or reaction to the examiner's questions, and no variation in biological sign for the instrument to read.
- Even normal persons of sufficient will can convince themselves of certain truths, and thus give no biological indicator of a "variation from the baseline" suggestive of deception.

The results of polygraphy are not evidence of innocence, guilt, or even deception, no matter how certain the examiner is of their interpretation. While

Figure 5-1

From the author's case files—The polygraph room in the West Memphis Police Department, in Arkansas. Note the baseball bat in the corner of the room behind the polygraph examiner's desk.

it is true that the polygraph measures objective biological indicators, it is not true that polygraph examiners can equate those indicators directly with deception or any other human emotion or response.

The philosophy of responsible polygraph examiners provide that (Chamelin, Swanson, and Territo, 2000, pp. 169–170):

> polygraph examination should not be under taken until a thorough investigation has been completed and all physical evidence processed by the crime laboratory. Without the benefits of such information, it is difficult for the examiner to formulate important questions and uncover inconsistencies in the subject's statements.

In all likelihood, if interviewers have worked to establish the facts of a case through an investigation, they will not need a polygraph to tell them if an individual is lying. Inconsistencies and breaks in logic should be apparent to the attentive and knowledgeable interviewer without the benefit of the box.

Sadly, the polygraph is commonly used as a substitute for a thorough investigation by less-than-skilled interviewers and investigators alike. It is a shortcut that requires less work and time than an actual investigation, and subsequently many polygraph examinations are administered without the appropriate foundation. Too often the result is the unwarranted exclusion or inclusion of a suspect, or the inappropriate disbelief of a victim.

The results may also be used by interviewers to suggest that deception has been indicated even when it has not, in order to seek a confession. In such instances, the polygraph is merely a prop. When abused or used without regard to the results of further investigation, this practice can result in coerced or false confessions that can become wrongful convictions. Consider the following case of Eddie James Lowery out of Ogden, Kansas, where he was convicted of raping an Ogden woman in 1982 ("Suspect wrongfully convicted . . . ," 2003):

After DNA testing showed Lowery didn't rape an Ogden woman, a Riley County District Court judge ruled in April that Lowery was not guilty of the crime for which he had served 10 years in prison before he was paroled in 1991.

The notice alleges that officers who interrogated Lowery denied his repeated requests for an attorney, provided him details of the rape and then coerced him into confessing to the crime.

Lowery was linked to the rape when he was involved in a traffic wreck in Ogden. Police questioned Lowery, then a soldier stationed at Fort Riley, because they knew he had been in the area. He denied any connection.

Lowery agreed to take a polygraph test, was told by police that he had failed and later confessed.

As a result of his DNA exoneration, Mr. Lowery is as of this writing suing the city and police department for $15 million. The lawsuit also seeks to reform the way that police interviews are done, requiring mandatory videotaping to "give an objective basis to determine whether a confession is the result of coercion or suggestive questioning" ("Suspect wrongfully convicted . . . ," 2003).

VOICE STRESS ANALYSIS (VSA)

Voice stress analysis (VSA) is widely used in law enforcement as a screening tool during hiring and an investigative tool during interviews. VSA machines are smaller, less expensive, and require far less training than the polygraph. Instead of reading multiple biological indicators, VSA devices measure only one: the voice. The theory is this: When the subject feels stress, as may be caused by lying, the muscles in the vocal cords tighten up, and the vibration of the vocal cords increases from a relaxed 8 to 9 Hz, to a stressful 11- to 12-Hz range. When this range is detected, a needle on the VSA (or whatever) dips into the red. Or a red light comes on. It's that simplistic.

The VSA and similar devices are so poorly conceived and unreliable that the American Polygraph Association, the Department of Defense Polygraph Institute, and the American Association of Police Polygraphists have all come out to denounce their use.

One study concluded, quite conservatively, based on the overall poor performance of VSA devices, that (Krapohl, Ryan, and Shull, 2002):

Over the last 30 years other researchers outside of the government have also researched voice stress for lie detection, and published their findings in scientific journals. The general conclusion has been that the accuracy is modest to poor for a handful of experimental approaches, and uniformly poor for those relying on the micro-tremor (see www.voicestress.org for a summary of the available research). This does not prevent some as-yet untried analytical approach from someday yielding a valid voice lie-detector, and the Government is still aggressively seeking such a capability for the important advantages it would afford. As a practical consideration, the poor validity for the current voice stress technology should provide a caveat to agencies considering adding voice stress to their investigative toolboxes.

So as poor as the polygraph is in terms of detecting deception, the VSA and similar devices are far less reliable.

STATEMENT ANALYSIS

Statement analysis is a method for examining written words independent of case facts, exclusively for the purposes of detecting deception. It is generally considered an investigative aid for developing leads and lines of inquiry, but not an end in itself (Adams, 1996). As discussed in the *Washington Post* (1998):

> Developed in the early 1980s and known variously as "content analysis," "statement analysis" or "linguistic forensic analysis," the technique is widely used to ferret out signs of truth or deception in patterns of words.

Responsible methods of statement analysis, such as those outlined by Stan Walters, are quite rigorous, readily accepting evident limitations and following strict guidelines for use. For example, Walters (1996) suggests that it will not be reliable when the subject writing the statement is mentally deficient, psychotic, mentally disturbed, suffering from a brain disease, or under the effects of drugs or alcohol. This of course requires extensive background information on a subject and competent writing samples. This method, then, cannot reliably be used to examine the opportunistically acquired statements of unknown offenders.

Other methods of statement analysis, however, involve treating any written statement as an individual crime scene with its own merits and inferences.

They may even regard statement analysis as a scientific process that gives the analyst unique, universal insight, and the ability to almost instantly solve cases:

> SCAN (Scientific Content Analysis) will solve every case for you quickly and easily. You only need the subject's own words, given of his/her own free will. . . .

SCAN will show you:

- whether the subject is truthful or deceptive
- what information the subject is concealing
- whether or not the subject was involved in the crime (LSI SCAN, 1998)

Written and verbal behavior is important evidence that demands attention, but it is not the only evidence. Moreover, it has limitations that are not readily admitted by those who use it:

> And of course, content analysis has its limits. It can detect whether someone is using cautious, hedged language or words that imply a greater intimacy with another than the speaker is willing to admit, but it cannot determine the precise intent behind such language. It can only point out promising lines of inquiry for investigators (*Washington Post*, 1998).

Statements should not be interpreted outside of, or independent from, the other facts of a case. They are a part, not a whole.

FALSE CONFESSIONS

Confession evidence is among the most powerful forms of proof of a defendant's guilt that can be brought forth at trial; judges rarely exclude it and juries almost never ignore it. It is the kind of evidence that can leave little doubt in the minds of those who hear it. In some instances, however, there is reason for doubt.

Though it is difficult for some to believe, false confessions can and do occur "when a suspect's resistance to confession is broken down as a result of poor police practice, overzealousness, criminal misconduct and/or misdirected training" (Leo and Ofshe, 1998).

Examples of false confessions abound, especially in recent years as the problem has gotten more attention from the press. One report explained the problem with this brief but helpful overview (Chapman, 2003):

> It's obvious that if you want to find a guilty person, you should look for one who has admitted his guilt. But if you want to find an innocent one? Same place. Contrary to what you might expect, we have discovered that many suspects who incriminate themselves are lying through their teeth.

> The number of cases where such incidents have led to erroneous convictions is long and growing longer. The Center on Wrongful Convictions at Northwestern University law school says that of 42 erroneous murder convictions documented in Illinois since

1970, 25—60 percent—stemmed from false confessions. Nationally, according to the Innocence Project at New York's Benjamin N. Cardozo law school, such admissions figure in 1 in 4 unjust capital convictions.

A local study conducted by the Miami Herald found the following (DeMarzo and DeVise, 2002):

At least 38 false or questionable murder confessions have been thrown out by Broward County courts, rejected by juries or abandoned by police or prosecutors since 1990. . . .

In the first comprehensive review of murder confessions in South Florida, The Herald found repeated examples of illegal interrogation, coercive questioning and flawed fact-checking. In at least six cases, innocent people languished in jail while likely killers escaped detection.

. . .

In case after case revisited by The Herald, Broward homicide detectives:

- Jailed people for confessions that were wrong on such basic facts as the year of the crime, the city, the name of the victim or the weapon used. Among them: Antwoin Ricks, who confessed in 1997 to killing a man in Pompano Beach. Broward sheriff's detectives charged him and a codefendant, Lamonda Giles, with a murder in Dania Beach. The men were cleared a few days later.

. . .

- Gained confessions from suspects who were in no condition to confess. When Moshe Bitoun confessed to the Fort Lauderdale police in 1997, he was high on morphine and didn't know what day it was. A jury acquitted Bitoun.
- Took questionable murder confessions from the homeless, from boys as young as 15 and from men with a mental age as low as 7. Jerry Frank Townsend, with an IQ of 58, confessed falsely to murders in Broward, Miami-Dade, Tampa and San Francisco.

For those who continue to doubt that this is a real occurrence, a list of "Proven False Confession Cases" is maintained by the Innocence Project, compiled by Dr. Richard Ofshe and Steven Drizin at: http://www.innocenceproject. org/docs/Master_List_False_Confessions.html.

Confronted with the problem, the first and most reasonable question that is asked about false confessions is *why*? Why would anyone confess to being a rapist or a murderer or any other kind of criminal when they are not? There are a number of circumstances that work alone or in concert to help elicit a false confession:

1. The innocent suspect may be mentally disabled in some way and unable to understand the nature and consequences of what they are agreeing to.
2. The innocent suspect may be presented with fabricated evidence that makes the case against them seem hopelessly overwhelming. This can be as simple as phony claims that the suspect failed a polygraph, or as involved as altered forensic reports.
3. The innocent suspect may be worn down by hours upon hours of uninterrupted, mentally exhausting interrogation that can break their will and lead to a false confession.
4. The innocent suspect may be physically threatened or abused by their interrogators, which can also break them down mentally and lead them to falsely confess.
5. The innocent suspect may give an ambiguous or equivocal statement that zealous investigators interpret incorrectly as a confession, such as a discussion about a dream related to the crime, or holes in their memory around the presumed time of the crime.
6. The innocent suspect gives a confession while under the influence of drugs or alcohol.

It is important to note that children, teenagers, and the homeless are particularly susceptible to giving false confessions. Children and teenagers are more susceptible because of their lack of appreciation for the consequences of their statements. The homeless are more susceptible because of the associated frequency of mental illness and drug and alcohol abuse within that group.

False confessions are most readily identified by a failure to accurately account for the circumstances of the crime. Moreover, they may even reflect law enforcement's misperceptions about how the crime occurred. In such ways, overzealous or incompetent investigators leave their mark on the confessions that they have induced. Either they have purposefully led the suspect to confess to a false version of events, or they have failed to adequately and competently establish the facts of the case and subsequently sign off on a confession to events that did not occur.

Good interviewers know the power that they wield; they know that during some interviews, with some suspects, they can get them to agree with just about any set of facts. Such is their skill. However, responsible interviewers in search of the facts of a case will use their skill to understand and accept when they have reached this point and not abuse their power.

INTERVIEW GUIDELINES

In agreement with some of what has been provided in McGrath (1990), the authors generally recommend the following guidelines should apply to interviews with witnesses, victims, and suspects alike:

Interviews should be done in private and without distractions.

Interviews must be done in a professional and tactful manner.

Interviewers should be non-judgmental and patient. Interviewers must create an environment that allows the interviewee to make statements willingly and naturally. Taking time with the interview and keeping an open mind will yield more information in the long run.

Interview collaterals separately. Interviewing anyone with family, friends, boyfriend, parents, spouses, or others present may give someone an overt opportunity to control or taint subsequent responses. One may also be less likely to be forthcoming in the presence of another. If there is someone present, a victim may feel uncomfortable asking them to leave. It is the investigator's responsibility to make this decision on their behalf. If the interviewer speaks with each interviewee separately, they have a better chance of getting more complete and reliable information.

Avoid multiple questions. Asking more than one question at a time encourages confusion, interrupts the flow of the interview, and allows the offender to dodge portions of the question.

Repeat questions. Asking the same question or variations of the same question at different times throughout the interview is a simple but useful interview strategy. Interviewees often disclose some aspects of their histories in response to questions that are posed early in the conversation and then add more details.

Don't tip your hand. Some interviewees will try to determine what the officer knows about the offense and their personal history, and will admit only to those facts. The officer should inform the interviewee that a great deal is already known about the case, while at the same time remaining vague on the specifics until the interviewee has told their story and has been encouraged to fill in any missing details.

Be open-minded. Do not focus on one theory and then try to prove that theory.

Use behavioral descriptors. Words such as "molester" or "rapist" mean different things to different people. Ask questions concerning the offender's specific behavior rather than using words or phrases that are prone to misinterpretation.

Listen carefully. To successfully accomplish any of the above, it necessary for the investigator to listen carefully during interviews and interrogations. The investigator's job involves talking to people, but during an interrogation many investigators take the opportunity to conduct a monologue, or even a rant of some kind. Such investigators would rather listen to themselves speak than to hear what the interviewee is trying to say. This is not a healthy or useful investigative practice.

Specifically, in regard to suspect interviews, the following guidelines should apply:

1. Have a plan. Investigators must have a clear picture of the information they want to elicit during the interview. What do they want to ask the suspect about? What do they need the suspect to say in response? It may help to have these written out in some fashion before the interview begins.
2. In most cases, one investigator should interview the suspect. A second interviewer may be used as a silent backup, to intimidate the suspect when necessary, or when new interviewers are being trained. More than that and the suspect may feel too defensive to talk, and rapport building becomes less likely. The second investigator can also take notes during the interview.
3. Utilize a small interview room with bare walls, shades on the windows, no furnishings, no telephone, and no distractions whatsoever. Limit anything that may distract or interrupt the interview.
4. The room should only contain two chairs. The interviewer should sit in a good-quality chair with the height adjusted a bit higher than the suspect's, and capable of rolling or sliding easily on the floor. The other chair should be a bit inferior and of a lower height adjustment. This chair should either be bolted to the floor or made very difficult to move. This keeps the suspect from moving away from the interviewer.
5. Do not use a desk. A desk is a barrier between the interviewer and the suspect.
6. Avoid taking written notes. Use a small audio recorder of any kind, placed out of direct view, to record the interview. Video recording is preferable for any future reference. This should, again, be done with a recorder out of direct view.
7. Situate yourself directly across from the suspect.
8. Before the interview ask the suspect if he wants a glass of water or needs to use the bathroom. If so, provide the opportunity. It is also important to provide food for the suspect. Some interviews can last for hours, and the investigator must provide and document food and drinks supplied for the suspect. If this is not done, the fact may be used to suggest that the suspect was abused or that statements were coerced at a later time. In addition, taking a break to sit and eat together in the interview room loosens the tension. It may also help with the task of building a rapport.

9. Do not allow the suspect to smoke. Smoking is a privilege, and a suspect should only be allowed a cigarette as a reward.

10. Read the suspect their Miranda warnings before the interview, *not after.*

11. If the suspect is under arrest, inform them of this fact at the time of arrest, *not after.*

12. Address the suspect in a respectful manner at all times.

13. Compliment the suspect when appropriate.

14. Try to find something you have in common with the suspect and build on it (sports, hobbies, hometown, etc.).

15. Yelling at, berating or otherwise browbeating the suspect usually causes them to put up their defenses and shut down. It does not result in legitimate confessions.

16. Always attempt to stop any suspect denials by cutting them short.

17. Do not promise the suspect anything that cannot be followed through with.

18. Blame the victim when necessary. Take the suspect's side and allow them to rationalize their behavior.

19. Minimize the crime when possible. Let the suspect believe that it's not that big of a deal.

20. Do not use a poorly contrived bluff; it may backfire. Once the interviewer has lost the suspect's trust, it may not be gained back.

21. Do not show disgust, dismay, or animosity toward anything the suspect has stated or about any aspect of the crime.

22. Attempt to get the suspect to admit that they were at or near the crime scene. This can be built upon with or without the suspect's further cooperation.

23. When a suspect does not confess to the crime at hand, it is just as important to detail their denial, especially should they be involved in a later trial.

24. Investigators must realize their own limitations; if they cannot get a statement, they should be willing to let someone else try. There is no shame in it. It may just be that the suspect did not bond with the first investigator, for any number of unforeseen reasons. One investigator can do everything right and still not get a statement. Another investigator may walk in afterward and get the suspect to start talking without much effort at all. It is important not to let pride get in the way when this happens. For example, one of the authors noted that during the interrogation of a serial rape suspect, the case detective did not have a rapport with his suspect. Subsequently, he was unable to elicit any information. Frustrated, he let his pride get in the way and did not want other investigators to attempt a separate interview. This was a missed opportunity. On the other hand, the authors are aware of cases where, under similar circumstances, and when a second

investigator was allowed to interview the suspect, a rapport was developed, and a confession was elicited.

All of this while bearing in mind that, barring legal issues, there is no limit on the amount of time that can be spent with the suspect, whether they are speaking or not. Even when the interviewer knows for certain that a statement is a complete fabrication, hours may be spent carefully drawing it out and documenting it. Once this has been done, the interviewer can go back and confront the interviewee with some of the inconsistencies in this first statement armed with the facts of the investigation.

Case Example:

"During the investigation of the rape of a young woman who was followed into her apartment building by an unknown male. He sexually assaulted her, and then choked her until she passed out, inside of the buildings elevator. When she came to, all of her belongings were missing including her cell-phone. Hour's later investigators were able to locate the individual as he was walking on the street using the victim's cell-phone. He had all of her jewelry and her credit cards in his pockets.

After interviewing the suspect and after about two hours listening to the suspect's story about how he met the victim in a bar. The suspect went as far as to name some friends they had been hanging out with. He said that after they drank together, they decided to go a hotel and have sex. He went on to say that after the hotel encounter, he borrowed her cell phone to make a call and he just forgot to return it.

The suspect did admit to robbing her other personal property. This statement was documented.

Investigators confronted him with the fact that they would be able to visit the bar and the hotel and would be able to prove whether or not the suspect was being truthful.

The suspect eventually admitted to following the victim into her building, sexually assaulting her, choking her, and robbing her. If confronted during the first interview, he may have shut down and not talked at all. This is a way to get someone comfortable with talking and then point out how far fetched their story usually is. Even if this suspect had not made a full confession, and had decided to stop talking when confronted with his inconsistencies, his recorded statement would have been powerful evidence against him to any jury. It would have been presented in court along with his numerous lies and refuted by evidence from the investigation. This is a reminder that any statement is worth taking, even if it is a complete denial.

The offender in this case pleaded guilty in light of all of the evidence against him and is serving a jail term of 32 years.

This interview lasted about six hours including a break for food. Again, remember, there are no time constraints or limits on interviews."

FRAME-BY-FRAME ANALYSIS: AN INTERVIEW TECHNIQUE[1]

In 1997, one of the authors was assigned to assist a detective with the investigation of a woman's claim that she had been raped and robbed in her apartment. The detective had taken a statement from the victim containing numerous breaks in logic. The detective in this case had explained away the victim's troubling statements and decided that it was not necessary to reinterview her. Among these were claims that her purse and welfare card had been stolen by the offender. Upon interviewing her husband, who was not home at the time of the attack, the author learned that the husband had found her purse and welfare card hidden in the apartment. The husband was unaware that the victim had hidden these items and wondered aloud why she would have placed them where they were found. When the alleged victim was confronted with the purse and the welfare card, she confessed that she had fabricated the story in an attempt to gain sympathy from her landlord, who was in the process of evicting her. Her husband was unaware of the fabrication.

In 2001, one of the authors was charged with investigating a case in which a 17-year-old girl claimed she was sexually assaulted on the grounds of a national park. The girl originally spoke with police officers and detectives. The portion of the police report pertaining to this girl's story was less than a paragraph in length and contained illogical statements. For example, she stated that she had been pushed to the ground in a muddy area. However, there was no evidence of mud on her clothing to support this. She also claimed that she was pushed to the ground from behind, but claimed elsewhere that she was pushed to the ground from the front. Both of these could not be true. The author personally conducted an interview of the girl and confronted her with these breaks in the logic of her statement. She quickly confessed to making the story up in order to gain attention after breaking up with her boyfriend.

Both of these cases are examples of the effective use of a *frame-by-frame analysis* of victim statements in criminal investigations. The purpose of this section is to outline and discuss this highly effective technique as used by the authors in the resolution of their casework.

---

[1] This section was adapted from an article originally published as Baeza, J., and Savino, J. (2001) "Frame-by-Frame Analysis: An Interview Technique," *Journal of Behavioral Profiling*, December, Vol. 2, No. 2.

DEFINITION

Frame-by-frame analysis (FFA) is term used by the authors in reference to an interview method applicable to interviewing the victim and, at times, even a suspect. The best way to understand this particular method is by comparing it to a movie. If we watch a movie in real time we may understand what is going on, but we might not observe all of the details. However, if we run the same movie in slow motion, frame-by-frame, we may better recognize the details of the action as it occurs. Investigators must use this concept if they wish to capture all the details of a crime during a given interview. Knowing the details of a reported crime is crucial to linking cases, solving crime, and prosecuting crime. It is also key to separating false statements from those that are genuine.

A review of the literature pertaining to interview and interrogation techniques (Aubry and Caputo, 1965; Gross, 1949; O'Connell and Soderman, 1936; O'Hara, 1972; and Walters, 1996) reveals that concepts equivalent to a *frame-by-frame analysis* are not presented, discussed, or referenced. Gross (1949) comes close to explaining the process when he writes:

> The object of an Investigator's interrogation of witnesses is to supply him with such complete and accurate information that he understands the case as if he had actually witnessed the events which he is investigating.

It also should be noted that this same literature does not cover the interrogation of false reporters or victims of crime. This speaks to an overall assumption of victim integrity in the criminal investigation process. As we will discuss, this assumption may not always be warranted.

USE

The authors have found that the FFA is used most effectively with victims of crime or those suspected of falsely reporting a crime. But it can also be used with suspects in criminal investigations. It is the experience of the authors that intensive, detail-oriented methods of interview and interrogation such as the FFA are rarely utilized because of several prevalent investigative circumstances:

- Investigator apathy: the indifference of investigators to their cases
- Investigator impatience: the desire for a quick and superficial resolution
- Investigator preconceived theories: the belief that the truth is already known
- Lack of investigator training and experience related to crime investigation

GOALS

Employment of the FFA provides investigative headway toward at least four equally important ends:

- The development of case information
- The identification of inconsistencies or breaks in the logic of both statements and crime reconstructions
- The elicitation of confessions from those who are, in fact, guilty of a crime
- Establishing the validity of a criminal complaint

To better comprehend the FFA and how it may be used, the reader should understand what takes place prior to the initiation of the FFA in a formal interview setting.

PRE-FFA VICTIM INTERVIEW

If the victim is at or near the scene, they should be taken to a safe, comfortable, and secluded location outside the crime-scene perimeter. If the crime was committed in their home, it may be best to have the victim taken to the hospital and then conduct a preliminary interview there. The initial or preliminary interview of the victim does not have to be detailed.

The initial interview need not be that detailed because of the following real-life considerations:

- Time constraints—the detective may need to get back to the scene because the crime-scene evidence and crime-scene personnel won't wait.
- There may be interruptions/distractions at the hospital.
- Depending on the nature of the crime, the victim may not be able to endure a sustained, detailed interview.
- A more detailed, formal interview, including the FFA interview technique, can always be arranged for at a later time.

Before beginning the initial interview, criminal investigators should introduce themselves by explaining where they work and what they do. Give the victim a business card with name, title, business address, and telephone number.

The investigator must get as much information as possible in this short period of time. In doing so, the investigator should make a note of the victim's emotional state for court purposes (this is usually asked of the investigator while on the stand). Some key factors to establish include:

- Who is the offender? Get as much detail and description as possible.
- What did the offender do to the victim? Explain to the victim that it is important to establish each act that the offender committed so that appropriate charges may be filed.
- When did the attack take place?
- Where did the attack take place?
- How did the offender gain access to the victim? Did the offender use a con, a ruse, or some form of surprise attack?
- What was the likely point of offender entry?
- How did the offender maintain control during the attack, if at all? Weapons, threats, physical intimidation, mere presence, etc.
- What physical assault did the victim suffer? Hit, punch, slap, burn, cut, bite, etc.
- Did the victim offer any resistance? Offender's reaction?
- Did the offender have trouble obtaining or maintaining an erection?
- What acts were demanded of the victim or performed by the offender?
- Did the offender ejaculate? Specific location—vaginal, anal, oral outside the body, etc.
- What was the sequence of sexual acts?
- What did the offender say to the victim?
- What did the offender demand the victim say, if anything?
- Did the offender take any personal belongings from the victim?
- Did the offender take any safeguards against being caught? Gloves, disconnecting the phone, mask, blindfold, washing or wiping up, binding victim, etc.
- What items/objects were touched by the offender?
- What are the potential locations of bodily fluids (blood, semen, saliva, etc.) at the scene and on the victim?
- How much time did the offender spend with the victim?

This is just some of the information that may be valuable in the early phases of a rape investigation. Note that that there are no "why" questions, such as "Why didn't you fight back?" or "Why didn't you report this right away?" These kinds of questions suggest an investigator bias and may put a victim off. It is more useful to ask a victim "What were you thinking or feeling?" rather than "Why didn't you scream or call the police?" and by extension accuse the victim of acting inappropriately.

This information can be relayed to the crime-scene unit personnel who are assigned to process the scene. They will then be in a more informed position to recognize, preserve, document, and collect any evidence at the crime scene.

A rape crisis counselor may be present when the victim is receiving medical treatment. These counselors are often volunteers and are there to help the victim in any way they can, providing emotional support and information. Criminal investigators and rape crisis counselors have had a somewhat rocky relationship when it comes to interviewing the victim with the counselor present. If criminal investigators would like to interview the victim outside the presence of the counselor, they should ask for the victim's permission. Abide by the victim's wishes. If the counselor becomes problematic during the interview by answering questions for the victim, asking the victim questions, or interrupting the investigator, it is best to stop the interview and say to the rape crisis counselor, "Can I speak to you for a minute?" Do not argue in front of the victim! The authors have had very few problems with rape crisis counselors and view them as hardworking, dedicated individuals. If they see the criminal investigator in the same light they will more than likely allow the investigator to do their job without interference.

FRAME-BY-FRAME ANALYSIS

Below is an example of a FFA conducted during a formal victim interview. One of the authors was interviewing a victim who reported that she had been raped after returning to her home from a night on the town. During the first part of the formal interview he asked the victim to tell him about her day, up to and including the incident, without interruption. She related the following:

> I woke up this morning in my apartment and left for work. I worked all day and when I left work I took the subway back home. I ate dinner at home and later on I went out with some friends to a party across town. After having some fun and a few drinks, I left the bar and headed home. When I got to my building a man came up behind me and put his hand on my face. He pushed me to the floor and pulled up my skirt. He raped me and after he was done he took my money. I ran upstairs and called the police.

The second part of the formal interview consists of the FFA and is typically much longer and serves to uncover more details of the crime or event in question.

The authors will use the above victim statement as an example of the detailed questions a competent criminal investigator must ask in the following frame-by-frame crime analysis.

> I woke up this morning in my apartment {**What time?**} and left for work {**What time did you leave, do you normally leave for work at this time, how did you get there, and where do you work? What was the exact route?**}. I worked all day {**What hours did you**

work, did you leave the workplace during work hours, did you have lunch anywhere?} and when I left work {**Did you leave alone or with someone? What time did you leave, what route did you take home, any stops along the way, do you normally leave at this time?**} I took the subway back home {**What subway station did you use and what was the route you took to get there, where did you get off the train, and how did you get home from the subway station? What was the exact route?**}. I ate dinner at home {**Alone? What time?**} and later on I went out with some friends {**Alone? What time? What was the exact route? Transportation? What are the friends' names?**} to a party across town {**What kind of party, for whom? Where exactly, any stops on the way?**}. After having some fun and a few drinks {**How many drinks, what kind of drinks, who was there?**}, I left the bar and headed home {**Alone? What time? What was the exact route? Transportation?**} When I got to my building {**Did you walk up, did a cab drop you off in front?**} a man came up behind me {**How did you notice him, when did you first notice him, where were you located at the time, how did you know it was a male?**} and put his hand on my face {**Where were you exactly at the time, did you see his hand (if so describe it), right hand or left hand, did he say anything?**}. He pushed me to the floor {**Where were you when this occurred, explain how he pushed you to the floor, what happened when you hit the floor, any injuries?**} and pulled up my skirt {**Precisely where were you and in what position when this occurred, did he use one hand or both, were you wearing underwear, if so what did he do to them? (move them aside, tear them off, pull them down)**}. He raped me {**What exactly did he do, frame by frame?**} and after he was done {**Done doing what, did he ejaculate, did he say anything?**} he took my money {**How did he take your money (threats, grabbed it, went through purse), how much did he take, did he take anything else, how did he leave?**}. I ran upstairs {**Had he left yet?**} and called the police {**Did you call the local precinct or 911, did you call anyone else?**}.

As the reader can see, these questions are not the limit of what may be asked. The interview can become extremely detailed and lengthy, with each new question leading to others. This is what the criminal investigator wants. Less information is not better.

Criminal investigators must also bear all of the known facts and physical evidence in mind as they go through the FFA. The thorough criminal investigator must be able to recognize and then account for any contradictions between the facts, the physical evidence, and any current statements. If the facts or sequence of events remain in question even after further investigation, the victim or offender should be reinterviewed. There is no shame in this.

This interview technique, besides giving the criminal investigator a clear understanding as to exactly what happened, may also assist in determining the validity of the complaint. Many investigators will start the interview with "What happened?" In cases of false reports, as well as suspect interviews, stories may be practiced and rehearsed in the storyteller's mind from the point of "what happened." Using the FFA interview technique, as developed by the authors, gives the investigator a chance to observe body language, and other nonverbal clues, when seemingly unimportant questions are asked. The storyteller has not prepared to answer questions like "What time did you wake up this morning?" or "What did you have for breakfast?" They do not understand the meaning and reason as to why these types of questions are being asked. The response the investigator will receive is usually truthful; this should then give the investigator the opportunity to observe the person's reactions when answering questions truthfully and then be able to note the difference when they are being deceitful.

Example

A recent example showing the utility of this method occurred during the questioning of a 14-year-old girl by one of the authors. She had been living in a group home and after an unsupervised home visit she reported being the victim of a crime to one of her counselors. She had gone to a local hospital and told a story of being grabbed off the street by her boyfriend and three other unknown males. She claimed she was being dragged and carried for blocks and then was brought into a building where she was gang raped.

Because of the sensitive nature of the complaint, responding officers and hospital personnel never asked her any detailed questions; they let her tell her practiced and rehearsed story from a "what happened" perspective, which did not contain many more details than just stated.

The author met her about 3 days later in her group home's common living room. When she entered the room, she went and sat in a chair that was three chairs away from where the author sat. There were two other chairs positioned closer, as the author had placed them there. The author had an idea where this was going just from her seat selection. After moving her closer, the author introduced himself explaining, "I am here to help with what happened to you."

She immediately went into her rehearsed story. She told the author how she had been walking on the street; her boyfriend rode up on his bike and grabbed her. She then described how the three other guys grabbed her and dragged her to some unknown building and then how her boyfriend "did what he had to do," never giving any details. While she spoke, she never looked up; she kept her head down and would not make eye contact.

The author stopped her and changed the conversation away from the crime. She was asked how long she had been in the group home, what school she went to, and how her grades were. She spoke about her counselors. She turned her body and faced the author and now looked at the author's face when she spoke. She knew this information could not hurt her and was speaking honestly. It showed in her face as well as her body posture.

Again going back to the day of the crime, the author started with what time she awoke, what she had for breakfast, did she shower, and her daily events before anything happened. Those questions were answered honestly, and again her reactions and postures when answering questions that could not hurt her were carefully noted. As she and the author detailed the rest of the day, they came to events before the alleged abduction. The author was able to learn that she was at a football game and the names of three girlfriends (possible witnesses) that she was with.

All the while the author was asking detailed questions. She was asked how she met her boyfriend and about their relationship, how many times they went out, and where they went for dates. Again these were not harmful questions in her mind; they could not hurt her story, and she answered these honestly. But when asked how strange it appeared that she did not know the guy's last name, pager number, or cell phone number her reaction quickly changed to "What does this have to do with anything?" Her body language changed, indicating her displeasure from this question.

The author again asked how they met, an innocent question. She answered honestly and said that her sister set them up. The author asked her what she had told her sister about the assault. She started getting nervous again, asking, "What does this have to do with anything?"

She had previously admitted to only telling her sister about the boyfriend assaulting her, but not the other guys. Because this was a harmful question, she had to improvise a reason why she only told the sister about one guy. Again, the author used detailed questions and she then alleged her sister belonged to a violent street gang and was dangerous, and if her sister found out about the other guys, she might do something to them. She had not practiced or anticipated any of these questions.

The story eventually broke down, and then so did she. She admitted that she had had intercourse with her 23-year-old boyfriend, believed she was pregnant, and needed a way to explain it. There had been no abduction and no gang rape.

The FFA is an effective interview technique that can lead to the successful conclusion of a case if used consistently and properly. In even the toughest cases, it can lead to admissions and confessions that may otherwise not have been obtained. Regardless of the outcome, the investigator should be well prepared to answer any questions about a crime, as may be needed in future investigative efforts, after an FFA is completed on witnesses, suspects, and victims.

REFERENCES

Adams, S. (1996) Statement analysis: What do suspect's words really reveal? *FBI Law Enforcement Bulletin*, October.

Aubry, A., and Caputo, R. (1965) *Criminal Interrogation.* Springfield, IL: Charles C. Thomas.

Chamelin, N., Swanson, C., and Territo, L. (2000) *Criminal Investigation*, 7th ed. New York: McGraw-Hill.

Chapman, S. Innocent truth about false confessions. *The Washington Post*, December 26, 2003.

Christoff, C., and Zeman, D. Confessions could prompt taping law. *Detroit Free Press*, April 24, 2001.

DeMarzo, W., and DeVise, D. Zealous grilling by police tainted 38 murder cases. *The Miami Herald*, December 22, 2002.

Gross, H. (1949) *Criminal Investigation*, 4th ed. London: Sweet and Maxwell.

Krapohl, D., Ryan, A., and Shull, K. (2002) Voice stress devices and the detection of lies. *Policy Review*, the official publication of the International Association of Chiefs of Police (IACP) National Law Enforcement Policy Center.

Leo, R., and Ofshe, R. (1998) The consequences of false confessions: Deprivations of liberty and miscarriages of justice in the age of psychological interrogation. *Journal of Criminal Law and Criminology*, Winter (88 J. Crim. L. & Criminology 429).

LSI SCAN Scan gets the truth. URL: http://www.lsiscan.com/brochure.htm, retrieved September 3, 1998.

McGrath, R. J. (1990) Assessment of sexual aggressors: Practical clinical interviewing strategies. *Journal of Interpersonal Violence*, Sage Publications, pp. 507–509.

O'Connell, J., and Soderman, H. (1936) *Modern Criminal Investigation.* New York: Funk and Wagnalls.

O'Hara, Charles E. (1972) *Fundamentals of Criminal Investigation.* Springfield, IL: Charles C. Thomas.

Suspect wrongfully convicted of rape files $15 million lawsuit. Associated Press, October 7, 2003.

Walters, S. (1996) *Principles of Kinesic Interview and Interrogation.* Boca Raton, FL: CRC Press.

The Washington Post, Follow the wording. April 26, 1998, p. C1.

CHAPTER 6

FORENSIC MEDICAL EVIDENCE: THE CONTRIBUTIONS OF THE SEXUAL ASSAULT NURSE EXAMINER (SANE)

Linda E. Ledray, RN, PhD, SANE-A, FAAN

Prior to the implementation of Sexual Assault Nurse Examiner (SANE) programs, when rape victims were brought to the emergency room (ER) for a forensic examination by law enforcement they sometimes had to wait for treatment as long as 4 to 12 hours in a busy, public area. Their wounds were seen as less serious than those of other trauma victims, and they competed unsuccessfully for staff time with the critically ill. Once a medical professional saw them, the forensic examination could take an additional 3 or more hours, during which the law enforcement officer was often expected to wait.

In many communities law enforcement was expected to pay the exam cost, but they were not allowed immediate or easy access to the medical evidence or medical records that result from the exam. In order to obtain access to the evidence and related medical records, some departments were even required by the medical facility to get a court order before the evidentiary exam records or evidence was released. In addition, all too often the medical evidence that resulted did not meet the current national standards because the doctors and nurses collecting the evidence were not sufficiently trained to do medical–legal exams. The medical professionals who complete the examination of the sexual assault victim were also less than cooperative when additional information or court testimony was necessary, and they sometimes lacked expert witness testimony ability as well (Lynch, 1993). In communities without SANE programs, unfortunately, many of these problems still exist.

In most communities today either law enforcement or the prosecutors' office pays for the cost of the medical evidentiary examination. This cost to the department is typically hundreds if not more than $1000 for each sexual assault evidentiary exam. Even if an investigator's department is not expected to pay for the medical evidentiary exam, investigators have both a right and a responsibility to know what medical evidence they should be getting from their community medical facility and to ensure immediate access to all appropriate medical forensic evidence, including the medical records related to the forensic examination. In addition, investigators and prosecutors should be able to

expect medical professionals to be cooperative, to provide additional information or explanation when needed, and to be readily available to testify as fact
or expert witnesses in court when this becomes necessary.

This chapter will provide you, the sex crimes investigator, with the information needed to decide when an evidentiary exam is necessary and what information and victim assistance it should provide, and to evaluate the evidence
that results. The chapter also provides options for improving your access to
medical evidence and related records. Since these forensic medical exams are
expensive and a significant time commitment, it is reasonable to ask if the cost
and time required is necessary and useful.

ARE FORENSIC MEDICAL EXAMS WORTH THE TIME AND MONEY?

It is very important to note that all sexual assault exams are *not* equal, and,
much like any crime scene investigation, the quality of the results is directly
related to the training and experience of the medical professional completing
the evidentiary exam. If the evidence resulting is not complete, you have a right
to demand your medical facility improve their response to victims of sexual
assault at their facility.

The implementation of Sexual Assault Nurse Examiner (SANE) programs
across the country has significantly improved the process and quality of evidence collected in participating communities. The advancements in DNA
recovery and analysis have also significantly contributed to the importance of
this physical evidence recovered in sexual assault evidentiary examinations, and
the utilization of this evidence for prosecution. Gray-Eurom, Seaberg, and
Wears (2002) correlated the legal outcomes of 355 cases in which a suspect was
identified by law enforcement. They identified three variables that were significantly related to the likelihood of a successful prosecution. These included the
following: a victim who was less than 18 years of age, presence of physical
trauma, and the use of a weapon. In a similar review of the records of 861 sexual
assault cases in a Minnesota study, no relationship was found between age and
the use of weapons; however, they, too, found the documentation of physical
injury to be significantly related to successful prosecution.

THE VICTIM AS A CRIME SCENE

In addition to the location where the sexual assault occurred, the victim is an
important crime scene. With the advances in DNA evidence collection (see
Chapters 8 and 9), the victim may in fact be the most important crime scene

in a sexual assault investigation. It is thus important that as a part of your initial investigation you take every step possible to ensure that the medical evidence is not missed or lost. This involves understanding the following:

1. Who should get a sexual assault evidentiary exam and when
2. What the SANE's role is and what the SANE can contribute
3. What should be included in a sexual assault medical evidentiary exam
4. How to interpret the medical evidence, including what the medical evidence does and does not confirm
5. How to obtain immediate access to all medical evidence, including the sexual assault examination medical record
6. How to ensure proper chain-of-custody is maintained for the medical evidence
7. How medical forensic evidence should be stored to maintain evidence integrity
8. How a rape crisis advocate can make your investigation easier

WHO SHOULD GET A SEXUAL ASSAULT EVIDENTIARY EXAM AND WHEN?

All victims of sexual assault or attempted sexual assault should be brought to the identified medical facility for a sexual assault exam within 72 hours of the reported incident. It does not matter if there was or was not any penetration; they should still be examined, as there is potentially still evidence. It is also possible that once the victim is in a safe location, with an experienced SANE conducting the exam interview, additional information will be revealed. Victims who are uncertain when the sexual assault occurred should also be brought in for an exam if there is any possibility they fit within the time guideline.

Medical evidentiary exams are also recommended for victims who report to law enforcement more than 72 hours after the sexual assault or attempted sexual assault in cases when there may be injuries that can be documented or when the victim has not changed clothes or showered and evidence may still be available for collection.

It is preferable that all victims who come forward within 72 hours of a sexual assault, or attempted assault, be encouraged to get a sexual assault evidentiary exam as soon as possible, even if they have not yet decided if they want to report the sexual assault. If they wait to be examined valuable evidence will be lost that cannot be recovered later. Studies have shown that the best medical evidence is collected within the first 12 hours after a sexual assault, so especially with immediate reports, every hour counts (Ledray, 1999). With reports made within the first 24 hours after a rape, the detailed law enforcement report should be delayed until after the medical evidentiary exam as well.

Although there have been isolated cases of evidence collected beyond 72 hours, and the advances in DNA recovery techniques from minute samples may eventually affect the recommended time frame for medical evidence collection, today most national, state, and institutional protocols continue to recommend that evidentiary exams be completed for up to 72 hours after a sexual assault (ACEP, 1999; Frank, 1996; Ledray, 1999). To date there is not sufficient or consistent evidence collected beyond 72 hours to justify the time, expense, or inconvenience to the victim. Routine evidentiary examination beyond 72 hours is uncommon. It is, however, important that you check the policy in your area.

THE SANE ROLE: WHAT IS A SANE AND WHAT CAN THEY CONTRIBUTE?

The SANE is a specially trained nurse who is available on call 24 hours a day, 7 days a week. Whenever a sexual assault victim comes to the ER the SANE is paged, arriving within a specified time, usually 30 to 60 minutes, and completes the entire medical legal exam. In 2002 the International Association of Forensic Nurses (IAFN) established a certification process. A nurse who has the designation SANE-A after her name has passed this rigorous examination and certification process (Ledray, 2002).

Health care facilities have only begun to recognize their responsibility to have trained forensic medical professionals available to provide specialized forensic evidence collection for victims of sexual assault. Treating injuries alone is not sufficient. In 2000, Coney Island Hospital was fined $46,000 by state regulators after a rape victim came to the medical facility and a sexual assault evidentiary examination was not accurately performed. She was made to wait 3 hours before being examined, and then potentially significant evidence, including her underwear and vaginal swabs, was lost. The Department of Health investigation also found that the hospital did not provide her with medication to prevent pregnancy and failed to provide complete care. The authorities believed that had correct evidence collection and chain-of-custody occurred, the evidence might have been useful to secure a conviction against the serial sex offender charged with her rape. As a result in 2001, New York passed the Sexual Assault Reform Act encouraging New York State medical facilities to develop specialized sexual assault examiner evidence collection programs (Chivers, 2000).

The Joint Commission on the Accreditation of Health Care Organizations (JCAHO) requires emergency and ambulatory care facilities to have protocols on rape, sexual molestation, and domestic abuse, and to develop and train their staff to use criteria to identify possible victims of physical assault, rape or other sexual molestation, domestic abuse, and abuse or neglect of older adults and children (JCAHO, 1997). Although JCAHO certainly does not require that specially trained forensic examiners or Sexual Assault Nurse Examiners (SANEs) be available to do the evaluation, these requirements mean it is no longer optional for medical facilities to identify and provide appropriate and complete services to victims of rape and abuse. These requirements have effectively set the stage for the further development of the SANE role as an important component of the emergency medical response to survivors of sexual assault.

To be most effective it is essential that the SANE work within a coordinated Sexual Assault Response Team (SART) model. At a minimum the SART should include the SANE (or medical care provider/forensic examiner), advocate, law enforcement officer, and prosecutor. Other members may include state crime laboratory specialists, domestic violence advocates, clergy, and social services (Ledray, 1999).

EVIDENCE OF SANE-SART EFFICACY

HIGHER REPORTING RATES

It is well established that the better a sexual assault victim knows the assailant, the less likely she is to report the incident to law enforcement (Rennison, 2002). In ERs without a SANE program available, survivors sometimes encounter busy, insensitive doctors or nurses and delays in treatment, and even if they were initially willing to report, they may decide it is not worth the effort or the wait. By providing the rape survivor with additional assistance, resources, and support, SANEs facilitate reporting and cooperation with the legal process (Frank, 1996). In one program 38% of 337 rape survivors were uncertain about reporting when they first came to the hospital ER for medical care after a sexual assault. After working through their fears and concerns with a knowledgeable SANE, an additional 12% decided to report and law enforcement was called to the ER, and an additional 23% agreed to have an evidentiary exam completed because they thought they might report later. Nearly one third of these made a delayed report, increasing the total reporting rate by 17%. Only 3% of the 337 survivors in this study refused to have an evidentiary exam (Ledray, 1999).

SHORTER ER TIME

Not only does a SANE program shorten the wait for the survivor before the exam is begun, but SANEs also shorten the time a survivor must ultimately spend in the ER. Unlike the ER physician who may be called away during the rape exam to see a more urgent case, the SANE is able to stay with the survivor until the entire exam is completed in from 1 to 3 hours.

In addition, most SANEs understand that the law enforcement officer has additional investigative responsibilities and do not expect the law enforcement officer to wait in the ER while the exam is being completed. The officers are called by the SANE when the exam is near completion to return for the victim, the evidence, and the exam records.

BETTER FORENSIC EVIDENCE COLLECTION

Just as with any other specialized clinical skill, competent forensic evidence collection is the result of both training and experience. The SANE model has demonstrated that it does not necessarily take a medical degree to complete an evidentiary exam or testify effectively as an expert witness. Unfortunately, forensic principles are not taught in most medical or nursing schools. Even when doctors and nurses who work in ERs are taught the basic forensic principles of evidence collection, few have the opportunity of conducting sufficient rape exams to develop or maintain this proficiency. A primary advantage of the SANE program is that with a limited number of dedicated nurses completing all of the evidentiary exams in a given hospital or regional area, they are able to complete an adequate number of exams to develop and maintain this proficiency.

As a result of periodic meetings with law enforcement officers, crime laboratory specialists, and prosecuting attorneys about the quality and use of evidence, evidence collected has evolved over the years of the SANE program operation and today is more complete and helpful in obtaining a conviction. For instance, one program now routinely collects an extra tube of blood at the request of the prosecutor that can be held and run for drug or alcohol analysis if the assailant claims the victim was so drunk that she doesn't remember giving consent or that she exchanged sex for drugs (Ledray, 1999).

In a study comparing 24 sexual assault evidence kits collected by SANEs to 73 evidence kits collected by non-SANEs, the SANE kits were overall better documented and more complete. A significant 100% of the kits collected by SANEs maintained proper chain-of-custody of the medical evidence collected, whereas only 52% the kits collected by non-SANEs did so. Thirteen kits, 18%, of the kits completed by non-SANEs either had no indication of who had collected the evidence or it was illegible, making the evidence available potentially useless. All the SANE kits were properly labeled (Ledray and Simmelink, 1997).

OBTAINING VICTIM CONTACT INFORMATION

The SANE should routinely ask for the name, address, and phone number of friends or relatives with whom the survivor might decide to stay after leaving the ER, and through whom they may later be contacted. With proper consent obtained in the ER, this information can be shared with law enforcement (Ledray, 1999). There is nothing more frustrating for everyone involved than to have a suspect in custody who must be released because the victim cannot be located to sign a formal statement.

IMPROVED PROSECUTION

The role of the SANE does not end with the initial collection of evidence. Courtroom testimony is also important. Concerns about SANE credibility are unfounded. In fact, there are several reports of county attorneys who were initially concerned, later finding that the SANE was an extremely credible witness in court as a result of their extensive experience and expertise in conducting the sexual assault exam. SANEs are also more accessible and more willing to adjust their schedules to testify, as it is an expected part of their chosen position (Ledray and Barry, 1998). Prosecuting attorneys have come to trust the competence of the SANE as a witness if the case goes to trial (Yorker, 1996). The testimony of the SANE is backed up by solid credentials and impressive numbers of victims seen (Lenehan, 1991). It was based on this solid SANE education, training, and experience that Tennessee more broadly interpreted their state laws to allow the SANE to testify in court (Speck and Aiken, 1995). A common concern of physicians turning over the exam to the SANE is that they will still be called to testify in court. Although physicians are called to testify about injuries that they treated, in thousands of cases there has not been one case where the testimony of the SANE alone was not sufficient and the prosecutor had to subpoena the ED physician to testify about the evidence collected (Ledray and Simmelink, 1997).

Results of research data collected by SANE programs on the incidence of injury to rape victims or the likelihood of collecting seminal fluid after a rape have also been helpful to prosecutors needing to explain that the lack of injuries or the absence of body fluid evidence does not mean the woman was not raped (Ledray, 1999). The Santa Cruz County Attorney actually believes that having the SANE collect evidence and be available to testify in court has resulted in more guilty pleas (Arndt, 1988). One SANE program reported a 100% conviction rate for over 3 years in cases that went to court and in which the SANE testified (O'Brien, 1996). Another SANE program had an impressive 96% conviction rate in cases in which the SANE did the exam (Smith, 1996). In New York City the prosecutor reported that an assailant continued to deny he had any sexual contact with the rape victim until he was confronted with the evidence collected by the SANE. He pled guilty to the maximum charge and accepted a 15-year prison sentence (Chivers, 2000).

WHAT SHOULD BE INCLUDED IN A SEXUAL ASSAULT MEDICAL EVIDENTIARY EXAM?

INITIAL MEDICAL EVALUATION

The ER triage nurse should do an initial medical evaluation to determine if there are any injuries requiring immediate medical attention. It is important, whenever possible, that the ER physician wait to treat injuries until after the SANE or forensic examiner documents injuries with pictures and collects evidence. Sometimes, even with serious injuries, it may not be detrimental to delay treatment until after the forensic exam (Speck and Aiken, 1995).

THE EVIDENTIARY EXAM

In 1987, California became the first state to standardize their sexual assault protocol statewide (Arndt, 1988). Few states have done so even today, and there is still significant variation in what evidence is collected and how it is collected in different locations even within the same state. In most medical facilities the complete exam is conducted within 72 hours of the sexual assault.

After obtaining a signed consent, the SANE/forensic medical examiner will conduct a complete exam including a medical forensic interview, followed by the collection of any evidence to confirm recent sexual contact; to show force or coercion was used; to help identify the suspect; and to corroborate the survivor's assault history provided (Frank, 1996; Ledray, 1996). This will usually include the following:

- Collection of any clothing potentially containing evidence
- Collection of biological evidence in a sexual assault evidentiary exam kit
- Further assessment and documentation of injuries, including pictures of injuries
- Preventive care for sexually transmitted infections
- Evaluation of pregnancy risk and offer of emergency contraception
- Crisis intervention and advocacy
- Referral for follow-up medical and psychological care

CLOTHING EVIDENCE

Even if the victim has changed clothing since the assault, the underpants should always be collected by the SANE/forensic medical examiner. Each piece of clothing collected should be placed in a separate paper bag to avoid cross-contamination and properly labeled with the time and date collected, the complete name of the victim and medical examiner, and a description of the evidence.

BIOLOGICAL EVIDENCE

The biological evidence collected in the sexual assault evidentiary exam kit examination will vary depending upon local protocol and the choice of evidence kit. It will, however, typically include the following:

- Collection of swabs from the orifices involved in the sexual assault to look for sperm, acid phosphatase, and most importantly, the offender's DNA
- Collection of swabs of the skin that may have body fluids of the assailant, including blood, saliva, or seminal fluid
- Buccal swabs or blood from the rape survivor as a standard to identify her or his DNA
- Collection of blood and/or urine for possible drug screen (especially in suspected drug-facilitated sexual assault)
- Pubic hair combing to look for the assailant's pubic hair
- Collection of debris from anywhere on the victim's body or clothing

Note: Most SANE programs no longer collect pulled head hair or pubic hair as this is seldom useful evidence, the collection is very painful, and when it is needed it can be obtained in those few cases at a later time. Some state crime laboratories still request this evidence, however, and it is essential that the forensic examiner be aware of the local standards.

DOCUMENTATION

Gray-Eurom, Seaberg, and Wears (2002) point out the importance of accurately documenting the forensic examination findings, and of quoting things the victim tells the forensic examiner. Precise documentation is important because statements made to the physician or nurse examiner during the medical–legal examination can be repeated in the courtroom as an exception to the hearsay rule and are very helpful in corroborating the victim's account of the sexual assault. This corroboration of the victim's statement is especially important because Gray-Eurom et al. found in their research that victim lack of credibility was the second most common reason that a sexual assault case was not prosecuted.

The SANE should ask only for information necessary to collect the proper medical evidence, to deal with the immediate physical and psychological needs of the survivor, and to collect and interpret the physical and laboratory findings. SANEs must remember they are conducting a medical forensic interview that centers on the survivor and not other assault details or investigative information that will be the focus of the law enforcement interview, such as the height or weight of the assailant. Details recorded by the nurse that differ from the police report may be used by the defense attorney to show discrepancies in the survivor's story. If this information is reported to the SANE they will of course record it; however, their focus is the medical–legal exam and the information necessary to guide that exam and treat the survivor. (Ledray, 1999; Slaughter, 1992).

Basic documentation should include:

- Site and time of assault
- Nature of physical contacts
- Race and number of assailants
- Relationship of victim to assailants(s)
- Weapons and restraints used
- Actual and attempted penetration of which orifice by penis, objects, or fingers
- Ejaculation, if known, and where
- Use of condom
- Activities of the victim that may have destroyed evidence, such as bathing, douching, bowel movement
- Consenting sex within the last 72 hours and with whom
- Use of tampon
- Change of clothes
- Contraceptive use
- Current pregnancy
- Allergies
- Victim's general appearance and response during exam
- Physical injuries

It is important to remember that in addition to the Sexual Assault Exam Medical Report, the entire ER chart is a part of the legal record and may be requested as evidence if the case goes to court. All statements, procedures, and actions must be accurately, completely, and legibly recorded. It is important to accurately and completely document the emotional state of the survivor and quote important statements made by the survivor, such as threats made by the assailant (Ledray, 1999). When appropriate, qualifying statements such as "patient states" or "patient reports" should be used by the SANE. If the exam findings match the history given by the survivor the examiner should also document "there is congruence between the victim's story and her injuries" or "the injuries are consistent with the story." The term "alleged sexual assault" should never be used in documentation of a sexual assault, as the term "alleged" has negative connotations and may be interpreted by judges and juries as indicating the victim exaggerated or lied (Sheridan, 1993).

EXAMINING FOR SEXUALLY TRANSMITTED DISEASES (STDS)

SANEs do not recommend testing adults or adolescents for STDs during the initial evidentiary exam, as this testing has no forensic value and little or no clinical value; results will only show if the victim had an STD prior to the sexual assault. If she did, this information may be accessed by the defense and used against her in court. While the CDC also states that the survivor and clinician may opt to defer testing for fear that the results may be accessed, they naively continue to recommend that sexual assault victims should be routinely tested for STDs as a part of the initial exam. They go on to state, "Laws in all 50 states strictly limit the evidentiary use of a survivor's prior sexual history, including evidence of previously acquired STDs, as part of an effort to undermine the credibility of the survivor's testimony" (CDC, 2002, p. 69). Unfortunately, while rape-shield laws were intended to "strictly limit" information of this nature from the courtroom and require that judges think hard about the relevancy of sexual history information that is allowed in testimony, many states have such broad exceptions that such laws are useless, or trial judges accept weak excuses for an exception (Murphy, 2003).

Since the early 1980s HIV has been a concern for rape survivors even though the actual risk still appears to be low (CDC, 2002). In a study of 412 Midwest rape victims with vaginal or rectal penetration, tested for HIV in the ED, at 3 months post-rape, and again at 6 months post-rape, not one became positive for HIV. The study also found, however, that even if the survivor did not ask about HIV in the ED, within 2 weeks it was a concern of theirs or of their sexual partner. Although the researchers did not recommend routine HIV testing, based on the recommendations of the study population they recommend that even if the survivor does not raise the issue of HIV or AIDS in the ED, the SANE or forensic examiner should, in a matter-of-fact manner, provide them with information about their risk, testing, and safe sex options. This will allow them to make decisions based on facts, not fear (Ledray, 1993). How to best deal with the issue of HIV is complicated and controversial. Because the rates of infection vary from state to state, so does the actual risk of infection. The antiviral agents that are used after possible exposure are toxic and have side effects that will likely make the victim very nauseated; as these prophylactic agents are still of uncertain efficacy, their use is not generally recommended (ACEP, 1999; CDC, 2002).

PREVENTIVE CARE FOR SEXUALLY TRANSMITTED INFECTIONS (STI)

In the past, forensic examiners tested for STIs in the ER and then again at follow-up. The rationale was that if a victim was negative initially and positive on follow-up, the assailant, if apprehended, could be tested as well. If he was positive for the same STI this could then link him to the crime. Because there are so many variables that could account for a positive STI test, this has not been useful forensic evidence and is no longer recommended practice for adult and adolescent examinations. It is, however, still recommended for ongoing child sexual abuse and can be useful forensic information in these cases (ACEP, 1999; Frank, 1996; Ledray, 1999).

STIs are a concern for victims from a clinical perspective and must be addressed as a part of the initial examination. Although one study found 36% of the rape victims coming to the ED stated their primary reason for coming was concern about having contracted a STI (Ledray, 1991), the actual risk is rather low. The CDC estimates that the risk of rape victims getting gonorrhea is 6% to 12%; for chlamydia the risk is 4% to 17%; for syphilis the risk is 0.5% to 3%; and the risk of HIV is less than 1% (CDC, 1993). STI testing is very expensive and time-consuming for the survivor, who must return two or three times for testing, and unfortunately, most victims do not return. In one study, only 25% of the survivors seen in the ED returned for the initial STI follow-up visit (Ledray, 1991). In another study, only 15% returned. Researchers were able to contact 47% of those who had not returned for follow-up, and they found an additional 11% of these went elsewhere for medical follow-up; however, only 14% told the physician they saw for follow-up about the rape (Tintinalli and Hoelzer, 1985). Most clinicians recommend prophylactic treatment for STIs. Except in child sexual abuse cases, the cultures taken for STIs need not be handled as evidence, because they are not used in court (Blair and Warner, 1992).

EVALUATION OF PREGNANCY RISK AND OFFERING EMERGENCY CONTRACEPTION

Although the risk of pregnancy from a rape is the same as the risk of pregnancy from a one-time sexual encounter, 2% to 4% (Yuzpe, Smith, and Rademaker, 1982), pregnancy is another concern of most sexual assault victims and must be addressed at the time of the initial examination even if the treating medical personnel or the medical facility does not support termination of an existing pregnancy. The National Conference of Catholic Bishops has agreed that "A female who has been raped should be able to defend herself against a potential conception from the sexual assault. If, after appropriate testing, there is no evidence that conception has occurred already, she may be treated with medication that would prevent ovulation, or fertilization" (p. 16, National Con-ference of College Bishops, 1995). The importance of offering complete care to sexual assault victims, which includes care to prevent pregnancy when the victim wants this care, was further strengthened by the fine against the New York City hospital, which did not ensure she received a full birth-control pre-scription to prevent pregnancy (Chivers, 2000).

Most medical centers offer pregnancy prevention care for the women at risk of becoming pregnant, if they are seen within 72 hours of the rape and have a negative pregnancy test in the ER. Sometimes referred to as "the morning-after pill," oral contraceptives such as Plan B (Levonorgestrel), Ovral, or Lovral are used for emergency contraception (ACOG, 1996). These drugs do not cause an abortion and will not harm an established pregnancy. When Plan B is started within 72 hours of unprotected intercourse, 85% of pregnancies were prevented in one study (Task Force on Post Ovulatory Methods of Fertility Regulation, 1998).

WHAT INFORMATION WILL THE MEDICAL EVIDENCE PROVIDE, AND WHAT WILL IT NOT TELL YOU?

DNA EVIDENCE TO IDENTIFY THE ASSAILANT

In 1987, the first man was convicted of sexual assault with the help of deoxyri-bonucleic acid (DNA) evidence. The case was upheld on appeal the following year (Lewis, 1988). In 1991, the Minnesota Bureau of Criminal Apprehension (BCA) Laboratory became the first state crime lab to identify a suspect on the basis of DNA alone. As a result of this valuable investigative resource, an oth-erwise unidentified rapist was found and convicted (Ledray and Netzel, 1997). The recognition of DNA as a valuable investigative tool, and the knowledge that many rapists are repeat offenders, led to the development of the FBI Combined DNA Index System (CODIS) (Miller, 1996). Today, with most state crime labo-ratories participating in the CODIS system, these databases are widely used to link serial cases, identify offenders of multiple assaults, and exonerate falsely accused suspects (Ledray and Netzel, 1997).

The forensic medical examiner should collect any possible body fluids, hair, or skin, evidence that could be from the assailant on the skin or clothing of the victim. If the survivor reports she scratched the assailant, fin-gernail swabs, not scrapings, should also be collected in hopes of collecting the assailant's skin or blood. DNA can also be obtained by swabbing the involved orifices with a standard-size cotton-tip swab for sperm and seminal fluid (Ledray, 1999).

In addition, when the SANE or forensic examiner completes the evidentiary exam, blood or saliva evidence must be collected from the survivor for DNA analysis to distinguish her DNA from that of the assailant. If the assailant had contact with the victim's oral cavity, blood should be used for comparison as a buccal swab may be contaminated with the assailants' body fluids.

SEMINAL FLUID EVIDENCE TO PROVE RECENT SEXUAL CONTACT AND TO SUGGEST THE LIKELIHOOD THAT DNA EVIDENCE IS PRESENT

It is important to remember that the absence of positive sperm or seminal fluid findings does not prove there was no recent sexual intercourse (Tucker, Ledray, and Stehle Werner, 1990). Studies have shown that 34% or more rapists are sexually dysfunctional (Groth and Burgess, 1977), and as many as 40% wear condoms (Larkin and Paolinetti, 1998). In one study of the results of 1007 rape survivors examined, sperm was found in only 1% ($N=3$) of the 369 cases involving oral rape. All of the positive oral specimens were collected within 3 hours of the rape. Of the 210 cases with rectal involvement, only 2% ($N=4$) were positive for sperm. These exams were all completed within 4 hours of the rape. In the 111 skin specimens collected, 19% ($N=12$) were positive. All but two of the positive specimens were collected within 4 hours of the rape. Of the 919 vaginal specimens, 37% ($N=317$) were positive. Of these the majority, 263 were examined within 5 hours and an additional 317 were examined within 12 hours of the rape. Only seven of the positive specimens were collected more than 20 hours after the rape (Tucker, Ledray, and Stehle Werner, 1990).

With the advances in DNA recovery and utilization, seminal fluid evidence today is primarily used by crime laboratory specialists to determine if a sample contains potential DNA evidence from the assailant. In some communities it may still be analyzed for sperm, motile (alive and moving when observed under the microscope) or nonmotile. It is rare to see motile sperm more than a few hours after a sexual assault, so this could help determine the time of the assault. It may also be analyzed for prostatic specific acid phosphatase (PAP 30). This enzyme is present in large quantities in seminal fluid and minimal concentrations in vaginal fluids; thus if a high level of acid phosphatase is collected in a sexual assault victim, this would be indicative that recent sexual contact occurred. Cases are typically negative for sperm and positive for acid phosphatase when the assailant had a vasectomy, but this is also possible in cases of chronic alcoholism (Enos and Beyer, 1979). Unfortunately, there has been little study of the results of sexual assault exams and the likelihood of getting specimens positive for sperm or acid phosphatase.

In the above study (Tucker, Ledray, and Stehle Werner, 1990), the acid phosphatase results were 10 times more likely to be positive than sperm evidence alone. Eleven percent ($N=40$) of oral specimens were positive; 12%

($N = 32$) of the rectal specimens were positive; 43% ($N = 72$) of the skin specimens were positive; and 62% ($N = 566$) of the cases involving vaginal assault were positive.

URINE EVIDENCE TO SHOW LACK OF CONSENT OR DRUG-FACILITATED SEXUAL ASSAULT (DFSA)

Although alcohol has long been used to facilitate sexual assaults, today newer, memory-erasing drugs such as flunitrazepam (Rohypnol), other benzodiadepines, ketamine, gamma hydroxybutyrate (GHB), gamma butyrolactone (GBL), 3,4-methylenedioxymethamphetamine (MDMA, or Ecstasy) and many others are being used in drug-facilitated sexual assault. Symptoms include a history of having only a couple of alcoholic beverages but quickly becoming extremely intoxicated. The victim can often remember very little of the incident other than flashes, sometimes referred to as "cameo appearances," until she awakens. With GHB the victim will often be unconscious one minute and fully awake minutes later. She may then find herself undressed, or partially dressed, with vaginal or rectal soreness making her believe she has been raped (Ledray, 2001).

Whenever a victim of a potential drug-facilitated sexual assault is seen within 72 hours of the likely assault, a urine specimen should be collected for a drug screen analysis (ACEP, 1999). Although 72 hours is the recommend time limit because most substances cannot be detected beyond that time, newer techniques of drug analysis are being developed and the time frames may change. These processes are currently only in the research stage, but, once developed, they will allow for the identification of substances as long as 28 days post ingestion of a single 2-mg dose of flunitrazepam (Negrusz, Moore, Stockham, Poiser, Kern, Palaparthy, B. Pharm, Le, Janicak, and Levy, 2000).

Even though there is little memory and perhaps no certainty of a sexual assault, whenever the victim's story is consistent with a DFSA, or raises suspicions of DFSA, the forensic examiner should collect a urine specimen for DFSA analysis as a part of the sexual assault evidentiary examination. If the victim calls before coming to the hospital or clinic, she should be told to not void unless necessary, and if she must void to collect her first voided urine in a clean container and bring it with her (Ledray, 1996; Anglin, Spears, and Hutson, 1997).

INJURY EVIDENCE TO CORROBORATE FORCE, COERCION, OR LACK OF CONSENT

Nongenital trauma evidence

Physical injuries can corroborate the victim's account of the assault, as well as demonstrate that force was used. A bruise on the arm may corroborate that the victim was grabbed by the arm and dragged into a car, or injuries to the inner thigh may corroborate that the victims' legs were forced apart during the rape. Physical injuries are probably the best proof of force and should always be photographed, described on body drawings, and documented in writing on the Sexual Assault Medical Exam Report (Ledray, 1999). Photographs are not meant to take the place of good charting (Pasqualone, 1996). Specific consent to photograph is necessary and should be included as a standard part of the exam consent. Two sets of pictures should always be taken. One set always remains with the chart. The second set should be given to law enforcement with the other sexual assault evidence. These will usually be the pictures used in court. When pictures are taken, the first picture should always be of the survivor's face and others should follow in a systematic order, such as head to toe, or front to back. They should be taken first without a scale to show nothing is being hidden, then with a scale to document size. Although a coin such as a quarter is sufficient, a gray photographic scale will also assist with color determination.

The type of camera used will vary from area to area. Today more programs are using digital photography as the fear of altering the image is resolved. Some programs make a hard copy in the ER for comparison purposes; others rely upon the testimony of the SANE or medical examiner. Many prosecutors continue to be uncomfortable with digital photography and continue to insist on 35 mm or Polaroid images. Each picture should include a label with the survivor's name and/or case number in the picture. When Polaroid pictures are used the SANE or forensic medical examiner should print the date, time, client number and/or name, and the examiner's name and title on the back of every picture. When using a 35 mm camera, it is recommended that photographic documentation of injuries be completed with a standard 50 mm lens and 100–200 speed (ASA) color film. A disadvantage of 35 mm pictures is that they must be sent out for developing and are often not available to the police when they investigate, or to the prosecutor when he or she is deciding to charge the case. All too often 35 mm images are never developed. Polaroid and digital pictures have the advantage of being available to law enforcement immediately during the initial investigation. Polaroid film is, however, very expensive (Sheridan, 1993). Although some examiners have historically been hesitant to take pictures of victims' breasts and genitals, not properly documenting injuries with pictures may result in liability for failure to document (Pasqualone, 1996). The survivor's dignity can be maintained and proper evidence made available by taking close-up pictures of the injury and by properly draping exposed areas.

It is always important to remember that the absence of injuries does prove the lack of force or coercion and does not prove consent. Most sexual assault victims are *not* injured. Significant physical injury from a sexual assault is rare and occurs in only 3% to 5% of rape survivors across studies. Fewer than 1% of rape victims have been found to need hospitalization. Even minor injury is usually documented in only about one-third of the reported rapes. Injuries, when they do occur, are, however, more common in stranger rapes and rapes by someone the victim knows intimately, such as a domestic partner, rather than in date rape or acquaintance rape situations (Kilpatrick, Edmunds, and Seymour, 1992; Ledray, 1999; Bownes, O'Gorman, and Saters, 1991; March-banks, Lui, and Mercy, 1990; Tucker, Ledray, and Stehle Werner, 1990).

In one study of 355 cases, nongenital traumatic injuries were identified in a total of 45% of the cases examined (Gray-Eurom et al., 2002). In another study of 351 rape victims, the overall injury rate was somewhat lower; however, the rate of physical injury for male rape victims (40%) was found to be higher than for female victims (26%). Although 25% of the men and 38% of the women in this study sought medical care after the rape for their physical injuries, only 61% of those seeking treatment told the treating physician they had been raped. The women expressed a strong preference for medical treatment and counseling by a woman. The male victims were, however, less likely to express a gender preference (Petrak and Claydon, 1995). A more recent study of 1076 sexual assault victims found nongenital trauma even more often, 67% of the time (Riggs, Houry, Gayle, Markovchick, and Feldhaus, 2000). It is important that the forensic examiner be aware of the likely pattern of injuries from violence so that she knows the appropriate questions to ask and where to look for injuries on the basis of the history given. Intentional injuries tend to be more central, and accidental injuries more toward the extremities. Especially if domestic violence is involved, injuries are most often inflicted where the victim can easily hide them. The most common injuries are broken eardrums from slapping, neck bruising from choking, punch bruising to the upper arm, and "defensive posturing" injuries to the outer mid-ulnar areas of the arms. Also common are whip or cordlike injuries to the back; punch or bite injuries to the breasts and nipples; punch injuries to the abdomen, especially in pregnant women; punch and kick injuries to the lateral thighs; and facial bruising, abrasions, and lacerations (Sheridan, 1993).

The literature cautions the forensic examiner against trying to estimate the age of a bruise by its color. Although we know that in people with light skin recent bruising is red or dark blue in color, older bruising may be green-blue or yellow-blue, and older still bruising may be barely visible, people vary greatly in their rates of healing. Medications may affect bleeding and healing response as well. Experts suggest that the size and color should be documented, eg. "2 cm × 3 cm, deep blue-purple bruising" without further interpretation (Ledray, 1999). It is also important to remember that it can be very difficult to even identify bruising in individuals with dark skin if alternative light sources are not available. Unfortunately, since these light sources are very expensive, most medical facilities do not have them available.

Genital Trauma Evidence

Trauma to the orifice reported by the victim as involved in the assault both will corroborate the victim's assault history and can be used to show force was used. The location of the genital trauma can be related to the position of the victim during the assault. For example, if a woman is raped in the "missionary position," the forensic medical examination of the vaginal area will be more likely to reveal injury to the external vaginal opening between 5:00 and 7:00, or the posterior fourchette area. If the medical forensic exam reveals a half-moon curved cut on the cervix or a scratch along the inner vaginal wall or external vaginal lips (labia minora), this would corroborate that digital penetration, or attempted digital penetration occurred (Ledray, 1999). The literature suggests that colposcopic genital examination is extremely useful to visualize and document genital abrasions, bruises, and tears, as they are often so minute they cannot be seen with the naked eye (Frank, 1996; Ledray, 2001; Slaughter, 1992). The colposcope magnifies the genital injury to make smaller injuries more easily visible with the naked eye and allows for photography of this detail. The colposcope is not being used to identify pathology. It is well documented in the legal arena that the use of the colposcope is an accepted practice in the forensic examination of adults and children (IAFN, 1996), and colposcope use for this purpose is within the scope of the SANE practice (Ledray, 2000). The colposcope is especially important as a part of the examination of children. When a colposcope is used the medical examiner should always document the magnification and the positions for examination, and a method of measurement should also be used (Soderstrom, 1994).

Most research on sexual assault documents that the likelihood of genital trauma identification without the use of a colposcope to magnify the trauma is similar to that of nongenital trauma: 1% severe injury and 10% to 30% minor injury across studies (Ledray, 1999). In a recent study Gray-Eurom et al. (2002) identified slightly more genital trauma, 34%, with gross visualization alone. Riggs et al. (2000), found genital trauma in 52% of the cases reviewed. Unfortunately, they did not indicate if a colposcope was used during the examination. With colposcopic examination genital trauma has been identified in up to 87% ($N = 114$) of sexual assault cases (Slaughter, 1992). Just as with nongenital trauma, the absence of genital trauma does not indicate consent.

It is also true that minor genital trauma does not prove rape. In a study that compared 311 sexual assault survivors to a group of 75 women who had consenting sexual contact, researchers identified genital trauma in 68% ($N = 213$) of the rape survivors. However, 11% ($N = 8$) of the women had injuries from consenting sex. It is important to note that only one injury was found in the consenting sex group and the sexual assault group had an average of three injuries each (Slaughter et al., 1997).

Both the colposcope and anoscope have been shown to improve the identification of rectal trauma; however, the colposcope may be less helpful than the anoscope. In a study of 67 male rape victims, all examined by experienced forensic examiners, 53% had genital trauma identified with the naked eye alone. This number increased only slightly, 8%, when the colposcope was used; however, the positive findings increased a significant 32% when an anoscope was utilized. The combination of naked eye, colposcope, and anoscope resulted in a total of positive findings in 72% of the cases (Ernst, Green, Ferguson, Weiss, and Green, 2000).

OBTAINING IMMEDIATE ACCESS TO ALL EVIDENCE AND MEDICAL RECORDS

SANE programs, working collaboratively as a part of a SART, can ensure law enforcement gets the completed sexual assault evidentiary exam kit and all related ER records of the exam immediately, and interpret the findings when necessary. When the evidentiary exam is completed, the SANE should review the findings of the forensic exam with the law enforcement officer. Confidentiality is not a barrier when the SANE knows to obtain all necessary signed consent for release of information to law enforcement prior to beginning the exam.

It is true that new consent and confidentiality laws have significantly restricted the release of medical records. It is not true, however, that these new laws now prevent medical personnel from releasing records of the sexual assault evidentiary exam to law enforcement immediately, or that a court order is now necessary. The consent for the exam must, however, specify which records will be released and to whom. If this consent is not now being collected, it needs to be added. Everyone needs to understand that the forensic medical exam is completed as a part of the investigative process and is of limited use unless all the evidence, including the medical records completed at the time of the forensic medical examination, which are also important evidence, is turned over to law enforcement for this purpose.

Ask the medical facility collecting your evidence what signed consent they need to be able to hand this evidence and the records over to your officer immediately. They will likely want the hospital attorney involved. The consent can be brought to the medical facility by the officer, or obtained as a part of the consent for the medical examination by the medical staff.

HOW DO YOU ENSURE PROPER CHAIN-OF-CUSTODY IS MAINTAINED FOR MEDICAL EVIDENCE?

As the study described earlier demonstrates (Ledray and Simmelink, 1997), it is reasonable to be concerned if proper chain-of-custody is being maintained by your medical facility if you do not have a SANE program. If you are not certain if proper chain-of-custody is being maintained with your medical evidence, check with your crime laboratory and prosecutor.

Maintaining proper chain-of-evidence is as important as collecting the proper evidence. Without this complete documentation, with signatures, of everyone who has had possession of the evidence from the individual who collected the evidence until it was entered into the courtroom, or analysis, the evidence may be inadmissible in court. If the SANE must leave the room for any reason during the exam, the evidence must go with her (Frank, 1996). It is the responsibility of your medical facility to ensure that their personnel are adequately trained to do their complete job, and this includes maintaining chain-of-custody for all forensic evidence collected in a sexual assault exam.

You can certainly help by letting them know if you identify a problem, and by offering to provide training for their medical personnel. Some law enforcement departments have decided that to ensure chain-of-custody is maintained, they will insist on being present during the medical evidentiary exam. Although this is certainly one solution, it is a very poor, inappropriate solution of last resort. It is not necessary, nor is it appropriate, for the police officer to be in the exam room when the evidence is collected to maintain proper chain-of-evidence. It is not your role to help collect medical evidence any more than it is the role of the medical forensic examiner to do your investigation.

If you take custody of the evidence from the SANE or medical examiner who collected it, both signatures on the chain-of-evidence document are all that is necessary. It is not, however, essential for law enforcement to take possession of the evidence immediately. If you cannot immediately return, the SANE or individual that collected the evidence can place the evidence in a locked storage area with limited access and sign that they placed the evidence in the storage area. This is often a locked refrigerator, a locked box that can be placed in a refrigerator (if there is whole blood), or a locked cabinet that only the charge nurse has the key to open. When law enforcement does return, any available nurse can sign that they released the evidence and the law enforcement officer who picks it up will, of course, sign that they received the evidence (Ledray, 1999).

HOW SHOULD MEDICAL FORENSIC EVIDENCE BE STORED TO MAINTAIN EVIDENCE INTEGRITY?

The requirements for maintaining specimen integrity will depend upon what is collected in the sexual assault evidence kit. In the past sexual assault evidence kits included whole blood that needed to be refrigerated to prevent deterioration of the specimen (Ledray, 1999). Many states have eliminated the whole blood because of the difficulty of storage and the changes in processing. Now most rape kits include only dried blood, which does not need refrigeration, and because DNA evidence can be recovered from a very small amount of dried blood indefinitely. Clothing evidence collected as part of the medical evidentiary exam should be turned over to law enforcement in paper bags to allow for continued drying (Ledray, 2001).

HOW A RAPE CRISIS ADVOCATE CAN MAKE YOUR INVESTIGATION EASIER

It is important to recognize that the rape victim will likely be in a state of extreme crisis after a sexual assault. No matter what the assault circumstances, even if it did not involve a weapon, even if he or she was not physically injured, it is likely that the victim feared for her life during the assault. The more time you take initially to make the victim feel safe and secure, the better able he or she will be to answer your questions and give you accurate details about the incident. Remember that your tone of voice can sound supportive or blaming, even though you may use the same words, and will also have an impact on the victim. If you take the time to explain to the victim why you need to ask tough or potentially embarrassing questions, you will also get better cooperation. The advocate can help with this explanation and support the victim through the process.

This is not a time to test the victim to see if they will make a good witness in court. This is the time to provide support and to make the victim feel safe and secure so that weeks or months later, when they may need to testify, they will be better able and more willing to do so. The reality is most sexual assault cases do not go to trial. Many more are solved in a guilty plea. All that is needed now is for the victim to cooperate with an initial report and to get a sexual assault evidentiary exam. The rape crisis center advocate will help work through the victim's reporting fears and provide her the support necessary for her to answer your questions and cooperate with the medical evidentiary exam.

In most communities the advocate will also keep in touch with the victim after she leaves the hospital. The advocate can help you locate the victim for the more detailed report and can help keep the victim informed about the status of the legal case. Although they may not be willing to give you the contact information for the victim if they do not have the victim's permission to do so, they should be willing to contact the victim and ask that she contact you ASAP. They should also be available to take the victim to the later investigative interview and provide her support to help her get through the interview. No matter how delicate you may attempt to be, remember there are tough, personal, and often embarrassing questions that will be difficult for most victims to answer.

Many communities have set up a system where a specially trained advocate is available on call. Should law enforcement of a community medical facility get a call from a victim of sexual assault, the advocate can be called to come to where the victim is, usually the medical facility, and provide crisis intervention services. Most advocates have 40 hours of specialized training, plus clinical experience. In most communities this advocate will work for your local rape crisis center or domestic violence center. If they do not yet have an outreach advocate system in place, they may be willing to establish one, as grant money is available to do so (Ledray, 1999).

In many communities across the nation, prosecutors and law enforcement agencies have found this so helpful in assisting the victim that they have established their own system-based advocate services that work with all crime victims, not just rape or domestic violence. Grant money is often available to develop these services. Your local rape crisis center will likely be a helpful resource for you.

Although providing crisis intervention is the primary role of the rape crisis center advocate when one is present, the SANE or medical examiner is also responsible for providing crisis intervention and ensuring that follow-up counseling services are available following sexual assault. When domestic violence is suspected as a part of the sexual assault, it is especially important to have a protocol in place for screening and/or referral. Many medical facilities have domestic violence advocates available who can be called to the hospital. They will know the availability of shelters for victims of domestic violence who may need a safe place to go after the evidentiary exam (Ledray, Faugno, and Speck, 2001).

Fear and anxiety resulting from the rape can significantly affect the survivor's life, including her work, school, and relationships with others, far into the future. However, even the crisis intervention that occurs during a one-time ER contact can have a significant positive impact on the recovery process (Ledray, 1999).

AFTER THE EXAM

Many medical facilities now have a place for the survivor to shower, brush her teeth, and change clothes after the exam. They often provide her with fresh clothes as well (Frank, 1996; Sandrick, 1996). It is not unusual for the victim to be afraid to return home alone, so it is important for the advocate or medical examiner to offer to call a friend or relative to be with the survivor during the exam and to take her home. Since the survivor may be in a state of shock in the ER, it is important to provide her with written information to take home with her (Speck and Aiken, 1995). The advocate or SANE should also make follow-up phone calls within 24 to 48 hours to check on her status and medical compliance and to assist with follow-up referrals that were recommended (Ledray, 1996).

SANE-SART DEVELOPMENT

HOW DO YOU GO ABOUT GETTING BETTER FORENSIC MEDICAL CARE?

It is important to remember that every medical facility, no matter its size or location, has a responsibility to provide complete and current state-of-the-art medical forensic care for victims of sexual assault. Doing a good job of caring for their injuries, but not properly collecting evidence, maintaining chain-of-custody, and documenting, is not acceptable and could, in fact, result in the medical facility being sued. If your facility is not providing this level of care, it is reasonable to expect that they make changes in their response to sexual assault victims. It may be that they are unaware of the SANE model.

If there is another facility nearby that does have a SANE program, you may want to consider taking your sexual assault victims to that hospital instead. If you do not know where SANE services are available you can contact your local rape crisis center, as they should have this information. Another resource is the National SANE-SART Web site, www.sane-sart.com. If your program is a member, contact information will be provided, but remember, not all SANE programs participate in this national program, so you may still have a local community program even if it is not listed. If there is a nearby SANE program, they may be willing to also provide services to the hospital you currently utilize. Many SANE programs provide services to multiple medical facilities. If you do not want to be the primary individual negotiating this change, you might want to ask your local rape center to do so.

If there is no SANE program in your area, your local rape center may also be willing to spearhead the development of a SANE program. It is very important that you remain involved in this process, however. You can get the helpful document *Sexual Assault Nurse Examiner (SANE) Development and Operation Guide* free of charge by calling the Office for Victims of Crime (OVC) at 1-800-627-6872. Ask for NCJ document #170609. Their Training and Technical Assistance Center (TTAC) can also provide you with funding for technical assistance to develop a SANE-SART program in your community. Your department, your local medical center, or your local rape crisis center can lead this effort.

SUMMARY

Significant advances in the medical–legal examination of the sexual assault survivor have occurred in recent years. Much of the improvement can be accredited to the development of SANE programs and SART teams. By working together SANEs, law enforcement, prosecutors, and advocates have improved services to the survivor, increased reporting rates, improved medical–legal evidence collection, and facilitated a seamless system response. The continued coordination of effort between the professionals working with the survivor of sexual assault is essential to furthering the advancement of our knowledge and to supporting survivor recovery.

It is important to remember the following when you get a call to a report of a sexual assault:

1. All sexual assault or attempted sexual assault victims should get an exam as soon as possible, within 72 hours of the incident (this time limit may vary depending upon local guidelines).
2. Whenever possible the exam should be completed by a Sexual Assault Nurse Examiner (SANE) or other trained forensic medical specialist.
3. You need a system established that allows law enforcement immediate access to all medical evidence, including the sexual assault examination medical record.
4. Know what the medical evidence does and does not confirm.
5. It is reasonable to expect your medical examiner to maintain proper chain-of-custody for the medical evidence.
6. The medical forensic evidence must be properly stored to maintain evidence integrity.
7. It is important to get the victim immediate support services from an advocate and for someone to maintain contact with the victim after the evidentiary examination.
8. The only way to get better forensic medical services is to ask your community medical center to provide them, if you do not currently have a SANE program or trained medical forensic examiner available.

REFERENCES

ACOG (1996) Practice Patterns: Evidence-based guidelines for clinical issues in obstetrics and gynecology, No. 3, December 1996.

American College of Emergency Physicians (ACEP) (June 1999) Evaluation and management of the sexually assaulted or sexually abused patient, Dallas, TX.

Anglin, D., Spears, K., and Hutson, H. (1997) Flunitrazepam and its involvement in date or acquaintance rape. *Academic Emergency Medicine*, Vol. 4, No. 4, pp. 323–326.

Arndt, S. (1988) Nurses help Santa Cruz sexual assault survivors. *California Nurse*, October.

Blair, T., and Warner, C. (1992) Sexual assault. *Topics in Emergency Medicine*, Vol. 14, No. 4.

Bownes, I., O'Gorman, E., and Saters, A. (1991) A rape comparison of stranger and acquaintance assaults. *MedSciLaw*, Vol. 31, No. 2, pp. 102–109.

Center for Disease Control and Prevention (1993) Sexually transmitted diseases treatment guidelines. *MMWR*, Vol. 42, No. RR-4, September 24.

Centers for Disease Control and Prevention (2002) Sexually transmitted diseases treatment guidelines. *MMWR*, Vol. 51, No. RR-6, May 2002.

Chivers, C. J. (2000) In sex crimes, evidence depends on game of chance in hospitals. *The New York Times*—Metropolitan Desk, pp. 1–6, August 6.

Enos, W. F., and Beyer, J. C. (1980) Prostatic acid phosphatase, aspermia, and alcoholism in rape cases. *Journal of Forensic Sciences*, Vol. 25, No. 2, pp. 353–356.

Ernst, A., Green, E., Ferguson, M., Weiss, S., and Green, W. (2000) The utility of anoscopy and colposcopy in the evaluation of male sexual assault victims. *Annals of Emergency Medicine*, Vol. 36, No. 5, pp. 432–436.

Frank, C. (1996) The new way to catch rapists. *Redbook*, pp. 104–105, 118, 120.

Frazier, and Hanley (1996).

Gray-Eurom, K., Seaberg, D., and Wears, R. (2002) The prosecution of sexual assault cases: correlation with forensic evidence. *Annals of Emergency Medicine*, Vol. 39, No. 1, pp. 39–46.

Groth, A. N., and Burgess, A. W. (1977) Sexual dysfunction during rape. *The New England Journal of Medicine*, October 6, pp. 764–766.

IAFN Statement (1996) Utility of the colposcope in the sexual assault examination. Fourth Annual Scientific Assembly of Forensic Nurses, Kansas City Conference, November.

JCAHO (Joint Commission on Accreditation of Health Organizations) (1997) *Comprehensive Accreditation Manual for Hospitals: The Official Handbook*. Oakbrook Terrace, IL: Joint Commission on Accreditation of Health Care Organizations.

Kilpatrick, D., Edmunds, C., and Seymour, A. (1992) Rape in America: A report to the nation. Arlington, VA: National Victim Center.

Larkin, H., and Paolinetti, L. (1998) Pattern of anal/rectal injury in sexual assault victims who complain of rectal penetration. IAFN Sixth Annual Scientific Assembly. Pittsburgh, PA, October 1–5.

Ledray, L. (1991) Sexual assault and sexually transmitted disease: The issues and concerns, in Ann Wolbert Burgess (ed.), *Rape and Sexual Assault III: A Research Handbook.* New York: Garland Publishing, pp. 181–193.

Ledray, L. E. (1993) Sexual Assault Nurse Clinician: An emerging area of nursing expertise, in Linda C. Andrist (ed.), *Clinical Issues in Perinatal and Women's Health Nursing,* Vol. 4, No. 2. Philadelphia: J.B. Lippincott.

Ledray, L. E. (1996) The Sexual Assault Resource Service: A new model of care. *Minnesota Medicine: A Journal of Clinical and Health Affairs,* Vol. 79, No. 3, pp. 43–45.

Ledray, L. (1999) *Sexual Assault Nurse Examiner (SANE) Development and Operation Guide.* U.S. Department of Justice, Office of Victims of Crime.

Ledray, L. (2001) Sexual Assault Nurse Examiner, in LeBeau, M., and Mozani, A. (eds.), *Drug Facilitated Sexual Assault: A Forensic Handbook.* London: Academic Press, Chapter 11, pp. 231–252.

Ledray, L. (2002) Do all emergency physicians have an obligation to provide care for victims of sexual assault or is there a more effective alternative? *Annals of Emergency Medicine,* Vol. 39, No. 1, pp. 61–64.

Ledray, L., and Barry, L. (1998) Sexual assault: Clinical issues: SANE expert and factual testimony. *Journal of Emergency Nursing,* Vol. 24, No. 3, pp. 284–287.

Ledray, L., Faugno, D., and Speck, P. (2001) Sexual assault: Clinical issues. SANE: Advocate, forensic technician, nurse? *Journal of Emergency Nursing,* Vol. 27, No. 1, pp. 91–93.

Ledray, L. E., and Netzel, L. (1997) Forensic nursing: DNA evidence collection. *Journal of Emergency Nursing,* Vol. 23, No. 2, pp. 182–186.

Ledray, L. E., and Simmelink, K. (1997) Sexual assault: Clinical issues. Efficacy of SANE evidence collection: A Minnesota study. *Journal of Emergency Nursing,* Vol. 23, No. 2, pp. 182–186.

Lenehan, G. P. (1991) Sexual assault nurse examiners: a SANE way care for rape victims. *Journal Of Emergency Nursing,* Vol. 17, No. 1, pp. 1–2.

Lewis, R. (1988) DNA fingerprints: Witness for the prosecution. *Discover,* June.

Lynch, V. (1993) Forensic nursing: Diversity in education and practice. *Journal of Psychosocial Nursing and Mental Health Services,* November, Vol. 31, No. 11, pp. 7–14.

Marchbanks, P. J., Lui, K. J., and Mercy, J. A. (1990) Risk of injury from resisting rape. *American Journal of Epidemiology,* Vol. 132, No. 3, pp. 540–549.

Miller, J. V. (1996) Letter to Virginia A. Lynch, October 11, 1996. Fourth Annual Scientific Assembly of Forensic Nurses Kansas City Conference, November 1996.

Murphy, W. (2003) The myth about rape shield laws. *Sexual Assault Report*, Vol. 7, No. 2, pp. 1 and 31. National Conference of College Bishops, 1995, p. 16.

Negrusz, A., Moore, C. M., Stockham, T. L., Poiser, K. R., Kern, J. L., Palaparthy, R., Le, N. L., Janicak, P. G., and Levy, N. A. (2000) Elimination of 7-aminoflunitrazepam and flunitrazepam in urine after a single dose of Rohypnol. *Journal of Forensic Sciences*, September, Vol. 45, No. 5, pp. 1031–1040.

O'Brien, C. (1996) Sexual Assault Nurse Examiner (SANE) Program Coordinator. *Journal of Emergency Nursing*, Vol. 23, No. 5, pp. 532–533.

Pasqualone, G. A. (1996) Forensic RNs as photographers. Documentation in the ED. *Journal of Psychosocial Nursing*, Vol. 34, No. 10, pp. 47–51.

Petrak, J., and Claydon, E. (1995) The prevalence of sexual assault in a genitourinary medicine clinic: Service implications. *Genitourinary Medicine*, Vol. 71, pp. 98–102.

Rennison, C. (2002) *Criminal Victimization 2001: Changes 2000–01 with Trends 1993–2001* (NCJ 194610). U.S. Bureau of Justice Statistics.

Riggs, N., Houry, D., Long, G., Markovchick, V., and Feldhaus, K. (2000) Analysis of 1,076 cases of sexual assault. *Annals of Emergency Medicine*, Vol. 35, No. 4, pp. 358–362.

Sandrick, K. M., Medicine and law (1996) Tightening the chain of evidence. *Hospital Health Networks*, June 5, Vol. 70, No. 11, pp. 64, 66.

Sheridan, D. J. (1993) The role of the battered woman specialist. *Journal of Psychosocial Nursing*, Vol. 31, No. 11, pp. 31–37.

Slaughter, L., and Brown, C. (1992) Colposcopy to establish physical findings in rape victims. *American Journal of Obstetrics and Gynecology*, Vol. 176, No. 3, pp. 83–86.

Slaughter, L., Brown, C. R., Crowley, S., and Peck, R. (1997) Patterns of genital injury in female sexual assault victims. *American Journal of Obstetrics and Gynecology*, March, Vol. 176, No. 3, pp. 609–616.

Smith, K., Holmseth, J., MacGregor, M., and Letourneau, M. (1998) Sexual Assault Response Team: overcoming obstacles to program development. *Journal of Emergency Nursing*, Vol. 24, No. 4, pp. 365–367.

Soderstrom, R. M. (1994) Colposcopic documentation: An objective approach to assessing sexual abuse of girls. *Journal of Reproductive Medicine*, Vol. 39, No. 1, pp. 6–8.

Speck, P., and Aiken, M. (1995) Twenty years of community nursing service. *Tennessee Nurse Focus*, Vol. 58, No. 2, pp. 15–18.

Task Force on Post Ovulatory Methods of Fertility Regulation, 1998.

Tintinalli, J., and Hoelzer, M. (1985) Clinical findings and legal resolution in sexual assault. *Annals of Emergency Medicine*, Vol. 14, No. 5, pp. 447–453.

Tucker, S., Claire, E., Ledray, L., and Werner, J. (1990) Sexual assault evidence collection. *Wisconsin Medical Journal*, Vol. 89, No. 7, pp. 407–411.

Yorker, B. (1996) Nurses in Georgia care for survivors of sexual assault. *Georgia Nursing*, Vol. 56, No. 1, pp. 5–6.

Yuzpe, A., Smith, R., and Rademaker, A. (1982) A multicenter clinical investigation employing ethinyl etradiol combined with dl-norgestrel as a post-coital contraceptive agent. *Fertility and Sterility*, Vol. 37, No. 4, pp. 508–513.

CHAPTER 7

INVESTIGATING DRUG-FACILITATED SEXUAL ASSAULT

Stephen M. Pittel, PhD and Laila Spina, PsyD

"Candy is dandy but liquor is quicker."

—**Ogden Nash**

INTRODUCTION

A publication of the American Prosecutor's Research Institute (APRI, 1999) on the prosecution of drug-related sexual assaults reflects the growing public concern with the use of such potent drugs as Rohypnol (flunitrazepam) and GHB (gamma-hydroxybutyrate) in the commission of sexual crimes. The same concerns are reflected in documentaries and extensive media reports on the use of these and other drugs in the commission of sexual assaults by dates or acquaintances of unsuspecting victims.

Google searches using combinations of such keywords as "date," "acquaintance," "rape," "sexual assault," "drug," "Rohypnol," "GHB," "ecstasy," "alcohol," etc., identified from 100,000 to 1.5 million Internet "hits" that focus on drug-facilitated sexual assaults allegedly perpetrated by dates or acquaintances of the victims. Included among these are literally thousands of articles in magazines and newspapers, law enforcement and criminal justice agencies Web sites, and many college and university sites. Among the resources listed on these sites are hundreds of local or nationwide organizations dedicated to warning potential victims of these crimes or offering assistance to those who have been victimized. Yet, according to the APRI report, fewer than 20 cases of drug-facilitated rapes had been brought to trial in the United States by the end of 1999.[1]

---

[1] A majority of these cases were prosecuted in Broward and Dade counties, FL, and in Los Angeles, CA. Most of the prosecutions involved the death of one or more victims; a few were based on videotapes recorded by the perpetrators to memorialize their acts; some were "stranger-rapes" in which the perpetrators drugged their victims, whom they met in bars. We have been informed by the director of the APRI Violence Against Women Unit that no information is available on additional prosecutions since the publication of the APRI Manual in December 1999.

Estimates of the prevalence of sexual assault vary greatly from source to source. A widely cited nationwide survey of 3187 female and 2972 male college undergraduates (Koss, 1988; Koss, Gidvez, and Wisniewski, 1987), for example, found that:

- Approximately 25% of female college students report being the victim of rape or attempted rape
- Almost 85% of victims knew their attacker
- Approximately 60% of the assaults occurred while on dates or at parties
- More than 55% of women who were assaulted were under the influence of alcohol or drugs at the time of the assault
- More than 40% of rape victims did not tell anyone about their sexual assault
- Only 27% of women whose sexual assaults met the legal definition of rape thought of themselves as rape victims
- Only 5% of rape victims reported the crime to the police
- Only 5% of rape victims sought help at rape-crisis centers
- At least 40% of the victims had subsequent sexual relations with their assailants

The study also found that almost 10% of male students reported that they had committed acts that met the legal definitions of rape or attempted rape, and that 85% of those men did not believe that their behavior was either criminal or improper.

Estimates from other sources (e.g., Berliner and Koss, 1992; Fitzgerald and Riley, 2000; Fairstein, 1997) indicate that as many as 60% of women between the ages of 16 and 35 have been the victims of at least one sexual assault, and almost all sources indicate that the actual prevalence of sexual assaults is likely to be considerably higher because of the failure of victims to report.[2]

When drugs or alcohol are used to facilitate a sexual assault, estimates of prevalence are even more likely to be inaccurate because, in addition to false reports and failures to report, in many—perhaps most—cases the alleged victim has little or no memory of what actually occurred.

Although news sources report many cases of drug-facilitated sexual assaults perpetrated by employers, co-workers, neighbors, or other acquaintances, the published literature and information we have obtained from prosecutors throughout California and other states suggest that the majority of reported

---

[2] Estimates of the prevalence of sexual assaults may also be inflated by false reports (e.g., Baeza and Turvey, 2002; McGrath, 2000). Most sources agree, however, that the number of false reports does not offset the underestimation caused by failures to report.

cases involve college- and high-school-aged women who believe they have been assaulted by dates or acquaintances who are either fellow students or mutual friends of their classmates.[3] These are the kinds of cases that are most likely to "fall through the cracks" of the criminal justice system because, as Campbell (1998) points out:

- Stranger rapes are typically investigated more thoroughly than acquaintance rapes (e.g., Fairstein, 1997).
- Assaults that involve the use of weapons or that result in physical injury to the victim are more likely to be investigated thoroughly than those that do not (e.g., Kerstetter, 1990).
- Victims of these crimes tend to be classified by investigators and prosecutors as "bad victims" because their impaired memory, reluctance to seek help, and other factors that are directly associated with the unique features of these crimes. These factors make them appear to be less credible than victims of other types of sexual assault (Madigan and Gamble, 1991; Schuller and Stewart, 2000; Schuller and Wall, 1998).

It is reasonable to assume that the vast disparity between the number of reported cases of drug-facilitated sexual assaults by dates or acquaintances and the number of defendants prosecuted for these offenses can be attributed to these and related issues. Yet, as we will try to show in this chapter, investigators who understand the unique features of these crimes can use the very factors that appear to make their task more difficult to their advantage in their pursuit of the truth.

UNIQUE FEATURES OF THE CRIME

Drug-facilitated date or acquaintance rapes differ from other cases of rape or sexual assault in many ways. These differences can be categorized under four major headings:

- The use and effects of a variety of drugs and/or alcohol
- Victim participation
- Perpetrator motives and behavior
- The social context

---

[3] It is worth noting that few if any cases of on-campus sexual assaults are reported by any of the colleges or universities whose annual crime reports we have reviewed. This includes many of the schools that maintain Web sites that provide information and warnings about the dangers of drug-facilitated sexual assault.

DRUG USE AND EFFECTS

Although most public attention has focused on Rohypnol and GHB as "date-rape" drugs, Lebeau et al. (1999) note that many other substances have been detected in victims of alleged sexual assaults. These include:

Ethanol (alcohol)	Amphetamines
Benzodiazepines	Methamphetamine
Alprazolam (Xanax)	MDMA (Ecstasy)
Clonazepam (Klonopin)	Barbiturates
Chlordiazepoxide (Librium)	Cocaine
Diazepam (Valium)	Marijuana
Flunitrazepam (Rohypnol)	Opiates
Flurazepam (Dalmane)	Muscle relaxants
Lorazepam (Ativan)	Carisoprodul (Soma)
Triazolam (Halcion)	Cyclobenzaprine (Flexeril)
GHB	Meprobamate (Equanil, Miltown)
Ketamine	Antihistamines
Scopolamine	Diphenhydramine (Atarax)
	Chloral hydrate

ElSohly and Salamone (1999) report that the substances found most frequently in urine samples of 1179 cases collected from alleged victims in 49 states, Puerto Rico, and the District of Columbia over a 26-month period were alcohol, marijuana, cocaine, benzodiazepines, amphetamine, and GHB. Thirty-nine percent of the samples tested negative for all substances. Alcohol was found to be present in almost 40% of the samples, whereas benzodiazepines (including Rohypnol) and GHB, the most frequently suspected "date-rape" drugs, were each found in slightly less than 4% of the samples.

These findings demonstrate the difficulty of relying on toxicological findings to determine the validity of victim's reports of drug-facilitated rape. They also lend support to the notion that alcohol remains the most likely substance to be involved in these crimes when they do occur (e.g., Ullman, Karabatsos, and Koss, 1999). They also suggest that the victims of these alleged assaults are willing participants in the consumption of alcohol and of other drugs that may be used to facilitate the offense. The role of alcohol in such cases is well documented in the literature (e.g., Abbey, 1991; Abbey, McAuslan, and Ross, 1998), whereas the use of other drugs is more often suspected than confirmed. (See below for a discussion of some of the reasons that failure to confirm the presence of drugs through toxicological testing does not necessarily mean that they were not used to facilitate a sexual assault).

Most of the drugs—including alcohol—that are commonly used to facilitate acquaintance rape have sedative–hypnotic effects that cause the user to lose inhibitions, to be more submissive, and ultimately to lose consciousness. Other effects commonly reported include confusion, dizziness, drowsiness, loss of muscle control, impaired judgment, and nausea (LeBeau et al., 1999). Drugs such as GHB, ketamine, and scopolamine produce similar effects even though they are not classified as sedative–hypnotics and they are not typically used to cause these effects. MDMA (Ecstasy) is often used because of its reputed ability to enhance feelings of intimacy and sexual desire.

In addition to the major sedative–hypnotic effects—loss of inhibitions, mental confusion, impaired judgment, and ultimate loss of consciousness—that lead to their use in cases of drug-facilitated sexual assaults, many of these substances, especially Rohypnol, GHB, and scopolamine, cause partial or total amnesia for events that occurred while the victim is under the influence of the drug. The same is true but to a lesser extent with alcohol and MDMA.

The investigator should be aware that the inability of the victim to recall much if anything of what actually occurred, or even to identify who may have assaulted her, is particularly common when drugs with a rapid onset such as Rohypnol, GHB, or scopolamine are involved. This should not occur when alcohol or drugs that take longer to have an effect are used unless the sexual assault took place after the victim had lost consciousness. It is also important for the investigator to recognize that in many cases the perpetrator of the sexual assault may be equally unsure of what actually took place because of his voluntary use of alcohol and/or other drugs.

VICTIM PARTICIPATION

In contrast to the vast majority of rapes in which an unwilling victim is forced to engage in sexual acts by threats of bodily harm, the alleged victim of drug-facilitated rape may or may not have been a willing and active participant in previous acts of consensual sex, may or may not have voluntarily consented to use drugs with the alleged perpetrator, or may engage in sexual acts in situations where they had sought to obtain drugs from the alleged perpetrator.

With the growing popularity of GHB and Ecstasy (MDMA) as "club drugs" that are commonly used by members of both sexes to enhance energy and to produce euphoria at all-night dances or "raves," it is also likely that at least some alleged victims of drug-facilitated rape were not drugged involuntarily, and that they may have encouraged or initiated sexual intimacies that they later regret or that they perceive to have been forced upon them.

In other cases, the victim may have met the perpetrator at a bar or party and had been willingly talking, dancing, and drinking with him before he slipped something into her drink. At this point, she may become noticeably more flirtatious and amorous, and most people would just assume that she is drunk.

People who observe her may believe that her increased sexual behavior is an indication of her interest in the person she is with.

However, it is important to note that if she had ingested Rohypnol, MDMA, or especially GHB, such behavior is very much part of the effect of the drug. It is also possible that during her intoxicated and disinhibited state, she will "voluntarily" ingest other recreational drugs. Such behaviors may appear to be "consensual" to others and in such cases, interviewing waitresses, and other witnesses may be important in determining if the victim was behaving uncharacteristically, even though her behavior appeared to be voluntary. In addition, an indication of a drug being slipped in a drink is that the alleged victim will notice that she feels far more "drunk" than expected, given the amount of alcohol she has ingested, particularly if she had a drink she usually consumes.

PERPETRATOR MOTIVES AND BEHAVIOR

In cases of drug-facilitated rape, the perpetrator does not typically use weapons, force, or threats to force his victim to engage in sexual acts; the victim is far less likely to be the victim of physical attack or to engage in defensive behaviors that may provide important physical evidence (e.g., fingernail scrapings, scratches, or bite marks).

Another critical difference—except, perhaps, in the case of repeat offenders—is that the perpetrator cannot easily be classified in terms of the commonly employed stratagems that rapists use to entice their victims (e.g., Douglas, Burgess, Burgess, and Ressler, 1992; Groth and Birnbaum, 1979; Douglas and Olshaker, 1998). Similarly, while many studies have demonstrated that rapists are typically motivated by power, control, sexual sadism, or other pathological motives (e.g., Groth and Birnbaum, 1979), in most cases of drug-facilitated acquaintance rape it is more likely that the perpetrator is motivated primarily by sexual desire.

As we noted in the introduction to this chapter, almost 10% of male college students admit that they have committed acts that met the legal definitions of rape or attempted rape, and 85% of those who did so did not believe that they had committed any crime. Although we are not aware of any published studies that focus on drug-facilitated sexual assaults, it is reasonable to believe that the findings would be comparable. Even when men admit that the use of alcohol and/or other drugs by their female partners raises their expectations of engaging in sex with them, they do not perceive that encouraging their dates to consume alcohol or drugs is improper, or that their partner's intoxication affects their ability to engage in consensual sex.

Moreover, a number of studies find that both male and female undergraduates believe that a woman's willing use of alcohol or drugs with male partners increases the likelihood that she will consent to having sex, and that women who allege that they have been sexually assaulted when they have voluntarily used only alcohol makes their allegations less credible (e.g., Schuller and Wall, 1998).

THE SOCIAL CONTEXT

The setting in which two people interact and eventually engage in sexual acts and the larger social network of mutual friends of both the alleged victim and perpetrator play an important role in cases of drug-facilitated acquaintance rape. In many cases the setting is a party or other social event at which others may have observed the alleged victim willingly touch, kiss, or fondle the alleged perpetrator. Others may have also observed both of them drinking or using drugs. In some cases, others may be aware that the couple had engaged in sexual activities on previous occasions, or that the alleged victim may have told others that she wanted or planned to do so. It is even possible that either or both of them were using drugs and alcohol for the explicit purpose of lowering their inhibitions and with the expectation that they would eventually have a sexual relationship. Although no romantic behavior or prior intentions of the alleged victim negate the possibility that she was, in fact, raped or sexually assaulted, what others know or observe may provide useful information in determining what actually occurred, especially when the victim claims partial or total amnesia for the events leading up to the alleged assault.

It is reasonable to assume that failure to report sexual assault, and the typical delays of 3 months to a year before making a report in many cases (e.g., Feldman et al., 2000), results from the alleged victim's uncertainty about whether any sexual activity actually took place or whether she had consented to whatever did occur. In some cases, others who observed the couple may be influential in convincing the alleged victim to report a sexual assault when she is uncertain about what occurred. In many other cases, others may discourage the victim of a sexual assault from making a report when doing so might alienate her from friends who may either disbelieve her claim or view it as a betrayal of personal and group loyalties.

The larger social context in which drug-facilitated acquaintance rape occurs also plays a role in cases of false accusations. High-school or college students, for example, may feel the need to make a false report to protect their reputations, to avoid punishment for violating curfews or other rules and regulations imposed on them by parents or school authorities, or to explain their behavior to boyfriends or other sexual partners. The same reasons may account for false accusations of rape in other cases, but it may be a more tempting alternative when the alleged victim's misconduct is either witnessed by or widely known by her friends and associates.

The same is true, of course, of false accusations motivated by anger or jealousy toward the alleged perpetrator, but again, this may occur more frequently in the case of a schoolgirl who believes that their reputation and/or social status may be irreparably damaged by her failure to retaliate against a young man who others know has treated her badly.

INVESTIGATION OF DRUG-FACILITATED ACQUAINTANCE RAPE

When a case of alleged drug-facilitated rape is reported to the police, the investigation should focus on:

- Determining if sexual acts that meet the legal definition of rape, attempted rape, or other types of sexual assault actually occurred
- Determining if the victim was under the influence of drug or alcohol to the extent that she was unable to consent to or to resist a sexual assault
- Determining the extent to which the victim was a willing or inadvertent participant in the use of drugs
- Identifying the alleged perpetrator
- Determining if the alleged perpetrator had access to the drugs that either were identified by toxicological findings or are consistent with the victim's account of the effects of the drugs that may have been used to facilitate the offense

The nature and course of the investigation will depend to a significant extent on how soon after the alleged assault a report is made. In cases where reports are delayed for even a few days, for example, neither toxicological evidence nor medical examination of the victim can provide any useful information. In such cases, the investigation must focus primarily on interviews with the alleged victim, the alleged perpetrator, and others who may have witnessed the events preceding the assault or the assault itself.

To the extent that the investigator believes that a sexual assault did take place, the investigation should focus on a search for other possible victims of the alleged perpetrator, and for friends of the alleged perpetrator who may have witnessed the assault or were told by the perpetrator that it did occur. A pretext phone call to the alleged perpetrator by the alleged victim may also be used to obtain direct evidence that the assault actually took place. If there is sufficient evidence to obtain a search warrant, the investigator may then conduct a search for videotaped recordings that some perpetrators use to memorialize their conquests or for evidence that the alleged perpetrator possesses illicit drugs that may have been used in the alleged offense.

Although the chances of obtaining sufficient evidence to prosecute a perpetrator are slim when reports are delayed, the investigator should not doubt the credibility of the reporting victim simply because she failed to make an immediate report or because her impaired memory of the events leave her uncertain about what actually occurred. While the investigator should take note of the "red flags" of false accusations discussed by Baeza and Turvey (2002), he or she should also be aware that victim confusion and delayed reports are more the rule than the exception in these cases. It is well worth remembering that many perpetrators—especially repeat offenders—are encouraged to use drugs to facilitate their sexual assaults because they believe themselves to be immune to prosecution for these very reasons.

When the report is made immediately after the assault or within a few days thereafter, toxicological findings may confirm that the victim had used drugs and/or alcohol that may have been given to her without her knowledge or against her will. Because all of the drugs—except alcohol—implicated in cases of drug-facilitated sexual assault are excreted from the body more or less rapidly, blood rather than urine samples should be submitted for toxicological examination. The presence of drugs in blood is indicative of relatively recent use, whereas their presence in urine does not.[4]

Because alcohol and many of the drugs—including Rohypnol and GHB—that are commonly used to facilitate sexual assaults are used recreationally, the detection of these drugs may lend credibility to the alleged victim's accusation, but it is not necessarily of any probative value. If the alleged victim has a history of recreational drug use, for example, positive toxicology findings are of little help determining that she was drugged without her knowledge or against her will.

It is important to note that many toxicology laboratories do not routinely test for GHB, MDMA, scopolamine, and some other drugs used to facilitate sexual assaults, and that when blood rather than urine samples are submitted for testing, the failure to detect the presence of drugs does not necessarily mean they were not used.

To determine if the alleged victim's belief that she was drugged is credible, the investigator should become familiar with the signs and symptoms of the use of all of the commonly used "date-rape" drugs so that he or she can determine if the victim's account of her experiences is consistent with their effects. The next section of this chapter provides information on Rohypnol and GHB—the

---

[4] Some inferences about how recently certain drugs were used can be made from urine toxicology findings when both the parent drug and its metabolites are detected.

two drugs that are most often believed to be used in cases of drug-facilitated sexual assault. Information on other drugs is readily available in the medical literature, on the Internet, and from numerous law-enforcement and criminal-justice system manuals and reports. The Vaults of Erowid Web site, www.erowid.org, is an excellent source of information on many drugs and is particularly valuable because it includes many first-hand accounts by users of their subjective experiences.

The importance of obtaining as detailed an account as possible of the alleged victim's experiences cannot be overemphasized, especially in cases where the drug or drugs that may have been used cannot be confirmed. The investigator should ask the victim to recall whatever she can prior to the time she began to experience the effects of drugs she may have been given, and then about her subjective feelings of intoxication. From this information the investigator may be able to make an educated guess about what drugs may be involved. If, for example, the victim reports that she felt very relaxed and drowsy before losing consciousness, she may have ingested Rohypnol or some other sedative–hypnotic drug. If she reports having felt giddy, "drunk-like," and then "nodded" off and on for a while before losing awareness of events, it is more likely that she had been given GHB.

No matter how little the alleged victim may recall, the investigator should not give any indication of doubt that her account is authentic. Because drug-induced amnesia is rarely either total or permanent, the investigator should be patient in probing for even seemingly trivial details that may trigger the recall of events that were previously lost to memory. Pressing for details of the alleged assault or focusing on information that is of greatest interest to the investigator too soon in the interviewing process is likely to be unproductive. A number of interviews over a period of weeks may be required before the victim is able to recall events that are critical to the investigation and that may be corroborated by other evidence.

As in the case of delayed reports discussed earlier, investigation of drug-facilitated sexual assaults should focus on interviews of the alleged victim, perpetrator, and others who either witnessed or have knowledge of what may have occurred. Pretext phone calls and a search for other possible victims and physical evidence should be considered also, if the investigator believes that there is sufficient cause.

Finally, when cases of drug-facilitated sexual assaults are reported soon after the alleged events, the investigator should consider a search for physical evidence at the scene of the alleged drugging and other locations at which the victim and perpetrator were together. Traces of drugs, for example, may be found on glasses from which the victim drank, in containers used to mix drinks, or in discarded bottles that may have contained drugs, especially those that are available in liquid form.

THE "DATE-RAPE" DRUGS

Rohypnol and GHB are most often referred to as "date-rape" drugs. Women who believe that they have been drugged and sexually assaulted are most likely to believe that one of these drugs was used to facilitate the assault. Although there is little evidence to demonstrate that this is the case, there is no question that the popularity, availability, and use of both drugs has grown dramatically in recent years.

The information we provide here about these drugs was obtained primarily from Web sites maintained by the Office of National Drug Control Policy (ONDCP), the Drug Enforcement Administration (DEA), the National Institute on Drug Abuse (NIDA), and a number of other governmental agencies and organizations. Additional information on these and on other drugs that may be implicated in cases of sexual assault is easily accessible from these and other Internet sites and in the medical and scientific literature.

ROHYPNOL

Background

The Swiss pharmaceutical company Hoffman-La Roche first developed benzo-diazepines in the 1950s. Since then, modifications of the basic benzodiazepine structure have led to the introduction of many related tranquilizers. Rohypnol was first introduced to the market in 1975. Although Rohypnol is reported to be the most widely prescribed sedative–hypnotic drug in Western Europe, it has never been available for medical use in the United States.[5]

Rohypnol, apparently brought in to the United States from Mexico, became available in Florida and Texas in the early 1990s. An increasing number of seizures of Rohypnol and related drugs by law enforcement officials led to the formation of a Texas–Florida Rohypnol Response Group that, in 1995, actually suggested closing the border to cut off the supply of these drugs.

The first reported case of the use of Rohypnol in a drug-facilitated sexual assault occurred in Florida in early 1992. Additional cases reported in Florida rose from 11 in 1992 to 38 in 1993, 144 in 1994, and 342 in 1995. Los Angeles began to identify cases of Rohypnol-facilitated rape in 1995. To date more than

---

[5] Hoffman-La Roche did not seek FDA approval for Rohypnol in the United States because other comparable drugs, including some that it manufactured, were already available on the domestic market.

2500 cases of sexual assault believed to involve the use of Rohypnol have been reported to law enforcement agencies throughout the country and reports of additional cases are reported by media news sources almost every day.

Common Names

Street names for Rohypnol include "R-1" (1.0 mg tablets), "R-2" (2.0 mg tablets), the "forget-me-pill," "rib," "roaches," "roofies," "rope," "ropies," "ruffies," "run-trip and fall," "Mexican Valium," and "pingas."

Appearance

Royhypnol tablets manufactured by Hoffman-La Roche come in the form of small, white tablets that are either single or double-scored on one side and are inscribed on the other side with the name "Roche" and the encircled number 1 to designate a 1.0-mg dosage.[6] It is commonly encountered in a clear plastic blister pack, but has also been found unpackaged or in containers marked "Roche Vitamins." Very rarely, it is found in liquid form, or crushed into powder form. In solution, the drug is colorless, odorless, and tasteless. The price of a single tablet ranges from $2 to $5.

Because of concerns about the illicit use of Rohypnol in sexual assaults and other crimes, Hoffman-La Roche reformulated the drug in 1998. The new Rohypnol is a hard green oval tablet with a coating that makes it dissolve slowly; it also contains a strong blue dye designed to color any liquid in which it is dissolved, making improper use more difficult. Although the green oval tablets in 0.5- and 1.0-mg doses are currently used throughout the world, except in Japan, the white tablets remain available to illicit users in the United States.

Uses

Rohypnol is a central nervous system depressant or sedative–hypnotic drug that was prescribed primarily for the treatment of insomnia and related sleep disorders. Its effects are similar to that of Valium, a closely related benzodiazepine, but it is estimated to be 10 times more potent. Rohypnol has also been used to relieve depression following withdrawal from the use of stimulants such as methamphetamine and cocaine. The use of Rohypnol and alcohol to enhance the subjective effects of heroin or to reduce the severity of withdrawal from heroin or methadone has also been reported.

---

[6] Hoffman-La Roche no longer manufactures the 2.0-mg tablet that was inscribed with the name Roche and the encircled number 2 but was otherwise identical to the 1.0-mg tablet in appearance. When the 2.0-mg tablet was available it was often confused with Klonopin (clonazepam) tablets, also manufactured by Roche, that were inscribed with the number 2 preceded and followed by a dot instead of being encircled as with the 2.0-mg tablets of Rohypnol. Klonopin is commonly used for treatment of panic and seizure disorders.

Effects

Rohypnol is typically ingested orally, but it may also be snorted (insufflated), smoked, or injected. Effects of the drug begin within 15 to 30 minutes after oral ingestion, peak within 2 hours, and may persist 8 to 12 hours or more. Symptoms include decreased blood pressure, drowsiness, visual disturbances, dizziness, confusion, impaired memory, nausea, gastrointestinal disturbances, and urinary retention. Many users experience amnesia for events occurring for as long as 8 to 10 hours after ingestion of the drug, while others report less dramatic impairment of memory.

Whereas most users fall asleep within two hours after using the drug, others may have experiences that resemble an alcoholic "blackout" in which they appear to be awake and able to function normally even though their conscious control of their behavior is significantly impaired and they are unaware of what they are doing. In many cases, the person is unaware that they are under the influence of a drug even when they are acting in an uncharacteristic manner (e.g., Dowd, Strong, Janicak, and Negruz, 2002). In cases of drug-facilitated assault this may result in the victim engaging in sexual behavior in a state of automatism or dissociation in which they lack the ability to either consent or resist. When the victim awakens 10–12 hours later, she may be fatigued, confused, and unable to focus attention for as long as 2 days thereafter.

The victim typically cannot give a full account of what occurred while she was under the influence of the drug, but she may have glimpses of memory where she recalls fragments of people, places, and events, many of which are trivial and incidental to the sexual assault. She may recall, for example, being in a dark place that had a pretty picture hanging over the bed, asking a tall man for a glass of water, having someone pull off her pants, and riding in a big car with nice music playing on the radio. The initial reports of these experiences may be related without regard for the order in which they occurred, without emotion, and without understanding what they signify. Only with the passage of time, and often with the assistance of others, will the victim begin to weave these fragments together, to recall additional details, and eventually to assist in the investigation of the offense.

Toxicology

Baselt and Cravey (1995) report that while the half-life of Rohypnol ranges from 9 to 25 hours, plasma levels of the drug drop off rapidly after ingestion. The drug may be detected in urine samples for 5 days or longer, but only if the level of detectability is set to 0.02 ng/ml rather than the 0.20-ng/ml cutoff level used in many laboratories. Although most laboratories test for benzodiazepines, they may not routinely screen for Rohypnol. Negative findings for Rohypnol, therefore, do not necessarily rule out the possibility of its use (Negruz and Gaensslen,

2003). Because the most commonly used presumptive tests (EMIT, FPIA, and Online) often yield false negative results for Rohypnol, it is always preferable to employ GC/MS analysis when the use of Rohypnol is suspected.

Legal Status

Until 1996, travelers could declare up to 180 doses of Rohypnol for personal use if they had a foreign prescription. This is no longer the case. Although Rohypnol is available as a prescription drug in more than 60 European and Latin American countries, it is not manufactured or sold legally in the United States.

A steadily increasing number of sexual assaults believed to be facilitated by the use of Rohypnol have been reported in the British Isles and other countries throughout Europe, Asia, and South America. Some European countries have already banned the use of Rohypnol or are in the process of enacting legislation to do so.

Rohypnol is currently classified as a Schedule IV substance under the Controlled Substances Act of 1970. Schedule IV drugs are considered to have legitimate medical uses, but also have a potential for abuse and for the development of physical or psychological dependence.

In 1995, Rohypnol was moved to Schedule III by the World Health Organization, requiring more thorough record keeping on its distribution. In 1997, the U.S. Sentencing Commission increased the penalties associated with the possession, trafficking, and distribution of Rohypnol to those of a Schedule I substance, a classification reserved for drugs that have no legitimate medical use, a high potential for abuse and addiction, and an unacceptable level of safety. The DEA is currently considering the possibility of classifying Rohypnol as a Schedule I drug.

GHB

Background

Gamma-hydroxybutyrate (GHB) is classified as a "nutrient" that is found in all mammalian tissue. It was first synthesized in the 1920s. It is a powerful, rapidly acting central nervous system depressant that has been investigated for the treatment of a number of disorders, including alcohol dependence. GHB was used as a general anesthetic in the 1960s and 1970s, but it never gained wide acceptance in clinical practice except in the treatment of narcolepsy.

More recently, GHB has been used by bodybuilders, who believed that it stimulates the body's production of growth hormone. GHB was sold in health food stores until the Food and Drug Administration (FDA) banned it in 1990.

The chemical "recipe" for GHB and kits containing precursor chemicals, equipment, and detailed instructions to make it are available on a number of Internet sites. The two basic ingredients of GHB are GBL (gamma-butyrolactone) and lye (sodium hydroxide). Muriatic acid or vinegar is also used in the manufacturing process. Because almost all of the GHB available to street users is made in home laboratories, samples of the drug vary widely in their chemical composition and purity.

When ingested, the precursor drug, GBL, produces a clinical picture very similar to that of GHB, but its effects persist for considerably longer. GBL is also sold in health food stores as a dietary supplement under such trade names as "Renewtriant," and "Revivarant"; it is known to users as "blue nitro" and "fire-water." GBL is also available as an industrial solvent used for stripping floors and degreasing machinery.[7]

Common Names

Street names for GHB include "aminos," "blue monster," "G," "Georgia home boy," "gh buddy," "goop," "great hormones at bedtime," "grievous bodily harm," "liquid X," "liquid ecstasy," "salty water," "soap," "scoop," and "water."

Appearance

GHB is a clear, liquid substance that looks like water. It is carried in water bottles, or any other container that can hold a small amount of liquid, including purse-size hair spray, children's bubble containers (very common at raves), or vitamin pill bottles. It is also starting to be seen in powder form, in capsules, or in a putty-like form.

Uses

GHB is now a drug of choice in the club and rave scene—especially in Los Angeles—where it is prized for its ability to cause euphoria without any residual "hangover" effects. Recreational users generally buy capfuls (the size of a water bottle cap) or sip on a diluted GHB mixture as they dance throughout the night. The price of a capful of the drug typically ranges from $25 to $40. Because it is naturally present in human tissue, many users assume that GHB is harmless.

In cases of drug-facilitated sexual assault, GHB is typically mixed into an already strong alcoholic drink to try to mask the salty and unpleasant taste of

---

[7] As the regulation of GHB has tightened, street users have turned to the use of GBL and other closely related drugs. Among these is another industrial solvent, 1,4-butanediol, whose effects are similar to that of GHB and GBL. Street names for this drug include "pine needle extract," "pine needle oil," "thunder nectar," and "serenity."

the drug. GHB is rapidly absorbed into the bloodstream, with peak levels occurring 20 to 60 minutes after ingestion.

Effects

Although it is known as a nutrient or steroid, GHB acts as sedative–hypnotic drug or central nervous system depressant. As with alcohol, low doses of GHB result in giddiness and lowering of inhibitions that may cause female users to be sexually aroused and to behave in an uncharacteristically flirtatious and provocative manner. Higher doses lead to relaxation and progressively increasing loss of consciousness as the user become drowsy, begins to nod off, and eventually falls asleep. Depending on the dosage, the victim may initially look and act "drunk" before passing out.

The ability of the drug to lower inhibitions, arouse sexual interest, and cause women to be more receptive to sexual advances may account for at least some of its popularity as a "club drug." Its ability to subsequently cause an increase in submissive and compliant behavior as the user begins to lose consciousness and to move from drowsiness to sleep may account for its use in the facilitation of sexual assaults.

The effects of GHB on memory are similar to those described earlier for Rohypnol, particularly when the dosage is sufficient to cause a loss of consciousness.

Toxicology

GHB is excreted very rapidly from blood. With its estimated half-life of only 20 minutes, it cannot be detected in blood samples within 4 or 5 hours after ingestion. It may be detected in urine for 72 to 96 hours.

When the use of GHB is suspected in a case of drug-facilitated sexual assault (or when no information points to any specific drug), it is important for the investigator to realize that most laboratories do not routinely test for GHB and that many are unable to do so. Because GHB is normally found in human tissue, especially careful evaluation of toxicology findings is required in the identification of GHB when it is used as a drug.

Legal Status

Prior to the passage of the bill H.R. 2130 that was signed into law by President Clinton in February 2000, laws regulating GHB and its analogs were enacted primarily at the state level. Since that date GHB, GBL and ketamine (another drug implicated in sexual assaults) are classified as Schedule I Controlled Substances. The continued medical use of GHB for the treatment of narcolepsy is still under consideration by the FDA.

GHB remains legally available in Europe and from other foreign sources, some of which continue to offer it for sale on their Internet sites.

Investigators should also be aware that the 1996 "Drug-induced Rape Prevention and Punishment Act" criminalizes the possession of GHB and other drugs by persons who "intend to commit a violent crime by covertly distributing a controlled substance to an unknowing individual."

REFERENCES

Abbey, A. (1991). Acquaintance rape and alcohol consumption on college campuses: How are they linked? *Journal of American College Health 39*(4), 165–169.

Abbey, A., McAuslan, P., and Ross, L. T. (1998). Sexual assault perpetration by college men: The role of alcohol, misperception of sexual intent, and sexual beliefs and experiences. *Journal of Social and Clinical Psychology 17*(2), 167.

APRI (1999). *The Prosecution of Rohypnol and GHB Related Sexual Assaults.* Alexandria, VA: American Prosecutors Research Institute.

Baeza, J. J., and Turvey, B. (2002). False reports. In Turvey, B. (ed.), *Criminal Profiling: An Introduction to Behavioral Evidence Analysis.* London: Academic Press.

Baselt, R. C., and Cravey, R. H. (1995). *Disposition of Toxic Drugs and Chemicals in Man,* 4th ed. Chicago: Year Book Medical Publishers.

Berliner, L., and Koss, M. P. (1992). Facts or advocacy statistics: The case of acquaintance rape. *Journal of Interpersonal Violence 7*(1), 121.

Campbell, R. (1998). The community response to rape: Victims' experiences with the legal, medical, and mental health systems. *American Journal of Community Psychology 26*(3), 355.

Douglas, J. E., Burgess, A. W., Burgess, A. G., and Ressler, R. K. (1992). *Crime Classification Manual.* New York: Lexington Books.

Douglas, J., and Olshaker, M. (1998). *Obsession.* New York: Pocket Books.

Dowd, S. M., Strong, D. S., Janicak, P. G., and Negruz, A. (2002). The behavioral and cognitive effects of two benzodiazepines associated with drug-facilitated sexual assault. *Journal of Forensic Science 47*(5), 1101–1107.

Dunn, P. C., Vail-Smith, K., and Knight, S. M. (1999). What date/acquaintance rape victims tell others: A study of college student recipients of disclosure. *Journal of American College Health 47*(5), 213.

ElSohly, M. A., and Salamone, S. J. (1999). Prevalence of drugs used in cases of alleged sexual assault. *Journal of Analytical Toxicology 23*(3), 141–146.

Fairstein, L. A. (1997). *Sexual Violence: Our War Against Rape.* New York: William Morrow.

Feldman, S. S., Cauffman, E., Jensen, L. A., and Arnett, J. J. (2000). The (un)acceptability of betrayal: A study of college students' evaluations of sexual betrayal by a romantic partner and betrayal of a friend's confidence. *Journal of Youth and Adolescence 29*(4), 499–516.

Fitzgerald, N., and Riley, K. J. (2000). Drug-facilitated rape: Looking for the missing pieces. Washington, D.C.: National Institute of Justice.

Groth, A. N., and Birnbaum, H. J. (1979). *Men Who Rape: The Psychology of the Offender.* New York: Plenum Press.

Kerstetter, W. A. (1990). Gateway to justice: Police and prosecutorial response to sexual assaults against women. *Journal of Criminal Law and Criminology 81*, 267–313.

Koss, M. P. (1988). Hidden rape: Sexual aggression and victimization in a national sample in higher education. In Burgess, A.W. (ed.), *Rape and Sexual Assault,* vol. II. New York: Garland Publishing.

Koss, M. P. (1993). Detecting the scope of rape: A review of prevalence research methods. *Journal of Interpersonal Violence 8*(2), 198.

Koss, M. P. (1996). The measurement of rape victimization in crime surveys. *Criminal Justice and Behavior 23*(1), 55.

Koss, M. P., Gidyez, C. A., and Wisniewski, N. (1987). The Scope of Rape: Incidence and prevalence of sexual aggression and victimization in a national sample of higher education students. *Journal of Consulting and Clinical Psychology 55*(2), 162–170.

LeBeau, M., Andollo, W., Hearn, W. L., Baselt, R., Cone, E., Finkle, B., Fraser, D., Jenkins, A., Mayer, J., Negrusz, A., Poklis, A., Walls, H. C., Raymon, L., Robertson, M., and Saady, J. (1999). Recommendations for toxicological investigations of drug-facilitated sexual assaults. *Journal of Forensic Science 44*(1), 227–230.

Madigan, I., and Gamble, N. (1991). *The Second Rape: Society's Continued Betrayal of the Victim.* New York: Lexington Books.

McGrath, M. (2000). False allegations of rape and the criminal profiler. *Journal of Behavioral Profiling 1*(3).

Negruz, A., and Gaensslen, R. E. (2003). Analytical developments in toxicological investigation of drug-facilitated sexual assault. *Annals of Bioanalytic Chemistry 376*, 1192–1197.

Schuller, R. A., and Stewart, A. (2000). Police responses to sexual assault complaints: The role of perpetrator/complainant intoxication. *Law and Human Behavior 24*(5), 535–551.

Schuller, R. A., and Wall, A.-M. (1998). The effects of defendant and complainant intoxication on mock jurors' judgments of sexual assault. *Psychology of Women Quarterly 22*(4), 555.

Ullman, S. E., Karabatsos, G., and Koss, M. P. (1999). Alcohol and sexual assault in a national sample of college women. *Journal of Interpersonal Violence 14*(6), 603.

CHAPTER 8

DNA FOR DETECTIVES

John M. Butler, PhD and Terilynne W. Butler

Deoxyribonucleic acid (DNA) is being used increasingly in criminal cases involving sexual assault to help identify the guilty and exonerate the innocent. This chapter will introduce the basics of DNA, the types of DNA tests available, and how to interpret results that might be obtained from a forensic DNA laboratory. In addition, the typical sources of biological material used in DNA testing will be described to aid detectives in knowing where they might search for evidence that could help in a case.

BASICS OF DNA

DNA is the genetic code found within every living cell. With the exception of identical twins, we are all genetically unique, a product of generations of genetic shuffling making us truly individuals. Our genetic material is inherited from our parents—one half from our mother and one half from our father, whose parents passed on their genetic patterns, and so on up the line. Children of the same parents differ from one another because the DNA passed on from each parent is really a jumble of different combinations of genetic patterns such that no two children get exactly the same mix.

DNA is made up of four major "building blocks" called nucleotides. They are adenine, guanine, cytosine, and thymine, or simply A, G, C, and T. These letters join to one another like four different-colored beads placed apparently randomly on a very, very long string. These patterns somehow account for the structure and function of our bodies. Like a computer code that looks mostly like gibberish to the untrained eye, the large majority of our DNA does not code for things we can physically identify such as hair color or diseases. It is within these vast nonsensical regions that are found discrete patterns that only differ somewhat from person to person and can be used for identification purposes.

Because DNA is in all of our cells that make up all of our parts and fluids, by collecting traces of these things it is possible to identify who left them behind.

Technology has been available since the late 1980s to enable testing of very small amounts of DNA recovered from a crime scene. Only a few cells are needed to perform a DNA test. The sensitivity of DNA testing now makes it more difficult to collect samples from many crime scenes because biological material that contains sufficient DNA cannot always be easily seen with the naked eye. A tiny drop of spittle or a single eyelash may be all that is needed to link the suspect to the crime scene. The trick is having a sharp eye and a careful hand in collecting things so small.

It is also easy for the investigator to accidentally contaminate the sample with his or her own DNA. For this purpose special precautions are in order including gloves and masks. Additionally, crime-scene investigation personnel should have their DNA on file with the lab so if there is contamination, the technicians can separate the investigators from the suspects or victims in the evidence sample. Otherwise a different DNA profile found at the scene may be pursued as another suspect, leading police on a chase that takes them right back to their own team of investigators, an embarrassing loss of critical time and resources that could have been spent finding the perpetrator.

DNA testing is always performed by comparing two or more samples to see if they match. A DNA profile from crime scene evidence is of little value without something with which to compare it. Like Cinderella's glass slipper there is a perfect "foot" that fits each profile. For example, two suspects may be developed in the course of an investigation. DNA profiles generated from blood taken from these suspects can be compared to the evidence from the crime scene to see if there is a perfect match.

The victim's DNA is also analyzed for two important reasons. First, if an unknown DNA profile is found at the crime scene it may be confused as belonging to another suspect or accomplice when really it is the victim's. Second, as is common in rapes, the DNA sample obtained is really a mixture of the victim's and the perpetrator's bodily fluids. A pure sample from the victim is needed in order to compare and separate the two profiles in the evidence sample. What is left then should be the perpetrator's DNA profile, depending on the sexual history of the victim. DNA samples from recent consensual partners of the victim may also be needed to eliminate these innocent individuals as potential contributors of the "unknown DNA profile" suspected to be from the perpetrator.

SOURCES OF DNA

Since every living cell contains DNA, any biological material left at a crime s cene can potentially be valuable in a DNA test. The most obvious potential sources of DNA that can be obtained from a sexual assault crime scene are

Source	Evidence	Collection
Victim	Semen and sperm may be recovered if the perpetrator ejaculated	Vaginal, anal, or oral swabs collected by sexual assault examination nurse
Suspect	Some of victim's cells may be present if a condom was not worn for the assault and the perpetrator has not cleaned up following the assault	Penile swab within a few hours of suspected assault
Condom	Fluids or skin cells from inside can confirm perpetrator; fluids or skin cells from outside can confirm victim	Swabs from inside and outside of condom
Victim's bed-sheets or panties	Semen stains	Submission of bedsheets or panties to crime lab

Table 8-1

Some potential sources of DNA evidence in sexual assault cases

semen and vaginal cells. Some ways to identify and collect this kind of evidence are described in Table 8-1. Other important sources include blood, urine, saliva, skin, hair root, fingernails (often in a struggle a victim will scratch the perpetrator, catching his skin under her fingernails), condoms, clothing, linens, carpet, ligatures, and tape (especially good because tape and ligatures are difficult to work with while wearing gloves, possibly forcing the suspect to temporarily remove them for the task). All can provide biological material that may prove very helpful in solving a case. Even a bite mark on a victim can be swabbed to collect DNA left by the perpetrator's saliva because saliva or "spit" often contains ample cheek cells to perform DNA testing.

Make careful choices in selecting what evidence is worth submitting. Backlogs grow when too many samples are submitted due to redundancy. Discuss all evidence with crime laboratory analysts to reduce submissions to only those samples that contribute the most valuable information to the investigation.

Several years ago the National Institute of Justice produced a pamphlet entitled "What Every Law Enforcement Officer Should Know about DNA Evidence." A copy of it can be obtained over the Internet at http://www.ojp. usdoj.gov/nij/pubs-sum/000614.htm. Here are a few of the important points from this pamphlet.

• First a law enforcement officer or crime-scene investigator should always wear gloves when collecting DNA evidence in order to avoid contaminating the crime scene. Disposable gloves that can be changed often are preferable so that the collector can avoid any potential cross-contamination of crime-scene evidence.

- Use disposable instruments or clean them thoroughly before and after handling each sample. Often moistened cotton swabs are used to collect biological evidence such as dried blood or semen stains. These swabs, which are essentially sterile Q-tips on a long wooden stem, should be moistened with clean water, *not the investigator's mouth*!
- Avoid touching the area where you believe DNA may exist.
- Avoid talking, sneezing, and coughing over evidence. Wearing a disposable dust protector over your mouth and nose can help protect the evidence from you.
- Avoid touching your face, nose, and mouth when collecting and packaging evidence.
- When possible, air-dry evidence thoroughly before packaging.
- Put evidence into new paper bags or envelopes rather than plastic bags. Condensation can easily form in plastic bags and water will promote bacterial growth as well as break down the DNA molecules in the biological evidence. Do not use staples in the paper bags or envelopes. These metal staples can accidentally draw blood from the crime scene investigator or the lab technician that would contaminate the evidence.

Maintaining a careful chain-of-custody with collected DNA samples is critical, especially if a case goes to trial. DNA evidence admissibility in court may hinge on this very point. Additionally, biological evidence should be kept dry and cool during transport to the forensic laboratory to help preserve the DNA present in the collected samples for accurate analysis. Water or moisture has the effect of degrading the DNA, destroying its ability to be analyzed and submitted as evidence.

TYPES OF DNA TESTS AVAILABLE

Once biological evidence has been collected from an examination of the victim and the crime scene, the samples are packaged and sent to a forensic DNA laboratory. More than 140 government (public) DNA laboratories exist within the United States at the state, local, or federal level. These laboratories participate in the Combined DNA Index System (CODIS), a computer database containing DNA profiles from convicted offenders that can be searched against crime-scene evidence to identify serial crimes or repeat offenders. CODIS can be searched on a local, state, or national level. If a rape is committed and the suspect's DNA profile is obtained from evidence, then this profile can be entered into the CODIS database as part of a search to see if there are any other cases containing this same DNA profile. Since many rapists are repeat offenders, the perpetrator of the crime in question may be located through this CODIS search and removed from the streets as the investigation continues. Remember that as reliable and popular as DNA evidence has become, it is usually only a part of the whole body of evidence presented in court. For instance, in the case of the NBA player Kobe Bryant, although his DNA in the form of semen was recovered, the argument arose as to whether the exchange was rape or consensual. DNA results provided by a laboratory must always be considered in the context of all other evidence.

State and local DNA laboratories are supported by taxpayers, mandated by law to accept evidence from their jurisdictions, and, unfortunately, woefully understaffed and underfunded. Federal labs include the FBI Laboratory (Quantico, VA), the Armed Forces DNA Identification Laboratory (Rockville, MD), and the U.S. Army Criminal Investigation Laboratory (Atlanta, GA). In addition, more than a dozen private laboratories are accredited to perform forensic DNA analysis (Table 8-2).

The cost of DNA testing from private laboratories can average about $1000 per submitted item. In addition, costs of courtroom testimony by a lab representative may exceed $1000 per day plus expenses. However, results will likely be returned within days or weeks from private labs rather than months or even years later for samples submitted to backlogged public laboratories. Costs in time versus money must be weighed case by case when considering DNA testing options. Private labs are often the choice in high-profile cases for their quick turnaround time, as, for instance, in the O.J. Simpson trial, which utilized the Orchid Cellmark laboratory in Germantown, Maryland.

STR TYPING

Forensic DNA laboratories perform DNA testing using a technology known as STR typing. The term STR stands for short tandem repeat, which is a region of DNA that has a short sequence repeated over and over. The number of repeated segments varies between individuals. Returning to our example of beads on a string, let us suppose the "repeat" is the pattern blue, red, red, green repeated twice, three times, or six times in a row depending on the person. Typically 13 different STR markers, or areas of repeated patterns, are examined to produce a DNA profile that is unique enough to establish a DNA identity. This profile is then searched against the CODIS database. These 13 sites do not provide information on any known genetic diseases and thus only provide a simple identifier much like a social security number. DNA tests named "Profiler Plus," "COfiler," or "PowerPlex 16" are used to generate the STR information described in a report (Table 8-3).

Table 8-2

Private DNA laboratories that perform forensic DNA analysis

Company	Address	Contact Information
Baltimore Rh Typing Laboratory Inc.	400 West Franklin Street Baltimore, MD 21201	800-765-5170 Fax: 410-383-0938 www.rhlab.com
Bode Technology Group	7364 Steel Mill Drive Springfield, VA 22150	703-644-1200 Fax: 703-644-7730 www.bodetech.com
DNA Print	900 Cocoanut Ave. Sarasota, FL 34236	Tel: 941-366-3400 Fax: 941-952-9770 www.dnaprint.com
DNA Reference Laboratory	7434 Louis Pasteur Suite 15 San Antonio, TX 78229	877-362-1362 Fax: 210-615-0100 www.dnareferencelab.com
DNA Solutions, Inc.	840 Research Parkway Suite 546 Oklahoma City, OK 73104	800-393-1595 Fax: 405-271-1174 www.dnasolutionsusa.com
DNA Testing Solutions, Inc.	11972 North Florida Avenue Tampa, Florida 33612	1-888-362-3228 www.dnatestingsolutions.com
Fairfax Identity Laboratories	3025 Hamaker Court #203 Fairfax, VA 22031	800-848-4362 www.fairfaxidlab.com
Genelex Corporation	3000 First Ave., Suite One Seattle, WA 98121	800-523-3080 Fax: 206-219-4000 www.genelex.com
Identigene	5615 Kirby, Suite 800 Houston, TX 77005	800-362-8973 www.identigene.com
Identity Genetics, Inc.	801 32nd Avenue Brookings, SD 57006	800-861-1054 Fax: 605-697-5306 www.identitygenetics.com
LabCorp	1912 Alexander Drive RTP, NC 27709	800-533-0567 www.labcorp.com
Myriad Genetics	320 Wakara Way Salt Lake City, UT 84108	800-469-7423 801-584-3600 www.myriad.com
National Medical Services	3701 Welsh Road Willow Grove, PA 19090	800-522-6671 Fax: 215-657-2972 www.nmslab.com
Orchid Cellmark— Germantown	20271 Goldenrod Lane Germantown, MD 20876	800-872-5227 Fax: 301-428-4980 www.orchidcellmark.com
Orchid Cellmark— Dallas	2600 Stemmons Freeway Suite 133 Dallas, TX 75207	800-752-2774 Fax: 214-634-3322 www.orchidcellmark.com
Orchid Cellmark— Nashville	1400 Donelson Pike Suite A15 Nashville, TN 37217	888-256-6383 Fax: 615-360-5003 www.orchidcellmark.com
ReliaGene Technologies	5525 Mounes Street #101 New Orleans, LA 70123	800-256-4106 Fax: 800-256-4556 www.reliagene.com

Table 8-3

Example DNA laboratory report

Results of Examination:
DNA recovered from the submitted samples was processed for short tandem repeat (STR) markers using the polymerase chain reaction (PCR) AmpFlSTR Profiler Plus and COfiler typing systems.

Conclusions:
The DNA profile detected from the evidence matches suspect 1.

The DNA typing results are as follows:

STR Marker	Suspect 1	Suspect 2	Evidence	Victim
Amelogenin (sex-typing)	X,Y	X,Y	X,Y	X,X
CSF1PO	10,10	10,10	10,10	10,12
FGA	21,22	22,23	21,22	21,25
TH01	6,6	6,9	6,6	6,9
TPOX	8,8	8,12	8,8	8,10
VWA	17,18	17,18	17,18	17,20
D3S1358	16,17	16,17	16,17	17,17
D5S818	12,13	8,14	12,13	11,13
D7S820	9,9	9,12	9,9	8,12
D8S1179	12,14	16,17	12,14	13,14
D13S317	11,14	11,14	11,14	8,12
D16S539	11,13	11,14	11,13	8,9
D18S51	14,16	14,14	14,16	14,17
D21S11	28,30	30,30	28,30	31,32.2

Population Statistics:
Population statistics are offered to estimate the frequency of occurrence of the reported DNA profile in the general population. The method used applies recommended procedures endorsed by the National Research Council (*The Evaluation of DNA Evidence*, 1996) and can be tested at the ProfilerPlus/COfiler RMP Calculator Web site: http://www.csfs.ca/pplus/profiler.htm (with the FBI Caucasian and FBI African American databases).

Using available population frequency data, the probability of selecting an unrelated individual at random from the population having a DNA profile matching the evidence is

Caucasian	1 in 1.56 quadrillion
African American	1 in 21.1 quadrillion

MITOCHONDRIAL DNA TESTING

Other DNA tests include mitochondrial DNA testing. Mitochondrial DNA (mtDNA) is a much shorter segment of DNA that is found outside the nucleus within another cellular structure called the *mitochondrion*. For various reasons this segment is much hardier than nuclear DNA and can remain intact for many years under harsh environmental conditions. It can be harvested from dead cells including hair, teeth, and bones. This can be quite valuable in cases where the victim is not discovered until many years later, long after cells have died and disintegrated. The limitations of the information available from this segment, however, greatly decrease its value for evidence. Because of its small size, there are comparatively very few areas to examine that differ from person to person. This would be like a social security number with only four or five digits. The chance that someone else has your same number increases dramatically. In addition, mtDNA is inherited entirely from an individual's mother, meaning that siblings and other maternal relatives will all have the same mtDNA type. Nevertheless, mitochondrial DNA results are still very useful in the absence of nuclear DNA information when sample degradation is an issue. However, its strength is much less than standard nuclear DNA tests, such as STR typing, and therefore other evidence may need to be more heavily relied on when evaluating an entire case.

Y-CHROMOSOME TESTING

Another DNA test that is rapidly gaining popularity is performed on the Y-chromosome. Women have the chromosome pair XX while men have the pair XY. By isolating identification patterns only found on the Y-chromosome, an analyst can separate out the male perpetrator's DNA from a mixture containing the female victim's DNA. Because rape kit evidence usually contains a combination of the biological fluids, this test is particularly useful. Again, because only one chromosome is examined (and this chromosome is directly passed on from father to all sons), the information from a Y-chromosome test is not as powerful as a standard STR typing result. Y-chromosome profiles can be searched against other Y-chromosome profiles in DNA databases to estimate probabilities of a random match to unrelated individuals.

INTERPRETING DNA TEST RESULTS

Generally the outcome of DNA testing falls into three categories: inclusion, exclusion, and inconclusive. Usually laboratory results will only include a description of the evidence received and a summary of examination results. Conclusions on the lab report might include words such as "the DNA profile obtained from evidence found at the crime scene matches the suspect" or "the suspect cannot be excluded as contributing the sample obtained at the crime scene," meaning the results support the possibility that the suspect is involved. If the suspect "*can* be excluded . . .", then his DNA profile is different from the one found at the crime scene and therefore most likely did not contribute it. Inconclusive results indicate that the DNA testing cannot include or exclude the suspect as the source of the biological evidence. If the quality of the submitted DNA samples is poor, or insufficient DNA was recovered from the evidence, or if the evidentiary sample contains a mixture of DNA from several individuals that cannot be easily interpreted, then results may be declared inconclusive.

Matching DNA results usually come with some sort of statistical analysis to estimate the frequency of the reported DNA profile in the general population. In other words, what is the probability for an unrelated person randomly selected from a population to have the DNA profile that matches that of the crime scene evidence and the suspect? A laboratory report will sometimes list the names of the various STR markers along with two numbers separated by commas (see Table 8-3). These values indicate the number of measured repeats present in the STR markers examined. Every individual has two copies of each STR being measured—one from their mother and one from their father; thus the two numbers.

ENSURING RELIABILITY OF DNA TEST RESULTS

In order to ensure accuracy and reliability of DNA testing results, the process is evaluated on the laboratory, analyst, and individual test level. The American Society of Crime Laboratory Directors—Laboratory Accreditation Board (ASCLD/LAB) accredits laboratories in the United States. This ASCLD/LAB accreditation process is performed at least every 5 years and involves demonstrating to external auditors that certain procedures are carefully followed and documented. In the United States, forensic laboratories must adhere to the National DNA Standards, which were established by the FBI's DNA Advisory Board in October 1998 (see full text at FBI Web site: http://www.fbi.gov/hq/lab/codis/forensic.htm).

Every DNA analyst who performs forensic casework is required to undergo a proficiency test at least twice a year. This proficiency test involves evaluating multiple DNA samples and reporting the results as though a case had been examined. If analysts fail their proficiency tests, then further training or a probationary period may be required before the analyst performs casework again. Standard operating procedures for each step in a DNA test are strictly followed in crime laboratories. In addition, standard samples are run as controls with each set of samples to ensure that the testing procedure is working properly.

The three-tiered checkpoints of laboratory accreditation, regular proficiency testing of analysts, and careful following of standard operating procedures with regular testing of control samples act as safeguards to ensure reliable DNA analysis. Finally our judicial system, which can include careful scrutiny of DNA test results by defense attorneys, acts as an additional safeguard on DNA evidence to make sure that the innocent are not falsely convicted.

SOURCES FOR FURTHER INFORMATION

The National Institute of Justice (http://www.ojp.usdoj.gov/nij) funds research in the area of forensic DNA typing technology and over the years has prepared a number of useful training guides regarding DNA testing. See *What Every Law Enforcement Officer Should Know about DNA Evidence* (Sept 1999): http://www.ojp.usdoj.gov/nij/pubs-sum/000614.htm and *Understanding DNA Evidence: A Guide for Victim Service Providers* (May 2001): http://www.ojp.usdoj.gov/nij/pubs-sum/BC000657.htm.

The National Institute of Standards and Technology maintains a Web site containing a more technical description of DNA typing using short tandem repeat markers for those who are interested: http://www.cstl.nist.gov/biotech/strbase/.

The Federal Bureau of Investigation's Combined DNA Index System is summarized at: http://www.fbi.gov/hq/lab/codis/index1.htm.

CHAPTER 9

DNA: INVESTIGATIVE APPLICATIONS

Alan Sandomir

From a single thin strand of hair, from a small innocuous stain hidden in a corner under a rug and regularly missed by the naked eye, from a fleck of skin on a windowsill or from the sweat of another man's brow—lives have been altered, changed dramatically and forever by DNA. DNA technology has revolutionized both the forensic and medical communities in a manner unimaginable just a few years ago. Forensics—commonly considered to be the application of science and technology to the law—has been radically changed in a way that has already surpassed the development of fingerprint identification and the revolution that had ushered in just a few short generations ago. DNA has allowed criminal investigators to reach back in time and snare perpetrators of violent crimes in cases that most thought long forgotten and buried deep within the dusty recesses of police stations or in basements of crime labs across the country. The long arm of the law has flexed its muscle. Suspects are being both convicted and exonerated. Violent predators are being tracked down, arrested, and prosecuted for cases that otherwise would have been impossible to successfully complete without the advent of DNA technology, for cases long since forgotten. Or, as aptly put by one DNA cop: "You can't hide anymore."

Part of the difficulty in the investigation of "cold cases"—and in many of the cases being solved with the assistance of DNA—is the fact that so much time may have passed. The victim may not want to cooperate or understand why, after being the victim of a violent sexual assault perhaps occurring well over a decade ago, the police want her to sit down and once again retell, and often relive, the horror of many years past. It might be difficult, awkward, or strange for a victim to understand the need to view a line-up or go meet with a prosecutor. In many of these unsolved cases the victims have moved on with their lives or have put this particular aspect of their past behind them. Many want to forget. Often, they never really do. Now they are being asked to recount a tragedy to an investigator, a prosecutor, and a jury of their peers whom they do not know—in short, to strangers.

Frequently, investigators knock on a door unexpectedly or after a brief but vague phone call. The victim is usually stunned. The last thing that they expected is an investigator at their front door to stir up images from long ago. Many victims have long harbored dual inner fears: (1) that their attacker is still lurking out there and (2) that the police have truly forgotten about them. Many of these cases begin with an investigation to locate the victim and obtain their cooperation. Most victims initially react with a stunned silence. Knees might shake. Faces might grow pale. But almost all victims will want to hear what the investigator has to say. And almost all victims will want to cooperate.

Unfortunately, this will not always be the case. There will be exceptions. There will be times when the victim might calmly ask the investigator to leave. Or there might be times when they'll ask the investigator to leave in a manner not at all calm, causing the investigator to retreat under a shower of invective.

Family and friends might intervene. This can work for or against the investigator. There might be times where the Investigator will have to work through a psychiatrist or psychologist in order to gain a victim's cooperation. This, too, can work for or against the case. Ultimately, an informed decision needs to be made by the victim. After all, it's the victim's well-being that is at stake and is one of the two goals that investigator is ultimately striving for. The second goal is to identify and remove a predator from our midst. Both are serious and oft times difficult goals, but are goals well worth the effort.

Every few years since James Watson and Francis Crick established the structure of DNA in 1953, advances in DNA science continued to expand and leave imprints upon the fabric of our society. In 1984 a British researcher, Dr. Alec Jeffreys, developed "DNA fingerprinting"—a term that he coined—which allowed scientists to identify individuals through their DNA (Nickel and Fischer, 1999).

In 1986, British investigators linked two rape/homicides that occurred almost 3 years apart. Although a suspect was apprehended and provided a confession, investigators wanted additional corroboration. Consequently, they contacted Dr. Jeffreys after hearing about this unique, albeit unproven, technique. The result of this contact was that they discovered that the wrong man was arrested: DNA tests revealed that they had the wrong suspect. Investigators continued their search using the first DNA "dragnet" to test all of the males in the community. The offender was identified by old-fashioned detective work; the suspect was flushed by the DNA dragnet and identified after he sent a co-worker to stand in his place. DNA analysis confirmed that Colin Pitchfork, the man who had shunned testing, was the elusive rapist/murderer that they sought. He was the first person to be convicted of a murder based on a genetic profile in 1987. He was sentenced to life in prison (Owen, 2000).

In November of 1987, a Florida man was convicted of rape based upon "DNA fingerprinting." The Circuit Court in Orange County, Florida, convicted Tommy Lee Andrews of rape after DNA tests matched his DNA from a blood sample with that of semen traces found in a rape victim. This was one of the first cases in the United States that used DNA to convict a felon (*U.S. News & World Report*, 2003). Detectives and prosecutors became smitten by the possibilities offered by DNA.

CODIS

As DNA technology improved, so did its applications to police work and criminal investigations. In 1994, Congress passed the DNA Identification Act. This enabled the FBI to establish a national DNA data bank whose goal was to expand upon a pilot project started in 1990 and to provide law enforcement agencies and forensic labs from around the country the means by which to compare DNA evidence electronically. In 1998, the FBI's DNA data bank became operational at the national level (McClintock, 2001). Federal, state, and local law enforcement agencies began to methodically collect and store DNA evidence from crime scenes, sexual assault evidence collection kits, and specified convicted offenders in DNA dedicated computerized data banks with the expectations of comparing their findings nationwide. These DNA data banks are frequently referred to as the CODIS (Combined DNA Indexing System) (U.S. Department of Justice, 2003).

The CODIS program is maintained at both the state and national levels. By 1998 all 50 states, Puerto Rico, and the District of Columbia had passed legislation allowing for the collection of DNA samples from specified convicted offenders. However, this does not preclude local police labs or coroner/medical examiner offices from maintaining their own DNA data bank of nonconvicted offenders or suspects (although this DNA group will not be compared at the state or national CODIS levels since the subjects are not convicted).

Both police labs and private labs utilized by law enforcement began to develop and compare these DNA fingerprints or "profiles" within their jurisdictions. After being compared at the local and state levels, the profiles are uploaded into the FBI's CODIS for nationwide search and comparison. These profiles, at both the CODIS and local levels, have churned out a wealth of information linking crimes and suspects by DNA. Not only have local and state law enforcement agencies been receiving DNA case links and matches from within their own states, but the national CODIS has linked and matched cases across state lines and across the country.

Previously identified DNA profiles found within the CODIS (i.e., those DNA profiles already associated with known individuals) are normally from the thousands of inmates and/or parolees who have been convicted of certain specified crimes (Ramsland, 2001). These convicted offenders are required to provide DNA samples. Although each state has its own list of crimes requiring DNA samples from individuals convicted of those specified crimes, not all the crimes requiring DNA samples are sexually related. Some of the specified crimes can include murder, assault, robbery, burglary, weapons possession, and felony narcotics. Each state has its own requirements.

When the CODIS began, it produced DNA matches to cases that were at times over a decade old. However, as the CODIS continued to develop, it began to uncover matches and links between cases both old and new. The CODIS' ability to match and link cases will always be based upon the evidence being offered to it. That is why the CODIS and local DNA data banks will always be the jewel in the crown of both cold case investigators and those seeking assailants in new cases.

THE EVIDENCE TRAIL

If there were one rule or maxim for criminal investigators to follow, particularly when forensic evidence is involved, it would be this: Follow the evidence trail carefully and completely. This is of critical importance when DNA evidence comes into play. Of utmost importance in a DNA-based investigation is both how and where the DNA evidence is obtained. Once that is established, its connection to the suspect needs to be clear, unwavering and unequivocal. There can be no room for ambiguity. The line between the crime and the offender needs to be unbroken. For that, attention to detail is paramount. Investigators must follow the evidence trail wherever it goes.

DNA evidence must be understood in its entirety—from the moment it is discovered and collected to the way it was transported and presented for analysis. Forensic authors W. Jerry Chisum and Brent Turvey coined a phrase to describe this concept: "evidence dynamics" (Turvey and Chisum, 2002). Evidence Dynamics simply refers to any type of change or influence that a piece of evidence might become exposed to that can relocate, obscure, or destroy it as a piece of the evidentiary puzzle. Other phrases such as "chain of custody" have been used to describe the path that evidence takes once it is collected and removed from the crime scene or human body. But the term "evidence dynamics" describes an investigative process that can be as much a part of the investigation as the investigation itself. Investigators must understand not only those who handled the evidence, where the evidence went, and how it got there (the "chain"), but what influences the evidence might have experienced or sustained during that time and how, if at all, that affected the value of that evidence (the "dynamics"). In other words: What changes, if any, did the evidence go through?

How did that happen? Why did that happen? How has its value as a piece of the puzzle changed—if at all?

DNA is biological evidence and is susceptible to change as a result. Its collection, transportation, and storage become important since biological evidence can degrade. If the evidence changes, so does its value. Consequently, DNA evidence needs to be collected in a manner that will stabilize and preserve it without changing or contaminating it. Before a man or woman is arrested and convicted based upon DNA evidence, all evidentiary-related questions and inferences need to be identified and answered completely. Investigators must anticipate both the questions and the answers before they can proceed. In short, they have to follow the evidence trail, wherever it takes them, and have all the answers ready before the questions are even asked. They have to know.

Example:

In the summer of 2002, a DNA link was established between an unsolved rape that occurred in 1993 and a man serving time for an unrelated arrest involving a weapon. Investigators were able to identify a second 1993 sexual assault case as a result of a similar M.O. and linked it to the first rape by M.O. only (not by DNA). Investigators also found an unsolved homicide that had some similarities—but in this third case the offender shot the victim in front of her young child and killed her.

The Sexual Assault Evidence Collection Kit from the second unsolved 1993 rape had previously been tested and the results indicated that there was no biological evidence discovered—there was no DNA. However, investigators were able to locate additional evidence from that second 1993 rape case that had never been examined or tested. That evidence was sent for testing and DNA soon proved that the two rapes in 1993 were indeed committed by the same offender. The tests also went on to positively identify the male convicted in the unrelated weapons possession case as the attacker in both cases. Although there was no biological evidence in the homicide case, this male could now be identified and charged with the murder using more conventional means of evidence. His arrest for both rape cases came a few months before the statute of limitations would have expired. Overwhelmed by the evidence against him, he pled guilty and will be spending the rest of his life in prison.

This example simply outlines the necessity of how following up on all of the evidence in detail can bring dramatic results to an investigation. The evidence trail was aggressively followed to the end—even when preliminary evidence related reports showed that the evidence trail was leading nowhere. *All* the evidence was reviewed and pursued until all the possible answers were known.

An error frequently made by investigators involved in a sexual assault case is the misreading of the sexual assault evidence collection kit results. Frequently, physicians or qualified medical staff will apply a cotton swab to the overall genital area without clarifying whether the specimen collected was from an external or internal exam. As a result, the investigator will interview a victim who will describe a rape. However, the hospital and lab report might show that a DNA profile was collected and established from another area of the victim's body that was also swabbed for evidence. This is where a careful understanding of the evidence trail, of "evidence dynamics," comes into play. At first glance, it would seem that the victim was either lying or too embarrassed to disclose that she had been sexually assaulted in more than one fashion. While that might be true, there can be another explanation as well: that DNA-laden fluids from the rape simply dripped down to either her buttocks or another area—or were transferred via tissues, towels, or undergarments that then had contact with either her buttocks or those other areas. Those other areas were later *externally* swabbed at the hospital by a physician who broadly categorized that swab as coming from other "areas" of her body without going into specific detail. Consequently, it would be easy to misinterpret the hospital and lab report unless one has a working knowledge of how sex-crime evidence works.

DNA SOURCES

DNA evidence can come from a variety of sources and can be found at crime scenes in a variety of places. In a sex crime, the victim's body is frequently the main repository of much needed evidence. Although investigators typically expect blood- or semen-based DNA to be recovered from a victim's genitals or mouth, other areas and sources should not be overlooked. Other areas would include pubic and head hair, dandruff, any expanse of skin, under fingernails or toenails, ears, ear wax, between the toes or fingers, under rings, earrings, or bracelets, and from any item of clothing or material that the victim and/or attacker came into contact with. Obviously, bedsheets, towels, tissues, condoms, *anything* in the bathroom wastebasket, and so forth needs to be collected—the obvious items. But often overlooked are such sources as ligatures: cord, rope, tape, wire, etc. can add an interesting and corroborative dimension to an investigation in that the ligature can potentially hold DNA from both the victim and offender along the same piece of evidence thereby locking them both together within the context of a crime. Additional yet easily overlooked sources also include bandages, contact lenses and eyeglasses, bullets that pass through bodies, toothpicks, inside sink traps, drains, or plumbing fixtures, and even drinking straws (Ramsland, 2001). Even leftover foods partially eaten by a hungry criminal may hold potential DNA. In short, anything that can acquire and hold biological evidence.

Often forgotten is the fact that seminal fluid does not contain DNA. The DNA in seminal fluid is found within spermatozoa. However, it is possible to recover seminal fluid containing absolutely no spermatozoa! In the absence of spermatozoa, the seminal fluid may contain skin cells or white blood cells (Hazelwood and Burgess, 1999). Skin cells and white blood cells are tiny repositories that can be treasure troves of DNA information.

Nor should investigators overlook saliva. Investigators should question the victim, if available, and determine if the attacker's mouth came into contact with any part of the victim's body. Items such as stamps, envelopes, cigarette butts, soda cans, drinking cups, and telephones also need to be considered (Silverstein, 1996). If the possibility of a DNA transfer occurred—if the attacker left behind any type of biological evidence—those areas should be treated and processed in a manner consistent with biological evidence collection. Usually, qualified personnel will examine and swab the area in order to collect and preserve the evidence. If the victim is dead, unconscious, or otherwise unable to communicate, and there are bite or teeth marks on the body, do not stop at merely swabbing that single area for saliva. Expand the search to include the victim's entire body. Saliva by itself does not contain DNA. However, saliva can contain epithelial cells (skin cells) from inside of the mouth or white blood cells (Hazelwood and Burgess, 1999). And that is where we can hope to find the attacker's DNA.

In the absence of victim feedback, always assume that other areas of the body might potentially have fluids or biological debris as a result of contact (i.e., saliva, semen, sweat, skin, hair, etc.). Care and scrutiny need to be employed so as to not overlook dried secretions. Dried fluids can, at times, be easily missed. Obviously, the victim should be questioned, if possible, about the presence of any unidentified fluids. These fluids, biological or not, should be documented and collected for further analysis. Fluid and evidence collection from a body or crime scene does not end with the collection of biological evidence alone. Latent (not visible) or patent (visible) fingerprint evidence, surveillance tapes, ballistic and fiber evidence, foot- and tire-print evidence, soil, leaf, and insect samples, paint, paper, and chemical samples, and so on all play a role in the completion of the crime-scene puzzle. Although teeth or bite marks can signal the possibility of saliva waiting to be swabbed and collected, the evidence collection effort should not stop there. The images or impressions of those marks should also be evaluated for collection or documentation. Bite marks can, at times, be as unique as fingerprints. DNA collection, though a major part of the puzzle, should not overshadow or exclude other avenues of evidence collection.

Often overlooked is the presence of human sweat, urine, feces, and tears as potential sources of evidence. These items, too, can turn up when least expected and can be similarly documented, collected, and sent out for analysis. However, these items are *not* usually promising and may *not* always be counted upon to provide DNA. Yet these items can act as transfer mediums for DNA material and, as such, cannot be ignored. Collection of these items will be a decision usually made either at the crime scene or at the hospital where the victim is being examined.

Crime scenes that occur in the woods or within campsites present interesting possibilities that will often require that the Investigator think "outside of the box," to ignore conventional textbook guidelines, to apply a very basic understanding of human nature and to simply go with what works. For example, it might be worthwhile to return to that wooded crime scene at night if the initial response was during daylight hours and shine an ultraviolet light on the surrounding areas. The investigator might very well discover DNA evidence in human urine left on the tree trunks in the vicinity (Genge, 2002). Latrine holes or trenches dug in the earth when the comforts of modern plumbing are absent also cannot be ignored. Although not exactly a preferred method of DNA collection—and not one that will automatically guarantee DNA evidence if human waste is actually found—it, too, needs to be considered as an evidence source that can perhaps help complete the evidence puzzle.

Thinking "outside of the box" should be the DNA investigator's maxim. Whether looking for a rapist' DNA inside of a victim's stab wound, between floorboards, on steering wheels, in matchbook covers, or on items used as ligatures, traces of the puzzle abound.

Sweat-based evidence is most useful when used as a means of skin cell transfer. While drops of sweat infrequently yield DNA, the sweat rubbed off on a hatband, shirt collar, bandana, handkerchief, or other article (usually cloth-based material) may act as a transfer medium and may contain the rubbed-off skin cells of its host. Simply put: If the attacker wore a hat and his head produced an amount of sweat, it is conceivable that any skin cells from his head rubbed off as a result of wearing that hat will be contained in the hatband along with the sweat. Consequently, that sweat now holds potential DNA as a transfer medium. Of value would be the collection of either that sweaty hat or an amount of that potentially DNA-laden sweat. Even the sweaty rough surface of a weapon can yield potential DNA if the person who held the weapon transfers an amount of sweat-holding skin cells to the weapon's surface. This may hold true even for the simple act of perpetrator's sweaty hand turning a doorknob to open a door before fleeing.

Hair and skin debris also hold value. Although their success rate is not as pronounced or as advertised as that for semen, blood, or saliva, their importance as a potential tool for offender identification cannot be ignored. The sexual assault evidence collection kits usually found in hospitals most always include collection tools for each of the biological categories listed in the paragraphs above. Hair can present a problem in that to gain the full benefit of a DNA fingerprint, the hair follicle needs to be recovered. That tiny pod at the base of a hair shaft holds all the vital DNA material. A partial hair shaft without the follicle can also present a partial DNA picture through mitochondrial DNA.

In cases that involve multiple offenders, the possibility of mixed DNA exists. However, crime labs have the capability to differentiate individual DNA profiles in multiple offender cases if the DNA is semen based. For example, if the victim had a consensual partner prior to the assault, his DNA profile can be separated once his standard is obtained and compared. This allows investigators to identify the DNA profiles of the offender(s) and separate the consensual partner from the suspect(s).

DNA IN THE CRIME SCENE

The crime scene is of critical importance. One of the most easily avoided problems is that of crime scene contamination by either the police officers or paramedics who respond to the initial emergency call. One of the best rules taught to novice police officers after a crime scene is safely established and secured, and one that often needs to be repeated to seasoned veterans, is to stuff your hands in your pockets if you find yourself inside of the crime scene and to carefully retreat to the outer perimeter if not needed within. Then there is the "do not" list: Do not touch anything! Do not use the phone if it is part of, or within, the crime scene. Do not smoke or deposit your cigarettes within the crime scene. Do not use the bathroom or sinks. Do not eat or drink in the crime scene. Do not track mud or debris into the crime scene—if you do track mud or debris into the crime scene, crime-scene investigators must be advised. Do not remove anything without authorization unless not doing so will cause an item to be lost as evidence. Document whatever you touched and why and be sure that the lead investigators are aware. Keep a log of *all* personnel who entered the crime scene perimeter. Be careful where you step and do not kick around any items on the floor. Be careful opening doors, closets, and windows (if safety and security concerns are no longer an issue). Do not use the crime scene as a temporary headquarters or operational center. Do not spit, cough, or sneeze near evidence. Try to keep the crime scene as pristine as possible without compromising physical safety. Don't touch anything.

Crime-scene investigators will frequently wear a paperlike one-piece jump suit and, many times, a mask to cover their nose and mouth. They will wear gloves and change them often. Paper and elastic shoe coverings may also be used. They will either clean the instruments they use to collect biological evidence to prevent cross-contamination between samples, or simply pick up a fresh new instrument when moving on to collect another sample. They will always package biological evidence in paper and never in plastic. Biological evidence sealed in plastic will break down and create bacteria that can potentially ruin a DNA sample as evidence. DNA evidence should be stored at room temperature and kept dry. Humidity (moisture), heat, and direct sunlight can, at times, degrade the value of the DNA sample as evidence.

Often, sexual assault evidence collection kits are stored in refrigerators.

Ultraviolet lighting has been traditionally used by law enforcement to illuminate certain forms of biological evidence causing some fluids to "fluoresce," or otherwise offer a visual signature when submitted to UV lighting. A semen stain, depending on its context, might even appear as a spot darker than the surrounding area when exposed to UV lighting. Consequently, detecting semen stains can be difficult since the room or area needs to be dark when using this detection method.

Investigators usually wind up looking for a stain under conditions that offer limited visibility at best while scrutinizing potential evidence under a blue glow and/or flashlight beam. Consequently, as useful as UV lighting can be, investigators need to be prepared to deal with "false positives" where suspect evidence produces a visual signature but later turns out not to be the type of evidence sought. Food stains and laundry detergent are the most common culprits (Hazelwood and Burgess, 1999). Even animal urine can give off a visual signature (U.S. Department of Justice, 2003). This is why the processing of a crime scene has to be both thorough and complete and why an investigator cannot rest on his laurels after encountering what appears to be the first piece of evidence.

Example:

In 1997, a partially naked female was found unconscious inside of a bathroom in a high-rise office building. The victim was beaten and left for dead by the offender. Because the victim was unable to communicate as a result of her injuries, investigators were not able to determine if the bathroom was the primary crime scene or if there was another location that contained critical evidence. Investigators, in an attempt to locate the crime scene, went around vacant offices with a UV light and a pair of scissors collecting any stains that "fluoresced" under the UV light. The lab later confirmed that these were not biological traces of a crime. In all likelihood they were food stains. The crime scene was later discovered after a suspect was identified and confessed to the crime.

Ultraviolet light is an extremely useful tool, but not everything that reacts to UV light is biological evidence or the result of a crime. For many years, ultraviolet light served as the primary method of fluorescence detection and the investigator often viewed the crime scene through optical filter glasses. Usually, the room or area had to be dark in order to have this evidence collection method work. Obviously, this has many drawbacks and can slow an investigation down (i.e., returning to an outdoor crime scene at night). And it is not a perfect method since many types of biological evidence would still remain hard to find and give off a weak visual signature.

However, in the late 1990s, a man named Colin Smithpeter developed an evidence illumination system while working at the Sandia National Labs called the "Criminalistics Light-Imaging Unit" (CLU). The CLU allows investigators to find fluorescing evidence such as DNA-laced semen in areas that are not darkened. The CLU can detect evidence under normal light. The CLU is designed to use various colors of light in conjunction with a strobe light, signal processor, and improved optics to locate fluorescing biological evidence such as semen. The CLU can also detect unprocessed latent fingerprints on dark, multicolor, or transparent surfaces (U.S. Department of Justice, 2003).

VEHICLES

Crime scenes involving the interior of a vehicle include their own unique challenges. Investigators should look for DNA in ashtrays; on or under the seats; on headrests, seat belts, seat belt fasteners, and floor mats; behind the rear seats; and on the steering wheel and gear shifts, door and window handles, any dials, switches, or knobs, and window glass. The exterior of the vehicle requires an examination of the tire, tire treads, wheel wells, mud guards, bumpers, and grills. If at all possible, and if the investigation's circumstances permit, have the vehicle removed and secured in an indoor facility such as a garage. A vehicle as a crime scene is best processed when dry, at room temperature, and shielded from external elements (i.e., inclement and/or changing weather). However, as each case is different, investigators at the scene need to confer with the crime scene investigators and forensic technicians to determine if moving the vehicle is beneficial in each specific case.

ACQUAINTANCE RAPE

When investigating an acquaintance rape (sometimes called "date rape"), investigators need to evaluate the merits of entering the offender's residence in order to collect evidence. If the investigator wants to enter the offender's residence in order to seize items such as a bedsheet for DNA analysis, keep in mind the that bedsheets would more than likely contain the offender's DNA anyway. After all, it is his bed and bed sheet. That his DNA is present in his own bed and sheets cannot be assumed unusual or indicative of a crime and so might be of little evidentiary value. The victim's DNA on the bedsheets will only prompt cries of a consensual encounter by the offender. Frequently, a search warrant would be needed to enter the residence and the offender possibly alerted to the fact that a police investigation is afoot. Consequently, any future efforts to establish corroboration in an acquaintance case (i.e., a controlled and tape-recorded conversation between the two or a letter of apology from the offender) would be tainted, if not improbable, or even cut off completely as a result. Additionally, any knowledge of police involvement by the offender can potentially cause him to flee (i.e., coming home to find a uniformed police officer at his front door posted to protect and secure his home as a crime scene—complete with yellow and black crime-scene tape draped around and cordoning off his house or apartment). That is why a crime-scene evaluation needs to be considered *before* the scene is surrounded and/or secured by the police and the offender consequently alerted.

There are, of course, exceptions. Exceptions would include the collection of the victim's blood or any other evidence that would establish a violent or non-consensual encounter. In investigations like these, every situation needs to be evaluated on its own merit and in a case-by-case basis. Every case is different.

SECONDARY EVIDENCE TRANSFER

Investigators frequently grab and hold onto evidence without stepping back and examining the entire picture. Forensic labs many times do the same thing. A situation that needs to be acknowledged is that of secondary evidence transfer, where noncriminal evidence, in this case biological evidence, is (or was previously) transferred from a source onto the crime scene or victim. Investigators need to be aware of this possibility and must be prepared to vigorously investigate any evidence that might fall into this category in order to properly include or exclude that evidence link. An example would be a semen stain on an old sweatshirt worn by a victim that does not match the DNA recovered from semen found on the interior of her underwear from the day of the attack. While the location of each sample might be easily latched onto and quickly explained away by a police investigator, a defense attorney and defense investigator can wreak havoc on a case unless each semen sample is explained. It could simply be that a secondary evidence transfer occurred weeks or months prior, leaving a semen stain from a noncriminal event on the sweatshirt. Or it might mean that the victim is being less that truthful. Regardless, all evidentiary questions must be confronted, investigated, and answered. As with all major case investigations, we have to know! We need all the answers to all the questions—even before those questions are asked.

DNA VERSUS LATENT FINGERPRINT COLLECTION

Every object touched by the offender is a potential source of evidence. If the attacker entered through a door, the door and doorknob should be examined. A determination should be made as to the benefit of dusting the area for latent fingerprints versus swabbing those surfaces for possible biological debris left behind as a result of that contact (sweat/skin cells, blood, etc.). Similarly, windows, window frames, and windowsills deserve equal scrutiny. While glass or Plexiglas windows can offer excellent surfaces for latent fingerprint recovery, a determination has to be made as to whether the surface can yield DNA-based evidence as well. At times, the collection of one type of evidence might preclude the collection of the other if the same surface is being considered. For example, swabbing a surface for DNA over a latent fingerprint will probably smudge and ruin the value of the latent fingerprint. Dusting for and tape lifting (as opposed to dusting for and photographing) a latent print might undermine the value of any DNA sharing that same surface unless sufficient trace evidence is left behind. Techniques need to be developed that can extract any possible DNA lingering within the latent print tape lift AFTER that fingerprint has been tape-lifted and adhered to a latent print viewing surface. As DNA technology improves perhaps there can be a technique developed in which that lingering evidence can be removed from the tape surface and developed into a DNA profile.

While examining windows and fire escapes for latent prints, these are also two areas that should not be overlooked for their usefulness in harboring blood or skin evidence—even if it is minute trace evidence.

If an item is found to contain both a potential source of DNA and a potential latent print, and the piece of evidence is evaluated as requiring chemical fuming to raise the print, the evidence should probably be first sent to the lab for chemical fuming. DNA analysis can frequently be performed after the fuming. This is because DNA processing will destroy the latent print, but chemical fuming will not necessarily destroy the DNA. However, this is by no means a maxim. There are no set rules here.

Investigators should avoid submitting evidence for any type of latent print processing that involves the physical immersion, or dunking, of that evidence into a liquid mixture. This process can usually guarantee the removal of any type of DNA evidence from the targeted surface. Consequently, it should be avoided when that particular piece of evidence is also being considered as a DNA source. However, the actual decision as to which process to submit the evidence to first rests with those responsible for the investigation. This is but one of many instances where the field investigator needs to reach out to and confer with the laboratory staff to determine the consequences of each test and what the sequence of collection and testing should be. At times, one will have to be forfeited for the benefit of the other.

When it comes to DNA collection versus latent fingerprint collection, each case has to be evaluated on its own merits. There is no one correct answer. Each lab has its own techniques, procedures, and standards. Some labs might even advise that the way they chemically fume latent prints can destroy the DNA evidence. Similarly, some DNA labs might object to working around latent fingerprint powders and chemicals to extract a DNA sample. Each case is unique and has to be evaluated on its own.

ELIMINATION DNA

Crime-scene investigations can produce investigative leads frequently not expected in a non-DNA investigation. Cigarettes and cigarette butts found at the crime scene need to be collected and sent out for DNA testing. If the lab report establishes that there is both male and female DNA developed from the cigarette butts, the investigator needs to establish who these people are, how they came to have access to that crime scene, why they were there, their relationship to the victim or crime, and who was smoking which cigarette. All of the people who had access to that crime scene need to submit an elimination DNA sample for identification (frequently from oral swabs)—this would include police officers and other emergency service personnel who responded to the crime scene.

Similarly, DNA analysis of bedsheets or bottles can come up with unexpected DNA profiles unless the investigator has a clear picture of who had access to that crime scene, when, why, and how. Bedsheets and other cloth material, and at times bottles and cigarette butts, can provide more than one DNA profile indicating more than one person present. Again, it is the investigator's responsibility to obtain elimination DNA samples and establish who had access to that crime scene. Again, investigators need to know.

THE CONDOM CONUNDRUM

Investigators at crime scenes should not overlook the importance of abandoned condoms. The obvious reason is that condoms serve as repositories for semen. However, since a sex crime may not always include ejaculation, used condoms lacking semen still have great value. While the attacker's semen might not be present, his DNA in the form of skin cells left within the condom's interior might be. It is also prudent to have the condom's exterior surface tested for DNA. The condom's exterior might carry traces of the victim's DNA. Consequently, if there is no biological evidence left on the victim's body, a discarded condom containing both the suspect's and victim's DNA turns into a positive physical evidence link connecting these two people within the context of a crime. Interior/exterior DNA profiles can become a very useful tool if the crime scene yields multiple condoms because of its location (i.e., secluded locations often used for sexual encounters). It allows the Investigator to determine which condom was used in the crime. Additionally, if a condom is found, look for the wrapper! Condom wrappers can potentially offer latent fingerprints and/or DNA from saliva if the attacker used his mouth to open it.

Example:

In August 1998 a 23-year-old woman was raped inside an elevator at knifepoint. With the exception of an unrolled condom found on the elevator floor, there was little evidence in this case. There were no witnesses, the victim was not able to identify her attacker, and there were no fingerprints to help identify the offender. However, DNA was found on the victim's body. In 2002 a DNA link was established letting investigators know that the same offender who committed the rape in 1998 was responsible for an unsolved murder in 1999. A few months after receiving news of the initial DNA link, a match was made to an offender who was serving time on an unrelated drug charge. The condom that was originally found at the scene was not tested since it did not contain semen. However, with this DNA link now established, investigators reviewed the evidence and had the condom tested. As a result, a DNA profile from the offender's skin cells recovered from the condom's interior was developed along with a DNA profile from the victim's skin cells found on the condom's exterior. The significance of this is that the condom further tied the suspect to the crime by placing him at the scene—an elevator. It can also help if he alleges to have had a consensual sexual relationship with the victim somewhere else when trying to explain his semen on the victim's body. By testing the condom that was documented, photographed and collected at the crime scene, a potential alibi defense was effectively eliminated. The offender pled guilty to both the rape and homicide.

FIVE BASIC DNA LINKS

There are five basic DNA links of concern for law enforcement. The labels used here are simply the vernacular used by the author to describe the types of cases investigated when working with DNA data banks.

DNA Hot Hit: DNA data bank identified an offender who is *not* in custody.

The investigator needs to locate the case(s), the victim(s), and the whereabouts of the offender. The investigator also needs to establish a clear, secured, and documented evidentiary link between the offender's DNA and the DNA recovered at the time of the crime. Several variables need to be considered: From where was the DNA recovered at the time of the crime? Does that match the case's expectations and the victim's statements? Is there any untested evidence? Is the identified DNA Hot Hit offender the victim's attacker or a past consensual sexual encounter associated with the victim? An Investigator should always consider such variables as the jurisdiction's statute of limitations, the prosecutor's position concerning the viability of the case, extradition, risk of suspect flight, the prospect of search warrants, arrest warrants, court ordered confirmatory DNA samples, and so forth.

DNA Case-to-Case Match/Offender Identified: The DNA data bank identified a series of cases as linked, and a suspect is named through sources other than a secured and confirmed CODIS identification.

A Case-to-Case match where an offender is identified usually involves two or more cases linked by DNA where the offender is either named on one or more police reports or had been previously arrested in at least one of the cases (and due to DNA linked to the other cases). However, caution needs to be exercised here. Just because an offender was named on a police incident or arrest report does not mean that particular person is the serial offender being sought in the other open DNA cases. Until there is a secure and positive evidentiary DNA link established to confirm that the person simply named on a police or lab report is the DNA offender being sought, the investigation needs to proceed with caution. This is not a confirmed CODIS or DNA databank identification, but possibly a DNA identification merely proposed by the DNA lab based on a DNA profile recovered from evidence submitted *and* the fact that a person was previously named as a suspect without a confirmatory test. Many times the DNA investigator will have to initiate the DNA confirmatory process in order to ensure that the suspect previously named is the offender being sought. There have been instances where the suspect named or arrested on the first case indeed sexually assaulted the victim—but the DNA recovered was not his but that of a person involved in a consensual encounter with the victim either before or after the rape. Consequently, that consensual partner will be the offender in the *other* DNA-linked cases. The evidence puzzle needs to be carefully displayed and examined. The person named and perhaps correctly arrested in the first case might not be involved with the other linked cases. It's just that his arrest created a situation where a legitimate victim was examined and had a rape kit prepared where DNA from a consensual encounter was recovered and linked to other nonconsensual attacks. The police then receive a break in their nonconsensual attack cases by circumstance.

Several questions obviously need to be addressed:

(a) How was this suspect named?
(b) Is his DNA in a CODIS? If so, why was he not linked through a CODIS?
(c) If his DNA is not in a CODIS, how can investigators confirm or exclude his involvement with this case or serial pattern?
(d) What was his actual involvement in the initial case that brought his identity to the attention of the DNA investigators?
(e) Does his DNA really match the evidence in the other DNA-linked cases, or is he simply a suspect "named on paper" by the victim, witnesses, or police in that very first case?

In cases where the offender is not in prison and is walking the streets freely, the investigator will have to abide by his or her jurisdiction's protocol for non-DNA suspect identification pending a secure DNA evidentiary link (i.e., suspect line-up, photographic array, confirmatory photographic ID, latent print or other forensic techniques, suspect interrogation, reverse photographic array or confirmatory ID, locating witnesses, etc.).

Example.

In the spring of 2003 investigators received notification of a Case-to-Case DNA match between a 1993 rape and a rape from 2002 in another part of the city where a perpetrator was arrested. Investigators located and interviewed the victims from the 1993 and 2002 attacks since the DNA identification was based upon the 2002 arrest without any confirmatory DNA testing. The 2002 victim reported that she had unprotected consensual sex with her boyfriend prior to the rape. This presented an interesting but expected problem for investigators: Was the 1993 attacker the man arrested in the 2002 case, or was the 1993 attacker the 2002 victim's boyfriend? Whose DNA was found in the 2002 case? This problem was compounded by the fact that the 2002 victim was a juvenile and refused to identify her boyfriend in fear that he'd be arrested for statutory rape as a result of having consensual sex with her. The 1993 case's statute of limitations was due to expire in a few months and time was critical. After investigators queried the 2002 victim and learned how both the consensual sex and the rape occurred, they became convinced that the man arrested in 2002 was the 1993 rapist. However, there was no official DNA link. A DNA buccal (oral) swab was obtained from the perpetrator pursuant to his 2002 arrest and, at the investigator's request, was compared to the 1993 rapist's DNA profile. It was a match. The same man committed both rapes. Investigators intercepted the perpetrator as he exited a courtroom after attending a DNA hearing on his 2002 case. He was arrested and charged with 1993 rape just 4 months before the 10-year statute of limitations was due to expire. He eventually pled guilty.

In summary, just because a suspect is named by the police on an initially non-DNA-based report (i.e., police incident or arrest report), and that name is later sent to the DNA investigator by the lab as being connected to that first case, that does not necessarily mean that he will become the offender wanted in connection with the other DNA-linked cases. Unless the offender is established through a secure DNA data bank procedure or confirmed CODIS identification, the investigator needs to obtain a DNA sample from the suspect in order to confirm the match and firmly establish that he is, in fact, the person being sought and not a person involved with the victim in a consensual or noncriminal encounter. Many of the DNA evidence shortfalls described in the Case-to-Case Match/Offender Not Identified section apply here as well. Again, "evidence dynamics" cannot be ignored since many DNA cases are, in fact, old or "cold" cases being reconstructed many months or years later. The foregoing example serves to illustrate how two crimes were reconstructed when two possible offenders emerged as the culprit with only one suspect simply named "on paper" without a secured DNA link.

Another avenue of approach to move further toward completing the identity of a rapist named but not confirmed in a DNA-linked case would be to approach the suspect's family. DNA samples obtained from confirmed biological relatives either can serve to keep the subject in the "active suspect" file, or can serve to eliminate him as a rapist altogether. Since investigators have been known to use this technique to identify murder victims (Hazelwood and Burgess, 1999), it would seem logical to extend this idea to the identification of perpetrators as well. However, the people sought to provide DNA samples need to be confirmed as actual biological relatives.

For law enforcement, DNA is all about correctly attaching previously obtained evidence to currently targeted victims and suspects in such a way that there is no room for error or doubt.

DNA Case-to-Case Match/Offender Not Identified: The DNA data bank links two or more cases through DNA without identifying a suspect.

This situation is similar to the Case-to-Case Match/Offender Identified in that the investigator is presented with a series of two or more crimes being linked by DNA. The link is usually discovered through the CODIS. However, a suspect is not identified. Again, all cases need to be reviewed, all victims and witnesses located and reinterviewed, and the entire evidence sequence scrutinized. It is crucial that the investigator reexamine all aspects of these previously unlinked cases for a common investigative thread. Case and victim/witness review can open up investigative leads previously unknown. Similarities and patterns of behavior can be uncovered. At this point, the uniqueness of this being a DNA-linked investigation falls into place as an investigative advantage when a suspect is developed. The investigations will more than likely take on the appearance of an otherwise linked serial attacker pattern with DNA coming into play only when a suspect is finally targeted.

In this situation there is no suspect readily identified. One of the concerns for law enforcement is that Case-to-Case matches either reveal or confirm that a serial offender has been at work and has not yet been identified. Since Case-to-Case matches might include incidents and investigations many years old and possibly long since forgotten and filed away, the investigator's task will include finding these old cases, piecing them together, and carefully reviewing all aspects of these investigations. Both victims and witnesses will need to be reinterviewed and their statements compared to what they said during the original investigation. All evidence—both tested and not tested—should be evaluated along with all crime-scene reports and photographs. A physical canvass of the crime scene, although now possibly years later, might also be warranted. All aspects of each individual case should be thoroughly reviewed then compared and contrasted to the other cases in the match set. Similarities and common themes need to be identified, researched, and examined (i.e., delivery men involved, suspect posing as a repairman, license plate canvass, same or similar commercial establishments involved, similar names and/or witnesses keep resurfacing, same or geographically connected cab companies, statements made by offender, cellular or hard-line phone records if applicable, credit card and/or bank card records if applicable, etc.). Ballistic and latent fingerprint evidence should also be reviewed and resubmitted for examination if appropriate.

An often overlooked investigative tool when searching for an unknown DNA-linked offender is the local DNA data banks maintained by certain jurisdictions or municipalities. These are non-CODIS DNA profiles maintained by local forensic labs but not provided to the CODIS. CODIS receives, compares, and archives DNA profiles from people convicted of certain and delineated crimes. Consequently, the CODIS might not have all the DNA profiles received at the local level that were developed from people who submitted DNA locally as suspects in other unrelated cases. Those DNA "fingerprints" are maintained at the local level since that suspect was never arrested and convicted for a delineated DNA crime. As a result, local data banks might have an offender on file that the CODIS does not. However, there might be unanticipated legal issues if an investigator in one jurisdiction or state requests that a DNA profile be run outside of the CODIS and through the local DNA data bank of another jurisdiction or state. Legal counsel is advised.

DNA Cold Hit: The DNA data bank identified an offender who is in custody.

Here, a suspect is identified through the CODIS as an offender linked by DNA to one or more crimes. The investigative protocols and potential problems are very similar to those outlined within the previous DNA links. The advantage here is that the offender's identity and location are known. Usually, the offender is in prison on an unrelated case—or at least in prison for a case not initially linked to the case under investigation. This affords the investigator time to reevaluate the case and establish the necessary contacts with both the victim(s) and witnesses. Similarly, evidence and crime scene documents can be located and examined. There are two things that an investigator needs to keep in mind when the offender is safely secured in a prison: (a) When is the offender due to be released? (b) When does the statute of limitations expire? Statute of limitation issues need to be considered in all old cases. DNA cases will frequently approach this issue in jurisdictions that have a statute of limitations.

Even when a Cold Hit is received, the investigator still needs to examine the details. The inmate in the Cold Hit might not be the offender wanted for the rape. He might be a past consensual encounter that the victim engaged at some point prior to her crime being reported. The most obvious advantage that a Cold Hit can offer is time. If the offender is in prison with no release date in sight and if the investigation is not constrained by statute of limitation issues, the investigator can methodically piece together and construct a case that can, perhaps, fortify any past weaknesses or shortfalls.

Example:

In the summer of 1995 a woman was dragged up to the rooftop of a building where she was beaten and sexually assaulted. Before fleeing, the perpetrator removed her clothing and tied her up with it. With her feet bound and hands tied behind her back, the victim crawled down several flights of stairs where she banged her body against a stairwell door to summon help. Several witnesses responded and discovered the victim bloody, naked and bound. The police were called but no substantive leads were developed. In the summer of 2003 a DNA Cold Hit identified her attacker as a man already in prison serving a lengthy sentence for a string of violent attacks. With time on their side, Investigators pieced the case together. They found the victim, the case reports, the crime scene reports and photographs, the medical records and the evidence reports. However, the witnesses that found the victim were never located and interviewed back in 1995! There was nobody to attest to the fact that the victim was originally found naked, crying, bound and injured. The Investigators anticipated that the perpetrator, once he learned that he was linked to the victim by DNA, might claim that his encounter with the victim was nothing more than consensual sex. Consequently, it became crucial to locate those missing witnesses. The Investigators canvassed buildings and knocked on doors. The witnesses were found and confirmed the circumstances under which the victim was discovered. As a result, her attacker was denied an alibi. He was also subsequently arrested and immediately sought to broker a plea bargain agreement with prosecutors.

DNA Warm Hit: The DNA data bank identified an offender who had already been linked to, or arrested for, this crime.

In this situation, law enforcement receives notice that an offender has been identified. The notice may or may not include the fact that the offender had already been identified and/or arrested for the crime(s). Upon receipt of a DNA hit notice where an offender is identified, the Investigator needs to run a background check on the suspect to confirm whether it is a Hot Hit, Cold Hit, or Warm Hit. If the suspect has been arrested or previously linked to this crime, it can be considered a Warm Hit. The prosecutor's office needs to be advised, whether or not the case is still being actively pursued in court. The investigator should then follow whatever administrative procedure is required by his or her jurisdiction. Frequently, a Warm Hit will be produced as a result of the original arrest: The offender was previously arrested for the Warm Hit crime and a DNA sample was obtained for a postarrest comparison, or as a result of compliance with state law requiring inmates or parolees convicted of certain crimes to submit DNA. The lab will develop a DNA profile and match it to the case that he was already arrested for. The lab may or may not know that the offender was arrested for the crime and will forward the DNA hit to the investigator as a fresh DNA match. It is up to the investigator to determine if it is a fresh DNA match or simply a confirmation of what is already known.

DNA PATTERNS

If one thing becomes clear, it is that DNA has the ability to uncover the hidden work of serial attackers years after the initial crimes. While investigators at the time may have had a hunch that the crimes they were confronted with were being committed by the same attacker(s), DNA now gives credibility to their foresight—or discounts their premonitions.

However, if investigators are confronted with a serial, or pattern, attacker, it is now incumbent upon them to aggressively engage these series of cases and piece together fragments of the puzzle. While serial, or pattern, cases have an investigative protocol of their own, a DNA-based case has the distinct advantage in that it can positively identify or exonerate a suspect. But before the investigator gets to that point, a suspect needs to be developed.

In a serial investigation there might be a case linked by the attacker's behavioral and physical similarities. However, there might be a situation where physical evidence at the time yielded little to corroborate this link. There might have even been evidence submitted at the time that was actually tested and came back with negative results for biological evidence. It would behoove the investigator involved to revisit *all* of the physical evidence and have items previously untested submitted for lab analysis. There have been documented cases of formerly untested evidence pulled from storage and sent to the lab years later only to confirm what the investigators felt years ago—that the cases were indeed linked by more than behavioral and physical similarities. They were linked by DNA.

Also a consideration when dealing with serial investigations that involve cases from years past would be to confer with the lab staff involved in the DNA analysis and profiling. The formats used for the profile comparisons have changed over the years. Evidence tested and submitted many years ago might have their DNA profiles formatted in a manner that can be incompatible with the computer language used to develop and format DNA profiles today. Consequently, there might be two cases sitting side by side and not linked because the DNA profiles in each were tested at different times using different formats. Therefore, if an investigator feels that an old case bears similarity to a case perhaps equally old but recently tested, he or she should confer with the lab to ensure that the case tested using an older format is retested and correctly compared to its potential companion case. This is a situation that will be corrected as DNA labs nationwide develop increasingly newer and more vibrant technologies.

When dealing with DNA evidence and labs that test for it, it is important to review from where the DNA profile was established—from where, physically, it was obtained. This applies not only to Case-to-Case investigations, but to all DNA investigations. This is where victim reinterviews, statement comparisons, and evidence examination become important. As a cautionary note, many labs will only test the primary piece of DNA evidence submitted and will not test any other submitted evidence if a DNA profile, *any* DNA profile, is quickly established. Consequently, the lab has no way of knowing if the DNA belongs to an offender or not. They just know that they were able to produce a DNA profile from what they considered to be a primary piece of evidence (i.e., a genital area or oral swab). For example, if a victim in a Case-to-Case Match/Offender Not Identified reports that the offender ejaculated on her clothing and the lab reports that the DNA was recovered from the vaginal swab, the investigator should recognize this discrepancy and have the lab test the clothing to ensure that it matches the DNA on the vaginal swab. If there is no match between the clothing and vaginal swab, another investigative lead to further identify the offender has just been established. If the victim's case is credible, then her attacker's DNA can be found on her clothing and that profile now needs to be entered into the CODIS for further comparison and, ideally, identification.

However, what this means is that the offender in the other Case-to-Case matches can be found on this case's vaginal swab and might be a person known to the first victim. If that is the case, an important lead was just uncovered and should be exploited to identify a potential serial offender, or at least an offender wanted in another open Case-to-Case match. In this instance, the victim's consensual boyfriend might be the DNA suspect wanted in the other case(s). His DNA was linked to the other crimes only after another man raped his girlfriend and she went to the hospital to be tested.

BUCCAL SWAB

Throughout this chapter references have been made to buccal swabs. A buccal swab is merely a swab, commonly a sterilized cotton swab at the end of a wooden or plastic stick, that is used to collect the skin cells that are normally sloughed off from the interior of the mouth. These cells are normally found in saliva, which is why DNA investigators frequently seek out such items as the cup that a suspect drank from or the gum he had chewed. However, in a formal and more controlled setting, the investigator would have the suspect rub the end of a cotton swab inside of his mouth against his cheeks and gums: This is called a buccal swab. Usually, two swabs are used. Each "rubbing" should last for about a minute. Ideally, upon removal of the swab, the swab should be allowed to air dry before being secured in a *paper* container (*never* plastic). Moisture might contaminate the swab if it is not allowed to dry properly. Different jurisdictions will have different means of securing a wet swab. Although there are specific buccal swab kits that resemble small sexual offense evidence collection kits manufactured for this very purpose, in the absence of these cardboard-contained kits, the investigator can simply place the completed swabs in a clean unused paper envelope. Caution needs to be exercised here: The investigator cannot afford to have his or her DNA left on the envelope. Protective gloves should be worn when handling the swabs and the suspect should seal the envelope himself if the envelope adhesive is gummed, requiring moisture to do so. The investigator should *never* lick the envelope adhesive lest there be a DNA transfer. In the absence of a gummed envelope, the paper container, envelope or otherwise, can be sealed with tape. Of course, a wet paper towel can be used to moisten the gummed edge. If the envelope has a self-adhesive, that too, can be used. But it is recommended that the envelope be ultimately sealed with tape—evidence tape would be preferred. It is also recommended that the container be marked for identification. The markings should include the suspect's name, date of collection, which investigator collected it, and the case number or any other administrative identifier that will attach those swabs to that investigation both at the lab and within that police department. The swabs should then be brought to the lab as quickly as possible.

Some police departments arm their investigators with DNA consent forms. These are simply permission forms that should be used whenever a court order to seize a DNA sample is unavailable or simply not required. It demonstrates that the swabs were voluntarily obtained. How the swabs were voluntarily obtained can potentially become a crucial part of the investigation. In the absence of a court order, a defense attorney will closely examine the conditions surrounding how his or her client voluntarily provided physical evidence that will become the linchpin of an investigation and prosecution that will seat his client in prison potentially for a lifetime. Frequently, the onus to demonstrate that the swab was obtained voluntarily and without coercion or false promise falls upon the investigator. Consequently, a signed DNA consent form becomes almost the equivalent of a signed Miranda warning document. The only possible exception here would be that some jurisdictions, and some prisons, will not allow the collection of buccal swabs from an inmate without a court order.

INDICTING "JOHN DOE"

Since DNA-based investigations can frequently turn into long-term investigations that may exceed the statute of limitations for prosecution, prosecutors have devised a strategy to "stop the clock" on case due to expire without an arrest or resolution. With this strategy, legal time constraints can be suspended and the case can continue until the offender is identified, located, and apprehended. The strategy is simple but not without drawbacks. Local prosecutors will bring the entire unsolved case, evidence and all, before a grand jury. The case is presented to the grand jury against an unknown assailant identified only by his DNA profile. If acceptable, the grand jury will indict this unknown offender based upon the DNA being offered as both evidence and proof of his existence. Some police departments and local prosecutors call this a "John Doe indictment" since they are indicting a person who is unidentified. The name "John Doe" is used because it is commonly employed by law enforcement to denote a person whose identity is not yet known. It is a commonly accepted slang term in many jurisdictions that has worked its way into both police and court documents to indicate that a person is not identified.

If the grand jury indicts the DNA profile, an arrest warrant can be issued based upon that indictment. An arrest warrant has no expiration date. Therefore, the perpetrator can be sought until captured. The statute of limitations no longer applies. However, the drawback is that since charges have been formally brought against this person in a court of law, the right to counsel usually automatically attaches. That means that the offender, when caught, usually has an absolute and automatic right to an attorney before being questioned. Although this might not stop investigators from talking to the assailant prior to the arrival of counsel, the statements given might not be able to be used in court. Each jurisdiction has its own set of legal requirements. Each investigator, therefore, needs to research the options available.

It is important to note that some jurisdictions have no statute of limitations for crimes such as rape. Consequently, these jurisdictions have no practical use for the "John Doe" indictment strategy. Other jurisdictions have statute of limitation "recipes" for designated felonies where a specific amount of time can be added on to the established time limit if the case experiences extenuating circumstances such as DNA or when the investigator can document that the suspect is out of the jurisdiction for a period of time. Additionally, there might be jurisdictions or agencies that will allow the suspect to be questioned after an indictment and/or arrest warrant has been handed down. Each jurisdiction and agency is different. "John Doe" indictments can only be used when it is legally and practically viable to do so.

However, in jurisdictions that have specific legal time constraints for misdemeanor and felony investigations, "John Doe" indictments on DNA-based cases can allow the investigator to clear the hurdles presented by the statue of limitations. These indictments, in effect, "stop the clock" when legally possible. It allows the hunt to continue.

THE VICTIM

When dealing with multiple cases and victims it is equally important to assess the victims themselves. Some law enforcement agencies call this "victimology." This is also an aspect of DNA investigations and has the potential to come into play when investigating both single and serial offenders. The reasons, motives, and circumstances of a person filing a sexual assault complaint are always significant. The various conditions present that are factored into one victim's motivation to come forward and contact the police can shed some light on a suspect regarding another unrelated attack. An extreme example of this would be where a victim presents herself to a hospital's emergency room and falsely reports being sexually assaulted. The victim does this with full knowledge of the fact that in certain jurisdictions by doing so he or she will jump to the head off the line as a sexual assault victim when asking for immediate placement in a drug treatment program. Past experience and refusals by hospitals and drug treatment programs, or being placed on long waiting lists in order to be accepted by various drug treatment programs, might drive this victim to such a tactic. Although this tactic does not in any way diminish the seriousness of this person's problem or predicament, it is a consideration investigators need to be aware of—including DNA investigators, because if the DNA in this person's sexual assault evidence collection kit matches DNA in other cases, then perhaps this person can identify his or her consensual partner (if this person is no longer being viewed as a victim), thereby identifying a single or a serial offender for the police.

Much has been written about crime victims. Within that context much, too, has been written about victims of sexual assaults. Literature abounds concerning both approach and interview technique. However, when approaching a victim in a potentially DNA-based investigation, investigators need to know certain facts because, as callous as it may sound, the victim is very much a part of the evidence trail. Consequently, all sex-crime victims need to be approached as partners in a complicated investigation. Until otherwise indicated, the investigator needs to treat the case as one that might potentially include DNA.

The interview with the victim should proceed as professionally as one would expect: with sensitivity, nonjudgmental support, and attention to detail. What becomes difficult for most Investigators and victims alike is the necessity to go over the actual physical elements of the crime in a graphic step-by-step fashion. Investigators need to know exactly what happened, when and where. Questions need to be asked: What did he do? Where did he place his penis? Did he ejaculate? Where did he ejaculate? Where did he touch you? Where did he place his mouth? Where did he place the knife or gun? Where did he place his hands or fingers? How many times did he penetrate you? If so, how? How was he positioned? What were you wearing? In what order was clothing removed? What did he use to tie you up? In certain instances the Investigator has to delicately pursue the possibility that the victim is withholding certain details out of fear or embarrassment. The interview needs to be both detailed and complete.

The investigator will have to learn if the victim had any type of sexual contact within the last 48–72 hours. The victim will have to describe what that sexual contact consisted of and with whom. If the victim had a consensual sexual partner within the past 48–72 hours, that person would need to submit a DNA sample for elimination purposes. Even if there was no ejaculation involved, even if the consensual partner was a female, these questions have to be answered since the DNA evidence recovered might not be semen based (i.e., saliva, hair, blood, etc.).

The victim might be reluctant to be entirely candid for many reasons. Among the reasons that the investigator needs to consider are not only the emotional issues, but issues that the victim might view as socially uncomfortable and embarrassing. The interview might reveal the fact that the victim was having an extramarital affair, a same-sex relationship, or that she/he engages in high-risk or unusual sex. It's not that the police are immediately concerned with the victim's social situation sexually, but investigators have to know what happened so the pieces of the puzzle can be put together correctly if there is DNA from a consensual encounter also found within the rape kit or crime scene. These are some of the difficult questions that need to be asked of a victim who had already suffered the intense trauma of a sexual assault. These are questions that have to be gently asked—but they have to be asked. While it is all about helping the victim, it is also about tracking a violent felon. Consequently, it is all about tracking the evidence.

Meeting with the victim also provides an opportunity for the DNA investigator to determine if there is any piece of evidence in the victim's possession that the police do not have (i.e., clothing or undergarments that fell behind a bed or furniture, soiled towel or tissue, unexpected items in a waste basket, key chain, pen, eyeglasses, etc.). It is not uncommon for a victim to discover something after the police had left. Usually, crime-scene investigations are thorough, but it is the victim (frequently not present during the processing of the crime scene) who knows what belongs and what does not. Consequently, if the crime scene were the victim's home, only she would know that an item of clothing found a week later under a sofa cushion in another part of the house did not belong to her or anybody she knows. Ask questions. That's what investigators do. Ask a question, solve a crime.

It might be useful to advise an understandably hesitant and anxious victim that there are reasons for each and every highly personal question that the investigator asks. However, the investigator should wait until the end of the interview before providing those explanations so as not to lead or bias the victim's answers during the interview process.

Frequently, a single sex-crime investigation is really two investigations operating simultaneously: one investigation to seek out the attacker and a second investigation to seek out the background of the victim. Prior police reports, arrests records, medical records, and psychiatric records—if any of these exist—need to be obtained. The victim's credibility and strategic utilization as a witness can be better assessed as a result.

Often, a DNA-based case involves an investigator contacting the victim of an attack committed a long time ago. Sometimes, it can be well over a decade or more later when the victim gets that knock on her door. While finding a victim after so many years might present a challenge in itself, so does confronting a victim and telling them that they've not been forgotten, and that recent developments either have revealed the identity of their assailant or have linked their case to others with no suspect identified yet. Each scenario poses its own set of vexing problems. But one single theme does resonate throughout: The police are now contacting the victim after some years and are requesting that they talk about a traumatic and emotionally searing event that they might have worked hard to forget or bury. Often, investigators confront a reality all too familiar to many victims: that sexual assault is akin to "murder of the mind." It is a physical crime that can smash the very foundation of a person's psychological being. Its emotional toll can be devastating and extends, all too frequently, to those associated with the victim. Families and friends are touched and suffer. The consequences can be far reaching and can destroy both the emotional and financial viability of the victims and their families. Here is where the talents, skills, compassion, and motivations of a sex-crime investigator come into play. This is what makes a sex-crime investigation—and a sex-crime investigator—so radically different from any other.

THE PERPETRATOR: INTERVIEW TECHNIQUES

Completing any type of criminal investigation is like trying to sit comfortably on a three-legged stool: It's only possible if the stool is built the right way, or else you'll either fall off or struggle to remain both seated and balanced. For an investigator, there are three legs of an investigation that need to be addressed to complete the stool: (1) victim and witness statements, (2) physical evidence, and (3) perpetrator statements. Obviously, successfully completing all three would be the ideal goal. However, that does not always happen. Still, these three areas need to be addressed regardless of the level of success achieved. Once addressed, these three areas need to be examined and affixed to the case in context. It's all about pieces of a puzzle.

Usually, the potentially weakest leg is the perpetrator's statement. Frequently, the other two legs of the stool can compensate for this so the investigation can still be completed. But these are the three components of an investigation. Each may or may not provide a degree of success in and of itself. However, it is how each component is constructed and attached to the case that counts. It is the piecing together of a puzzle. Talking to and listening to the perpetrator, even through his soul-wrenching and adamant denials, can add a piece to the investigative puzzle that the investigator never had before he walked into that interrogation room.

Much has been written about interrogation techniques, and so much of that literature is useful. Since each case has its own unique components, investigators should adjust their methods and approach, however slightly, for each and every case. DNA simply adds a unique twist to this mixture that obviously favors the investigator: We know the perpetrator was there in some capacity. It is now the investigator's job to find out the truth and to both construct and document a situation, through a conversation, that will prevent the perp from later recanting or denying what he told you. Whether the perp issues a full denial, provides a full confession, or offers that the sexual encounter was consensual, the investigator needs to lock him into that statement, document it, and ensure that he cannot change it to suit his needs when the case and its evidence later proves that it is to his dishonest advantage to try and do so.

There are usually only three responses that a suspect can provide an investigator when accused of a sex crime: (a) "It wasn't me, you got the wrong guy," (b) "It was consensual," or (c) "Yeah, I did it just the way you said I did!" Interestingly enough, when confronting an offender in a DNA-based criminal investigation, we walk into the interview room already armed with an advantage. But it is one advantage that cannot be freely advertised or squandered. Frequently, there is no advantage to letting the perpetrator know that there is DNA evidence unless the investigator feels that the perpetrator has said all that he is going to say. Introducing DNA into the conversation is a strategic decision that may or may not add to the interrogation or not. If the perpetrator hears "DNA," he might simply just shut down, shut up, or request a lawyer. He now knows what you know and knows that he has been caught. Sometimes, it can be advantageous at the end of an interrogation to tell the perpetrator that he has been identified through DNA and have him try to explain just how that happened. It might be useful to compare his post-DNA statement to his pre-DNA statement to see where his inconsistencies, if any, are. Each case is different.

"IT WASN'T ME, YOU GOT THE WRONG GUY"

This is a common response when interrogating a suspect in a sexual assault case—whether it's a DNA-based case or not. But in a DNA case it's the best response to hear other than "Yeah, I did it just the way you said I did!" Frequently, locking the suspect into a denial statement in a DNA-based case is as good as getting a complete confession. This puts him in the position of having to explain how his DNA came to be found in or on a victim, or crime scene, if he claims to have no connection to either. This is why it might be prudent to wait awhile before telling the perpetrator that he has been linked to the attack by DNA. It often pays to wait and see how the suspect plans to structure his response before bringing up the subject of DNA.

One strategy commonly used would be to sit down with the suspect and advise him that his name came up in an investigation. It's not always helpful to tell him that the investigation is a sexual assault or DNA based. Since he'll be curious, tell him that he will definitely be told of the case's particulars—but only after the investigator is satisfied that he is being truthful and can be trusted to offer an exchange of ideas. Ask him about himself, about his family, hobbies, cars, jobs, favorite restaurants, and so forth. Buy him lunch. Get him to tell you if he has a brother who is an identical twin. This can simply be accomplished by asking him the age and sex of his siblings. If a brother's age matches his, ask if it's a biological or a stepbrother. Obviously, if it's a biological brother we need the date of birth. If the date of birth matches his, we need to know if he is an identical twin. In a DNA case, the only other possible suspect will be the offender's identical twin since identical twins share the same DNA profile. This is an issue that needs to be addressed at the beginning during the "getting to know you" first phases of the interview. If an identical twin does exist—rare as that may be—find out where this twin was around the time of the crime. Camouflage the intent of your questions by casting a wide net and ask about all of his family and friends at the time under the pretext of learning more about him. In a DNA-based case, an identical twin brother is of obvious great interest.

Try to learn about the suspect's lifestyle and patterns during the time of the crime. Did he live in the area, have prior arrests in that area, work in that area, walk or ride through that area? Does he drive, own a car, ride a bicycle, or take a bus or train through that area? Did he have family or friends in that area? Did he go to school? Where? What were his work or school hours? The investigator needs to paint a picture of how this suspect lived his life and where. If it's an old, or cold, case reopened, the investigator has to reconstruct the suspect's lifestyle, often from many years past. In jurisdictions that have no statute of limitations, this can be a potentially arduous history lesson as the effort to recreate the suspect's life can reach back decades.

At some point it might be useful to show the perpetrator non-crime-scene type photographs of the area in question. It might be a park, an apartment building's exterior, or a hotel's identifying façade. But it needs to show the area in question in a simple and nonsuggestive manner. Ask the perpetrator if he is familiar with the area. Have him sign his response on the actual photograph. If he claims that he has never been in that building, park, or hotel in his life, then he will later have to explain how his DNA was found either in that area or in a person who has been documented as having been in that area and picked up his DNA within. If the perpetrator confirms that he is indeed familiar with the area shown in the photograph, have him sign the photograph confirming that, too. This will prevent him from later retracting that statement in order to distance himself from a crime scene where his DNA was found.

One technique that usually has some value is the "reverse photo ID." This is where the investigator shows the suspect a photograph of the victim as she looked during the time period in question. Ask him if he knows her. Document his response and have him sign the actual photograph (or a copy) to further confirm his response. The benefit here is that if the suspect does not know the victim, or insists that he does not, and his denial is recorded on the investigative report, case notes, and actual photograph, a potentially powerful piece of evidence was just created. Somehow the suspect, or his attorney, will have to explain how the suspect's DNA was found in a woman that he does not know.

This tactic is especially useful in "stranger rapes" where both the perpetrator and victim do not know each other anyway. However, the investigator needs to be prepared in case the perp claims that he does know the victim and recognizes the photograph.

"IT WAS CONSENSUAL"

If the perpetrator claims that he knows the victim or that the sexual encounter was consensual—it might have been! Or the perp is lying. This is where a thorough knowledge of the case, victim's statements, witness statements, evidence trail, and medical records come into play. The way a sexual assault investigation develops in the beginning with outcry witnesses, victim demeanor, area canvass, visual observations of physical injuries, 911 tapes, surveillance tapes from commercial establishments, comments by doctors, nurses, and paramedics, and responding uniformed police officers can paint a picture that can counter the perpetrator's claim that the event was consensual. But every investigator needs to be made aware that it just might, indeed, have been a consensual encounter. Or not.

> *Example:*
>
> In December 2002 a DNA match identified a suspect for the brutal sexual assault of a woman in April of 1993. The suspect was in prison serving time on unrelated charges. With the statute of limitations due to expire in April 2003, it took almost all of that time to find the victim and obtain her medical records. But the wait paid off.
>
> The victim had been savagely beaten with a metal pipe, her head lacerated and bleeding. The offender had raped her while she was unconscious.
>
> When interviewed, the offender admitted to frequenting the area in question. He would have had a hard time doing otherwise since his arrest record indicated numerous arrests in and around that area. However, he adamantly denied knowing the victim. As the interview progressed the investigator's strategy changed and aimed to have the offender admit that he knew the victim and had sex with her—but only after his initial denial was documented!
>
> Investigators felt that after the victim's injuries were revealed to the offender, he'd more than likely have an epiphany and remember that he knew her casually from the area. He might then claim that he had consensual sex with her before an unknown assailant beat her. And that was how, he might claim, his DNA came to be associated with the victim.
>
> Shortly, he admitted that he knew the victim and did indeed have sex with her—but it was consensual. This revelation was documented. No mention had yet been made

of the victim's extensive injuries, surgery, and hospitalization. By this point, the investigator had documented the offender as being prone to lying. The offender had first said that he never saw the victim before and denied having sexual contact with her; he later admitted to knowing the victim and having consensual sex with her. After the victim's injuries were brought up, the offender denied attacking her.

As the interview progressed, he admitted to having an argument with the victim but never hitting her. The story soon changed to the victim, a petite 5′2″, attacking the offender who stood hulking at 6′2″. The offender claimed that he wielded a metal pipe in self-defense but never struck her. As he was pressed for details and his contradictions pointed out, he admitted that they had consensual sex, argued afterward, and that he hit her with the pipe in self-defense.

The facts of the case show that the victim stated in the hospital in 1993 that the man who beat her was the man who raped her. She bore witness to her own rape, as she was fading and losing consciousness. The offender ultimately pled guilty to rape and assault charges.

This case illustrates the need to have the entire case file available for review and analysis and to have at least two interrogation strategies ready with a plan to change directions mid-interview when it seems likely that the offender will claim a consensual encounter and the investigator knows otherwise. Documentation of the suspect's contradictory responses is very important and can be brought up later on in the interview to either cajole the truth out of him or to catch him in another lie. The aim of any interrogation is twofold: to gain the truth, and to paint the suspect into a corner so he is unable to get out either in the interview room or in the courtroom.

"YEAH, I DID IT JUST THE WAY YOU SAID I DID"

Obviously, every investigator would prefer that a suspect simply confirm and document that he did indeed commit the crime as it was reported and described. Actually, this does happen. And it happens with some frequency. However, it would be prudent for investigators not to expect that type of response all the time. Interview preparation is a very important part of any investigation. This is particularly true with a sex-crime investigation, where the suspect might be loath to admit that he is a rapist because sexual predators do not fare very well in prison. He'll admit to murder, assault, robbery, burglary, and drug dealing—but to admit to a rape carries a dangerous prison stigma.

Often, full and complete confessions—or partial admissions—come after a period of time talking to and getting to know the perpetrator. Documentation of the perpetrator's statements, admissions, denials, and contradictions cannot be stressed enough. If a perpetrator is prone to fully confess, it will usually be after he is confronted with the myriad of case evidence arrayed against him along with the prospect of future photographic or physical line-ups with confirmatory DNA testing to later damn his cause.

To cajole a partial admission out of a reluctant perpetrator, try working around his upbringing as a child. If he had any sort of religious background at all, invoking the power of truth, guilt, and the value of remorse can be useful. Ask him to at least write a letter of apology to the victim if he cannot bring himself to admit it all to you. Probe his answers and prod his defenses. Find the weak link in his armor.

Again, the literature on interrogation and interview techniques abound. But in DNA-based sex-crime cases a sound denial can often be as good as a complete confession.

> *Example:*
> In late 2003 a suspect was interviewed by investigators after DNA had identified him
> as the offender in two gunpoint rapes. The interrogation lasted several hours, and
> the suspect offered countless inconsistencies that were gently pounced upon and
> offered back to the suspect to explain. In the end, the suspect knew that he was in
> deep trouble that he could not back-pedal out of. He was a man who had spent
> most of his life talking himself in and out of situations. But he still kept trying.
>
> Even after he was told that DNA linked him to both attacks, he still tried to con the
> investigators. When he realized every time he opened his mouth he was, in effect,
> building a case against himself, he stopped, got up, shook the investigators' hands,
> said "Good job, gentlemen, good job," and walked out defeated. He knew that he
> was going to spend the rest of his life in prison.

CONCLUSION

When investigating violent and pattern/serial crimes where the offender is not identified, even the smallest link can lead to a breakthrough that can identify a potential suspect. These are some of the most difficult types of cases a criminal investigator can encounter. Consequently, attention to detail is paramount when investigating violent or serial crimes. The circumstances surrounding a DNA-based serial crime investigation makes that point obvious.

Criminal investigators following DNA trails often pursue the most violent and elusive of predators. Often, they are repeat, or pattern, offenders—serial rapists. These cases create a uniquely vexing problem for law enforcement and a unique challenge for DNA investigators. Many rapists do not strike just once. Many lash out and attack repeatedly. Some do so in short brief violent spurts lasting days, weeks, and at times even months. Others pace themselves and burst out in fits of violence only after years of lying dormant. Perhaps their dormancy was the result of imprisonment, hospitalization, military service, and/or travel. Perhaps their psychological trip-wires lay taut but hidden, waiting for an event to trigger them.

The challenge for the DNA investigator—whether the offender is still lurking among us and walking the streets as a free man yet to be linked to these crimes, or removed from the community as a prison inmate waiting to be discovered by DNA while incarcerated—is not only to identify him, but to build a case against him that will stand the test of both an arrest and prosecution. Often, this means locating and/or re-creating a case from years past. Both victims and witnesses have to be tracked down. And the hunt for crime-scene photographs, evidence, case notes, and files still hangs over the investigator's head. Locating innocent victims and witnesses might at times prove as daunting as finding the criminal offender himself.

DNA is a powerful forensic tool that will only continue to grow as science develops newer technologies that will allow for better and more sensitive evidence collection and analysis. This will allow us to identify even smaller bits of genetic material at crime scenes, collect it, and send it to labs technologically adept enough to quickly extract and develop a DNA profile. As DNA technology progresses, we can expect that the turnaround time—the time from the collection of the evidence to the time there is a DNA match—will similarly improve with impressive speed.

DNA allows us to identify the guilty. But of equal importance is that it also allows us to exonerate the innocent. DNA is one of the most useful tools to have entered the investigator's toolbox in the history of law enforcement. It has been making the bad guys constantly look over their shoulders. It gives a refreshed and reinvigorating meaning to the phrase "the long arm of the law."

REFERENCES

Genge, N. (2002) *The Forensic Casebook.* New York: Ballantine Books, pp. 146–147.

Hazelwood, R., and Burgess, A. (1999) *Practical Aspects of Rape Investigation.* Boca Raton, FL: CRC Press, pp. 83–84, 95.

McClintock, T. (2001) "D.C. Bar Criminal Law and Individual Rights Section Newsletter: The power of DNA typing," Fall, p. 9.

Nickell, J., and Fischer, J. (1999) *Crime Science: Methods of Forensic Detection.* Lexington, KY: The University Press of Kentucky, p. 201.

Owen, D. (2000) *Hidden Evidence.* Buffalo, NY: Firefly Books, p. 209.

Ramsland, K. (2001) *The Forensic Science of C.S.I.* New York: Berkley Boulevard, pp. 65, 108.

Silverstein, H. (1996) *Threads of Evidence*. New York: Twenty-First Century Books, p. 46.

Turvey, B., and Chisum, W. (2002) *Criminal Profiling*. San Diego: Academic Press, p. 102.

U.S. Department of Justice (2003) "Advancing justice through technology," March, p. 2.

U.S. Department of Justice (2003) Without a trace? Advances in detecting trace evidence. *National Institute of Justice Journal*, Issue 249, pp. 6–8.

U.S. News & World Report, February 24, 2003, p. 41.

FURTHER READING

U.S. Department of Justice, DNA Evidence: What Law Enforcement Officers Should Know, **National Institute of Justice Journal**, Issue 249, July, 2003, pp. 10–15.

CHAPTER 10

VICTIMS OF RAPE

Brent E. Turvey, MS

> We are threatened with suffering from three directions: from our own body, which is doomed to decay and dissolution and which cannot even do without pain and anxiety as warning signals; from the external world, which may rage against us with overwhelming and merciless forces of destruction; and finally from our relations to other men. The suffering which comes from this last source is perhaps more painful than any other.
>
> **Sigmund Freud,** *Civilization and Its Discontents,* **Chapter 2 (1930)**

It is widely understood that victims of rape and sexual assault may continue to suffer through betrayals of the legal system if they choose to report the offenses that have been committed against them. First they must convince law enforcement responders and investigators that their situation is real—that they have indeed suffered a sex crime. This in order to get an investigation started in earnest. Second, they must convince a prosecutor to try the case in front of a jury—the victim's background and the circumstances of the attack play a role in whether this will actually occur. Third, they must convince a jury to convict. While this process is going on, they may suffer the stigma and disbelief from friends, family, and relatives. This is to say nothing of the weight imposed by potential public scrutiny should their identity come to light. Then there is always the potential of a not-guilty verdict. These are just some of the cumulative betrayals that victims are exposed to once they file a complaint.[1]

Investigators should be forewarned that victims dismissed by police indifference and blatant acts of negligence have the ability to hold law enforcement agencies and their civilian supervisors accountable in a civil court.

---

[1] These and other factors may lead to the many unreported sex crimes that exist beneath the known data. In 2001, it was calculated that only 39% of rapes and sexual assaults were reported to law enforcement officials, which is a little more than one in every three (Rennison, 2000). In 2001, there were 248,250 reported victims of rape, attempted rape, or sexual assault; 2002, there were 247,730 reported victims of rape, attempted rape, or sexual assault (Rand and Rennison, 2003). These numbers do not include victims 12 or younger.

Consider the Sparks, Nevada, case of Jennifer W., a 23-year-old student at the University of Nevada at Reno (see Sonner, 2001; "Woman sues police . . . ," 1999; "Rape victim . . . ," 2001). She called 911 in November of 1998 to report that a man she had met via the Internet after receiving an unsolicited email had abducted and raped her. As reported in "Woman: Police ignored . . ." (1999), Jennifer W. told police that after she received the unsolicited email:

> she went on to date Mobly several times, but she decided to break off the relationship Nov. 6.
>
> She said she invited Mobly over to her home on that day, and [his roommate Aaron] Cross accompanied him there.
>
> "They kidnapped me at my home," she said. "I was thrown into the trunk of their car like a suitcase" then sexually assaulted.
>
> But she said police did not arrest Mobly or Cross after she reported the incident. Instead, she said, police refused to believe her until after [a] 17-year-old girl was similarly assaulted.

The sexual assault took place in Mobly's home. She threatened to go to the police, but Mobly told her that nobody would believe that a rapist would drive her home; it would be her word against his. He was absolutely right.

Detectives from the Sparks Police Department interviewed Jennifer W. for 3 hours, accused her of lying, and threatened to prosecute her unless she immediately withdrew her complaint. She continued with the complaint and directed them to look for DNA evidence in his trunk, at which point detectives laughed at her. When she was taken to the hospital for a sexual assault examination, detectives warned her that she would have to pay for laboratory tests if the results came back negative for sexual assault, which they did.

Unfortunately, Mobly, and his roommate Aaron Cross, went on to commit another attack in January of 1999. They lured a 17-year-old girl to their apartment using the Internet and raped her in the same manner as Jennifer W. She escaped the next morning.

In March of 1999, Timothy Mobly (shown in Figure 10-1) and Aaron Cross pleaded guilty to attacking Jennifer and the 17-year-old girl. After their admissions, Mobly became a fugitive. He skipped bail and failed to appear at his sentencing hearing. He was facing life in prison. He was discovered and detained by Mexican authorities in January of 2002 and extradited back to the United States.

Figure 10-1
Timothy Mobley is extradited
back to the United States
from Mexico.

As a result of their conduct, Jennifer W. sued the city of Sparks, the Sparks Police Department, three detectives, and the police chief for damages of more than $900,000. She claimed that she had been humiliated when she tried to report the crime and was shunned by authorities until the second victim surfaced in January 1999. In August of 2000, she was awarded a $24,999 judgment (Sonner, 2001). She also reached an undisclosed settlement with the detectives and the chief of police ("Rape victim . . . ," 2001).

Consider also the case of a 41-year-old woman in New Port Richey, Florida, twice raped by the same stranger in her own home between 1998 and 1999, as reported in Davis (November 2002):

> The first attack occurred in the victim's New Port Richey home on Dec. 5, 1998. The woman, her left eye swollen shut and her mouth bloody with 15 broken teeth, told police she had been brutally beaten, bound, gagged, and raped at knifepoint by a stranger.

New Port Richey police detectives, however, did not believe her account and accused her of not telling the truth. "I believe that you were battered," Det. Jackie Pehote told the victim, who had a black eye and 15 broken teeth. "But I do not believe it happened the way you say" (Davis, February 2002).

Subsequently, a semen sample taken from the victim sat in a refrigerator at the department instead of being sent to the forensic laboratory for testing. New Port Richey police also failed to test evidence collected from the woman's house. Two weeks later, the NPR Police Department declared the investigation inactive (Davis, June 2003).

Twenty-nine days after the first attack, the same offender raped the victim again—but not before tripping a burglar alarm installed after the first attack, which the NPR police responded to. The rapist hid inside the victim's home until the police left; they did not enter the premises. Once the police were gone, he attacked the victim (Davis, May 2003).

While interviewing the victim after this second rape, NPR Police Detective Jackie Pehote asked her: "How could you be so stupid to move back into your house?" Pehote is currently NPR PD's lead detective, having more than 10 years with the department, but having served as a detective starting 1998 when the first rape occurred. Det. Pehote remained in doubt of the victim's rape allegations because of inconsistencies in her statements. Det. Pehote was convinced that a lover had battered the victim after consensual sex (Davis, June 2003).

Three days after the second attack, a milk crate filled with items stolen during the rape was delivered back to the victim's house with a note asking her for a date.

Four months after the second rape, the victim recognized her attacker in a convenience store. His name was John A. Casteel, and he lived 3 blocks from her home. Casteel had recently been released from prison after serving 14 years for a 1983 rape.

In August of 2001, after a 4-day trial, a jury took less than an hour to convict John A. Casteel (shown in Figure 10-2) of raping the woman. DNA tests linked him to both crimes. He was sentenced to life in prison without parole.

In November of 2002, the victim filed suit against the city of New Port Richey and the two detectives who handled her complaints, alleging that the second rape could have been prevented if police had properly investigated the first. The victim accused them of negligence and intentional infliction of emotional distress. According to reports (Davis, November 2002):

> New Port Richey Detective Jackie Pehote was accused by the victim of negligence and gross insensitivity.

Figure 10-2
John Casteel is sentenced to
life in prison without parole.

"I believe that you were battered," Pehote told the victim, who was left with a black eye and 15 broken teeth after the first attack. "But I do not believe it happened the way you say."

The attorney for the victim argued, among other things, that police failed in their duty to protect the victim (Davis, November 2003):

. . . given the totality of the circumstances, police had a responsibility to protect the woman after the first rape, especially when they responded to the burglar alarm just before the second attack.

The attorney for the city of New Port Richey argued that no such duty exists (Davis, May 2003):

Peter Walsh, the city's attorney for the civil case, argued Thursday that under the law, "there is no duty that New Port Richey owes to a citizen to protect them from a criminal."

The detectives, he said, "owed no special duty to catch this crook and perform a perfect investigation."

Both of the detectives that worked the case were cleared after an internal affairs investigation conducted by Captain Martin Rickus found no wrongdoing (Davis, February 2002):

"Some people may not feel that this approach should be used when dealing with a rape victim," Rickus wrote. "But it is also important that investigators make logical connections between what they are told by victims and what they observe."

The report criticized another detective, William Barrus, for waiting seven months before submitting for testing a semen sample taken from the woman after the first rape.

The report recommends that officers be given clear guidelines outlining the steps to be followed in submitting evidence. It also recommended a sergeant be added to the detective bureau to supervise investigations.

However, Det. Barrus was cited for failing to submit the semen sample from the cases in a timely fashion. He waited 7 months. John Casteel's DNA had been in a state database since 1996.

Furthermore, the internal affairs report also uncovered false testimony that Det. Pehote had given in an unrelated death investigation. She claimed under oath that she had not threatened to arrest the wife of the primary suspect in that case during an interrogation. A videotape of the interrogation proved otherwise. Captain Rickus said that she simply became confused under cross-examination and forgot about the threat. When this false testimony from Det. Pehote came to light, the suspect, who had originally been charged with first-degree murder, was allowed to plead guilty to manslaughter (Davis, November 2002).

Det. Pehote was also found to have given false testimony in the Casteel case (Davis, 2001):

In the Casteel case, she testified in a deposition that the Police Department at one time had no tape recorders. In fact, the department has never been without tape recorders, [Capt. Darryl] Garman [New Port Richey Police Department spokesman] told the Times for a story last month.

In June 2003, Pasco-Pinellas Circuit Judge Stanley Mills begrudgingly ruled that no matter how poor any investigation might have been (Davis, June 2003), the police cannot be held liable for negligence. Florida courts have made it clear, the judge said, that public safety agencies and their employees cannot be sued over discretionary judgments made during the course of an investigation, regardless of the consequences.

As of this writing, the rape victim's case against the city of New Port Richey is proceeding to trial on the victim's remaining claim of intentional infliction of emotional distress.

The collective lesson for police investigators is that the law may or may not provide them with protection in the form of immunity from liability related to negligence or false testimony. It depends entirely on state and local statutes, and subsequent case law. Furthermore, the surest way to incur liability is to form preconceived theories about the crime and victim culpability, and then to use these beliefs as a basis for investigative inaction. The surest way to alleviate liability is to treat each victim as equal and each complaint as valid until a thorough investigation has been completed. In this way preconceived theories will not provide for a failure to investigate, and victims have a better chance at justice.

VICTIMOLOGY

Victimology is the study of victims.[2] It is a general term that includes victims of any circumstance, including crime, accidents, and natural disaster. For the purposes of this work, we will be concentrating on victims of rape and sexual assault, and the term *victim* will refer to individuals who have suffered harm, injury, loss, or death.

WHY STUDY THE VICTIM?

Thorough investigators will spend at least as much time investigating victim history as they will the offender. As stated clearly and succinctly in the NIJ's *National Guidelines for Death Investigation* (1997):

Establishing a decedent profile includes documenting a discovery history and circumstances surrounding the discovery. The basic profile will dictate subsequent

---

[2] Most researchers trace the modern study of victimology to the seminal works of Hans von Hentig and Benjamin Mendelsohn, in which they established victim typologies and explored various aspects of the victim–criminal relationship (Tobolowsky, 1999). According to Karmen (1984), Mendelsohn actually coined the term *victimology* in an article written in 1947.

levels of investigation, jurisdiction, and authority. The focus (breadth/depth) of further investigation is dependent on this information.

Victimology is first and foremost an investigative tool, providing context, connections, and investigative direction. In an unsolved sex crime, where the offender is unknown, a thorough victimology defines the suspect pool. The victim's lifestyle in general and their activities in particular must be scrutinized in order to determine who had access to them, what they had access to, how and when they gained and maintained access, and where the access occurred.

If we can understand how and why an offender has selected known victims, then we may also be able to establish a relational link of some kind between the victim(s) and that offender. These links may be geographical, work related, schedule oriented, school related, or hobby related, or the victim and offender may be otherwise acquainted. These links provide a suspect pool that includes those with knowledge of or access to the linked areas.

Furthermore, if we can understand how and why an offender has selected their previous victims (by studying the complete victimology, as it changes or fails to change over time and throughout incidents), then we have a better chance of predicting the type of victim they may select in the future.

Even if we come to understand that an offender's victim selection process is random, or more likely, opportunistic, this is still a very significant conclusion. Victimology is all about getting to know the victim as a real person. Unless we know *who* a victim is, or was, and how they lived, we cannot say that we truly know the context of their demise, or the events leading up to it.

THE VICTIM AS A REAL PERSON

There is a tendency with some investigators, administrators, and forensic personnel to deify or vilify the victim in a given case.

Deification involves idealizing victims, who are perhaps young school children, missing adolescents, or those who arrive pre-deified by the press and public opinion. Because of the political or public culture of a certain area or region, certain victim populations tend to be more politically or publicly sympathetic. This view facilitates rationalizations about time expended on the case while other investigations suffer, and does not allow for an unbiased victimology by virtue of depriving the crime, and the investigation, of true victim context.

Vilification involves viewing certain victim populations as worthless or disposable by their very nature. This view presumes that it is okay, or not as bad, to commit crimes against people of certain lifestyles, races, religions, or creeds. This can include people of a certain ethnic origin, people of a certain social class, prostitutes, drug dealers, drug addicts, or even runaways. Ultimately, this tends to be defined by an investigator's subjective sense of personal morality. This view facilitates investigative apathy.

Investigators who hold this view of certain victim populations may not feel the need to investigate any crime committed against them thoroughly. The irony is that some of the most skillful serial offenders exploit these attitudes of law enforcement. They choose their next victim, in part, based on whether or not law enforcement perceives them as disposable.

The reality is that victims of crime are human beings. They are not the fictional constructs of our prejudices and biases born of our own morality, true crime novels, or films. As we have always secretly feared, and must be willing to admit, they are not unlike our own daughters, sons, mothers, fathers, sisters, brothers, wives, husbands, or friends. They are no more or less deserving of our attention because of their lifestyle choices or situations. If we idealize them, or vilify them, we will not learn who they were. We will not have the context for a complete investigation, and we will not be able to glean investigative direction based on victim–victim and victim–offender connections. Subsequently, if we proceed with the mindset that any victims are more or less deserving of our attention, then we do so at the risk of failing to serve justice. And we will most certainly speed ourselves away from our own humanity.

RISK ASSESSMENT

One of the many lenses that may be used to examine the victim–offender relationship is in terms of the *risk* involved. The amount of risk is defined by the amount of exposure to a possibility of suffering harm or loss. The question of risk is a matter of perspective. That is to say, there is victim risk and there is offender risk. Both must be considered when performing any type of victimological assessment.

RISK VERSUS BLAME

The terms and definitions provided in this chapter are designed to help investigators describe the relationship of a victim to their lifestyle and environment, and subsequently of a given offender to that victim. They should provide the investigator with a language to characterize the facts of a case as established by the behavioral evidence. They also provide insight into the defenses that an offender is willing go up against in order to sexually attack their victim.

It is important to remember that victims are not responsible for the predatory acts of sex offenders. This may seem like an obvious concept, but unfortunately, many people do blame the victim as being partially or wholly responsible for certain crimes committed against them. On this point, Groth

(1979, pp. 7–8) details common myths regarding victims of sexual assault which merit our attention, including:

- The victim in some way was party to the offense, by being seductive or provocative.
- If the victim wanted to, they could have prevented an assault.

This kind of judgmental, and often moral, reasoning has no place in criminal investigation.

To help further elucidate this concept of inappropriate bias and judgmental reasoning, we can contrast the risk of a prostitute with that of a student who lives in a secure building.

A prostitute, working in a major metropolitan city, lives a lifestyle that exposes them to a relatively high possibility of suffering harm or loss at any given moment. The risk-increasing hazards involved with such work include the overall criminal environment, the hours of operation (nighttime), the exposure to a constant barrage of strangers with potentially violent intentions, and the association of prostitution with the drug culture, to name but a few.

A student living in a college town, in a secure building, may live a lifestyle that conversely exposes them to a relatively low possibility of suffering harm or loss at any given moment. However, there are moments of vulnerability for the student. One such moment would be the 5 to 7 seconds that the student takes to get from a vehicle, through their locked front door, into their secured building, or vice versa into a locked vehicle. In either case there is a moment of distraction, when all attention is focused on finding one's keys and using them to open the door of the building or vehicle. There are many offenders who literally plan to lie in wait for those moments of vulnerability in such instances, and then exploit them for some criminal gain (robbery, sexual assault, etc.).

This contrast demonstrates that choices made by a victim to ensure personal safety, despite their best efforts, are only going to be sufficient for an offender of a certain skill level. Put another way, whether or not a victim is going to fall prey to an offender is not exclusively a function of their efforts to maintain personal safety. It is also a function of the amount of skill and time a particular offender is willing to put into their method of approach and method of attack.

Investigators might blame the prostitute in the foregoing example for allowing themselves to become the victim of a violent crime. The same investigator might view the student in the same example as an unfortunate victim of circumstance. However, establishing victim "blame" does not add anything to the investigative effort. All citizens have moments of vulnerability, no matter what type of lifestyle risks they take. Criminals are not entitled to commit crimes just because citizens have these moments of vulnerability. As we will discuss, this begs understanding the difference between *lifestyle risk* and *incident risk*.

RISK: THE VICTIM'S POINT OF VIEW

Victim risk is the amount of exposure to a possibility of suffering harm or loss that investigators perceive for a given victim. It is not necessarily the victim's perspective. It is also very subjective, depending upon the knowledge and experiences of the investigator examining a given case.

Surprisingly, differences in investigator knowledge and experience do not tend to account for the majority of the varying opinions that can exist regarding victim risk in a particular case (though they certainly are factors). When there is a disagreement regarding victim risk between two investigators, the biggest difference between them tends to be their thoroughness. Many investigators approach their victims with a great deal of prejudice, born out of preconceived theories developed from incomplete initial victim information. This initial information, if unchecked by a thorough victimology, can easily become the basis for underinformed assessments of victim risk.

Another influence on a victim risk assessment, sadly, can be the political kind. If the investigator feels that a certain victim risk suggests a certain offender type (the type that is suspected by others involved in the case), there is the danger that the investigator may tailor the risk assessment by ignoring risk factors in their assessment.

To guard against any of these pitfalls and projections, the best defense is always going to be thoroughness and reliance upon fact, rather than supposition, as the basis for all conclusions in an assessment. The veracity of an interpretation, or conclusion, should always be judged by how well it accounts for all of the known facts.

CATEGORIZING VICTIM RISK

The terms and definitions in the next paragraph are adapted from, but not identical to, terms from Hazelwood (1995, p. 171).

The term *low-risk victim* refers to an individual whose personal, professional, and social lives do not normally expose the individual to a possibility of suffering harm or loss. The term *medium-risk victim* refers to an individual whose personal, professional, and social lives can expose that person to a possibility of suffering harm or loss. The term *high-risk victim* refers to an individual whose personal, professional, and social lives continuously expose him or her to the danger of suffering harm or loss.

But know that victim risk is relative.

The question to be investigated and answered here is what a particular victim is specifically at risk for. Ask how a particular victim's lifestyle places them in harm's way, if at all. For example, a young teen male may have a high victim risk of domestic violence by virtue of living with a parent who is an abusive alcoholic. At the same time, they may have a low victim risk of being abducted, raped, and killed by a stranger, by virtue of a very fixed schedule with a great deal of group activity and adult supervision.

If that is not complicated enough, victim risk can, and should, be categorized even further still in terms of *lifestyle risk* and *incident risk*.

VICTIM LIFESTYLE RISK

Lifestyle risk is a term that refers to the overall risk present by virtue of an individual's personality and personal, professional, and social environments. The belief is that certain circumstances, habits, or activities tend to increase the likelihood that an individual will suffer harm or loss. Furthermore, it is also affected by the personality traits possessed by the victim. Lifestyle risk, then, is a function of who the victim is and how they relate to the hazards that their environment contains. The following is a list of general personality traits that can increase victim lifestyle risk. It is not an all-inclusive list but rather a place for the investigator to begin. The more prevalent or intense the trait in the victim's history, the greater the overall lifestyle risk:

- Aggressiveness
- Anger
- Emotional outbursts
- Hyperactivity
- Impulsivity
- Anxiety
- Tendency toward addictive behavior
- Tendency toward self-destructive behavior
- Phobias or irrational or inexplicable fears
- Difficulty with authority
- Personal space or privacy issues
- Passivity
- Low self-esteem
- Depression or hopelessness
- Negativity

- Emotional withdrawal
- Listlessness
- Need for attention or sympathy
- History of self-injury
- History of suicide threats and/or attempts
- Aberrant sexual behavior

These traits should be viewed in the context of the victim's age, occupation, criminal history, and any previous history of being a victim of crime.

VICTIM INCIDENT RISK

Victim incident risk is a term that refers to the risk present at the moment an offender initially acquires a victim, by virtue of the victim's state of mind, and the hazards of the immediate environment.

Factors that can increase victim incident risk include, but are not limited to, the following:

Victim Lifestyle Risk: Discussed previously, this must be established to help place the incident in context and begin to assist in establishing victim state of mind.

Victim State of Mind: This refers to the victim's emotional state before, throughout, and subsequent to an attack (when applicable) as evidenced by convergent patterns of behavior and any reliable witness accounts. An agitated or distressed emotional state, for example, may increase victim incident risk. Additionally, a victim who feels safe in a particular environment or situation will act differently from a victim who does not.

Time of Occurrence: Certain times of day can be more risky than others, but the interpretation of the impact of this factor is highly dependent on the location of the occurrence. It can affect elements such as available light for certain activities and the number of people present in public environments.

Location of Occurrence: Location is one of the most important factors to affect victim incident risk. Certain environments contain more criminal activity, others may place a victim out of the immediate reach of assistance, and still others may physically isolate the victim, all of which can increase the incident risk of victims at the lowest lifestyle risk.

Number of Victims: It is generally true that there is safety in numbers. Those who engage in activities with others are often at lower risk of victimization. This tends to be true as long as the people that an individual is with are not at a high lifestyle or high incident risk. Each case must be examined and evaluated separately.

Drug and Alcohol Use: The use of mind-altering substances may decrease one's physical reaction time and impair one's judgment. In either case, victim incident risk is increased dramatically, even for otherwise low-risk victims.

These factors inform the overall context of the crime, and each one on its own has meaning only when placed in the context of all of the known facts in a case. The examination of one factor on its own cannot in itself be used to gauge victim incident risk.

RISK: THE OFFENDER'S POINT OF VIEW

Offender risk is the amount of exposure to a possibility of suffering harm, loss, or identification and capture that an offender perceives when attempting to acquire a victim. It is not the same as the investigator's perspective, or the victim's perspective; an offender can only evaluate a given situation using their own knowledge and experience. This should be gauged and assessed by an evaluation of the behavioral facts of the case as indicated by the physical evidence.

Like victim risk, offender risk is also relative.

The question to be investigated and answered here is what obstacles did the offender perceive, or consider, in terms of acquiring a particular victim and avoiding identification and capture? And, how did the offender subsequently plan to defeat those obstacles, if at all? Ask of each incident, how much risk did the offender believe they were taking?

To fully understand the nature and extent of offender risks taken in a given incident, they should be categorized in terms of *modus operandi risk* and *offender incident risk*.

MODUS OPERANDI RISK

Modus operandi risk is a term that refers to the nature and extent of the skill, planning, and precautionary acts evidenced by an offender before, during, and after a crime to achieve their goal, and avoid detection by law enforcement. The more skill, planning, and precautionary acts evidenced by an offender, the lower they may perceive their own risk to be.

Low MO Risk

Low MO risk is a term that applies to offenders who evidence a high amount of skill, planning, and precautionary acts before, during, and after a crime. This term can refer to incidents where victims are selected who will not be immediately missed should they fall prey to misfortune, if they are missed at all. It may also be applied to incidents where the offender has more control, or where there is a low possibility of the offender being noticed and later identified. Examples include:

- Dark or poorly lit locations
- Times during the day; late at night or early in the morning when few people are around to witness offender activity
- Offense locations far away from where an offender resides
- Offenses where an offender abducts a victim to a remote or secluded location
- Offenses where a stranger victim is selected by virtue of lifestyle
- Availability (i.e., a runaway or prostitute)

It is important to keep in mind that high-risk victims are not necessarily low MO risks (i.e., unattended children are high-risk victims, but they can also be a high risk to an offender because they are missed almost immediately by parents, caregivers, or guardians).

High MO Risk

High MO risk is a term that applies to offenders who evidence a low amount of skill, planning, and precautionary acts before, during, and after a crime. This term may be applied to offenders who acquire victims who will be immediately missed should they fall prey to misfortune, and who are very well monitored by their environment and/or those who care for them. It may also be applied to incidents where there is a high possibility of the offender being noticed, and later identified, when acquiring a victim (such as someplace very public during the daytime, or where there are security monitors).

High MO risk is a term that also describes instances where an offender increases their chances of being recognized, identified, or apprehended by commission or omission. This can include, for example, actions such as allowing the victim to see their face, letting the victim survive an attack, and attacking victims who are known to the offender and can easily be linked back to them.

The offender's perceptions of risk regarding offense behavior can dictate their actions during any offense planning, during the offense itself, and after the attack has been completed. It is important to recognize that the offender's perceptions regarding an offense can be incomplete or downright wrong. In any case, assessing *modus operandi* risk gives investigators direct insight into the offender's perspective regarding what planning, skill, or precautionary acts are necessary and what are not.

OFFENDER INCIDENT RISK

Offender incident risk is a term that refers to the amount of exposure to a possibility of suffering harm or loss that investigators perceive for a given offender. It is not necessarily the offender's perspective. *The offender does not necessarily operate with the same insights into victimology and crime-scene characteristics as the investigator.*

> *Example:*
>
> The author was asked to consult on a case where a 21-year-old female victim, dressed in tight pants, a gold chain belt, lots of makeup, and glamour nails, was walking back and forth on a street just after midnight on a cold winter evening. The offender, who just happened to be driving by after an evening of drinking at topless bars up the freeway, believed that she was a prostitute. He drove around the block once, parked his van in a quiet residential area, and then made his approach on foot. He engaged her in some initial conversation and then attacked her, dragging her down the block, back into the residential area. He then proceeded to bind her, sexually assault her, and torture her over the next 2 hours inside of the van. When he was through he wrote down the information from her ID, helped adjust her clothing and jewelry (which he had torn), warned her not to tell anyone, let her out, and then drove off.
>
> In point of fact the victim was not a prostitute, but rather a young lady who was on her way to a nightclub when her vehicle had broken down. The offender perceived that this victim put him at low risk. He perceived that she would not likely report the incident, as she was a prostitute. He also perceived that she would not be missed by anyone, so he did not have to take her to a remote location to engage in a prolonged assault, even though he could have easily done so.

The lesson here is to try to understand the offender's perspective. What does the offender see, and how does that influence their behavior (if at all)? Establish the offender's MO risk level. Then compare those behaviors with the offender incident risk and determine the level of knowledge that the offender appeared to be operating with.

It should be noted that not all offenders will tender themselves to the considerations of blatant or obvious risks, and in such cases that information can be very useful. What kind of risk an offender is willing to take in order to acquire a certain victim tells you not only a great deal about what that offender desires, but what the offender is willing to do in order to achieve that desire.

INVESTIGATE THE OBVIOUS

Offenders of any kind may know, be acquainted with, or have some form of undiscovered connection with their victims. Investigate the obvious connections between all victims and potential suspects. Proceed by questioning all investigative assumptions related to the established victimology when first presented with the facts of any case. Get multiple sources of independent corroboration before accepting something as fact. If a fact cannot be established, then it should not be assumed.[3]

VICTIMOLOGY: GENERAL GUIDELINES

In terms of what is required for a thorough victimology, the NIJ's *National Guidelines for Death Investigation*, Section E: "Establishing and Recording Decedent Profile Information," is a good place to start. However, the author does not recommend that readers confine themselves to any single victimology checklist. Rather, an investigator should treat nothing about a victim as trivial. This means analyzing each characteristic that presents itself until it is an exhausted possibility, to see how it relates to the rest of the victim information.

Weston and Wells (1974, p. 97) provide a quick checklist of preliminary victimological queries that have proven to be most useful in eliciting investigative information.[4] This is the kind of information that should be gathered immediately, ideally before the investigator arrives at a given crime scene. The queries include:

- Did the victim know the perpetrator?
- Does the victim suspect any person? Why?
- Has the victim a history of crime? A history of reporting crimes?
- Did the victim have a weapon?
- Has the victim an aggressive personality?
- Has the victim been the subject of any field [police] reports?

The following are some basic victimological inquiries that this author has found useful when applied to actual casework. Gathering this information, along with

---

[3] For specific texts devoted in part or whole to victimology, the author strongly recommends that readers reference the following works:

- Finkelhor, D. (1979) *Sexually Victimized Children*. New York: Free Press.
- Haugaard, J., and Reppucci, N. (1988) *The Sexual Abuse of Children*. San Francisco: Jossey-Bass Publishers.
- Herman, J. (1981) *Father–Daughter Incest*. Cambridge, MA: Harvard University Press.
- Monteleone, J. (1996) *Recognition of Child Abuse for the Mandated Reporter*, 2nd ed. St. Louis: GW Medical Publishing.
- Strong, M. (1998) *A Bright Red Scream*. New York: Viking Press.

[4] Prior to this, O'Connell and Soderman (1935, p. 258) discussed victims primarily in relation to the issue of victim identification without delving into psychological or investigative issues.

the careful examination of physical evidence, provides the starting point for investigative activity. Again, no one checklist can suffice; the investigator must be willing to sift through each victim's history carefully, with no preconceived theories. This list is inclusive of items found in *National Institute of Justice* (1997):

1. Determine the victim's hard physical characteristics (race, weight, height, hair color, eye color, etc.).
2. Determine the victim's occupation or place of work, and their shift schedule.
3. Compile the victim's criminal history.
4. Compile a list of the victim's daily routines, habits, and activities.
5. Compile a complete list of victim family members with contact information. Interview each of them.
6. Compile a complete list of victim friends with contact information. Interview each of them.
7. Compile a complete list of victim co-workers with contact information. Interview each of them.
8. Compile the victim's medical history.
9. Compile the victim's psychiatric history—interview all of the victim's mental health care providers.
10. Compile a list of the victim's medications. Compare this with known victim toxicology.
11. Compile the victim's financial history (credit card usage, tax returns, insurance policies, etc.).[5]
12. Compile the victim's educational history.
13. Compile a residence history of the victim (where they have lived, when, with whom, etc.)
14. Spend time, when possible, with the victim's personal items, in their personal environments (hangouts, work, school, home/bedroom, etc.). Examine any available photo albums, diaries, or journals. Make note of music and literature preferences. Do this to find out who the victim seemed to believe they were, what they wanted everyone to perceive, and how they seemed to feel about their life in general.
15. Compile all available information regarding the victim's computer and Internet usage. When available, at least the following should be attempted:

   • Determine the victim's ISP
   • Determine the victim's email addresses

---

[5] This kind of information and documentation is generally available in the victim's home. If the victim's home is not the primary scene, it must still be examined as though it were involved in the crime.

- Examine the victim's address book/contact database
- Examine the victim's incoming and outgoing email
- Examine all documents on the victim's computer
- Determine the last known usage of the computer and various software applications

16. Create a timeline of the victim's last known activities, factoring in all witness statements and physical evidence.
17. Travel the last known route taken by the victim in whatever manner they did. Try to see that route from their perspective, and then from the potential perspectives of the offender. Keep these perspectives separate.
18. Look for security video cameras along the victim's route, or potential route, that may have documented the victim's activities, or even the actual crime.

CREATING A TIMELINE: THE LAST 24 HOURS

Retracing a victim's last known actions and creating a timeline are critical to understanding the victim as a person, understanding their relationship to the environment, understanding their relationship to other events, and understanding how the victim came to be acquired by an offender.

The general purpose here is to familiarize the investigator with the last known activities of the victim and subsequently determine, if possible, how a given victim got to a place and time where an offender was able to access them. This picture needs to be built from the ground up. It is a rewarding and illuminating process that is not to be overlooked.

A good approach to creating this timeline of locations and events includes at least the following steps:

- Compile all available forensic and factual data.
- Compile all of the crime-scene photographs.
- Compile all witness data.
- Create a linear timeline of events and locations.
- Create a map of the victim's route for the 24 hours prior to the attack, as detailed as possible.
- Physically walk through the victim's last 24 hours using the map and forensic evidence as a guide.
- Document expected background elements of the route in terms of vehicles, people, activities, professionals, etc., for the time leading up to, during, and after the victim was acquired. It is possible that the offender is, or was masquerading as, one of those expected elements.

Attempt to determine the following:

- The point at which the offender acquired the victim
- The place where the offender attacked the victim
- How well the attack location can be seen from any surrounding locations
- Whether or not the offender would need to be familiar with the area to know of this specific location, or get to it
- Whether or not the acquisition of the victim was dependent on some sort of routine or schedule, and who could be aware of that schedule
- Whether or not knowledge of the route would require or indicate presurveillance
- Whether or not this route placed the victim at higher risk or lower risk
- Whether or not the acquisition of the victim on that route placed the offender at higher risk or lower risk

THE SUSPECT SKETCH

If the victim did not know or otherwise recognize their attacker, investigators should have them review photographs of known sex offenders, burglars, those arrested for property crimes, and other viable suspect groups. Once a specific suspect has been identified, it is important to view them as just that—a suspect. The correct procedures for employing photo line-ups and live line-ups of suspects are discussed in Chapter 13.

When no suspect is generated otherwise, investigators may consider asking a victim to work on a suspect sketch with a police artist. Though not always productive in terms of generating actual suspects, either activity draws the victim into cooperation with investigators and can be a positive and empowering experience. However, this alone is not sufficient reason to have one drawn up.

The suspect sketch is a common feature in modern investigations, but there are some who question its use. Their complaints are not unreasonable. In some cases, the use of an accurate sketch has led to good tips from the public and the capture of suspects who were later convicted. In other cases, the use of a suspect sketch has derailed the investigation for years, bearing little or no resemblance to the true offender. And in still other cases, suspect sketches have helped to implicate the innocent as in the case of Christopher Duffy and Troy Graves. See Figures 10–3 and 10–4.

The problem with suspect sketches, as with any form of eyewitness ID, is that they are rendered from the tenuous, fallible memories of traumatized witnesses. Furthermore, they are an interpretation of what the artist is being told, not a precise depiction. The sex-crime investigator should therefore use this resource with the utmost care and reserve. Suspect sketches can be a useful guide to general suspect features, help raise public awareness about an unsolved case,

Figure 10-3

Pictured at left, 31-year-old Christopher Duffy shared similar features with the composite of the Center City serial rapist in Philadelphia, PA. Tipsters contacted authorities about Duffy at least seven times during their investigation. DNA evidence eventually cleared him and convicted the true rapist, 30-year-old Troy Graves.

Figure 10-4

Air Force Airman Troy Graves, the Center City Rapist. He targeted young women living in ground-floor apartments and often entered through unlocked doors or windows in the early morning hours. He would not use a weapon and spoke in a friendly and gentle manner to his victims. He also confessed to the strangulation murder of 23-year-old Wharton MBA student Shannon Schieber. Graves was married and was described as shy, socially awkward, and a soft talker with a lisp.

and sometimes they can lead to an arrest. But when used inflexibly, like a photograph, they may cause more harm than good. And that is how the general public will view it.

The decision to release a sketch once it has been rendered is always a judgment call. Remember that any suspect sketch is only as reliable as the memory of the victim or witness, that person's ability to articulate accurate descriptive information, and the skill of the artist rendering the sketch. If there are doubts about any of these, releasing a sketch may not be advisable.

RAPE TRAUMA SYNDROME

Ann Burgess and Lynda Holmstrom first coined the term Rape Trauma Syndrome (RTS) to describe a recurring pattern of postrape symptoms in victims of rape and sexual assault (Burgess and Holmstrom, 1974). In that work, they describe RTS as "the acute phase and long-term reorganization process that occurs as a result of forcible rape or attempted forcible rape."

As explained in DelTufo (2002):

> Rape Trauma Syndrome is considered a post-traumatic stress disorder consisting of four elements. The term Rape Trauma Syndrome originates from a 1974 study conducted by Drs. Ann Burgess and Lynda Holmstrom. For one year the study followed ninety-two women, who initially came to the Boston City Hospital Emergency Ward because they were raped. Burgess and Holmstrom interviewed the women at the hospital and then later counseled them by phone and through home visits, keeping detailed notes of symptoms reported and changes in thoughts, feelings, and behavior. Upon analysis of their findings, Burgess and Holmstrom applied the term "Rape Trauma Syndrome" to the reactions and coping mechanisms that rape victims may use to deal with the aftermath of rape. Rape Trauma Syndrome is the "acute phase and long-term reorganization process that occurs as a result of . . . rape or attempted . . . rape. This syndrome of behavioral, somatic, and psychological reactions is an acute stress reaction to a life-threatening situation."

According to Burgess and Holmstrom (1974):

> In the first hours, victims may show behavior such as crying, sobbing, smiling, restlessness, tenseness, and joking. Or they may have feelings that are masked behind a calm, composed, or subdued façade.

> In the first weeks, victims may suffer from physical trauma, skeletal muscle tension, gastrointestinal irritability, and genitourinary disturbance. Emotionally they may show signs of shock, numbness, embarrassment, guilt, powerlessness, loss of trust, fear, anxiety, anger, disbelief, shame, depression, denial, re-triggering, and disorientation.

After 3–4 months, victims may show signs of generalized anxiety and fear, as well as:

- Disturbance—of eating, sleeping, thoughts, relationship.
- Impaired social functioning.
- Difficulty in maintaining/establishing relationships.
- Guilt for not preventing assault.
- Sudden, unpredictable changes of residences and disappearances.

After as many as 4 years, victims may show signs of:

- Anger towards offender, legal system, family, and friends.
- Diminished capacity to enjoy life.
- Hypervigilance to danger.
- Continued sexual dysfunction, such as decreased desire and arousal, and even flashbacks.

Contrary to the way that some experts have presented it in court, Rape Trauma Syndrome is not a type of scientific test that accurately and reliably determines whether or not a rape has occurred. The symptoms of RTS may follow any psychologically traumatic event. Just because someone has these symptoms does not necessarily mean that they have been raped. It is only when the initial traumatic event is known to be rape that a patient may be diagnosed with Rape Trauma Syndrome. As explained in DelTufo (2002):

> Rape Trauma Syndrome lacks the scientific precision to prove causation because studies have not been able to demonstrate a specific link between particular symptoms and rape: not all victims of rape react the same way; some victims of rape do not show signs of Rape Trauma Syndrome behavior; and other factors unrelated to the rape can also affect psychological and emotional trauma after a rape. Furthermore, Burgess and Holmstrom intended their Rape Trauma Syndrome theory not to provide prosecutors with a legal analysis to prove rape, but rather to provide a therapeutic tool to aid in the diagnosis and treatment of psychiatric patients.

Additionally, RTS describes symptoms that occur with some frequency among typical victims, but does not describe every single case. Victim reactions to rape vary. Failure to show these symptoms is not evidence that a rape has not occurred.

REFERENCES

Burgess, A., and Holmstrom, L. (1974) "Rape Trauma Syndrome" *American Journal of Psychiatry*, September, 131(9): 981–986.

Davis, C. Detective's actions face inquiry, *St. Petersburg Times*, October 2, 2001.

Davis, C. Handling of rape cases is upheld, *St. Petersburg Times*, February 7, 2002.

Davis, C. Victim sues in handling of rape, *St. Petersburg Times*, November 19, 2002.

Davis, C. Judge may toss suit in rape, *St. Petersburg Times*, May 30, 2003.

Davis, C. Victim of rape dealt setback in court, *St. Petersburg Times*, June 26, 2003.

DelTufo, K. (2002) Resisting "utmost resistance": Using Rape Trauma Syndrome to combat underlying rape myths influencing acquaintance rape trials. *Boston College Third World Law Journal*, Spring.

Groth, A. (1979) *Men Who Rape*. New York: Plenum Press.

Hazelwood, R. (1995) Analyzing the rape and profiling the offender, in Burgess, A., and Hazelwood, R. (eds.), *Practical Aspects of Rape Investigation: A Multidisciplinary Approach*, 2nd ed. New York: CRC Press.

Karmen, A. (1984) *Crime Victims: An Introduction to Victimology*. Pacific Grove, CA: Brooks/Cole Publishers, pp. 2–3.

National Institute of Justice (1997) *National Guidelines for Death Investigation*, Research Report 167568, Washington, DC: Author.

O'Connell, J., and Soderman, H. (1935) *Modern Criminal Investigation*. New York: Funk & Wagnalls.

Rand, M., and Rennison, C. (2003) Criminal victimization, 2002. *Bureau of Justice Statistics: National Crime Victimization Survey*, NCJ 199994, August.

Rape case reveals pattern of poor police work, *St. Petersburg Times*, August 29, 2001.

Rape victim looks to move on after sentencing, Associated Press, February 20, 2001.

Rennison, C. (2000) Criminal victimization 1999. *Bureau of Justice Statistics: National Crime Victimization Survey*, NCJ 182734, August.

Sonner, S. Fugitive in jail on $5 million bond for Sparks rapes. *Las Vegas Review Journal*, January 12, 2001.

Tobolowsky, P. (1999) Victim participation in the criminal justice process: Fifteen years after the President's Task Force on Victims of Crime." *New England Journal on Criminal and Civil Confinement*, Winter.

Weston, P., and Wells, K. (1974) *Criminal Investigation: Basic Perspectives*, 2nd ed. Englewood Cliffs, NJ: Prentice Hall.

Woman: Police ignored suspects' earlier assault, *Las Vegas Review Journal*, January 17, 1999.

Woman sues police who disbelieved rape charge, *The Holland Sentinel*, March 24, 1999.

CHAPTER 11

FALSE REPORTS

Brent E. Turvey, MS

The conscience of the world is so guilty that it always assumes that people who investigate heresies must be heretics; just as if a doctor who studies leprosy must be a leper. Indeed, it is only recently that science has been allowed to study anything without reproach.

Aleister Crowley, *The Confessions of Aleister Crowley*, **Chapter 17 (1929)**

In his seminal work on criminal investigation, in a section dedicated to a discussion of the dangers of preconceived investigative theories, Dr. Hans Gross provides one of the earliest and arguably most informed segments on the subject of those who make false allegations of sexual assault (Gross, 1924, pp. 13–14). His discussion includes topics such as the various motivations for filing false reports, the occurrence of self-injury, and the related responsibilities of the investigating officer. In a more recent text on the history of rape, a discussion of the conceptualization and consequences of such false reports provides little more insight into these and associated problems (Palmer and Thornhill, 2000, pp. 159–161). Here the topic is couched in a general discussion of deceitfulness and sex differences, with some statistics. Their conclusion is that there are social factors and sex differences that may contribute to a general reluctance to believe female rape allegations (Palmer and Thornhill, 2000, p. 160).

An even, illustrative, and modern perspective of false reporting was recently provided from the pen of a prosecutor turned defense attorney turned news commentator, in the wake of sexual assault allegations made against a very popular sports figure (Spilbor, 2003):

The statistics on false rape reports in the U.S. are widely divergent, and often too outdated to be meaningful. Not surprisingly, the numbers also depend on whom you

This chapter has been adapted from material originally published in Baeza, J., and Turvey, B. (2002) False reports, in Turvey, B. (ed.), *Criminal Profiling: An Introduction to Behavioral Evidence Analysis*, 2nd ed. London: Academic Press.

ask. Organizations that tout a feminist agenda claim the number of false rape reports to be nearly non-existent—about two percent. But other organizations, taking the side of men, claim that false reports are actually very common—citing numbers ranging from forty-one to sixty percent.

Amid the statistics, the truth is impossible to ascertain—but it's plain that false reports are indeed made, and that they can ruin the life of the accused, whether or not a conviction follows.

Falsely reporting any crime is shameful. Falsely reporting a rape is especially heinous. The liar who files the false claim dishonors—and makes life all the more difficult for—the many true victims who file genuine rape claims because they have been terribly violated, and seek justice for it. At the same time, and perhaps even more seriously, the false report begins to destroy the reputation, and sometimes the life, of the accused from the very moment it is made—a fact of which many accusers are keenly aware.

At this point, a review of the literature is in order.

THE LITERATURE

Every so often false reports will be mentioned in the press, and unofficial false report rates will be disclosed to the public.[1] However, the professional literature on the subject of false reports is sorely lacking. There have, for example, been very few scientific studies conducted to ascertain false report rates or percentages. Further still, there is a dearth in the published literature on even the subject of false reports. Put another way, those studying rape and sexual assault do not typically examine false reports, let alone talk about them. This is due in no small part to the fact that many researchers fear being maligned, blacklisted, or threatened with sanctions should their results not agree with the prevailing sexual–political climate.[2]

---

[1] An editorial in *The New York Post* on the now-infamous Oliver Jovanovic false report case (Dunleavy, 1999) quoted District Attorney Linda Fairstein from an interview in *Penthouse* magazine where she stated, "There are about 4000 reports of rape each year in Manhattan, of these half of them didn't happen." In a more recent article, it was stated that out of 2000 uninvestigated cases in Philadelphia, PA, from 1995 to 1997, investigators determined that "600 were false reports or allegations that did not amount to crimes" (Inquirer Staff, 2000).

[2] This opinion is based on discussions with fellow investigators and forensic examiners. It is also based on the fact that a number of the articles reviewed for this chapter received scathing commentary from the professional community unrelated to reliability and validity. A common complaint was that the identification and prosecution of false reporters causes legitimate victims to fear reporting their crime to law enforcement. Thus, it has been argued that presenting the false report numbers, any numbers, harms victims and casework by preventing legitimate victims from coming forward for fear of not being believed, or even being prosecuted for a crime.

MacDONALD

MacDonald (1973) shows that, in 1968, the national average for false reports of forcible rapes was 18%. He further shows that, in a 1-year period in Denver, Colorado, 25% of all forcible rapes were unfounded. He goes on to explain that this is a conservative figure, as the police in Denver did not record as false reports any cases where there was a doubt as to the veracity of the complaint. In the same study, MacDonald (1973) states that 20% of the forcible rape complaints were actually in doubt. He does not footnote or otherwise reference this information.

TWO PERCENT FALSE REPORT RATE

There is no shortage of politicians, victim's advocates, and news articles claiming that the nationwide false report rate for rape and sexual assault is almost nonexistent, citing a figure of around 2%. This figure is not accurate.

In researching this issue, Haws (1997) has prepared a brief but detailed account of his failed attempt to find a legitimate and accurate study supporting the claim that 2% is the right number:

> If you talk to sexual assault counselors, you'll most likely hear the low figure: that 2 percent of all accusations of sexual assault reported to law enforcement across the country are later found to be false, which, the counselors say, is the same rate as for other crimes. Of all the numbers out there, this has been cited most often, appearing in publications from *The Boston Globe* to *The Houston Chronicle*, *The Christian Science Monitor*, *The Minneapolis Star Tribune*, *Newsweek*, and *Editor & Publisher*.
>
> Sometimes the figure is attributed to a particular source, but that's still no guarantee the numbers can't be challenged. Marcia L. Roth, the author of the 1996 op-ed article in *The Louisville Courier-Journal*, attributed the 2 percent rate to the 1993 book *Rape, the Misunderstood Crime*, by Julie Allison and Lawrence Wrightsman. But Allison and Wrightsman weren't so unequivocal. Noting that the frequency of false rape reports is difficult to assess, they didn't do their own study; instead they looked at a synthesis of research findings from a 1979 book, *Understanding the Rape Victim*, by Sedelle Katz and Mary Ann Mazur. Katz and Mazur, it turns out, had reviewed studies dating back to 1956 that showed the frequency of unfounded and false rape reports ranging from a low of 1 percent to a high of 25 percent. Allison and Wrightsman simply chose the study that showed 2 percent.
>
> Another named source for the 2 percent figure has been *Against Our Will*, the groundbreaking book on sexual violence by Susan Brownmiller published in 1975. She was reporting on the phenomenon that in New York City, the rate of false

accusations dropped "dramatically" to 2 percent as soon as the police began using policewomen instead of men to interview complainants.

Sometimes the 2 percent figure appears without any attribution. It simply floats out there, as in a 1994 article in *The Houston Chronicle* that cites a women's center official as the source for the false-rape-report figure of "between 2 and 3 percent." Period. And sometimes the attribution is vague but credible-sounding, like "federal statistics" or "the FBI." In 1992, The Boston Globe reported that a rape counselor stated the 2 percent rate for false reporting of rapes is the same as for false reports of other crimes—"according to the FBI."

But the FBI has been saying since 1991 that the annual rate for the false reporting of forcible sexual assault across the country has been a consistent 8 percent (through 1995, the most recent year available). That's four times higher than the average of the false-reporting rates of the other crimes tracked by the FBI in its *Uniform Crime Report*. The agency's guidelines define a report as false when an investigation determines that no offense occurred. A complainant's failure or refusal to cooperate in the investigation does not, by itself, lead to a finding of false report.

The writings of Susan Brownmiller, published three decades ago, stand out on this issue. In her work *Against Our Will*, she argues (Brownmiller, 1975, p. 435):

> A decade ago the FBI's *Uniform Crime Reports* noted that 20 percent of all rapes reported to the police "were determined by investigation to be unfounded." By 1973 the figure had dropped to 15 percent, while rape remained, in the FBI's words, "the most underreported crime." A 15 percent figure for false accusations is undeniably high, yet when New York City instituted a special sex crimes analysis squad and put police *women* (instead of men) in charge of interviewing complainants, the number of false charges in New York dropped dramatically to 2 percent, a figure that corresponded exactly to the rate of false reports for other crimes.

First, the statistic cited appears specific to New York City, so its use as a number representing national trends is inappropriate. Secondly, to support the 2% statistic provided, Brownmiller (1975) references "'Remarks of Lawrence H. Cook, Appellate Division Justice, before the Association of the Bar of the City of New York,' Jan. 16, 1974 (mimeo), p. 6." In response to criticisms for using this non-peer-reviewed remark at a public meeting as the basis for professional arguments and opinions, she wrote this brief response some 20 years later (Brownmiller, 1995):

> The cite from the New York City Rape Analysis Squad was reported by Judge
> Lawrence Cooke to the NY Bar Association in 1974. Cooke was a leading appellate

justice at that time. Cooke, the Bar Association, and the NYC Rape Analysis Squad were impeccable sources. The information was fresh & exciting. It had appeared nowhere else. The person who attempted to discount it in the post you reproduced denigrated New York State's leading appellate justice, a city agency, and me.

Ultimately, we are left to conclude that there is no published study or data to support any claim that the false rape allegation rate is or was ever down around 2%—not anywhere, even according to those who originally cited that number. Rather, the number comes from a judge giving a speech to some attorneys 30 years ago whose source has, to date, not been validated.

Unfortunately, this 2% figure has found its way into legitimate research and texts on the subject. For example, an otherwise excellent text on the subject of police culture and sexual assault recently surprised the author by referring to false reports as a "myth" (Gregory and Lees, 1999, p. 90):

> Behind the mutual recriminations about the handling of rape and sexual assault cases, the dominant discourse on male and female sexuality, shared by most police officers, lawyers, magistrates, judges and juries, gives rise to the myth of false allegations and to misunderstandings around the notion of consent.

It is not inappropriate to think that it is time we moved forward and away from the citation of this figure to newer, more reliable data.

McDOWELL

Charles P. McDowell, a Supervisory Special Agent serving with the United States Air Force, studied false reports extensively. Although his study is unpublished, McDowell examined 1218 cases that were initially reported as rapes. He found that 460 rape allegations were proven, 212 rape allegations were disproved, and 546 rape allegations were unresolved. The total percentage of false reports for all reported rapes was 17.41%, or 212 out of 1218. The total false report rate for all resolved rape allegations was 31.55%, or 212 out of 672 (McDowell, 1985).

KANIN

Professor Eugene Kanin of Purdue University in Indiana conducted one of the few published studies on false reports. Professor Kanin studied all rapes ($n = 109$) occurring in an unnamed midwestern city with a population of 70,000 from 1978 to 1987. Kanin found a 41% false report rate (Kanin, 1994). It should be noted that in Kanin's study a false report could only be identified by virtue of a confession from the alleged victim. In the same paper, Kanin also discussed the results of an unpublished study he conducted in 1988. This study examined all forcible rape complaints during a 3-year period on two midwestern college campuses. The false report rate in that study was 50% (Kanin, 1994).

DIETZ AND HAZELWOOD

During testimony at the Tawana Brawley grand jury, Dr. Park Elliot Dietz, a forensic psychiatrist, proposed 20 false report red flags that he had developed along with retired Supervisory Special Agent Roy Hazelwood of the Federal Bureau of Investigation (FBI) (*Court TV*, 1997). During this testimony, Dr. Dietz specifically mentioned the existence of false report red flags and stated that, based on his own research and his consultation with Hazelwood, there are 20 characteristics that have appeared in false allegation cases. These are provided below[3]:

- The story tends to be bizarre or sensational.
- The pseudo-victim injures herself, sometimes seriously, or simulates injury for the purpose of gaining support.
- The pseudo-victim presents herself in such a way that people believe no one would do this to herself.
- The pseudo-victim does not initially report the incident to police.
- A stranger is accused.
- The pseudo-victim claims that overwhelming force was used or that she resisted greatly or that there were multiple assailants.
- The account is either overly detailed or very vague.
- The pseudo-victim reports having her eyes closed during the attack or that she was unconscious, or passed out, or has no memory of what happened or was drugged, and so cannot provide details.
- The pseudo-victim is indifferent to her injuries.
- The expected laboratory findings are absent.
- The pseudo-victim is vague about the location of the assault or there is no evidence at the scene to corroborate the complaint.
- Damage to the clothing is inconsistent with the injuries.
- There are escalating personal problems in the life of the pseudo-victim.
- The pseudo-victim has been exposed in the past to accounts of similar things.
- The pseudo-victim's post-assault behavior is inconsistent with the allegations.
- The pseudo-victim is uncooperative with the investigation.

---

[3] Most of these red flags also appear in Aiken, Burgess, and Hazelwood (1995). More specifically, the section regarding false report red flags, "Red flags of false rape allegations," was written by Charles P. McDowell and Neil S. Hibler (Hibler and McDowell, 1995).

- When the pseudo-victim talks to the authorities, she tends to steer the conversation away from the specific to the unprovable.
- There is writing on the body of the pseudo-victim.
- There is a history of making other false allegations.
- There is a history of extensive medical care.

Clearly, some of these red flags have value. However, some of the red flags are much too vague and open to interpretation to be of investigative use. Consider this examination of the language used by Dietz (*Court TV*, 1997):

> *Delay in reporting*: What constitutes a delay? Does a delay constitute a victim calling a friend before calling 911, or is it a delay if a victim reports the crime three months later? This is a highly subjective criterion that requires more explanation to be useful as a potential indicator.
>
> *Post-assault behavior*: The post assault behaviors need to be spelled out. Are the authors referring to the victim laughing, becoming hysterical, crying, and/or not crying at inappropriate moments? Without some kind of detail and elucidation, this red flag will be difficult to apply to an actual case.
>
> *Accusing a stranger*: Many false reporters will actually name a suspect in their complaint. This may not constitute the majority of false report cases, but there have been far too many to agree that accusing a stranger is a red flag. It begs serious study before more can be inferred from its mere occurrence.
>
> *Writing on the body*: While this occurred in the Tawana Brawley case, it has occurred infrequently in the authors' case experience. If it can be determined through crime reconstruction and/or wound pattern analysis whether the victim could have made the injury, then this behavior has value to the investigation. If it cannot, merely the existence of such evidence would seem to indicate little. This too is a behavior that begs serious study before more can be inferred from its mere occurrence.

HIBLER AND McDOWELL

Hibler and McDowell (1995) propose a strategy for interviewing a potential false reporter. They suggest that the investigator utilize a supervisor or co-worker to act as a "second opinion" by having this person speak with the victim, and perhaps confront them with inconsistencies, during or after the interview. As for the initial interviewer, they write, "It would be counterproductive for this person to voice any doubts as to the veracity of her report." They point out that the principal investigator needs to be available to the person alleging rape and should maintain a nonjudgmental, supportive, and sympathetic relationship with her. Issues regarding unresolved inconsistencies, conflicts, or the lack of supporting data should be made by an investigative supervisor or coworker. In this way, the vital relationship between the complainant and the principal investigator can be maintained and perhaps even improved.

There are several problems with this suggestion:

First, if there are any doubts about the veracity of the victim's story, the person in the best position to examine those doubts is the one who knows the most about the case. This should be the principal criminal investigator. A coworker or investigative supervisor very often lacks knowledge of the details of the case in question. With false reports, a working knowledge of case details is everything.

Second, if there are doubts, and these doubts are supported by physical evidence, the investigator must explain to the alleged victim that they know that the alleged victim is not telling the truth. This is where interviewing skills come into play. There are many ways to let someone know you are aware that they are lying. And it is possible to be nonjudgmental, supportive, and sympathetic at this point in the interview. The investigator does not have to blurt out, "I know you are lying!" Other, more gentle tactics can be used. In fact, these are the same tactics an investigator might use when interviewing a suspect in a rape case.

Third, Hibler and McDowell (1995) fail to address the issue of Miranda warnings. Miranda warnings are typically read to a suspect when there exists custody and interrogation. The courts have interpreted custody and interrogation in many different ways. In some jurisdictions Miranda warnings do not have to be read to a suspect who is being interrogated in a police facility unless he is not free to go. In others it is common practice to issue the warnings to any suspect interviewed in a police facility, whether they are free to go or not. At some point in the interview the investigator may have evidence that disputes the alleged victim's story. This evidence may be so strong that the investigator plans to arrest the alleged victim. In this case, in some jurisdictions, it is best to read the alleged victim (who is now a suspect in a criminal investigation) his or her Miranda warnings. This action alone may be effective in obtaining a confession from a false reporter.[4]

[4] This occurs because once the alleged victim knows that the investigator is aware of their deception, and that the situation is serious, they may realize that it would be a grave error to continue with their fabrication. In such instances, it is best to read the alleged victim their Miranda warnings, leave the room, and then give them an opportunity to reflect on the gravity of their circumstances. Upon reentering the interview room, an investigator may find the alleged victim eager to confess. At this point, the victim should be charged with some kind of crime along the lines of falsely reporting a crime.

Fourth, an investigative supervisor may lack the skills necessary to conduct a proper interview of the alleged victim. Although this is not always the case, many investigative supervisors have backgrounds in patrol, or other duties unrelated to criminal investigation. Just because someone has a higher rank or a greater number of years of experience does not mean that they have experience in criminal investigation, interviewing, or the requisite knowledge of the case at hand.[5]

Fifth, quite often the relationship of the investigator and the alleged victim, now the perpetrator, is improved after the victim has been confronted and has subsequently confessed. The victim may feel relieved of a burden and may actually thank the investigator for helping them through a troubled time in their lives. This occurs regularly in the advent of a false reporter who was given the opportunity to confess by a deliberate and thorough interview. In short, the belief that bringing in another investigator or supervisor to interview the alleged victim will prove any more successful than having the principal investigator conduct the interview is false, and furthermore a waste of investigative time and manpower. The principal investigator should be capable of conducting the interview and confronting false reporters, as long as the investigator has been well trained and has the support of his or her agency.

---

[5] Law enforcement agencies in every country and in every part of government have varied internal workings and duties. In U.S. law enforcement, the duties typically break out thus: Patrol officers are at least in charge of traffic enforcement and first response to crimes (rendering aid, responding to citizen complaints, securing any crime scenes, then waiting for detectives to arrive). In some departments, they may inherit investigative duties when detectives are not assigned to certain types of cases such as burglaries or domestic violence (it is a little-known fact that some law enforcement agencies do not actively work these types of cases . . . ever—see the U.S. DOJ Bureau of Justice Statistics and note the 0% solve rate of certain types of crimes like burglary and auto theft). Detectives are in charge of criminal investigations. In many agencies, these are merely patrol officers who have passed an exam and have received nothing in the way of additional, formal training in criminal investigation.

The irony here is that large agencies handling a great deal of crime have little room in their budgets for such training, resulting in highly experienced investigators with little actual training (placing into question the quality of that experience). Conversely, smaller agencies with less crime to contend with have more money available for training, often resulting in highly trained investigators with little or no experience applying what they've learned (hence, when the big case comes along they don't have enough practice to do things properly). Sergeants who are overseen by lieutenants supervise detectives and patrol officers. These supervisors are in charge of reviewing the cases and performance of those out in the field. It is possible that these supervisors may receive their positions without any achievement in, or knowledge of, the work performed by their subordinates. This by virtue of having only performed non-case-related administrative duties during their careers.

As this is meant to suggest, being in law enforcement does not necessarily make one an authority on the subject of criminal investigation. Only detectives with the right mix of training and experience can or should make this claim. The truth is that those who can make this claim usually have a more humble attitude, and those who shouldn't often wind up giving interviews on CNN.

BROWN, CROWLEY, PECK, AND SLAUGHTER

Brown, Crowley, Peck, and Slaughter (1997) conducted research to address the issue of genital injury in female sexual assault victims. This study examined 311 rape victims who entered San Louis Obispo General Hospital's emergency room in California between January 1985 and December 1993. The study also examined a control group of 75 women, from the same location and time period, who had engaged in consensual intercourse. Of those 75 women, 48 had initially been evaluated as victims of rape, but later admitted that their encounters had been consensual. Though not conducted to address the issue of false reports specifically, this study ultimately revealed a 13.37% rate of false rape reporters. This study, it should be remembered, involved victims and alleged victims who presented to an emergency room. This is necessarily a different sample than presents at police departments to merely file a report; we would expect a lower percentage of false reporters to willingly submit to a physical examination.

INVESTIGATIVE SUGGESTIONS

The literature review just given demonstrates two things. First, investigators and forensic examiners are very likely to encounter a false report if they work sex crimes. Second, because of the dearth of literature and the limited investigative experience behind it, investigators and forensic examiners will be unprepared when this happens. The section that follows is intended to be a general guide until such time as better and more vigorous research can be published on the subject.

A FRAME-BY-FRAME ANALYSIS

The interview with the alleged victim of sexual assault is perhaps the most vital part of a sex crime investigator's effort to establish the facts of a case. Unfortunately, it is common for even seasoned investigators to accept an alleged victim's statement or story without question or suspicion. This may arise out of a fear of disturbing the alleged victim, being viewed as politically incorrect by victim advocates and colleagues, or lack of knowledge about the investigation of potential false reports. It may also arise out of a common problem that inhabits much of police culture: investigative apathy.[6] Many investigators

---

[6] It is important to note that there are other considerations motivating investigators, forensic examiners, and researchers away from the identification and study of false reports. Aside from apathy, an overall political environment that sanctions such identifications and investigations can promulgate a fearful investigative mindset. This fear of political reprisal routinely provides for the failure to correctly identify and investigate false reports to their fullest conclusion. As discussed in Palmer

will go to great lengths to explain away factual inconsistencies in an alleged victim's story. Inconsistencies that have been explained away by the investigator or criminal profiler in this manner, rather than actually investigated, should be treated as suspect. Whatever the case, there is no legitimate reason to avoid a detailed, frame-by-frame examination of the logic and rationale in any victim's statement. Regardless of the consequences, every alleged victim's statement must be examined thoroughly and enthusiastically. If there are breaks in the logic, they must be explained through a rigorous process of investigation. As stated in Gross (1924, pp. 14–15):

> In order to know exactly the attitude to be maintained towards what has passed, all the circumstances of the crime must be clearly taken into account and submitted to strict logical examination from their commencement to their last stage. If at a given moment something has not been explained, suspicion is justified and pause must be made at the point where the logical sequence is broken, for the purpose of examining if there is no better way of explaining the fact. If one is found the rest of the inquiry is easy.

Frame-by-frame analysis is a very important interview concept that all sex crimes investigators should consider when interviewing a victim (or an offender for that matter). The best way to explain this concept is to compare it to a film. If we watch a film in real time, we may understand what is going on, but we might not see all of the details. If we then run the film in slow motion, frame-by-frame, we are better able to recognize the minute details of the action. Sex crimes investigators must use this concept if they wish to capture all of the details of the crime. A thorough *frame-by-frame analysis* can act as the gateway to identifying false report cases.

FALSE REPORT INTERVIEW STRATEGY

False reporters may report their allegations to the police in the same way that real victims do. The interviewer will want to treat the potential false report case the same as any other, up until the point of the second part of the formal interview, the frame-by-frame analysis. This is where the interviewer should confront the alleged victim with any contradictions between their statement and the physical evidence. Any contradiction in the victim's statement needs

---

and Thornhill (2000), "To some feminists, the concept of false rape allegation itself constitutes discriminatory harassment." It is not unreasonable in such an environment for investigators and criminal profilers to be terrified that the investigation of a false report will bring about the brutal derision of colleagues, superiors, the media, victim advocates, and the general public.

to be explained by the victim, *not* the interviewer. The interviewer should never accept contradictions in the victim's statement because the victim was upset or experiencing trauma. These contradictions must be explained logically.

Upon encountering a contradiction in the alleged victim's statement, the interviewer will want to say something along the lines of the following:

> I have been investigating sex crimes for X amount of years and I have interviewed many girls/guys who have for one reason or another not told the whole truth. I know you're not telling me the whole truth, but I also know that you seem like a good person. I'm sure there is a perfectly good reason why you are not telling the truth. Without the truth I can't help you with your problem. I know you have a problem or you wouldn't be here today. The problem with not telling the whole truth is that it starts off like a small snowball rolling downhill and as it picks up speed it gets bigger and bigger. In the end it can crush you. Let's stop the snowball before it gets too big because right now it is out of control.

At some point it may be fruitful for the interviewer to explain that knows the alleged victim is not telling the whole truth and then leave the room for a few minutes so that the alleged victim can think about what has transpired. Quite often, upon re-entering the room, the interviewer will find the victim crying and the confession will be near.

If the victim does not confess right away, the interviewer must keep at it. The interviewer should maintain a neutral affect, as to show annoyance or anger will only serve to make the alleged victim more defensive. The interviewer should remain calm and confident throughout the interview. The most important thing to remember when dealing with a false reporter is to remain confident. When the interviewer is not confident, the false reporter will undoubtedly see this, and in turn they will feel more certain that the truth will not be revealed.

At some point during the interview, the interviewer may be convinced that the false reporter is lying. In this case, it is recommended that the investigator inform the false reporter that they are now a suspect in a criminal investigation, and then read them their Miranda warnings.

THE BAFRI

As suggested by the dearth of research in the area of false rape allegations, and the lack of professional awareness and willingness to investigate such instances, the need for tools to assess potential false reports is not being met or even pursued. The authors, harnessing their collective education, training, and experience, have devised the following index to help meet that need.

THE BAEZA FALSE REPORT INDEX (BAFRI)

BY DET. JOHN J. BAEZA (RET.)

Provided below is a list of false report red flags that every investigator, criminal profiler, and attorney should be aware of when examining or investigating any case that involves an alleged sex crime.

One or more of the circumstantial red flags described in this index has surfaced in most, if not all, of the false reports investigated by the authors[7]:

1. A female victim has demanded to speak with a female officer or investigator (this excludes those cases in which a male officer or investigator has acted inappropriately toward the female).
2. A female victim's husband, boyfriend, or other intimate partner has forced her to report the alleged crime, rather than having reported the crime of her own volition.
3. A victim's parents have forced the victim to report the alleged crime, rather than having reported the crime of his or her own volition.
4. A victim, most often under age (less than 18 years old), has returned home after curfew.
5. A victim states that he or she was abducted at a busy intersection (or some other very public location) during the day, and there are no witnesses to the incident.
6. A victim states that he or she was attacked by a masked offender in the middle of the day on a busy street (paradoxical offender behavior).
7. A victim is in a drug rehabilitation program and is out past curfew.
8. A pregnant female victim is forced by a parent or guardian to report the crime to police.
9. A victim cannot describe the suspect or provide details of the crime.
10. A victim has previously been charged with falsely reporting an incident.
11. A victim has previously reported a similar crime to the police.
12. A victim focuses on relocating to a new home or apartment during the investigation.
13. A victim focuses on initiating a lawsuit or on monetary gain during the investigation.
14. A victim displays "TV" behavior when initiating a complaint, mimicking the way that stereotypical victims act on television and in film (hysterical, demand female officer, catatonic, etc.).

---

[7] Although clearly an inductively rendered list, it has tremendous value to the investigator or criminal profiler. This value is felt by virtue of identifying areas that require further investigative attention. They can and will exist in legitimate cases, but when these elements are present, they must be examined, understood, and explained.

15. A victim cries at crucial points in the interview to avoid answering key questions.
16. A victim has a long psychiatric history.

At this point it must be made absolutely clear that this index should be used as a guide only. The items are not 100% foolproof indicators that the victim is falsely reporting a crime. To the sex-crimes investigator or forensic examiner, these red flags suggest only the possibility that the allegations may be false, and that further investigation is needed. There is no substitute for a thorough investigation.

MOTIVATIONS FOR FALSE REPORTS

Svensson and Wendel (1965, pp. 373–367) wrote about the motives of false reporters, warning:

> Where a woman alleges she has been raped or that an attempt has been made to rape her the police officer should always bear in mind the possibility that she is making a false charge. Her allegations against a man she names may be in revenge or due to mental derangement.
>
> The accusation may also be made after the woman had voluntary intercourse with a man but later, fearing pregnancy, claims she was raped. The motivation for the accusation may be an attempt to excuse her conduct or create grounds for a legal abortion.
>
> Cases coming under the first two conditions have occurred where the woman, with the intention of providing evidence against the man, has made arrangements which give the impression of having been produced by the alleged rape. Such arrangements may consist of torn clothing, minor injuries to her own body, contamination of the sexual organs with blood, etc.

As with any list of potential motives for human behavior, there is no bright yellow line between them. Human behavior is multidetermined. Hence, multiple motives may reside in the actions of a single false reporter. Some of the more common motivations that can impel the false reporter are provided next. It is certainly not intended to be an exhaustive list.

REVENGE

This includes situations where the reporter is angry at the accused and expresses that anger as a false report. Typically, a prior relationship with the accused is involved. It often occurs in child custody cases and in subordinate relationships.

Example

Seven sixth-grade girls from Germantown, MD ("Falsely accused," 2003):

> The students—six girls and a boy—allegedly accused a gym teacher of staring at the girls' breasts and fondling them in a locker room last month. Ronald Heller was suspended with pay and ordered to leave Roberto Clemente Middle School in Germantown.

> But police discovered the students made up the incident, reportedly angry because Heller had yelled at them for bad sportsmanship in front of the class. Under police questioning, their story collapsed and they admitted they had made the whole thing up.

According to Farenthold, Miller, and Shaver (2000), the actual victim in this case suffered great personal harm and felt compelled to leave teaching forever:

> Police said the seven girls eventually recanted the allegations, but the teacher, Ronald Heller, of Roberto Clemente Middle School, said the incident led him to retire after 32 years. [Montgomery County District Court Judge Dennis] McHugh called the lies a "cold act" that could have landed the teacher in jail.

NEED FOR ATTENTION

This category may include those who are said to be "crying out for help" as well as those with some degree of personality disorder or mental illness. It can include those who want attention from friends, relatives, or spouses, or even wish the attention of the media.

Example:

Nicole Armitage, 18, of Norfolk, Massachusetts. She was a University of Maine at Farmington student who claimed she had been raped by a stranger in a campus parking lot sometime in October of 2002. Authorities described the motive for her false report as a "cry for help" (Jespersen, 2003):

> Armitage's claim that a man with a tattoo on his arm attacked her attracted statewide attention and triggered concern over personal safety at UMF and in the community.

> . . .

> Armitage retracted her claim two weeks later and following disciplinary action, left school.

In a letter to Farmington residents, she apologizes for causing panic. She said she is now working full-time, going to school at night, and is getting medical help and support from friends and family.

"I have had the opportunity to rebuild my life from the ground up and feel I am well on my way to becoming a much better person as a result," she wrote.

Robinson said he weighed several issues before deciding not to prosecute. "One major consideration was that she did not implicate anyone and an innocent person was not dragged through the criminal process."

He was also convinced Armitage disclosed the story in confidence with the expectation it would go no further.

"But several well-meaning organizations and people pressured her to file a report. Then the investigation took on a life of its own," he said. "I am convinced she never intended for this result to occur."

Robinson said when someone is "desperate enough to tell a shocking lie to get attention, you have to ask why. I considered this a cry for help."

MEDICAL TREATMENT

Often this motivation is utilized to obtain drugs or treatment for a sexually transmitted disease. It can also occur when the reporter seeks treatment for AIDS or a pregnancy.

PROFIT

This may include the filing of a lawsuit by the reporter as well as the desire for new and better housing. For example, crime victims can reap enormous financial rewards by suing property owners (and their insurance companies) in what are referred to as premises liability lawsuits. In such a lawsuit, the victim argues that their attack could have been foreseen by the property owner, and subsequently prevented. Property owners and in some cases landlords are subsequently held financially responsible for criminal attacks on their property, when judgments favor the victim. Judgments in such cases can range into the millions of dollars, which is a powerful financial incentive to make a false report.

Example:
A 29-year-old woman from Vinton, VA. She was apparently motivated by profit, and was also concealing a consensual relationship with her attacker (Hammack, 2003):

Federal authorities say a Vinton woman falsely claimed she had been raped in order to receive disability benefits.

Elizabeth M. Gray, 29, was indicted Thursday in U.S. District Court in Roanoke on charges of health care fraud, mail fraud, perjury and making false statements to the Social Security Administration.

Gray claimed in 1998 that she had been raped by a co-worker . . . while in fact she was having a consensual relationship with the man and was planning to leave her husband, the indictment says.

Gray said that the man raped her in a company-owned truck at an interstate rest stop. But an Augusta County grand jury declined to indict the man, Assistant U.S. Attorney Tom Bondurant said.

Gray quit her job as an office clerk for . . . a company that collects and disposes of hospital-waste products, and then sought unsuccessfully to get her job back, according to the indictment.

For the next four years, Gray claimed that she suffered post-traumatic stress disorder as a result of the rape and was unable to work. As a result, she received about $22,000 in Social Security disability benefits and about $2,900 from Medicare, the indictment claims.

FAILURE OF CUSTOMER TO PAY PROSTITUTE

In such a case, a prostitute may not have received payment from his or her customer or "john." To get back at them, the prostitute may allege that they were raped. Ironically, a prostitute who actually is raped is unlikely to report it, considering such attacks part of the cost of doing business.

EXPLANATION FOR PREGNANCY OR SEXUALLY TRANSMITTED DISEASE

An unwanted or unexpected pregnancy or sexually transmitted disease may be explained by claiming rape. Although this is seen more commonly in juveniles, this reasoning motivates adults as well.

Example:
A 16-year-old girl from Victorville, CA (*Berg*, 2003):

A 16-year-old girl's report that she was violently raped in broad daylight Monday morning turned out to be a lie, wasting Sheriff's detectives' time and energy, San Bernardino County Sheriff's officials said.

After several hours of interviews and inconsistencies in her statements, the Victorville teenager admitted to detectives she made it up because she thought she was pregnant, said Sgt. Rick Roelle of the Sheriff's Victorville station.

. . .

This isn't uncommon with initial rape reports. There is often more to the story, Roelle said.

"This one seemed so believable, because she was so distraught, and she really had injuries on her," he said.

Roelle wasn't sure how she'd gotten the bruise on her forehead and a fresh scrape on her thigh.

The girl told deputies an unknown man attacked her after she dropped a child off at a preschool at Mojave and Jeraldo drives about 7:50 a.m.

The imaginary attacker supposedly threw a cloth over her face, so she was unable to describe him to detectives, Roelle said.

Example:
A 19-year-old girl from East Lansing, MI (Hassett, 2003):

[East Lansing Police Captain Juli] Liebler said the 19-year-old Farmington Hills woman made up the rape report because she was afraid she may have gotten pregnant from a recent unrelated sexual experience.

The woman told police that early July 20 she was walking to a friend's house in the 300 block of Division Street when she was forced into a sport utility vehicle and sexually assaulted.

False reports are very rare, Liebler said.

Filing a false sexual assault report is a felony punishable by up to four years in prison and up to $2,000 in fines.

There were a number of factors that led investigators to suspect the report was false, Liebler said.

"They didn't talk to her under the impression that it was a false report," she said.

"Our investigators have taken enough sexual assault reports to notice basic similarities. (And) a lot of these were not here."

Liebler emphasized that all sexual assault reports are considered true unless proven otherwise, but officers discovered too many red flags while questioning the woman.

Investigators found her description of the incident vague, and she couldn't remember where her friend's house was, Liebler said.

"We asked her to go back with us and show us where it happened, and she couldn't remember," Liebler said.

"(Just) because you can't remember the exact spot doesn't mean that it's false," she said. "But you put all these things together."

After speaking with the woman, investigators came to the conclusion that the incident didn't happen, and gave her the opportunity to confess, which she did, Liebler said.

ALIBI FOR INAPPROPRIATE ABSENCE

This is a common motivation for juveniles and adults alike. False reporters may be so desperate for an alibi to explain their absence that they will claim that a rape has occurred. This is common among those living in group homes or in treatment programs while under conditions of parole, where the consequences for failing to return prior to curfew can be severe. It may also be used by teenagers out past curfew, or by an adult to conceal infidelity.

Example:
A 44-year-old woman from Pittsburgh, PA, involved in multiple false reports against police officers (Ove, 1999):

> A South Side woman who filed a complaint against a Pittsburgh police officer claiming he had raped her was arrested Friday night on a charge of making a false report in an incident in which she said three carjackers had tied her up, fondled her and forced her to smoke a drug.
>
> Police believe the 44-year-old woman lied about the incident to explain to her husband why she disappeared for two days last week.
>
> In July, the same woman told police that a South Side station patrolman who had answered a call for a domestic dispute at her house returned when he was off duty and raped her.
>
> . . .
>
> The investigation into the latest incident began when a man walking in Lawrenceville late Friday night found the woman lying in the grass in Leslie Park, bound with a section of clothesline.
>
> When police arrived, the woman said three men had hijacked the car she was driving Wednesday while she was parked in the lot at the CoGo's convenience store on Carson Street on the South Side.

She said the men fondled her, pulled her hair and forced her to smoke a drug that made her feel as though she would pass out. She said they held her captive in an apartment for two days before tying her up and dumping her in the park.

She was taken to St. Francis Medical Center, according to reports, but left before she could be examined by a doctor.

NEW HOUSING (ESPECIALLY IN MORE POPULATED CITIES)

A desire for new housing will often motivate individuals to falsely report a rape to authorities. This is especially common in areas where rent-controlled housing is offered by the government. There are long waiting lists to get into the most desirable housing projects. Some residents believe that a way to jump to the front of this list is to claim that a rape or other attack occurred inside the individual's current apartment.

CHILD CUSTODY

Child custody battles are among the most heated and divisive legal disputes that can occur. When character and parental fitness are the issue, be ready for the accusations to fly. They can, and sometimes do, include allegations of rape or sexual abuse, made by one side or the other, in an attempt to gain custody of the child in question. Some have merit; some don't. The purpose of an investigation is to find out which is the case. Ideally, this will take place before things get before a jury.

Example:
Lesley Nickel and his wife, Lisa, filed suit in Ottawa County Common Pleas Court against his 15-year-old daughter, Mindy Fenton; his nephew, Daniel Fenton; and his sister, Robin Carter. According to the suit, the children told a guidance counselor at Port Clinton Junior High School in April of 1999 that her father had sexually abused Mindy since he gained custody of her and Daniel Fenton in 1992 ("Dad sues . . . ," 2001):

Mr. Nickel was indicted on felony charges of rape and gross sexual imposition and a misdemeanor charge of sexual imposition. He was acquitted in May, 2000.

. . .

After the charges were filed, Mr. Nickel was placed on a leave without pay from his job with the Ottawa County sanitary engineer's department; he was reinstated after his acquittal.

ATTEMPT TO VEIL A REOCCURRENCE OF DRUG OR ALCOHOL USE

This category includes individuals who have abstained from the use of drugs or alcohol for some period of time and then suddenly relapse making it necessary for them to develop an excuse for their behavior. They may claim that they were raped and forced to ingest drugs or alcohol against their will. They may also claim that they returned to using drugs or alcohol to deal with the pain of the incident.

Example:

A 27-year-old woman from Dearborn, MI, caused a chief of police to resign (*Warikoo,* 2001):

> The woman who falsely accused former Dearborn Police Chief Ron Deziel of rape is now the one being accused of a crime.
>
> Tammy Divetta, 27, of Taylor was charged Tuesday with filing a false police report. . . .
>
> "She admitted the allegations were untrue," Wayne County Prosecutor Mike Duggan said Monday. "It does a terrible disservice to Chief Deziel."
>
> . . . On Friday, Tammy Divetta admitted she had lied to State Police about being raped in the basement of a Dearborn hair salon.
>
> Divetta told the Free Press on Friday, "No, there was no sexual intercourse."
>
> She added that she wasn't sure what happened Jan. 18, the day she had claimed she was raped. Divetta, Deziel and the owner of the hair salon, where Divetta worked, had lunch that day in a Detroit restaurant. Divetta had claimed that Deziel assaulted her after lunch.
>
> Deziel, who resigned the day before the allegations surfaced, has said his only relationship to Divetta was that she washed his hair twice.
>
> . . .
>
> Duggan said Divetta might have made up the story because she was "trying to deflect her husband's anger that she had been drinking" the day of the lunch with Deziel.
>
> "She lied to her husband," Duggan said.
>
> The prosecutor said extortion does not appear to be a motive.

CHANGE OF HEART AFTER A CONSENSUAL SEXUAL ENCOUNTER

This is common in juvenile dating situations in which one of the parties of a consensual sexual encounter later feels guilty, angry, and/or vexed. In order to conceal and/or explain this behavior to themselves or to others, especially parental figures, they falsely claim that they were raped.

CONCLUSIONS

False reports are a problem for all of the professional communities that encounter them, and they are more frequent than those with pro-victim political agendas would have us believe. False reporters span all ages and all walks of life, and they are capable of staging both injuries and evidence to support their claims. A thorough investigation of the evidence has traditionally been the best way to reveal the false reporter, who is more likely to confess when confronted with logical inconsistencies in his or her statements and behavior. Unfortunately, law enforcement resources are drained away from actual victims by such cases. Innocent citizens are exposed to the possibility of false accusations and damage to their personal and professional lives. Legitimate victims of sexual assault are exposed to the possibility of encountering overtaxed law enforcement resources that are inadequate to the task of investigating their cases thoroughly or competently. Building owners, private companies, and insurance companies are exposed to the threat of costly liability lawsuits. As stated in Gross (1924, p. 14),[8] "Not only must the self-made victim be exposed, but innocent people who may be suspected must be protected."

Furthermore, research relating to sexual assault, which is often used as the basis for law enforcement resource and budget allocations, not to mention expert forensic testimony, is necessarily biased or otherwise compromised when such cases go unidentified. This is a problem in both criminal and civil cases. Hence, the need for more and better research in this area cannot be emphasized too strongly. Nor can the need for objectivity, thorough investigations of each complaint, and strict adherence to the forensic evidence.

---

[8] This sentiment is echoed today by Manhattan Sex Crimes Prosecutor Linda Fairstein, who states, "False reports of rape do occur . . . [and] have made it difficult for legitimate victims to be taken seriously. . . . For all prosecutors . . . it is critical to acknowledge that false accusations of rape are made."

REFERENCES

Aiken, M., Burgess, A., and Hazelwood, R. (1995) False rape allegations, in Burgess, A., and Hazelwood, R. (eds.), *Practical Aspects of Rape Investigation: A Multidisciplinary Approach.* New York: CRC Press.

Berg, E. Teen claims daytime rape, then recants: Authorities say bogus sexual assault reports are not uncommon, *Victorville Daily Press*, August 5, 2003.

Brown, C., Crowley, S., Peck, R., and Slaughter, L. (1997) Patterns of genital injury in female sexual assault victims. *American Journal of Obstetrics and Gynecology*, March, pp. 609–616.

Brownmiller, S. (1975) *Against Our Will: Men, Women and Rape.* New York: Fawcett Columbine.

Brownmiller, S., Personal email communication to David R. Throop of the Men's Issues Page, Jun 27, 1995, URL: http://www.menweb.org/throop/falsereport/commentary/brownback.html.

Court TV Online—Legal Documents (1997) Report of the grand jury concerning the Tawana Brawley investigation. Available online at: http://www.courttv.com/legaldocs/newsmakers/tawana/part3.html#sexual.

Dad sues daughter, kin over sex allegations. *The Toledo Blade Company*, March 28, 2001,

Dunleavy, S. Cybersex victim's kin: She's a liar. *New York Post*, July 26, 1999.

Falsely accused. ABC News.com, March 14, 2003.

Fairstein, L. (1993) *Sexual Violence.* New York: William Morrow and Co., Inc.

Farenthold, D., Miller, B., and Shaver, K. Girls ordered to do community service. *The Washington Post*, October 17, 2000, p. B2.

Gregory, J., and Lees, S. (1999) *Policing Sexual Assault.* New York: Routledge.

Gross, H. (1924) *Criminal Investigation*, 3rd ed. London: Sweet and Maxwell.

Hammack, L. She received $22,000 in disability funds: Authorities say woman made false rape claim. *Roanoke Times*, July 19, 2003.

Hassett, K. Charges urged in false report of sex assault: Woman said she was raped in East Lansing. *Lansing State Journal*, July 29, 2003.

Haws, D. (1997) The elusive numbers on false rape. *Columbia Journalism Review*, November/December.

Hibler, N., and McDowell, C. (1995) "Red Flags of False Rape Allegations," from Aiken, M., Burgess, A., and Hazelwood, R., False rape allegations, in Burgess, A., and Hazelwood, R. (eds.), *Practical Aspects of Rape Investigation: A Multidisciplinary Approach.* New York: CRC Press.

Inquirer Staff, Timoney commends rape-squad reforms. *Philadelphia Inquirer*, December 13, 2000.

Jespersen, B. Student fined for false report. *Kennebec Journal*, April 5, 2003.

Kanin, E. (1994) False rape allegations. *Archives of Sexual Behavior*, Vol. 23, No. 1, pp. 81–92.

MacDonald, J. (1973) False accusations of rape. *Medical Aspects of Human Sexuality*, May, pp. 170–194.

McDowell, C. (1985) *Chicago Lawyer*, June; cited online at: http://www.coeffic. demon.co.uk/descrim.htm.

Ove, T. Woman in police rape case charged with filing false report in another. *Pittsburgh Post-Gazette*, September 28, 1999.

Palmer, C., and Thornhill, R. (2000) *A History of Rape.* Cambridge, MA: MIT Press.

Racher, D. Cleared of raping mom of 3. *Philadelphia Daily News*, December 26, 2000.

Spilbor, J. (2003) "What if Kobe Bryant has been falsely accused?" Findlaw.com, August 11th.

Svensson, A., and Wendel, O. (1965) *Crime Scene Investigation*, 2nd ed. New York: American Elsevier.

Turvey, B. (2002) *Criminal Profiling: An Introduction to Behavioral Evidence Analysis*, 2nd ed. London: Academic Press.

Warikoo, N. Chief's accuser charged with filing false report: Arraignment set for today in recanted rape tale. *Detroit Free Press*, March 14, 2001.

CHAPTER 12

RAPIST MODUS OPERANDI AND MOTIVE

Brent E. Turvey, MS

> I wonder, Mr. Bone man, what you're thinking of your fury now, gone sour as a
> sinking whale, crawling up the alphabet on her own bones.
> **Anne Sexton, "The Fury of Beautiful Bones,"** *The Death Notebooks* **(1974)**

Understanding the methods and techniques criminals use to commit crime is the best way to solve cases. The best rape investigators, as evidenced by high clearance rates, are living encyclopedias of sex crime and rapist behavior. They have studied all kinds of rapists, what they do, and why they do it. They know how to examine a series of rapist choices for vulnerability, and a crime scene for signs of their passing. They are not afraid to assemble and understand all elements of the extreme violation that is rape. The best rape investigators have learned to uncover and read the facts in each case, and then turn it to a tactical advantage with which to ensnare the rapist.

Maples (1999, p. 38) is unequivocal in his support of this tried and tested investigative practice, explaining:

> A cop who's in the game understands that each choice the predator makes, each
> step of the criminal's method of operation, represents an opportunity. He will prowl
> the predators' hunting grounds. He'll trail potential victims. . . .

He goes on to say that (p. 62):

> the cop will appreciate how important it is to further his or her education by getting
> to know as much as possible about the predatory criminals on his or her watch—
> including their identities, habits, methods, hangouts, and hunting grounds.

In essence, this practice is the study of *modus operandi* and *motive*.

UNDERSTANDING RAPIST MODUS OPERANDI

Modus operandi (M.O.) is a Latin term that means *method of operating*. Investigators use it in reference to the manner in which a crime has been committed (Gross, 1924, p. 478). A rapist's modus operandi is made up of choices and behaviors that are intended to assist in the completion of a rape. Their *modus operandi* reflects *how* they commit their crime. It is separate from their motives, or *signature*, as these have to do with *why* the rape was committed.

The examination and storage of rapist modus operandi information can be investigatively relevant for the following reasons (with help from Weston and Wells, 1974, p. 110; and DeForest, Gaensslen, and Lee, 1983, p. 29):

- Investigative linkage of unsolved rapes and sexual assaults by modus operandi
- Suspect identification by comparing known rapist modus operandi with the modus operandi evident in unsolved rapists
- Development of investigative leads and/or rapist identity in unsolved cases by virtue of accumulating modus operandi information
- Suspect prioritization and/or elimination
- Clearance of unsolved cases[1]

To the rape investigator, M.O. is relevant because it can provide an array of information about rapists. This includes the involvement of choices, procedures, or techniques used during the rape that are characteristic of, or reflective of:

---

[1] After making a burglary, robbery, or sex crime arrest, law enforcement will often attempt to connect that suspect to other cases in their file for which there is tangible evidence. Similarities in other crimes may be uncovered and then thoroughly investigated. This is a legitimate investigative practice. However, historically, the procedures followed by the Washington, D.C., Metropolitan Police Department, as well as many others throughout the United States, allow (Feeney, 2000):

> individual officers to clear offenses without any assurance that the identity of the offender is reliably known. Officers are able to use the modus operandi method of clearance even where charges based on the cleared offenses are not filed, where the offender denies his involvement, and where no other evidence exists to connect him with the crimes. In one instance three thefts were cleared by a police officer because he "felt sure" a suspect arrested for a different theft was responsible, even though the suspect had not confessed to the thefts, there was no other evidence linking him to the thefts, and the modus operandi was different from the crime for which he was arrested.

In the author's view, this is not a legitimate investigative or forensic practice for what should be very obvious reasons. Even when the M.O. in otherwise unconnected cases is precisely the same, a reasonable level of certainty has not been reached with respect to the absolute identity of the rapist. Only physical evidence can provide that level of certainty. Similar M.O.'s across unconnected cases suggest a need for further investigation. Such an occurrence is a lead to follow up on, not a conclusive result with which to close a case.

- A particular discipline, trade, skill, profession, or area of knowledge (criminal and noncriminal)
- Knowledge particular to the victim, suggesting planning, prior contact or a prior relationship
- Knowledge particular to a crime scene, suggesting varying levels of planning or familiarity

General types of M.O. behaviors can include actions such as, but are not limited to (with help from O'Connell and Soderman, 1936, pp. 254–260):

- Number of rapists
- Amount of planning before a crime
- Selection of rape location
- Route taken to rape location
- Presurveillance of a crime scene(s) or victim
- Involvement of a victim during a crime (non-fantasy-related)
- Use of a weapon
- Use of restraints to control the victim
- Nature and extent of injuries to the victim
- Nature and extent of precautionary acts
- Location and position of the victim's clothing
- Items taken from victim or crime scene(s) for profit
- Items taken from victim or crime scene(s) to prevent identification[2]
- Method of transportation to and from crime scene(s)
- Direction of escape/route taken from the crime scene

THE ELEMENTS OF RAPIST M.O.

A rapist's M.O. is composed of learned behaviors that can evolve and develop over time. It can be refined, as a rapist becomes more experienced, sophisticated, and confident. It can also become less competent and less skillful over time, decompensating by virtue of a deteriorating mental state, or increased used of controlled substances (Turvey, 2000).

In either case, a rapist's M.O. behavior is functional in nature. It most often serves (or fails to serve) one or more of three general pur-

---

[2] It is common for all different types of rapists to take driver's licenses or other forms of photo ID off their living victims as an overt threat to victim safety should they report the crime. By doing so, they hope to achieve a level of intimidation. Such rapists are trying to send the message: "I know what you look like, I know where you live, and if you go to the police I will be back and they will not be able to protect you. I will remember you."

poses:[3] the protection or concealment of rapist identity, the successful completion of the rape, or the facilitation of escape.

1. **Protection of rapist identity.** Examples include:
   (a) Wearing a mask or covering a victim's eyes with an article of clothing so that the victim can't see their face and recognize them later
   (b) Wearing gloves to prevent fingerprints from transferring into the crime scene
   (c) Wearing a condom or getting a vasectomy to prevent sperm and semen transfer
   (d) Washing or wiping down the victim after the rape
   (e) Choosing a physically (i.e., blind) or mentally disabled victim
   (f) Destruction of transfer evidence through removal, disposal, or burning
   (g) Disposal of a vehicle involved in the commission of a crime

Case Example:

On April 24, 2001, 26-year-old Jesus Macias plead *nolo contendere* to one count of rape against Lena B., a 35-year-old woman suffering from cerebral palsy and mild mental retardation, with the subsequent mental age of a 9-year-old. Macias was a van driver for Tina's Transportation, a company that transports developmentally disabled passengers.

According to court records (*California v. Macias*, 2003):

> The victim reported on December 22, 2000, the defendant transported her to and from school [the Creative Center in Visalia]. The victim was usually dropped off first based on the current bus route, however, on this particular day was not dropped off until the end of the route. The victim reported the driver transported her to a desolate roadway on the outskirts of Visalia, and requested to have sex with her. The victim reported understanding what this meant, however, indicated she told him she did not want to. However, he told her to remove her clothes, at which point she complied by removing her undergarments and pants. Further, she indicated the defendant pulled his pants down and told her to touch his penis with her hand. She stated she did so out of fear, however, did not want to. She then reported the defendant put on a condom and placed his penis inside her vagina and had sex with her one time.

[3] There are by far more foolish and ignorant criminals than there are criminal masterminds. Investigators throughout history owe a great deal of their case resolution to the sheer stupidity of criminals. As explained in Gross (1968):

> The cleverest people do the most idiotic things. He makes the most progress who keeps in mind the great series of his own stupidities, and tries to learn from them.

> She indicated she did not want to have sex with him, however, was nervous and thought if she denied him, he would force her to anyway. The victim stated when the sexual act was complete, the defendant threw the condom out of the window of the van. She indicated he then drove her home and prior to dropping her off told her not to tell anyone what had just occurred.

The rape was not reported until several days later, and then only because the victim confided in her sister, who immediately contacted the authorities. Lena B. was able to lead investigators back to the location where the van had been parked during the attack. At the crime scene, investigators were able to locate tire marks and a used condom with bodily fluids and blood inside of it.

A search of the Macias' van, identified by the victim, revealed an opened condom wrapper in the side pocket of the driver's side door, matching the brand of the discarded condom from the scene. Macias was asked for a DNA sample that he consented to give, denying that any sexual contact had occurred between him and Lena B. When the results of the DNA test came back positive, Macias was confronted with those results, denied sexual contact, and then finally admitted to having sex with the victim. He explained that it was consensual, and that she had requested it. He denied ejaculating, however, and denied having any other sexual contact with the victim.

Of interest in this case are the results of further investigation, suggesting a history of intense fantasy and possible elements of planning for future sex crimes (*California v. Macias*, 2003):

> On December 31, 2000, officers served a search warrant on the defendant's residence and located extensive amounts of pornographic materials consisting of magazines, photographs, pornographic video tapes, a rubber vagina, a rubber dildo, condoms, and a package of .35 millimeter photographs randomly taken, which appeared to be of young women and girls throughout the city streets

In this case, the rapist chose a victim who was mentally and physically disabled, with whom he held a position of trust and authority. She was less able to resist a sexual attack and less likely to be believed if she reported it. The rapist further used a condom to prevent transfer of sperm and semen evidence, and then discarded the condom at the remote location (a "desolate roadway") that he had preselected for the attack.

2. **Successful completion of the rape.** Examples include:
   (a) Using a gag to silence a victim
   (b) Using ligatures to restrain the victim
   (c) Using a weapon to control a victim

(d) Making a list of potential victims with pertinent victim information (phone numbers, addresses, occupation, schedules, etc.)

(e) Choosing a physically (i.e., wheelchair/elderly) or mentally disabled victim

(f) Pretending to be a law enforcement officer to gain victim trust and deliver the victim to a preselected location for an attack

Case Example:

In 2001, Edward Simmons was convicted in the District Court, Orleans Parish, of aggravated burglary of an inhabited dwelling, false imprisonment while armed with a dangerous weapon, sexual battery, and possession of cocaine. On January 27, 2001, he had broken in to the residence of Mr. and Mrs. Dubberley. According to court records, Mrs. Dubberley reported the following to investigators at the scene (*Louisiana v. Simmons*, 2003):

> She told him that shortly after midnight on January 27, 2001, she awoke to the sound of her husband struggling with an intruder. The intruder forced his way into the bedroom, knocking Mr. Dubberley, who was trying to hold the bedroom door shut against the intruder, to the floor. The intruder grabbed Mrs. Dubberley by her arm, and informed her and her husband that he had a knife. The intruder tied Mr. Dubberley's hands with a pair of black pantyhose, and told Mrs. Dubberley to lead him to the valuables. The intruder dragged Mrs. Dubberley into the hallway. Mrs. Dubberley broke away from the intruder, and ran to the telephone. The intruder overpowered Mrs. Dubberley, pushed her against the wall, and punched her in the face. He dragged her back into the bedroom, where he proceeded to further tighten the bindings on Mr. Dubberley's hands. Next, the intruder blindfolded Mrs. Dubberley, held a knife to the back of her neck, and once again took her into the hallway. He pushed her to the floor, and inserted his finger into her vagina, after which he fled the house with a few articles. After speaking with Mrs. Dubberley, the detective transported her to the hospital for a sexual assault examination.

Mrs. Dubberley testified to the following (*Louisiana v. Simmons*, 2003):

> Her husband attempted to keep the door closed; however, the intruder over-powered her husband. The intruder tied up Mr. Dubberley with a pair of panty-hose, and ordered Mrs. Dubberley to bury her face in her pillow. The intruder told the Dubberley's he was looking for valuables, and proceeded to ransack the bedroom looking for her purse and Mr. Dubberley's wallet. Mrs. Dubberley got a good look at the intruder's face as he searched for valuables. The Dubberley's directed the intruder to Mr. Dubberley's wallet in the bedroom, and told him Mrs. Dubberley's purse was in the front room. The intruder blind-

folded Mrs. Dubberley, tied her hands behind her back, and walked her to the front room. As they walked, the intruder held a knife to her throat, and began rubbing his genitals against her buttocks. He told her to relax and asked her, "What's the matter? I know you've been f—ed before." The intruder drove away from the Dubberley residence in Mrs. Dubberley's car.

According to Deborah Ratterree, the Director of the Sexual Assault Nurse Examiner Program at Charity Hospital (*Louisiana v. Simmons*, 2003),

> She examined Mrs. Dubberley on January 27, 2001. Ms. Ratterree testified that Mrs. Dubberley suffered multiple contusions and bruising on her left side, left knee, head, chest and soreness of her jaw. Ms. Ratterree also noted ligature marks on Mrs. Dubberley's wrists. During the exam, Mrs. Dubberley was very upset, weepy, shaky, and had difficulty talking about her ordeal.

> Both victims identified Edward Simmons from a photo line-up, and also identified their house and car keys, which had been found on his person at the time of his arrest. Simmons had an extensive criminal history dating back to 1980, including burglary and attempted rape.

> In this case, the rapist chose to combine rape with burglary. He selected a time early in the morning when residents would be home but likely sleeping, brought a knife to control them once they woke, used available materials as a ligature to control the victims during the rape (pantyhose), and used a blindfold to limit any subsequent identification. He also had the confidence to handle two victims, controlling the male somewhat using the threat of harm to the female.

3. **Facilitation of rapist escape.** Examples include:
   (a) Use of a vehicle after the commission of the rape
   (b) Tying up victims and discarding their clothing to prevent escape and attempts to get help
   (c) Selection of a remote location to leave the victim after the commission of the rape
   (d) Dressing in jogger's attire when attacking victims on jogging paths in a public park, to blend in before and after the attack

Case Example:

In 1999, 23-year-old Alva Cepriano was convicted in the 24th Judicial District Court, Parish of Jefferson, of attempted second-degree murder and aggravated rape. The victim in the case was C.C., a 15-year-old babysitter. She had fallen asleep in the bedroom of a home where she was babysitting for Cepriano's stepbrother and the stepbrother's wife. C.C. was there to watch over four girls between the ages of 1 and 8, none of whom were attacked. According to her testimony (*Louisiana v. Cepriano*, 2000):

> She heard a knock on the bedroom door. She opened the bedroom door to find the defendant, whom she knew as Ali. The defendant had entered the house. The defendant asked her if Josh was home, and she replied that he was not and went back to sleep. Later that evening, the defendant returned and asked the victim to go into the kitchen and write Josh a note for him, which she did, though she thought it strange that he told her to make it from "Jack" when she knew that was not his name.
>
> . . .
>
> While she was in the kitchen with him, the defendant grabbed her from behind, and dragged her, struggling, to another bedroom in the house. C.C. testified that the defendant was choking her, and punched her in the eye, telling her to "shut up." C.C. told the jury that, when they reached the bedroom, the defendant threw her on the ground, unzipped his pants, and forced her to perform oral sex on him. Next, the defendant took her clothes off and had forcible sexual intercourse with her. C.C. testified that she was struggling, "trying to get him off of" her. After the rape, C.C. felt the defendant cut her neck with something. She screamed and tried to get up, but the defendant started strangling her. Being strangled was the last thing C.C. remembered before falling to the floor unconscious. The defendant testified that, once she fell to the floor, he wrapped a wire around the unconscious victim's neck.

According to Dr. David Dunn, an expert in the field of obstetrics and gynecology who performed the sexual assault examination (*Louisiana v. Cepriano*, 2000):

> His examination revealed trauma consistent with forced intercourse. His examination also revealed that C.C. had a black eye, bruising around the eye, ligature marks on her neck, and marks on her neck, that appeared to have been made by a serrated knife. Dr. Dunn took vaginal swabs from C.C. and submitted those swabs for testing. The swabs were tested by a forensic scientist from the Jefferson Parish Crime Lab, who testified that the vaginal swabs and the sample taken from C.C.'s underwear tested positive for sperm and seminal fluid. The samples were submitted to Relia Gene, a testing company for DNA analysis, and that analysis revealed the DNA found on the vaginal swabs and on C.C.'s panties matched the DNA of the defendant.

Alva Cepriano testified and admitted to raping C.C., but explained that he did not hit her. He further explained to the jury that (*Louisiana v. Cepriano*, 2000)

> although he put a wire around C.C.'s neck, held a steak knife to her neck, and placed a bag over her head and choked her, he was not trying to kill C.C.

The defendant testified that he was only trying to "knock her out" so that he could leave.

In this case the rapist bound the victim, brutalized her physically and sexually, and then engaged a neck ligature (a wire) that he would have others believe was merely intended to subdue her. Given the facts, circumstances, and the contradictory physical evidence, the jury believed that he was attempting to kill her in order to silence her as a witness. Either way, with the victim unconscious or dead he was more able to flee the scene without arousing the attention of neighbors.

INFLUENCES ON MODUS OPERANDI

A rapist's M.O. choices and behaviors are learned, and therefore dynamic and malleable. They are affected by the passage of time, changing as the rapist learns or deteriorates. In one case, a rapist may realize that some of the things they do during a rape are more effective than others. They may subsequently repeat them in future offenses and become more skillful, refining their M.O. However, M.O. behavior may also change due to a rapist's deteriorating mental state from the influence of controlled substances, or due to an increased confidence that law enforcement will not successfully apprehend them. These circumstances can cause a rapist's M.O. to become less skillful, less competent, and more careless.

Over the course of a rapist's career, they may also incorporate behaviors into their crimes to refine their M.O. that unintentionally reveal something about their identity, character, or experience. Common ways that a rapist may learn how to more skillfully commit crime, evade capture, and conceal their identity include, but are certainly not limited to, those provided next.

The persistent rape investigator will ask of each rapist choice and behavior: What does it tell me about any of the following issues?

EDUCATIONAL AND TECHNICAL MATERIALS

Until they are captured and convicted, rapists have equal access to the same learning opportunities as any other citizen. Professional journals, college courses, textbooks, and other educationally oriented media available at a public library, or now via the Internet, can provide information and knowledge that is useful in refining a rapist's particular M.O. The important lesson for the investigator is that the rapist's M.O. may reflect familiarity or proficiency with specialized knowledge or techniques, and this can provide investigatively relevant direction by narrowing the suspect pool.

TRADE OR PROFESSIONAL EXPERIENCE

Rapists may have been or may currently be employed in trades or professions that utilize special knowledge, or require proficiency with specialized techniques (i.e. electrician, plumber, telephone company, delivery person, computers, military, law enforcement, etc.). Such specialized knowledge may find its way into a rapist's M.O. and be reflected in their offense. The offense may also reflect an opportunity created by the rapist's profession, by virtue of time, place, or victim availability.

CRIMINAL EXPERIENCE AND CONFIDENCE

As a rapist commits more of the same type of crime, they may become more proficient at it. They may act more confidently, be able to handle the unexpected more smoothly (or even be more prepared for it), or they may have tailored their precautionary acts to the type of criminal activity they expect to engage in. It is important to establish, in any crime, what the rapist had planned for by virtue of what they brought with them, and by virtue of the behaviors they engaged in. The question that investigators need to ask here is whether the materials brought and the behaviors committed were appropriate to the crime. The next question is whether or not the materials brought and the behaviors committed are suggestive of proficiency with another type of crime (suggesting a criminal history apart from the crime at hand) (Turvey, 2000).

CONTACT WITH THE CRIMINAL JUSTICE SYSTEM

Being arrested just once may teach a rapist an invaluable lesson about how to avoid detection by law enforcement in the future. Further still, and with some great irony, a prison term in the United States is referred to by some in both law enforcement and the criminal population as "going to college." This is because younger and less-experienced rapists have the opportunity in prison to network with older and more experienced rapists who have already accumulated a great deal of criminal knowledge. Subsequently, a prison term of only a few years has the potential to advance a rapist's skill level far beyond their original M.O. Once released, that rapist may take their "education" and embark on criminal enterprises that before would have been beyond their ability.

THE MEDIA

Some rapists monitor investigations into crimes by paying close attention to media accounts in the newspapers and on television. It is important that investigators pay close attention to the release of any such information to the media, when it was released, and how that may affect the future crimes of a given rapist in serial cases. Not only may information relating to a case provide a rapist with insight into future precautionary acts, but it may also provide other rapists with adequate information to "copycat" a particular series, and defer investigative suspicion from themselves.

MOOD

A rapist's mood on a given day can influence their aggression level going into an offense, and the manner in which they subsequently reacts to victim and crime-scene influences. For example, if a rapist has a heated argument with their relationship partner an hour prior to attacking a victim, their aggression level may be higher than during previous offenses where such an argument was not a factor. Subsequently there may be less planning or control evident in crime-scene behavior.

X-FACTORS

An X factor, for our purposes, is any unknown or unplanned influence that can affect crime-scene behavior during an offense. The successful completion of any offense, from a rapist's perspective, is dependent upon the event conforming to their fantasies or expectations. Under real-life conditions, crime scenes, victims, and other extrinsic influences (i.e., weather, witnesses, scheduled events, and so on) may not always conform to rapist expectations. The presence of any number of X-factors, such as victims under the influence of controlled substances, unexpected witnesses, and unexpected victim responses (compliance, noncompliance, death, etc.), may force the rapist to improvise or to make a hasty retreat, resulting in an interrupted/incomplete offense, or an offense gone wrong.

> *Example:*
> A rapist attacks women in the park by approaching them from behind and dragging them into the nearby woods. He uses one arm around their necks to control them, and puts their shirts up over their faces during the attack to conceal his identity. When he is finished, he manually chokes them until they pass out and leaves them unconscious.

An *interrupted/incomplete offense* is one that does not contain enough M.O. behaviors to complete the offense. An incomplete event might include the following: The victim in the example, instead of being easy prey, turns around and kicks the rapist in the groin. The rapist may be stunned and limp away or the victim may create an opportunity to flee the scene. Or, during the attack on his victim, the rapist might be unwittingly witnessed by a passerby and flee the scene. Either way, the event would not have included the full potential range of rapist M.O. behaviors, and would therefore be incomplete.

An *offense gone wrong* is one that contains unintentional, unplanned M.O. behavior, which increases the rapist's risk or legal consequences. An event gone wrong might include the following: In the example given, the rapist might accidentally use too much force, or the victim response might be too violent for them, and the rapist's control-oriented choking could result in the victim's death. This turn of events can transform a serial rape investigation into a homicide investigation, increasing the rapist's legal consequences.

THE DEVOLUTION OF M.O.

As discussed, M.O. behavior does not always evolve to become more competent as the rapist progresses through their criminal career. Because of a deteriorating mental state, the use of controlled substances, or increased confidence that law enforcement will not successfully apprehend them, a rapist's M.O. behaviors can devolve over time to a *less* competent and *less* skillful level than when they first began.

Understanding how and why a rapist's M.O. evolves or devolves is crucial to the development of investigative strategy. A rapist's M.O. tells the investigator what the rapist has considered, what they have not considered, and what they were subsequently prepared and unprepared for. This means that an investigator must be open to considering all possible influences on a rapist's behavior, and what those influences may suggest.

RAPIST SIGNATURE

In general investigative terms, the word *signature* is used to describe distinctive behaviors or patterns of behaviors committed by a rapist that serve psychological and emotional needs. Through an analysis and interpretation of a particular rapist's signature behaviors, in combination with other elements such as modus operandi and victimology, investigators may investigatively link cases and develop an understanding of a rapist's *motive* for committing the crime.

DEFINITIONS

The term *signature* has been used in legal parlance to refer to an unusual, distinctive criminal modus operandi. An early court decision, where M.O. evidence was inappropriately allowed by the trial court to show rapist identity (but dismissed by the court as a harmless error), cites *McCormick on Evidence* from 1954 (*California v. Haston*, 1968):

> Professor McCormick states: "Here [i.e. in the matter of proving identity by means of other-offenses modus operandi evidence] much more is demanded than the mere repeated commission of crimes of the same class, such as repeated burglaries or thefts. The device used must be so unusual and distinctive as to be like a signature." (McCormick, Evidence (1954) 157, p. 328.)

An *offender signature* is a pattern of distinctive behaviors that are characteristic of, and satisfy, emotional and psychological needs. There are two separate but interdependent parts to the concept of signature. First, there is the general *signature aspect* of a crime. The overall signature aspect represents the emotional or psychological themes that the rapist satisfies when they commit a rape. These include, but are not necessarily limited to, the following general motivational categories:

- Profit
- Anger/retaliation
- Reassurance/experimentation
- Assertiveness/entitlement
- Sadism

   The second part of signature is that signature aspects are manifested or evidenced by *signature behaviors*. Signature behaviors are those acts committed by a rapist that are not necessary to commit the rape, but that suggest psychological or emotional needs. The problem for the investigator is distinguishing between M.O. behaviors and signature behaviors. The bigger problem is that signature needs and M.O. needs may be satisfied by the same behavior. This conundrum is best elucidated by what are perhaps the two most important axioms of behavioral evidence analysis (Turvey, 2002):

- Different rapists do similar things for different reasons.
- Individual rapist behaviors are multidetermined; they can be the result of multiple rapist motivations and multiple external influences.
- Because of the differences in the ways that rapists express their psychological needs, differences between the manifestation of modus operandi behaviors and signature behaviors are not always readily apparent to even the most competent investigators.

In the case of one rapist, for example, the act of covering a victim's face with her own shirt during a rape may be a part of a psychological desire, facilitating a fantasy that the victim is another person. This would be a signature behavior.

In the case of another rapist, the act of covering a victim's face with her own shirt during a rape may be a part of a functional need to keep the victim from seeing his face and identifying him at a later time. This behavior would then be considered a part of the rapist's modus operandi.

In the case of yet another rapist, behavior being multidetermined, the same act could be intended to satisfy both of the above needs, and therefore could be a part of both the rapist's M.O. and signature.

To address the issue of whether a behavior is part of the M.O. or part of the signature, investigators must look for behavioral patterns and convergences. They must not fall into the trap of interpreting behavioral meaning based on typical meanings from unrelated offenses. They must further not fall into the trap of interpreting a single behavior outside of the context of the facts of a given case, and apart from the other behaviors in the offense. As already discussed in the previous chapter, the meaning of a behavior to a rapist can only be interpreted when it is in the context of the rape.

RECOGNIZING RAPIST SIGNATURE

A rapist's signature is sometimes referred to inappropriately as a "calling card" or a "trademark" (Keppel, 1995). Those terms evoke the vision of a static, inflexible, indelible psychological imprint of rapist behavior on the crime scene. This is a misleading comparison.

There are important limitations on the concept of signature that must be understood. Many serial or predatory rapists do have a need to engage in personal expressions of emotion during offenses that are very distinct to their individually formed personality. However, despite this distinctiveness, which is a result of the many different variables affecting the human developmental process, it is not truly appropriate to state that two crime scenes related by signature alone are psychologically "identical." The terms "identical" and "match" can be misleading to those who do not fully understand the concept and psychology of signature.

The term "match" may be used to suggest "identical," shared characteristics between two things. But by their very nature, *crime scenes and crime-scene behavior cannot be precisely the same across offenses even when the same rapist is responsible for them.* Not only are the locations likely to be different, but the victims are most certainly different people with their own responses to rapist behaviors that will in turn influence the rapist's expressions, both M.O. and signature oriented. One of the other primary reasons for the lack of absolute certainty in interpreting signature behaviors as unique to a specific rapist is the subjectivity of the interpretation itself. Although rapists may be psychologically distinct, investigators cannot see through the eyes of a rapist with perfect, objective clarity. They can show the most likely perspectives and needs of the rapist by demonstrating a strong convergence of the physical and behavioral evidence, but they cannot go so far as to call it a "psychological fingerprint."

There are many variables to consider when interpreting signature behaviors that must be factored into any complete analysis. It is important to understand that it may not always be possible to link or unlink cases with signature, for the following reasons:

- A rapist may not always leave their signature behaviors behind.
- A rapist may engage in precautionary acts that conceal the evidence of signature behaviors (burning evidence, removing unknown fantasy items from the crime scene, staging the crime scene, etc.).
- Evidence of rapist behavior may be lost, overlooked, or destroyed by forensic personnel and criminal investigators.

The mere repetition of a behavior across multiple offenses is not enough to make it signature in nature. It may simply be a part of the rapist's M.O. Generally, the following will be true of signature behaviors:

- Takes extra time to complete, beyond more functional M.O. behavior
- Unnecessary for the completion of the crime
- Involves an expression of emotion
- May involve an expression of fantasy

If a behavior satisfies these criteria, then it is more than probably signature in nature. That is to say, it is related to psychological needs (fantasy and motive) rather than functional M.O. needs.

RAPIST MOTIVATION

For the purposes of this work, we will define *motive* as the emotional, psychological, and material needs that impel and are satisfied by behavior. *Intent* will be defined as the aim that guides behavior. Motive is the general need, and intent is the specific plan, or aim.

For example, many rapes are committed to satisfy a rapist's emotional or psychological need for power, anger, and control (Groth, 1979, p. 2). For the rapist, forced sexual acts of various kinds are used to satisfy the variations of those needs. Power, anger, and control are the motives, and rape is the intent.

Reasoning from the facts developed during an investigation best reveals a rapist's motive. Sometimes the motive is apparent, and sometimes it requires a great deal of investigation to reveal. An investigation that has not yielded the motive for the rape is incomplete.

Though it is not always necessary to solve or try the crime in court, determining the motivation behind a rape provides several advantages to an investigation and subsequent prosecution (or defense, for that matter):

1. Reduces the suspect pool to those individuals with a particular motive.
2. Assists with the investigative linkage of unsolved rapes with a similar motive.
3. Along with other class evidence (i.e., means, opportunity, associative evidence), motive can provide circumstantial bearing on rapist identity.
4. Along with other contextual evidence, motive can provide circumstantial bearing on rapist state of mind.
5. Along with circumstantial evidence, motive can provide circumstantial bearing on whether a rape has actually occurred.

Writing on legal issues related to character and motive evidence, Leonard (2001) defines motive by offering a number of similar definitions:

> Motive is a state of mind. A general dictionary defines it as "something that prompts a person to act in a certain way or that determines volition," and equates the term with inducement and incentive. *Wigmore* classified "motive" as a desire or emotion and treated it along with evidence of "feeling" and "passion." *Wright and Graham* assume that the "other crimes rule" uses the term motive "in the generally accepted sense of an emotion or state of mind that prompts a person to act in a particular way; an incentive for certain volitional activity." A turn-of-the-century court defined motive as "the moving power which impels to action for a definite result." Another source defines motive in the relevant context as "an inducement or state of feeling that impels and tempts the mind to indulge a criminal act," and notes that emotions such as hostility and jealousy can be the source of motives to act in a particular way.
>
> When it is defined in these similar ways, motive appears distinct from other states of mind that might be at issue or relevant in a particular case, such as intent. It would also appear to be distinct from the state of mind of one who possesses a "plan." . . .

Leonard (2001) goes on to argue that motive cannot be proven directly. It is something that only the rapist knows for certain, and often has every reason to lie about (consciously and unconsciously). Motive can, however, be inferred from criminal behavioral evidence present within given or established circumstances. As explained in Leonard (2001):

The inferential steps from the evidence to the existence of a motive, and then from the motive to the behavior at issue, can be strong or weak. In some cases, the evidence gives rise to a strong inference of a specific motive, and the likelihood of the motive gives rise to a strong inference of action in conformity with that motive or the existence of a relevant state of mind. In other cases, one or both of the inferences is hardly persuasive. One reason such an inference is often weak is that the motive is too general and too unlikely to be acted upon to be useful. As an English commentator noted, "almost every child has something to gain from the death of his parents, but rarely on the death of a parent is parricide even suspected."

In agreement with the basic approach offered in Leonard (2001) to infer motive, O'Hara (1970, p. 14) states that:

[Motive] may be inferred from circumstances. . . . Evidence relating to motive or state of mind is usually obtained by interviewing witnesses. A study of the crime scene and a reconstruction of the occurrence, including the suspect's prior and subsequent acts, may often be helpful.

Not discussed in Leonard (2001) or O'Hara (1970), but necessary to motive determination, are attempts to falsify motive theories and document the absence of evidence suggesting alternative and additional motivations.

In order to understand the motivations of violent, predatory rapists, A. Nicholas Groth, an American clinical psychologist working with both victims and rapists, conducted and published a study of more than 500 rapists (Groth, 1979). The purpose of his work was treatment oriented. He wanted to classify the motivations of rapists to assist with the development of effective treatment plans. In his study, Groth found that rape, like any other crime that satisfies emotional needs, is complex and multidetermined. That is to say, the act of rape, and its associated behaviors, can serve more than motive (pp. 12–13).

Groth originally described three types of rapists (pp. 13–58): the anger rapist, the power rapist, and the sadistic rapist. The *anger rapist* uses sexual acts as an extension of an overall physical assault, as a means of expressing and discharging feelings of cumulative anger and rage (p. 13). The *power rapist* has no desire to harm the victim. Rather, he has a need to possess, control, and own the victim sexually. By achieving sexual mastery and authority over the victim, he is compensating for underlying feelings of inadequacy (p. 25). The sadistic rapist achieves sexual gratification only through victim pain and humiliation. In such instances, suffering, hatred, and control are eroticized, with physical and psychological torture inflicted upon the victim (pp. 44–45).

Groth's research was adopted and expanded by others (Burgess, Burgess, Douglas, and Ressler, 1997; Hazelwood, 1995; Rosenberg, Knight, Prentsky, and Lee, 1998; Turvey, 2002), who generally describe the following rapist motivational typology:

Power-Reassurance (Compensatory): Involves nonaggressive behavior that normalizes an attack for a rapist, in an attempt to restore a rapist's doubts about his prowess and desirability.

Power-Assertive (Impulsive/Exploitative/Entitlement): Involves aggressive but nonlethal behavior that shows an outward macho facade of confidence and masculinity, restoring a rapist's inner doubts and fears regarding same.

Anger-Retaliatory (Displaced Aggression): When brutal levels of physical and sexual force service feelings of cumulative rage.

Anger-Excitation (Sadistic): When victim pain and suffering give the rapist sexual gratification.

THE BEHAVIOR—MOTIVATIONAL TYPOLOGY

The following typology is offered as a guide to help investigators classify rapist behavior, in context, in relationship to the rapist need it serves. It is not intended for use as a diagnostic tool, where rapists are crammed into one classification or another and conclusively labeled. Therefore, it is not investigatively helpful to think of this as a rapist typology, but rather as a *behavior–motivational* typology.

Also, readers are admonished not to interpret a single rapist behavior outside of its context. For example, a rapist who says, "Is your boyfriend home?" to a victim during the approach phase of a sexual assault may be doing so for M.O.-related reasons. However, if a rapist says the same thing while performing a sexual act on the victim, it may be fantasy related, and subsequently related to rapist signature. It is not just about what a rapist says or does, it is about how and when they say or do it.

POWER REASSURANCE (AKA COMPENSATORY)

These include rapist behaviors that are intended to restore the rapist's self-confidence or self-worth through the use of low-aggression means. These behaviors suggest a lack of confidence and a sense of personal inadequacy on the part of the rapist. This may also manifest itself in a belief/rationalization that the offense is consensual, or that the victim is somehow a willing or culpable participant.

Method of Approach
Surprise.

Method of Attack
Verbal threat and weapon.

Verbal Behavior
Examples include signature behaviors:

- Reassures victim that they do not wish to harm them. "Don't worry, it will be over soon. I'm not going to hurt/rape you. I'm not that kind of guy."
- Compliments victim. "You're beautiful, I bet you have a lot of boyfriends/girlfriends. You have nice breasts. You have a pretty face."
- Asks for emotional feedback. "Do you like me? Tell me that you won't leave me. Tell me that you love me."
- Self-deprecation. "You couldn't love me; nobody could. I'm so ugly, you're so beautiful. I don't have anything to offer anyone."
- Voices concern for victim welfare: "Am I hurting you? Do you need me to move this? Am I on your hair?"
- Apologetic: "I didn't mean it. Please forgive me. I know I wasn't supposed to do this. I hope you will be okay."
- Asks about victim sexual interests. "Are you a virgin? Do you do this to your boyfriend/girlfriend? Does your boyfriend/girlfriend do this with you?"
- Asks victim to evaluate their sexual skills—sexual reassurance. "Do you like this? Does this feel good? Are you going to be getting aroused?"

Sexual Behavior
Examples include signature behaviors:

- Foreplay attempt with victim (kissing, licking breasts, cunnilingus and analingus, etc.)
- Involvement of the victim in sexual activity
- Allowing the victim to negotiate sexual activity
- Not forcing the victim to physically comply with sexual demands

Physical Behavior
Examples include signature behaviors:

- Does not harm the victim, physically
- Minimal force used to intimidate victim
- Relies on threats or the presence of a weapon to get victim compliance

M.O. Behavior

- Selects victims who live in the same general area, often near rapist's home, work, or other places where they feel comfortable
- Targets several victims in advance
- Engages in surveillance of victims
- Attacks occur in late evening or early morning
- Victims are alone or with small children when attacked
- Attack lasts a short period of time: duration increased with victim passivity
- Vicinity of the attacks remains within same general area
- Terminates the rape if the victim resists

Signature Behavior

- Engages in voyeuristic behavior of victim before or after attack
- Takes personal item from the victim, such as an undergarment, ring, or photograph
- Keeps a record of attack
- Makes obscene phone calls to the victim
- Contacts the victim after the attack (phone calls asking the victim out on a date, flowers sent to their home, messages on their answering machine telling them what a good time they had)

Rapists evidencing this type of behavior may attempt to recontact their living victims after an attack. They might have expected the victim to respond erotically to their advances. In the rapist's mind the victim might even be in love with them and have enjoyed the attack. From the rapist's point of view, it was more of a date.

The core fantasy motivating this rapist is that the victim will enjoy and eroticize the rape, and subsequently fall in love with the rapist. These stem from the rapist's own fears of personal inadequacy; hence; the term commonly applied to this rapist is "an inadequate personality." The rape is restorative of the rapist's doubts about himself, and therefore sexually and emotionally reassuring. It will occur as his need for that kind of reassurance arises.

> **Example:** *Albert Arredondo*
> Referred to by some investigators as the "apologetic rapist," in June of 2002, 31-year-old Albert Arredondo **(shown in Figure 12-1)** confessed to at least 10 sexual assaults in apartment complexes and condos in Fort Worth, Arlington, Weatherford, and Longview, Texas. He brought a knife with him to the rapes, but rarely used it. He only used force when victims tried to escape. He also made victims undress

Figure 12-1
Albert Arredondo, the
"Apologetic Rapist."

themselves, adding to his fantasy that the women were willing participants. According to reports (Boyd, 2002):

> One investigator dubbed him "the apologetic rapist."
>
> Victims told police that the man who had forced his way into their homes was polite and conversational and routinely said he was sorry after raping them.
>
> He rarely brandished a knife and used physical force only when his victims struggled or tried to escape.
>
> "He was like, 'I have to do this, but I'm sorry to do this to you,'" said Longview police Sgt. Don Jeter. "It was weird. Like he had a foot on the gas and a foot on the brake, all at the same time."
>
> Investigators had long suspected that the man who was preying on women in Fort Worth, Arlington, Weatherford and Longview was a power reassurance rapist, apologetic, polite and indulging in a delusional fantasy that the rape was consensual.
>
> Of the four types of general personality profiles for serial rapists, at least 80 percent are power reassurance rapists.

. . .

> "In some of the cases, he acted really like kind of a nice guy while he was raping them," Jeter said. "It was an attitude he was trying to maintain: 'I'm going to be nice to you after I've done this, even after I've raped you and darn near choked you.'"

> Police say the man took items from the victims that he considered "trophies" or "souvenirs," behavior that is also characteristic of a power reassurance rapist.

The quick thinking of a victim's boyfriend led to Arredondo's capture. He had entered the victim's home while she was on the phone with her boyfriend. The boyfriend heard her scream and called police.

When they searched Arredondo's vehicle (a Kia Sportage), investigators found driver's licenses, school identification cards, and credit cards belonging to some of the other victims.

Arredondo appeared concerned about his victims, telling police that he would confess "because he didn't want to put the victims through the stress of a trial." He did confess and was convicted in 2003.

Of note is that Arredondo was only one of at least two known serial rapists operating in Tarrant County, Texas, at the same time.

POWER ASSERTIVE (AKA ENTITLEMENT)

These include rapist behaviors that are intended to restore the rapist's self-confidence or self-worth through the use of moderate- to high-aggression means. These behaviors suggest an underlying lack of confidence and a sense of personal inadequacy that are expressed through control, mastery, and humiliation of the victim, while demonstrating the rapist's sense of authority. They show a lack of experience with intimacy. For these rapists, sex is a commodity to be bought, sold, or stolen. As discussed in Baker (1997):

> For some, sex is a commodity, and if sex is a commodity, then taking it is theft. The definitions of lovemaking discussed above may attempt to resist the classification of sex as a commodity, but most people rarely, if ever, discuss the personal, intimate, and shared experiences of sex. We live in a culture that rarely discusses sex as anything other than a commodity. Indeed, the more objectified and commodified the conversation, the easier it is for most people—especially young people—to talk about sex. Some people are never able to talk about the intimate aspects of sex, even if they do understand them. It is hardly surprising that most young people neither talk about nor understand sexual intimacy.

Instead, youths, particularly young men, are bombarded by a culture that sexualizes commodities and commodifies women's sexuality. Companies sell products by selling the sexuality of the women endorsing the product. The product and the sex are purposefully conflated. Sex is also purposefully commodified. Men can easily buy sex, even though all but one state prohibit prostitution. Men can also buy pornography and purchase tickets to peep shows. What motivates many rapists may not be substantively different from that which motivates men who go to prostitutes or purchase tickets to peep shows. None of these acts requires mutual enjoyment or emotional intimacy, and they are all called sex. Thus, men are able to satisfy a desire for sex without having to incorporate the complexities of sexually intimate communication.

. . .

Rape necessarily involves an assertion of power. As discussed above, some men use this power instrumentally, to get sex, or to get sex in order to relate to other men. Other men use power for its own sake. Power rapists rape because they want to establish control over their victims. They rarely exert more strength than is necessary to force their victims into submission. Rape—the act of controlling—not sex, is critical to their motivation to rape.

Assertive and reassurance behaviors are known to occur during the same offense, making it difficult for some to discriminate between the two. Originally, Groth did not. He referred only to the "Power Rapist" in his original typology.

Method of Approach
Con or surprise.

Method of Attack
Verbal threats, physical force, weapon.

Verbal Behavior
Examples include signature behaviors:

- Does not want the victim to be verbally or otherwise involved in the attack
- Gives sexual instructions/commands. "Suck this. Bend over. Hold still. Don't move. Shut up."
- Rapist's pleasure is primary
- Acts "macho"
- Uses a great deal of profanity, language is offensive and abusive
- Demeans and humiliates the victim. "You are a whore. You are a slut. I own you. You're not so pretty now."

- Verbally explicit about sex. "I'm going to put my cock in your cunt. I'm going to cum in your ass. You are going to suck my dick."
- Verbal threats. "Do what I say and you won't get hurt. Shut up or I'll kill you. I don't want to have to teach you a lesson."

Sexual Behavior

Examples include signature behaviors:

- Rapist does whatever they want to the victim, sexually or otherwise
- Lack of fondling foreplay behavior
- Repeated attacks with a single victim
- Rapist sexually punishes or abuses victims
- Rapist engages in pulling, pinching, or biting behaviors
- Rapist's goal is capture, conquer, and control
- Victim is a prop only: an object for his sexual fantasy

Physical Behavior

Examples include signature behaviors:

- Rapist rips or tears the victim's clothing
- Rapist engages in the use of corrective force
- Rapist engages in moderate, excessive, or brutal levels of force that increase with victim resistance or his level of sexual dysfunction during the offense
- Rapist chooses locations for the attack that are convenient and safe

M.O. Behavior

- The victim is preselected or opportunistic (too good to pass up)
- Victim chosen by availability, accessibility, and vulnerability
- The location of the offense is victim dependent
- Weapon is involved, or substituted with higher levels of force
- Physical aggression is used to initially overpower the victim
- Victim is held captive in some fashion while being raped

Rapists evidencing this type of behavior have absolutely no doubt about their own adequacy and masculinity. In fact, they may be using their attacks as an expression of their own virility. In their perception, they are entitled to the fruits of their attack by virtue of being stronger.

   This rapist may grow more confident over time, as his egocentricity tends to be very high. He may begin to do things that might lead to his identification. Law enforcement may interpret this as a sign that the rapist desires to be caught. What is actually true is that the rapist has no respect for law enforcement. He has learned that he can commit his offenses without the need to fear identification or capture, and subsequently he may not take precautions that he has learned are unnecessary.

It is not this rapist's desire to harm his victims, necessarily, but rather to possess them sexually. Demonstrating power over his victims is his means of expressing mastery, strength, control, authority, and identity to himself. The attacks are therefore intended to reinforce the rapist's inflated sense of self-confidence or self-worth.

Example: *John Alexander Scieszka, the Five Points Rapist*

In October of 1996, an interstate task force was formed to investigate a series of 20 rapes of young women in and around Athens, Georgia, and Gainesville, Florida. This led to matching DNA evidence and the arrest of John Alexander Scieszka (shown in Figure 12-2) on January 29, 1997, in Alpharetta, Georgia.

The Georgia Police Department had first arrested Mr. Scieszka in 1977 on a burglary charge. In 1980, he was convicted of raping a woman in Florida. He also pleaded guilty to a second 1980 rape, and admitted in a police interview that he committed that attack while out on bail after being arrested for the first attack. He served only 11–12 years of a 25- to 30-year sentence.

In 1993, Mr. Scieszka attacked two women in Lullwater, Georgia, but they managed to escape. His third victim, on Memorial Day of May 1994, was a daytime jogger on a run. He held her at knifepoint, dragged her to a remote location, then raped and sodomized her for the next 30 minutes.

Figure 12-2

John Alexander Scieszka, the "Five Points Rapist."

In police interview on January 16, 1998, then 46-year-old John Scieszka further admitted that he was responsible for at least 11 sexual assaults in the Gainesville area. Collectively, Mr. Scieszka has admitted to assaulting 17 women—12 in Florida and 5 in Georgia. He is accused of assaulting more.

Mr. Scieszka targeted women 18–22 years old, but their actual ages ranged from 13 to 27. He did not know any of his victims and typically attacked while they were jogging or at home alone. At least three of his victims resisted and were beaten until they stopped. In one case, he beat a victim with a heavy metal flashlight. He also covered his face during the attacks, but on one occasion he wore a hood; when he bent over the victim in that case she got a full view of his face.

In terms of motive, his background and police interviews provide some insight, and a lot of self-serving rationalizations (*Shearer*, 1998):

> "I'd just be driving around and drinking and I would end up in Athens. I wouldn't consciously set out for Athens," Scieszka said.

> Five Points not only offered a mix of people that he could blend in with, he explained, but provided areas of dense shrubbery and trees that made it easy for him to stalk his victims.

> "I watched them first. I wouldn't just jump on them. I was able to go to the rear of the apartment, check it out, make sure it was safe, check out the person inside," he said. "In all these situations, there was places where I was able to stand and observe."

> Scieszka's technique in the Athens attacks was to come in through a window, and one simple measure would have deterred him, he said.

> "Oh, yes" he replied when the detectives asked if bolted windows would have stopped him.

> And asked what he would do to protect his own daughter if he had one, Scieszka listed three things. If possible, get an upstairs apartment. If she lived on the first floor, he said, he would pay to have burglar bars installed. And lastly: advise her to "just be aware when she goes from the car to the front door."

> "People shouldn't have to watch their back like that," he said. But his advice is to "be more conscious of the fact that you can't leave the door unlocked for five minutes. You can't open the windows for a breath of fresh air."

> Scieszka said in the interview he worries now about the young woman he was living with at the time of his arrest.

> "I worry that somebody like me would choose her as a target," he said.

"What am I doing?"

Scieszka told the investigators he had no intention to rape or hurt his Athens victims.

"It wasn't premeditated," he said. "I didn't plan to do it. I more or less tricked myself into going. The next morning after I woke up, I'd go, 'God! What am I doing? I can't do that no more. I'll swear I'll never do it again.' I kind of felt like Dr. Jekyll and Mr. Hyde. I hated it.

"Then I'd be drinking and say, 'Why don't I just cruise over to Athens and see what's happening?' I would lead myself into it one step at the time. And I really hated it.

"I had everything I ever needed. I loved the life I was leading. I loved the business I had. That's why I hated what I was doing, because I had everything I wanted," he said.

Scieszka had learned welding and metal work in his nearly 12 years in Florida prisons, and thoroughly enjoyed the work, he said.

"We actually built fire trucks, rescue units," Scieszka said. "We took old bookmobiles and converted them into SWAT command units. We did some beautiful work. I enjoyed it because I felt like I was contributing."

Scieszka got a job with an Atlanta fencing company after his 1992 release from prison, but soon was making $700 a weekend in free-lance work, nearly twice as much as the $400 a week he got from his job, he said in the interview. He started his own company, and in the weeks before his arrest last Jan. 30, he said, had begun to bring in some very profitable jobs: $98,000 for a six-week job, $139,000 for a two-month job, and larger contracts on the way.

Scieszka, asked why he raped, was vague, but mentioned several factors, most prominently alcohol. Determined to make a new start, Scieszka told the detectives he refrained from drinking for a while after his release, but started going out drinking with co-workers when he found a job and soon was up to a 12-pack of beer a day.

He also said a man fondled him in a theater when he was young.

"That really affected me. I think a lot of these crimes I committed here (have roots in that)," he said.

He also explained his rapes as a kind of fallout from the easy sex of the 1970s.

"From about '73 to '77, it was like the sexual revolution was going on. Every night I was going out with another college girl and I got addicted to it. As soon as herpes came along, the sexual revolution was over, and I wouldn't stop," he said.

In prison, Scieszka said he learned there are three kinds of rapists: the angry rapist who "goes berserk," the sadistic rapist who "wants to destroy," and power rapists—the category Scieszka said he belongs in.

"Me, I just wanted control. That's where my fantasies are," he said, describing his fantasy of having a harem. "In my fantasies, I wouldn't hurt them. They're just there to do whatever my wishes are. I wouldn't let myself think about what I was really doing."

To Scieszka, his rapes "were like coming home drunk and . . . getting in bed with the old lady."

Scieszka, married twice before his 1980 imprisonment, described one wife as a rich girl he couldn't materially satisfy and the second as a woman who "wanted a meal ticket."

In a 1998 trial, Mr. Scieszka was convicted of five attacks on University of Georgia women between 1995 and 1996. As of this writing, he is serving eight consecutive life sentences for the crimes.

ANGER RETALIATORY (AKA ANGER, REVENGE, OR DISPLACED)

These include rapist behaviors that suggest a great deal of rage, toward a specific person, group, institution, or a symbol of any of these. These types of behaviors are commonly evidenced in stranger-to-stranger sexual assaults, domestic homicides, work-related homicide, and cases involving political or religious terrorists.

Method of Approach
Blitz or surprise.

Method of Attack
Brutal physical force, extreme violence, weapons, explosives.

Verbal Behavior
Examples include signature behaviors:

- Verbally selfish—is not interested in hearing the victim
- Does not negotiate
- May blame victim for events and perceived events. "If you wouldn't have struggled I wouldn't have had to beat you like that. You think you are so hot. You think you're better than I am. It's people like you that are the problem. You don't understand; you have to be made to understand."
- Other angry, hostile language

Sexual Behavior

Examples include signature behaviors:

- Sexually selfish
- Sex is violent, an extension of the physical attack
- No foreplay
- Attempts to force victim to perform acts that they perceive as degrading or humiliating (fellatio or sodomy)

Physical Behavior

Examples include signature behaviors:

- Ripping of victim's clothing
- Dresses for the event (full military dress uniform, face paint, battle dress uniform [khakis or camouflage material], etc.)
- Excessive or brutal levels of force with high amount of injury to the victim

M.O. Behavior

- Attack is unplanned: a result of an emotional reaction on the part of a rapist
- Attack is skillfully planned and focused on a particular victim or victim population
- Offenses appear sporadic over time, occurring at any location, at any time of day or night (whenever the rapist gets pissed off or whenever a particular victim type is accessible)
- Uses weapons of opportunity, or if planned will prepare for the event with excessive weaponry and ammunition
- Rapist knows the victim, or the victim symbolizes something specific to the rapist

Signature Behavior

- There is an immediate application of direct physical force to the victim; the rapist attacks first, then continues into any other behavior as an extension of that attack
- Duration of attack is very short—ends when the rapist is emotionally spent
- Results in the rapist intentionally surrendering their life as part of a social, political, or personal message to others
- There is a lot of anger evident in the crime scene

- Collateral victims in the crime scene as a result of anger and lack of planning, other victims surprise the rapist in the heat of the moment or just get caught in the "crossfire" (very often unintentional, but if it is intentional it will be evidenced by rapist planning behavior)

Anger retaliation behavior is just what the name suggests. The rapist is acting on the basis of cumulative real or imagined wrongs from those that are in their world. The victim of the attack may be one of these people such as a relative, a girlfriend, or a co-worker. Or the victim may symbolize that person to the rapist in dress, occupation, and/or physical characteristics.

The main goal of this rapist behavior is to service their cumulative aggression. They are retaliating against the victim for wrongs or perceived wrongs, and their aggression can manifest itself spanning a wide range, from verbally abusive epithets to hyper-aggressed homicide with multiple collateral victims. As discussed in *Baker* (1997):

> The anger rapist assaults his victim completely. He attacks all parts of her body, often forces her to engage in repeated, nonsexual degrading acts, and uses much more violence than is necessary to force her into submission. "The aim of this type of rapist is to vent his rage on his victim and to retaliate for perceived wrongs or rejections he has suffered at the hands of women. . . . This offender displays a great deal of anger and contempt toward women." The offender "does not seek out a specific victim but instead discharges his anger onto someone who is immediately available."

It is important not to confuse retaliatory behavior with sadistic behavior. Although they can share some characteristics at first blush, the motivations are wholly separate. Also, a distinct lack of planning and overall rapist preparedness will likely be apparent in conjunction with nonterrorist anger retaliatory behavior.

> **Example:** *California v. John J. Park et al.*
> John J. Park, Hyun Gu Kang, aka "Eddy," and other Korean associates were convicted of being engaged in a criminal conspiracy against particular escort services and dance clubs whose female employees also provided sexual services to clients. Throughout 1996, they had conducted a series of interrelated robberies, abductions, and rapes that were motivated by revenge or the desire to damage the competitors of a coconspirator's escort agency, or both, and to gather funds for that agency. The evidence against them included eyewitness ID, DNA, fingerprints, a coconspirator's confession, and cell phone records.

According to *California v. John J. Park et al.* (2002):

> There were four female victims: Christina R., Seong H., Margarita Z., and Colleen O. After being lured to a hotel room, each was beaten, tied up, robbed, and subjected to violent sexual crimes, including forcible rape. In furtherance of the count 1 conspiracy, Ji Tae Kim, David Lee, and Dean Kim were robbed of their respective driver's licenses. These identity thefts were perpetrated in order to obtain identification to protect the true identity of the conspirator registering for the room where the female victim was attacked. Additionally, Seong H. discovered $300 had been stolen through her ATM card, which had been taken during the first attack on her. Also, during the attack on Margarita Z., her home was burglarized and $1,800 taken.

Because of the brutal nature of these crimes, the uncharacteristically intricate nature of the planning and precautionary acts involved, and the insight that the details lend into the various Korean gang and escort service culture, the specifics are provided for the benefit of the dedicated student of crime. Taken entirely from *California v. John J. Park et al.* (2002):

> In March 1996, Jennifer Nam, a former "hostess" at the Club Starlight, told Kang, with whom she was romantically involved, that she had received a large inheritance and wanted to use $10,000 to start a nightclub. Kang introduced Nam to the owner of Mamma Lion, a Korean nightclub where Kang worked as a manager, and the three discussed opening a new club.
>
> About two and a half weeks later, Nam admitted that she did not have $10,000. Kang threatened to have her put in jail for fraud and demanded that she earn the money by working for an escort agency. She agreed to do so.
>
> During her approximate four-month employment with Amore, the escort agency selected by Kang, Nam earned approximately $25,000 a month, all of which she turned over to Kang, who gave her back enough money for necessities.
>
> Amore was nominally an escort service whose services were limited to "strictly massage." However, the "escorts" were allowed to provide sex to male customers for "tips," which were paid directly to the escort along with the $150 basic hourly massage fee, of which $50 went to Amore. The procedure followed required the "escort" to check in upon arrival and check out upon finishing with Amore by telephone. Nam engaged in sexual relations with many of her clients.
>
> Nam was driven to the location where she met her clients. At first, Kang was the driver. He then arranged for his brother Jason Kang to drive her. After

Jason started school, Kang introduced Nam to Moses who drove her for awhile. Nam then met Park through Kang, and Park would "switch-off" with Moses. Although Yun was also a driver, Nam did not meet Yun, whom she referred to as "Peter" until close to the time she quit Amore. Kang would fill in, however, if no one else was available as a driver.

. . .

Nam quit Amore, because she was tired of "selling [her] body to get money." She told Kang, however, she was fired. Kang became very angry. He wanted to destroy Amore and said that Amore's owner, Jennifer H., was "going to pay." He also directed Nam to help him lure away Amore escorts and customers for his own escort service. Amore refused to rehire Nam when Nam asked at Kang's insistence. Kang became "very mad" at Amore.

. . .

Nam knew through Kang that some of the women going out on calls were getting beaten and robbed. After returning around 4:00 or 5:00 a.m. after the first meeting, Kang, with Park and Kim present, related to Nam that after the female involved, who was Hispanic or Armenian, entered the Days Inn hotel room, the men tied her up, beat her unconscious, took her money and driver's license, and then burglarized her residence. "[T]hey left her unconscious because she was really beaten up."

. . .

Following the conspirators' return after the second meeting, around 3:00 or 4:00 a.m., they talked about what they did. Kang spoke about what happened to a young woman at a hotel room. He explained that "[t]hey just beat the victims and take their money, take possessions." Nam saw the victim's driver's license.

On September 6, 1996, around 5:00 a.m., Christina R., an Amore escort, arrived at the conspirators' room at the Days Inn in Los Angeles's Koreatown. At least three conspirators then began beating and kicking her. When she started screaming, they warned her in an Asian accent to stop, and something round like a gun barrel was pressed against her head. At one point, she was tied up. Christina R. was digitally penetrated, sodomized, and raped as she lay on her stomach. Afterwards, they robbed her of $750, her checkbook and her identification. One asked if her checkbook address was correct and if she resided with anyone. She responded in the affirmative to both questions. When asked, she denied having any money in the house.

. . .

On September 11, 1996, late in the evening, at the request of her colleague Mina, Seong H. accompanied Mina to a Best Western Hotel. The two worked for the "Pretty Girl Dating Service," which provided "massage, entertainment, dancers, and escort service." When they arrived at the designated room, two conspirators came out. Mina immediately ran away, and the two men dragged Seong H. into the room while hitting and threatening her. A gun was held to her head. At some point, she was tied up. They took the small amount of money in her purse, perhaps $30, a hand phone, a pager, and her bank ATM card. At their demand, she revealed her secret PIN number. One spoke Korean. The other spoke English. The conspirators then left the room to confirm her PIN number. Seong H. subsequently learned that her ATM card was used to take $300.

On September 19, 1996, around 5:00 p.m., Seong H. went to the Days Inn on a "dating job[.]" When she knocked on the door, a man told her in Korean to enter. Once inside, a group of three men exited the restroom and confronted her. Both Korean and English were spoken.

They placed her on the bed and began questioning her about her home location and whether she kept money there. She gave them the address on her driver's license but not her home address and said there was no money there. The men who left to check out her information discovered her lie. The conspirators then threatened to kill her if she did not disclose her true address and where her money was. A knife was placed on her arm, chest, and thigh. A gun was placed against her body. Seong H. responded by telling them there was no money in her home and that her boyfriend had money at his home.

Seong H.'s face was covered and she was tied up part of the time. The four conspirators took turns raping her. As the fourth man raped Seong H., a fifth man who acted like he was the "boss" entered the room. Speaking in Korean, he said, "[W]ell, since you are all finished, I'm going to do it, too." He then also raped Seong H.

. . .

Although the conspirators left Seong H. her purse, they took her phone and pager.

On September 29, 1996, around 10:30 p.m., Ji-Tae Kim left his Pasadena store and drove his Mazda MPV to his home in a townhouse complex at 49 North Parkwood Avenue. Around 10:50 p.m., as he pulled into the secured parking garage area another car followed closely. When Kim exited his assigned space, the passenger of the other car pointed a gun at Kim's chest. Kim was told in English and Korean to do as he was told and he would not be killed. In Korean, Kim told them to take his money, about $100, and leave. Before leaving, in addition to his money, they took his "genie" garage opener and his "Marlboro bag," which contained his driver's license, personal checkbooks, and other items. A checkbook belonging to Ji-Tae Kim was found during a subsequent search of Yun's apartment.

. . .

On September 30, 1996, at 2:09 a.m., a man registered for room 223 at the Ramada Inn at 3900 Wilshire Boulevard. He identified himself as "Jitak Kim" and listed 49 North Parkwood Avenue as his residence. When asked, however, he denied having any identification. He appeared drunk and smelled of alcohol. In a photographic lineup, the hotel clerk identified Jason Kang, codefendant Kang's younger brother, as the man who registered.

Around 3:00 a.m., Margarita Z., who worked for Amore, knocked on the door of room 223 at the Ramada Inn. An Asian man wearing only boxer shorts opened the door, turned around, and walked to about the center of the bed. Another man then exited the bathroom, grabbed her by the hair, stuck a gun to her head, and shoved her in a closet. They took her personal checkbook, pager, and about $400 or $500. At some point, she was blindfolded and tied up, but she could see just under the blindfold.

The conspirators took her driver's license which listed her address. The man with the gun demanded her true home address and asked her to identify which key was for the garage, the building, and her apartment. After she complied, he told her his "home boys" were going to go to her house while he stayed with her. She admitted no one was home. He threatened to kill her if she had lied. At this time, there were four or five more men in the room. The conspirators then conversed together in Korean. When asked about money in her apartment, she responded by telling them the amount and exact location of the money. About 10 or 15 minutes later, the new arrivals left.

The man with the gun then raped Margarita Z. three times during which his cellular telephone rang several times. He answered in Korean and asked Margarita Z. first for additional directions to her place and on the second occasion why the lights were on in her apartment. She explained that she left the lights on just so it would not be dark when she returned.

The man who opened the door then raped her. About a minute or two later, the others returned. After the conspirators conversed together in Korean, a third man raped Margarita Z. The conspirators then left.

Subsequently, she discovered her apartment had been ransacked and the $1,800 she had hidden between some magazines in her bedroom had been stolen.

At a photographic lineup and at trial, Margarita Z. positively identified Park as the man who had the gun and the first to rape her. Moses Kim's fingerprints were found on the bottle of baby oil which had been in her purse.

. . .

On October 16, 1996, at 2:54 a.m., an Asian male registered as "Jason Kim" for room 313 at the Ramada Inn. The hotel clerk identified him from a photographic lineup and at trial as Kang. Sometime between 2:00 and 5:00 a.m., a "Pretty Woman" employee received a call from a "Jason Kim" requesting an Asian female be sent to his room. Instead, the employee recorded several calls with "Jason," because she suspected he might be involved in the incidents where Asian males requested Asian females late at night.

About 1:00 p.m., various police officers went to room 313. Kang, who answered the door in boxer shorts, allowed them to enter to conduct a criminal investigation. During a consensual search, a large knife, three pairs of pantyhose, and two gloves, black and blue, were found in Kang's briefcase. After Kang's arrest, a coil of very thin white rope, which had been cut into various eight shorter lengths, was found in a slightly ajar drawer next to the bed. Kang was taken to the station for questioning. He was later released.

Subsequently, Kang instructed Nam to buy a 12- to 20-inch white rope and a knife; take the items to their escort office; and spread them around "like we were moving boxes and packing up to move."

On December 14, 1996, around 11:00 p.m. in Koreatown, three of the conspirators robbed Dean Kim and David Lee of their respective driver's licenses. When the Korean attackers demanded their California "I.D.'s," Lee and Dean Kim complied. The attackers then left taking only the victims' driver's licenses. They were not interested in the victims' money.

. . .

On December 17, 1996, sometime after 11:30 p.m., Colleen O., who worked for "Unlimited Connections," which booked dancers for embarrassment birthday or bachelor parties, arrived at the Days Inn. Colleen O., who was neither Japanese nor Asian, knocked on the room door. A man with an Asian accent answered and asked if she were Japanese. She replied that she was both Japanese and American. When she began to respond to his inquiry about what took her so long, she was tackled by five men who exited the bathroom and shoved her to the floor. She was beaten and a gun was shoved in her face by the man who answered the door.

Colleen O. was tied up during part of the attack. They took her money, about $80, her car keys, and her California driver's license. Someone then asked where she lived and with whom and if there was any money there. She replied that she lived with her parents and there was no money. They announced their intent to go there and, if she had lied, to kill her.

The man to her left and closest to the bathroom door digitally penetrated Colleen O. and then raped her. All six attackers were Asian males with accents, but the one who sexually attacked her also spoke English clearly.

. . .

During a police interview, Moses Kim stated that Kang was like a "big brother." He made the following statements regarding the crimes he and his coconspirators committed. Either he or Park would usually make the telephone call to the agencies for a female. He stated that only Park and Kang were involved in those incidents also involving himself. He admitted having sex with women whom he tied up with duck tape in hotel rooms.

When asked about the incident involving a Hispanic woman, i.e., Christina R., Moses Kim denied beating up anyone. He also denied he was there. He admitted, however, being at the Days Inn one time. When asked about the incident involving Colleen O., he spoke about the woman being "pure white" but she appeared to be Asian. He also mentioned "[a] folding knife" being used. He recalled another incident involving a Korean woman who spoke Korean at the Best Western. There were two girls. One went inside, and the other ran away. This was the September 11, 1996, Seong H. incident.

He recalled the Ramada Inn incident, which involved Margarita Z., more than the others. He admitted that he was the one who answered the door in his underwear. He identified Park as the one hiding in the bathroom and who had the gun. Park also had sexual intercourse with the woman. He recalled silver duct tape was used to restrain the woman, and that Kang at some point came into the room.

Additionally, according to *Lota* (2001), the father of 32-year-old Hyun Gu "Eddie" Kang posted a $2.5 million bond at the conclusion of his trial, and he fled to South Korea on Feb. 26, 1999. At the time, the United States did not have an extradition treaty with South Korea. Two years later, in November of 2001, South Korea returned Mr. Kang to the United States to serve a life sentence for his crimes. He was the first person to be extradited back to the United States under the new treaty, which was signed in December of 1999.

SADISTIC (AKA ANGER EXCITATION)

These include behaviors that evidence rapist sexual gratification from victim pain and suffering. The primary motivation for the behavior is sexual; however, the sexual expression for the rapist is manifested in physical aggression, or torture behavior, toward the victim. In other words, for these rapists, violence is sexualized and eroticized.

Method of Approach
Con.

Method of Attack
Surprise, physical force, weapons, explosives.

Verbal Behavior
Examples include signature behaviors:

- The rapist says things meant to gain the victim's trust and confidence—things that will lower the victim's guard. "Can you help me with this? I'm lost. Do I know you? You remind me of a friend I had back in school."
- The rapist says things to entice the victim away from safe areas—"I have something I want to show you. Let me offer you a ride. Can I give you help with that heavy load up to your apartment?"
- During the attack, the rapist demands to be called a certain name or title to indicate victim subservience (Sir, Master, Lord, etc.).
- The rapist asks, "Does it hurt? Did that hurt? Can you feel that?" when engaged in rough sex acts or inflicting victim injury.
- The rapist demands that victim scream during the attack.
- The rapist calls the victim demeaning, humiliating names to reinforce his view of their worthlessness, such as "bitch," "slut," "whore," and/or "cunt."

Sexual Behavior
Examples include signature behaviors:

- The rapist has an extensive collective of pornography
- The rapist is sexually stimulated by the victim's response to the infliction of physical and/or emotional pain
- The rapist rehearses attacks in private, and with compliant victims (i.e., wife or girlfriend)
- The rapist involves the use of sexual bondage apparatus and behaviors during the attack
- The rapist performs sexual torture on victim, including repeated biting, insertion of foreign objects in vagina or anus, and the use of sexual torture devices on a conscious victim
- The rapist prefers rough anal sex followed in frequency by forced fellatio
- The rapist prefers ejaculation on specific parts of the victim's body
- The rapist is sexually selfish; the victim's primary function is to suffer, sexually

- The rapist records the attack for later fantasy activity (video, photos, journal, audio, maps, calendars, diaries, media clippings)
- "Souvenirs" and "trophies" are kept and hidden in secret, but accessible places (home, office, vehicle, storage space, etc.)

Physical Behavior

Examples include signature behaviors:

- Brutal or high level of force used to inflict victim injury over a prolonged period of time
- Injuries inflicted against specific areas of the victim's body of sexual significance to the rapist (feet, nipples, anus, vagina, mouth, etc.)
- The intensity of specified sexual injury increases with the rapist's anger (i.e., response to a noncompliant victim, or a victim who is too compliant), which increases with the level of sexual arousal

M.O. Behavior

- The rapist chooses or impersonates an occupation that allows them to act as an authority figure, placing them in a position to identify and acquire victims (i.e., law enforcement, security guard, youth counselor, coach, etc.).
- Offenses planned in exacting detail—victim type; location for selecting victim; con; location for attack; signature behavior; disposal site—all are thought of in advance.
- Offenses executed methodically.
- Rapist assesses and selects victim by emotional vulnerability, and gains their confidence through seduction.
- Victims are vilified by law enforcement (prostitutes, drug addicts, runaways, etc.).
- Victims are nonaggressive and have low self-esteem.
- Victim is lured to a concealed area where the rapist has a great deal of control (vehicle, basement, garage, hotel room, etc.).
- This rapist increases aggression with each successive attack.
- The rapist kills the victim as a precautionary act.

Signature Behavior

- Special offense materials brought with rapist to the scene, containing weapons, bindings, and any sexual apparatus.
- The sexual attack lasts for an extended period of time.
- Rapist is good at presenting the image of a loving and sincere individual.

- Victims are strangers to the rapist (facilitates both M.O. and signature—it is easier to torture and humiliate and make to suffer those that one has no personal connection to; however it is also less likely that law enforcement will link the rapist to the crime).

This offense behavior is perhaps the most individually complex. This type of behavior is motivated by intense, individually varying fantasies that involve inflicting brutal levels of pain on the victim solely for sexual pleasure. The goal of this behavior is total victim fear and submission. Physical aggression has been eroticized. The result is that the victim must be physically and psychologically abused and degraded for this rapist to become sexually excited and subsequently gratified.

> **Example:** *James Warren, Beth Loschin, and Michael Montez*
> In August of 2001, James Warren, 41, of Hampton Bays; Beth Loschin, 46, of Farmingdale; and Michael Montez of New York City were charged with kidnapping and sexually assaulting a 15-year-old girl with whom Warren and Loschin had been chatting over the Internet.
>
> According to reports (*"Teen's horrific . . . ,"* 2001; *"Three arrested . . . ,"* 2001), the victim had been exchanging emails with Warren for several months after meeting him in an online chat room that catered to people interested in sadomasochism. When she expressed desire to run away from home, Warren arranged to meet her on August 3rd at the Wrentham, Massachusetts, outlet mall where she worked. In short order, reality set in. She was taken to a motel, handcuffed, tied up, placed in a closet, and sexually assaulted. Furthermore, (*"Three arrested . . . ,"* 2001):
>
> > The girl told authorities she was handcuffed much of the time and was kept under constant surveillance. She was taken back and forth between Farmingdale and Hampton Bays on Long Island, and at one point was taken to Montez's home in New York City, police said.
> >
> > According to a criminal complaint in Queens, Warren and Loschin told the girl that if she didn't do what Montez wanted, they "would beat her more than they already had done and would kill her and get rid of her."
> >
> > The complaint said Montez stuffed toilet paper in the girl's ears, wrapped bandages over her eyes and ears, put her in a closet, attached a rope to a collar around her neck and tied it and her arms to a clothes rack. She was later returned to Warren and Loschin.
>
> The victim was left alone on Friday long enough to make a phone call to a friend for help before her abductors returned.

James Warren was charged with kidnapping, sodomy, rape, and sexual abuse and held without bail. Beth Loschin was charged with sodomy and sexual abuse and held in lieu of $80,000 bail. Michael Montez was charged with kidnapping, rape, sodomy, and sexual assault.

Beth Loschin, a bookkeeper turned phone sex operator turned prostitute, testified against James Warren at his trial in 2002 (*Crowley and Hunter*, 2002):

> Loschin, 46, told Assistant District Attorney Gregg Turkin that Warren had hinted at bringing a younger woman into their twisted relationship in August 2001.
>
> At first, Loschin hesitated. Then Warren said he had a 18-year-old and she finally agreed.
>
> Loschin said the gruesome twosome took an array of sex toys to meet the girl in Wrentham, Mass.
>
> Loschin said Warren had told the teen to raid her bank account and stuff the money in her private parts. When the teen got into the car, she said, "He reached in between her legs and pulled money out."
>
> The trio arrived at a Rhode Island hotel room, and the young woman was naked and handcuffed. Inside the room, the brutality and sadism began.
>
> Kneeling at the foot of the bed, Warren backhanded the teen, knocking her to the ground, Loschin said, adding that he was infuriated the teen had not shaved her pubic hair.
>
> He choked the girl with a belt, Loschin said, before repeatedly raping and sodomizing her. Loschin then put on a strap-on dildo and also sexually ravaged the teen. The couple took numerous photos of the attacks.
>
> Loschin said Warren also used a lighter to burn the teen's nipples and used needles to pierce various private parts.
>
> Loschin also admitted she and Warren loaned the teen to a Queens man, Michael Montez, who raped her over two days. Montez pleaded guilty to rape and is serving a nine-year prison term.

Michael Montez pled guilty prior to Warren's trial and received a 9-year sentence. Beth Loschin also pled guilty and was sentenced to 4 years in January 2003, receiving a reduced sentence for her cooperation with prosecutors against James Warren. Warren was convicted in December 2002 of 63 counts of kidnapping, rape, sodomy, sexual abuse, assault, and endangering the welfare of a child (*Lam*, 2003).

REFERENCES

Baker, K. (1997) Once a rapist? Motivational evidence and relevancy in rape law. *Harvard Law Review*, January.

Black, H. C. (ed.) (1990) *Black's Law Dictionary*. St. Paul, MN: West Publishing.

Boyd, D. Suspect fits common profile of serial rapist. *Dallas-Ft. Worth Star-Telegram*, June 16, 2002.

Burgess, A., Burgess, A., Douglas, J., and Ressler, R. (1997) *Crime Classification Manual*. San Francisco: Jossey-Bass.

California v. John J. Park et al. (2002) No. B132915 (Super. Ct. No. BA109553), July 30, 2002.

California v. Odell Haston (1968) Crim. No. 11710, Aug. 19, 1968 (70 Cal. Rptr. 419).

California v. Macias (2003) No. F038745 Aug. 15, 2003 (Super. Ct. No. 01-68325).

Crowley, K., and Hunter, B. Rape horror a laugh for "Net perv" gal. *DA*DA.org*, retrieved November 22, 2002, from http://www.dadi.org/net_perv.htm.

DeForest, P., Gaensslen, R. E., and Lee, H. (1983) *Forensic Science: An Introduction to Criminalistics*. New York: McGraw-Hill.

Feeney, F. (2000) Police clearances: A poor way to measure the impact of Miranda on the police. *Rutgers Law Journal*, Fall.

Gross, H. (1924) *Criminal Investigation*. London: Sweet & Maxwell.

Gross, H. (1968) *Criminal Psychology*. Montclaire, NJ: Patterson Smith.

Groth, A. (1979) *Men Who Rape*. New York: Plenum Press.

Hazelwood, R. (1995) Analyzing the rape and profiling the offender, in Burgess, A., and Hazelwood, R. (eds.), *Practical Aspects of Rape Investigation: A Multidisciplinary Approach*, 2nd ed. New York: CRC Press.

Keppel, R. (1995) Signature murders: A report of several related cases. *Journal of Forensic Sciences*, Vol. 40, No. 4, pp. 670–674.

Lam, C. Woman gets four years in sex abuse case. *Newsday*, January 11, 2003.

Leonard, D. (2001) Character and motive in evidence law. *Loyola of Los Angeles Law Review*, January.

Lota, L. (2001) Gangster be gone. *Asian Week*, Nov. 8–Nov. 15.

Louisiana v. Cepriano (2000) No. 00-KA-213, Aug. 29, 2000 (767 So.2d 893, 00-213 (La. App. 5 Cir. 8/29/00)).

Louisiana v. Simmons (2003) No. 2002-KA-0253, May 14, 2003 (848 So.2d 58, 2002-0253 (La. App. 4 Cir. 5/14/03)).

Maples, J. (1999) *The Crime Fighter*. New York: Doubleday.

O'Hara, C. (1970) *Fundamentals of Criminal Investigation*. Springfield, IL: Charles C. Thomas.

O'Connell, J., and Soderman, H. (1935) *Modern Criminal Investigation*. New York: Funk & Wagnalls.

Rand, M., and Rennison, C. (2003) Criminal victimization, 2002. *Bureau of Justice Statistics: National Crime Victimization Survey*, NCJ 199994, August.

Rosenberg, R., Knight, R. A., Prentky, R. A., Lee, A. "Validating the components of a taxonomic system for rapists: a path analytic approach," *Bulletin of the American Academy of Psychiatry Law*, 1988, 16(2): pp. 169–185.

Shearer, L. Serial rapist found Athens "a neat place"—Scieszka interview adds details to crimes. *Athens Online*, January 25, 1998.

Teen's horrific ordeal. *ABC News*, August 14, 2001.

Three arrested in Internet kidnapping, assault case. *Associated Press*, August 14, 2001.

Turvey, B. (2000) Modus operandi, in *Encyclopedia of Forensic Science*. London: Academic Press.

Turvey, B. (2002) *Criminal Profiling: An Introduction to Behavioral Evidence Analysis*, 2nd ed. London: Academic Press.

Weston, P., and Wells, K. (1974) *Criminal Investigation: Basic Perspectives*, 2nd ed. Englewood Cliffs, NJ: Prentice Hall.

CHAPTER 13

SERIAL RAPE: INVESTIGATIVE ISSUES

John O. Savino and Brent E. Turvey, MS

Commit a sin twice and it will not seem a crime.

Jewish proverb

After the first blush of sin comes its indifference.

Henry David Thoreau, "On the Duty of Civil Disobedience" (1849)

Habit starts at the second crime. At the first one, something is ending.

Albert Camus, "The Mother in the Misunderstanding," Act 1, Sc. 1,

Gallimard **(1958)**

A *serial rapist* is a rapist who has committed two or more attacks against unrelated victims at different times. The reason for this definition is that there are serial rapists who have attacked more than one victim in the course of a morning, afternoon, or evening. It might be more appropriate to refer to this type of offender as a *spree* rapist, but making that distinction is not necessary for investigators to do their job and determine how to allocate resources such as equipment, lab time, and manpower. In other words, for investigative casework, and until some legitimate research has been published, the term serial rapist will do.

By definition, the serial rapist is successful at what they do because law enforcement has failed to identify and apprehend them before multiple offenses have been committed. There are a variety of causes and cures for this circumstance. The most prevalent causes and effective cures will be discussed in this chapter.

Serial rapists are not limited to committing the crime of rape, or even sex crimes in general. Their range of criminal activity can vary greatly. In the rush to investigate, it is easy to think of rapists as just rapists and forget that they can and likely have been involved in other crimes.

An example of the harm that ignorance of this possibility can cause is given in Simon (1997), regarding the "Prime Time Rapist":

In the late 1980s, Tucson, Arizona, was terrorized by a serial rapist called "the prime time rapist" because he would break into people's homes during the evening news and rape, rob, and terrorize whole families. This rapist was able to avoid detection for several years until an informer turned him in. Unfortunately, law enforcement officials focused on looking for someone with a prior record of sexual offenses. The rapist, when apprehended, turned out to have no record for sex offenses, but did possess multiple convictions for other types of serious offenses including drug offenses, burglaries, and robberies. As this example illustrates, focus on the most serious crime(s) an offender has committed can obscure the fact that he or she commits varied and less serious crimes as well. This, in turn, can hamper law enforcement efforts to apprehend a dangerous offender.

Another example includes the case of John J. Royster. In 1996, New York City Detectives arrested Mr. Royster for a series of crimes that took place during a two-week period in June of 1996. The first assault took on June 4, inside New York City's Central Park, during the early afternoon. A young woman was found beaten beyond recognition, near death, and her clothes in disarray in what appeared to be a sexual attack.

The next morning a 50-year-old woman was attacked as she walked along an Eastside jogging path. Her head was bashed into the ground and she required a 3-day hospital stay.

On June 7, a young woman was found beaten on a highway overpass just north of New York City and in another jurisdiction. She was in a coma and was also the victim of an apparent sexual assault.

On June 11, a 65-year-old woman was attacked and murdered as she opened a dry cleaning store. She was found slumped in the entranceway bleeding from her head. A latent fingerprint developed from the entranceway led to the identification of Mr. Royster.

His only prior brush with the police was an arrest in March 1996 for jumping a turnstile in a subway station and failing to pay the fare. Had it not been for this minor brush with the law, his fingerprints would not have been in a database and investigators might not have been able to link Mr. Royster to these events. He was arrested on June 13 and confessed to all of the crimes.

The first question that arises, then, is how do investigators know that they have a serial rapist, also known in some areas of the country as a *pattern rapist*, operating in their area? In other words, how does an investigator identify a serial rape pattern?

Sometimes you have to think outside of the box; some of the most important information is developed directly from patrol officers who work in the area where the assaults are occurring. They are out there 24 hours a day, 7 days a week. They may have noticed something; they may have stopped someone; they may have heard something. It is important not to overlook this simple and effective resource.

IDENTIFYING SERIAL RAPES

For obvious reasons, it is important to identify a serial rape pattern as soon as possible. This may be very easy, or it may be extremely difficult. Each case is different.

The individual cases in pattern rapes are commonly not linked, or overlooked by investigators, for the following reasons:

1. Inaccurate victim descriptions of rapist
2. Inaccurate or misleading suspect sketches
3. Rapist movement within or between jurisdictions
4. Large cities or geographical locations with poor departmental communication
5. Poor communication between law enforcement agencies
6. Uncritical reliance on victim statements
7. Overreliance on behavioral indicators (M.O. and signature)
8. Failure to collect or test physical evidence
9. Lack of communication between investigators

To avoid these pitfalls, each individual sex crime must be investigated as though it may be part of a series or become the starting point of a pattern as opposed to a single or isolated case. Every crime scene must be examined and processed every time. Every victim must be examined for biological trace evidence. Every victim must be carefully interviewed and the facts of the case reliably established. Then, both behavioral information and the results of forensic (i.e., DNA) testing need to be placed in to a database of some kind so that:

1. Solved crimes may be compared with the results for case linkage
2. Unsolved crimes may be compared with the results for case linkage
3. Everyone that needs to search the database can do so without difficulty

The Federal Bureau of Investigation maintains what is intended to be a nationwide database of solved and unsolved cases known as VICAP (Violent Criminal Apprehension Program). VICAP is designed to assist with collecting, collating, and analyzing violent crimes. Many states use similar programs and then submit the information to the FBI. For these types of programs to be effective, information needs to be collected and forwarded to a national database of some kind for analysis.

VICAP takes information on solved and unsolved crimes. Once a case is submitted, it is continually compared against all other cases in the database on the basis of certain aspects of the crime. When a similarity in modus operandi or signature aspects of the crime is detected, and if patterns are found, the investigating agencies involved are notified. This may assist investigators with investigative leads and may explain dormant periods of activity in one jurisdiction, while the offender was somewhere else committing crimes.

According to information provided on the FBI's Web site (http://www.fbi.gov/hq/isd/cirg/ncavc.htm):

What is VICAP?

VICAP is a nationwide data information center designed to collect, collate, and analyze crimes of violence—specifically murder. Cases examined by VICAP include:

- solved or unsolved homicides or attempts, especially those that involve an abduction; are apparently random, motiveless, or sexually oriented; or are known or suspected to be part of a series;
- missing persons, where the circumstances indicate a strong possibility of foul play and the victim is still missing; and,
- unidentified dead bodies where the manner of death is known or suspected to be homicide.

For VICAP to work effectively, it needs an invitation and coordination with local law enforcement. Therefore, the FBI provides, free of charge, the software to set up the VICAP database. The program has been embraced by many agencies, with busier operations in cities including Los Angeles, Chicago, Detroit, Dallas, and Kansas City. Other cities, including New York City, are in the process of becoming fully operational.

The Process

Cases with an arrested or identified offender can be submitted to the VICAP system by local law enforcement investigators for comparison and possible matching with unsolved cases.

Once a case is entered into the VICAP database, it is compared continually against all other entries on the basis of certain aspects of the crime. The purpose of this is to detect signature aspects of homicide and similar patterns of modus operandi (MOs), which will, in turn, allow VICAP personnel to pinpoint those crimes that may have been committed by the same offender. If patterns are found, law enforcement agencies involved will be notified.

Again, this program can only be effective if information is submitted to the database. As of this writing, there is no legislation that requires all agencies to submit information to the VICAP program, and the number of cases in their database is limited.

In Canada, the Royal Canadian Mounted Police (RCMP) have a similar program, the Violent Crime Linkage Analysis System (ViCLAS). All Canadian provinces are required by law to submit all cases of solved and unsolved sexual assaults to the database.

According to information provided on the RCMP's Web site (http:// www.rcmp.ca/viclas/viclas_e.htm):

How it Works

When a serious crime occurs that qualifies as a ViCLAS reportable case, an investigator completes the questionnaire/booklet. The booklet is then sent to the ViCLAS centre responsible for the area the offence is reported in. The booklet then undergoes a quality assurance review, and some centres actually perform this twice. If the booklet passes the quality assurance review it is entered into the ViCLAS computer system by a trained data entry person. If the book does not pass the quality review the investigator may be contacted directly to clear up some minor points or the book maybe returned to the originator to be resubmitted when completed correctly.

Once the book has been entered on the system, the ViCLAS specialist begins the analytical process. This involves conducting extensive background research on both the victim and offender, if he or she is known. A typical analysis will involve the specialist reviewing all data that was available on the subject(s) including information from computerized police information retrieval systems, parolee files and any other reliable information source. They will review all statements, reports and photographs available and in some cases speak to investigators.

Once they have conducted their background research they will draw upon their experience and expertise by conducting various structured queries of the ViCLAS computer system. Each analyst will have his or her own approach to this process, but all will in some way, be looking at victimology, the offender, modus operandi, behavioural and forensic data found at the scene for clues that may link cases to each other and/or reveal the identity of the offender.

In order to provide the investigators with feedback, they are advised, usually in writing, the results of the analysis, whether it is positive or negative. In the case where a potential link is made the investigators are asked to provide the ViCLAS unit with the results of their investigation. A potential link is a situation where the ViCLAS specialist has reason to believe that a specific person, known, or unknown, may be responsible for one or more crimes. When this occurs the ViCLAS specialist connects the cases on the database in the form of a series. The ViCLAS record is then updated in the database accordingly when the investigator confirms or rejects the link by virtue of his/her investigation.

Until everyone is sharing information in some fashion, pattern cases will remain concealed within the unsolved case folders of detectives everywhere.

Case Example: Miscommunication in Miami

In Miami, the police department admitted that they shelved a rape kit, containing a DNA sample collected from the Sept. 17, 2002, rape of a 21-year-old woman, for almost 9 months before submitting it to the police lab for testing. The failure to establish the results of this sample prevented them from knowing with certainty that a serial rapist was working a 20-block area in Coral Way. The next attack occurred on Dec. 3, 2002, and involved the rape of a 55-year-old woman in the same neighborhood. Six months later, the still unlinked pattern included three girls, ages 11, 12 and 13, who were each attacked in their homes after school.

Miami police detectives explained, however, that they shelved the first DNA sample because, in their experience, the Miami-Dade police lab routinely refuses to conduct DNA testing unless a suspect has been identified. According to reports, a spokesman for the crime lab sort of denied this, but not exactly (Kidwell and Corral, 2003):

> The DNA supervisor of the Miami-Dade police lab denied the charge, saying almost every piece of evidence from violent crimes is analyzed and processed "as soon as possible."

> "To do otherwise would defeat the purpose of the entire DNA database," said Willard "Bud" Stuver. "I don't know what's going on over there at the Miami Police Department, but I have no idea where this is coming from."

> Stuver said the only times DNA samples are rejected are when the lab determines the labor-intensive test "will provide no meaningful benefit to the investigation" or when detectives improperly file their request.

> "You can't waste valuable resources, both in time and people and everything, to chase a bunch of needless leads," he said. "You need to have some idea of what investigators have developed, what seems to be the value of the evidence submitted. That is called good case management."

> . . . [Frank] Fernandez, Miami's deputy chief, said . . . that his detectives say the county crime lab frequently declines to conduct DNA tests when there is no suspect identified or when there is no DNA from a suspect to use in comparison.

His investigators claim the lab uses a screening process for DNA tests—which could take days or even weeks to perform—that gives priority to cases in which an arrest is most likely.

Stuver acknowledged there is a priority screening, but that violent crimes—including rapes by strangers where there are no suspects—take precedence.

"That's why there is a DNA database, to locate unknown suspects," Stuver said. "To do anything else wouldn't make sense."

Stuver said his office sometimes returns Miami's untested samples because of documentation problems and overly broad requests. For instance, he said if a detective sends him a bedsheet and asks him to check it for DNA from a rapist, it makes the lab's job almost impossible if the request doesn't include specific information on what to look for and where.

One Miami investigator, who spoke on the condition of anonymity, said rape-squad detectives likely would have shelved the Dec. 3 sample as well, except that details of the crime matched a serial rape case Miami-Dade police were investigating.

"The thinking was that we'd sent it over and they might be able to use it in their case," the source said. "We knew they wouldn't run the test for us because we didn't have a suspect. We didn't have anything for them."

Miami police sources said there were no obvious similarities between the September and December rapes other than their proximity. The ages of the two victims were different, their descriptions of the suspect were different and there were differences in the crime methods.

Unfortunately, this is not a unique or even uncommon circumstance because of the DNA backlogs that exist around the country at the present writing. When confronted by a police crime lab that refuses to do DNA testing unless there is an adequate suspect, investigators should consider sending the sample to a private lab. It is not as expensive or difficult as it sounds. Doing this one time sends a powerful message, especially if it results in a hit on a major case. When those in charge ask the question of why the private lab was necessary, attitudes and priorities have a way of changing very quickly.

INVESTIGATIVE STRATEGY, THE DUTY TO PROTECT, AND LAW ENFORCEMENT LIABILITY

There are some in law enforcement who regard the existence of a serial rapist in their jurisdiction as something to be kept secret from the public. The following logic is often found behind such thinking:

1. Notifying the public that a serial rapist is at work in a given area indicates a lack of police ability—serial rapists are strong evidence of unsolved crime, and this is bad for departmental image.
2. Notifying the public that a serial rapist is at work in a given area creates an expectation from the public that it should be thoroughly investigated and solved, and this could put a strain on limited departmental resources. A public that knows nothing expects nothing.
3. Notifying the public that a serial rapist is at work in a given area could cause unnecessary panic.
4. Notifying the public that a serial rapist is at work in a given area could generate too much publicity, and the serial rapist may stop offending or move to another jurisdiction; this would deprive the department of opportunities to catch them using information from future offenses.

None of these arguments are legitimate for at least the following three reasons: First, and most important, no desire for secrecy outweighs the danger presented to the public by a serial rapist—the public has a right to know when a sexual predator is actively targeting victims in a particular jurisdiction. Second, nothing is more corrosive to the relationship between a law enforcement agency and the community that it is sworn to protect than an abuse of trust by the willful withholding of information vital to public safety. And third, law enforcement agencies that withhold this kind of information may not be entirely immune from liability if they fail to notify the public and a victim is subsequently attacked.

In the opinion of the authors, the duty here is very clear: If a serial rapist is active in a given jurisdiction, law enforcement has a duty to notify the public and vigorously investigate the pattern until every investigative avenue is an exhausted possibility.

Case Example: Jane Doe and the "Balcony Rapist", Toronto

The following case summary is excerpted entirely from *Griffiths* (1999, pp. 18–19):

> In the summer of 1986, police knew that a rapist was at large in a downtown Toronto neighbourhood.

> While the then-Metro Police were aware that there were many similarities in the mode of the attacks, and had concluded that in fact the crimes were those of a serial rapist, they made a deliberate decision to not warn women in the neighbourhood, nor to take any other steps to protect them.

> In August of that year, Jane Doe (whose pseudonym used to protect her privacy became her public identity) was raped in her bedroom in the neighbourhood where the rapist was known to be active.

As a result of that rape, Jane Doe successfully sued the Board of
Commissioners of Police of the then Municipality of Metropolitan Toronto.
Judgment in the case by Madam Justice Jean MacFarland of the Ontario Court
of Justice was released on July 3, 1998.

Madam Justice MacFarland found that women in the area had not been
warned of the rapist because police believed they would become "hysterical"
and thus somehow jeopardize the police investigation. She further found that
had Jane Doe been aware of the serial rapist in her neighbourhood, she would
have taken steps to protect herself, and that those steps most probably would
have prevented her from being raped.

Although the police say they took the crime of sexual assault seriously in
1985–1986, I must conclude, on the evidence before me, that they did not, as
Madam Justice MacFarland concluded, detailing many longstanding problems
in the investigation of sexual assaults.

In particular, she accepted Jane Doe's allegation that she and other women
had been used as "bait" and that the police investigation in the case was
motivated by "serial rape mythology and discriminatory sexual stereotypes."

While the police in their defence attempted to show that steps had been taken
to improve the identified problems within the service, Madam Justice
MacFarland rejected this evidence and found that the status quo had
remained. She said that the police had engaged in "impression management"
to attempt to improve their public image, but that this effort did not represent
an "indication of any genuine commitment for change."

The judge found that the police investigation was "irresponsible and grossly
negligent" and that the police had failed "utterly" in their duty to protect
women.

In addition to finding the police liable for negligence, the judge also held that
they had breached sections 7 and 15 of the Canadian Charter of Rights and
Freedoms. She held that, "as a public institution with a crucial role to play in
the protection of all members of society, the police must act without
discrimination in carrying out its duties and responsibilities and must ensure
that its actions do not deprive individuals of their rights to security." Women's
rights to equality and security had been violated, the judge held.

At the end of the civil trial, in July of 1998, the judge awarded Jane Doe $220,000
and $20,000 annually for the next 15 years. A few days later, the Toronto City
Council voted 51–1 not only to apologize to Jane Doe for the way that the Toronto
police had used and mistreated her, but to apologize to all women in Toronto as

well. However, the public deception and poor conduct of the Toronto Police Department continued.

First, most cities have liability insurance to cover this sort of thing: to pay for attorneys, investigators, mediators, depositions, and experts in the cities defense. Taxpayers didn't think this was going to cost them a dime.

However, Toronto's private insurance companies hadn't made the decision to litigate the Jane Doe case for 12 years. In 1998, the press discovered that Toronto and its municipalities became uninsurable back in 1986 because of a number of big liability claims, requiring them to become self-insured. Subsequently, the money to pay for 12 years of litigation and the settlement awarded to Jane Doe was coming directly from the taxpayers. And the decision to continue litigation was made by a group of treasurers representing the former municipalities of Metropolitan Toronto. The chief of police had been telling everyone that a private insurer was making all the decisions, relieving him of any involvement or responsibility.

Second, the Toronto City Council did vote 51–1 to apologize to Jane Doe, stating "That city council issue an apology to Jane Doe and the women of Toronto regarding the handling of this case; and that City Council requests the Police Services Board to also issue an apology" (Gombu, 1998). However, less than a week later, chairman of the Police Services Board Norm Gardner came out to say that there would be a statement, but that it would not necessarily be an apology, citing future liability issues. Then the very next day Toronto police Chief David Boothby issued a full apology, and shook the hand of Jane Doe in front of the media.

As a result of her experiences, Jane Doe authored the book *The Story of Jane Doe: A Book About Rape*, published in 2003.

CASE LINKAGE

The identification of a serial rape case requires that a connection of some kind be demonstrated between different cases. This is referred to as *case linkage*: the process of demonstrating tangible connections between two or more previously unrelated cases. It commonly involves the examination of victimology, M.O., and signature behaviors. It should also involve witness statements and the results of forensic testing.

An *investigative link* is a connection between one or more solved or unsolved cases that serves to inform the allocation of investigative resources. This link is preliminary and, as the name suggests, requires further investigation before it may be confirmed. Examples of investigative links include:

- Consistent victimology
- Consistent M.O. behavior

- Consistent signature behavior
- Consistent location selection
- Consistent witness descriptions (voice, clothing, vehicle, physical characteristics, etc.)
- Consistent forensic class evidence (hair, fiber, glass, soil, footwear impressions, etc.)[1]
- Positive PCR DNA comparison results

A *probative link* is a connection between one or more solved or unsolved cases that is sufficiently distinctive as to support the conclusion that the same person is responsible. Examples of probative links include:

- A repeated pattern of M.O. and signature behaviors that is unique to a particular rapist
- Positive RFLP or STR DNA comparison results
- Positive fingerprint comparison results
- Positive bite-mark comparison results
- Positive results from comparison of other individuating forensic evidence
- Positive eyewitness IDs

Case Example: Serial Rapist

In September of 1994, in the early morning hours, a young lady was walking home from her shift at a local restaurant; she would become the fist victim of a serial rapist operating in a large metropolitan city. Living only a few blocks away, and having walked home many times before, she felt safe. A male she later described as Hispanic followed her into her building. He produced a silver handgun and forced her into the stairwell. Once inside the stairwell, the victim was able to talk the male out of raping her, but he demanded oral sex. He ejaculated inside the victim's mouth, and she had the forethought to deposit the evidence in the stairwell after the offender left. The responding officers collected the evidence themselves; trained evidence technicians never processed the scene.

A month later, in late October of 1994, 15 city blocks south of the fist crime, another woman was followed into her apartment building and was forced into a stairwell by a male with a silver handgun. As with the first victim, she was orally sodomized and raped. This victim, however, described the offender as a black male. The same two

---

[1] Forensic identification is a general term that refers to the methods used to classify or individuate items of evidence for court (aka forensic) purposes. An item is identified when it can be placed into a class of items with similar (aka class) characteristics. However, an item can only be individualized if it has some unique feature or property that distinguishes it from all other items in the universe (Kirk, 1974, p. 10).

investigators who responded to the September assault also handled this case. These investigators did not link the crimes at this time, although the M.O. was similar but in the 2nd case the victim described the offender as a black male. Again this incident did not have trained technicians' process the scene.

Then in March of 1995 a 3rd woman would be assaulted only 11 blocks from the first assault. A black male with a silver handgun followed her into her building. She was forced into a stairwell where she was raped and orally sodomized. Again, the offender ejaculated inside the victim's mouth.

It was now brought to light that there was the possibility a serial rapist was responsible for these three crimes, all occurring inside of a four square mile area in this major City. As a result of the fact that DNA testing was not as readily available as it is today, and the fact one of the victims described the offender as Hispanic, a task force was not established to investigate these three similar cases. The cases were vigorously investigated with no resolution.

Then again in August of 1995, the rapist attacked another victim, only this time it was in a completely different area of the City. A black male with a silver handgun followed a woman into her building, forcing her into a basement laundry room. The victim was raped and orally sodomized; again the offender ejaculated inside the victim's mouth. In this case the offender took some of the victim's jewelry and identification. Although biological evidence had not been tested to positively link these cases, it was now understood by detectives close to the investigations that one male was probably responsible for at least three of these crimes. However, there were some who did not think that one offender could be responsible.

More victims would follow. In September of 1995, as two females were entering their building, they were chased into their apartment by a black male. Able to make it safely into their apartment before anything happened, they waited a while, until they thought it was safe. Unfortunately, the bathroom was located outside the apartment in the hallway for all of the tenants of the floor to use. One of the victims opened the apartment door to go out to the bathroom and was forced back inside by a black male with a silver gun. The offender took control of both victims and made them lay face down on the floor. The offender then ransacked the apartment looking for money and jewelry. He sexually assaulted both of the females and then fled the scene.

This case generated a lot of publicity, and within three days a suspect was arrested and identified in line-ups by both victims. The other victims did not make an identification of this suspect. A search warrant was executed and numerous weapons were recovered inside the suspect's apartment, including several silver handguns. The suspect denied any involvement or knowledge of the sexual assaults.

As this case went forward to a possible trial, a biological sample was obtained from the suspect. His DNA sample, along with biological material from the rape he was charged with, were sent to a laboratory and tested. As test results were pending, there had been no reported assaults of a similar nature in the City. In 1996, the results from the DNA test were completed. They excluded the suspect that had been arrested. He was subsequently released.

Now having a DNA lab run by the Office of the Chief Medical Examiner. Evidence submitted for testing from the September 1994, March 1995, August 1995, and the September 1995 cases were tested. DNA proved that the same offender committed three of the attacks. The evidence from the September 1994 was inappropriately packaged and degraded; it was of no value.

A small task force was put together to re-investigate these four cases.

The rapist would strike again. In September of 1996, a black male with a silver handgun followed a female into her apartment building. He brought her inside to an isolated location where she was raped and orally sodomized. No biological evidence was obtained from the victim's examination.

At this time, a full time task force was developed to investigate these cases.

In April of 1997, this rapist would attack again. After a DNA match to another assault of a young woman in a stairwell, a team of ten detectives, and a task force of over 100 uniformed and plainclothes officers, were put together to apprehend this offender. This offender has been attributed to at least 11 other incidents where a black male had followed women inside their building. Many of the other incidents did not result in sexual assaults. As a result of these facts, the community was warned about this offender in their midst. A public awareness campaign was launched to warn residents of the rapist and the way they could assist with the investigation.

The fact that this pattern was not established after the second incident in 1994 may be critical to the apprehension of this offender. It is thought serial rapists can make more mistakes during their early crimes, because he has not yet had time to perfect his tactics. The chance for detection is therefore greater during the beginning of the pattern, or when he gets careless and sloppy later on.

As a result of the lack of attention that this case received early on, and the failure to identify it as a pattern, investigators had to play "CATCH-UP" and go back to review the early cases, some being three years prior, to see if anything crucial had been missed. But time takes its toll on everything, including memory and evidence. This offender is last known to have struck in September of 1998, and is still un-apprehended at the time of this writing.

CATCHING SERIAL RAPISTS

Most of the published work on the subject of serial rape investigation gives little or no attention to demonstrating how cases are solved. The reality is that good suspects most commonly come to light by the following mechanisms:

1. A confession
2. Another criminal informing on the serial rapist
3. The coming forward of a rapist's spouse, family members, friends, co-workers, or neighbors to report evidence of aberrant, suspicious, or overtly criminal activity (anonymously or otherwise)
4. The identification of a rapist by a witness
5. The identification of a rapist by a victim who has eluded or evaded an attack
6. The identification of a rapist by a victim who has suffered an attack but was subsequently released by the offender
7. The identification of a rapist by a victim who has suffered an attack but subsequently escaped from captivity
8. The routine stop of a rapist for a minor violation (expired vehicle tags, traffic violation, parking violation, and so on)
9. The arrest of a rapist for an offense unrelated to rape (burglary, purse snatching, indecent exposure, assault, and so on), and subsequent linkage to physical evidence on file associated with unsolved crimes such as fingerprints, photo ID, or DNA
10. The linkage of a known rapist to a series of offenses by the use of databased information or evidence such as gun registrations, driver's licenses, fingerprints, or DNA
11. Good detective work, which includes following up on all tips, investigating all leads to their conclusions, sharing information and collaborating with other law-enforcement agencies, and working the physical evidence until it is an exhausted possibility (which necessarily includes acting on the information developed from circumstances described in items 1–10)

Investigating a serial rape or pattern case can be a daunting task. There are many obstacles and pitfalls put in the investigator's way. These can be as simple as a supervisor who does not agree with investigative decisions, or as complex as a damaged or nonexistent relationship with a victim that has to be repaired by a new case investigator. During serial investigations, political pressure may be applied as a result of the attention that they commonly bring. This pressure usually flows down the ranks and is felt most by the investigator. Every available resource and tool should be utilized during this type of investigation, including the press. Print media and TV shows, such as *America's Most Wanted*, are able to reach a large number of people with facts of the investigation. Every tip, every lead must be fully exhausted before the case is allowed to go cold, or even closed.

CRIMINAL PROFILING

Criminal profiling is the process of investigating and examining criminal behavior in order to help identify the type of person responsible by identifying and then narrowing the suspect pool. It involves the inference of offender traits from physical and/or behavioral evidence. From physical evidence left behind in relation to a crime, such as offender hair and offender semen, the criminal profiler may deduce that the offender is a male with a particular color of hair, perhaps even of a particular race. Similarly, from behavioral evidence, inferences about the offender's lifestyle and personality may also be possible. Any good criminal investigator is more than likely a good criminal profiler.

The decision to use a criminal profiler not already attached to the case is always a judgment call and should only be made when all other investigative options have been exhausted. If investigators decide that a criminal profile might assist with an unsolved case, consider the following:

1. Do not use a law enforcement profiler simply because they are free. Take a look at their other case involvements and see what kinds of help they have provided others. A bad profile is worse than no profile at all.
2. Do not look for a yes man to simply ratify current investigative thinking; investigators should seek outside thoughts and ideas to refresh their perspectives.
3. Demand a resume from your profiler. Investigators need to know that the profiler has the background to go to court if needs be. If it is stacked with media appearances, true crime publications, or an absence of any court time, be suspicious.
4. Do not announce the use of profiling to the media; there is no up side to discussing this specific tactical decision with the press. Such an announcement, absent the profile, is merely a publicity stunt to enhance the public image of the department and assuage a public demanding some kind action.
5. Require that the profiler visit the crime scenes; if the profiler doesn't understand why this might help, thank them for their time.
6. Require a written profile for distribution and future reference; verbal profiles are investigatively useless. If the profiler is not willing to write their profile down, thank them for their time.

7. If the profile that is submitted reads a lot like profiles that have been published in the paper, do not use it, and certainly do not have it published in the media.

If investigators do decide to publish a profile in the media, focus on those elements that distinguish the rapist from others. Do not publish a profile that is general and nonspecific.

CASE EXAMPLES

Consider the following examples, provided to demonstrate the variety of serial rapes that can occur, the various M.O.s, the various motives, and the manner in which cases were linked and ultimately solved.

Darryl Thomas Kemp: Serial Rape with Homicide

Darryl Kemp was tried and ultimately convicted of charges relating to the murder of Marjorie Hipperson on June 10, 1957; the rape and kidnapping of E. Helen Shelton, on July 15, 1959; and the rape of Lelah D. Sherman on May 12, 1959. He pled not guilty by reason of insanity.

Regarding the murder of Marjorie Hipperson, the record provided in *California v. Darryl Thomas Kemp* (1961) provides the following details:

> Marjorie Hipperson was raped and murdered sometime during the early morning hours of June 10, 1957. Prior to her death Miss Hipperson lived in an apartment in Los Angeles, was employed as a nurse in a nearby hospital, and was engaged to be married to Dr. Deike, an intern at the hospital. On the evening of June 9, 1957, the employees at the hospital gave a combined stag party and shower for Dr. Deike and Miss Hipperson. At about 11:30 p.m. Miss Hipperson left the hospital in her automobile, alone, stating that she was going to her apartment. The doctor could not accompany her because he was on duty at the hospital that night. The next morning when Miss Hipperson did not show up for work, Dr. Deike went to her apartment to investigate. He discovered that the front door to the apartment was chained from the inside (there was no back door), that a screen had been removed from a rear window, and that the window was open. He entered the apartment through that window and discovered the dead body of Miss Hipperson lying on the bed in her bedroom. She was lying on her back with her nightgown bunched up around her upper body. There was a stocking wrapped around her neck, another stocking wrapped around one wrist, and a washcloth near her face. Her mouth was bruised, and she had numerous other bruises on different parts of her body. Subsequent investigation disclosed that she had been raped,

and had died of strangulation. It was obvious that the washcloth had been used as a gag and that the stocking on her wrist had been used to tie her hands. Investigation by fingerprint experts disclosed a portion of a palm print on the wall beside the bed, which had been pulled out from its normal position, and another palm print on the window ledge where entry had obviously been made. The palm print on the wall was about 18 inches directly across from the buttock of the victim, and the palm print on the window ledge showed that the fingers were facing into the house when the print was made.

. . .

The autopsy established the cause of death as asphyxiation due to strangulation. The lacerations in and about the vagina, and the presence of the semen and spermatozoa indicated a forcible entry into the vaginal canal.

The fact that appellant was familiar with the apartment where Miss Hipperson lived was established by the testimony of Marie Weber, who lived in the apartment directly across from that of Miss Hipperson. She testified that sometime in 1956 a handprinted note was slipped under the door of her apartment. This note stated that the writer had observed Miss Weber undress, that he had seen her body, and suggested that they get together for mutual satisfaction. . . . After appellant's arrest, specimens of his handwriting were secured, and a handwriting expert testified that the note had been printed by the appellant.

Regarding the rape of Lelah D. Sherman, the record provided in *California v. Darryl Thomas Kemp* (1961) provides the following details:

Mrs. Sherman testified that on May 12, 1959, she was in Griffith Park in Los Angeles, sketching. At about 3:45 p.m. she started to walk towards her bus stop, when appellant, whom she positively identified, drove up beside her and offered her a ride. When she got in the car appellant turned the car around and started towards the mountains. When Mrs. Sherman protested he told her that he wanted to show her the view because there were nice things to sketch up there. When they were high in the hills appellant stopped the car and Mrs. Sherman got out. Appellant indicated to her a path and told her that the view was in that direction. When she had progressed down the path a short distance he told her to stop, and started to push her. He then told her that resistance was useless, and that she might as well do what he wanted because otherwise he would throw her down the mountain, which was very steep in that area. She was frightened. He forced her to the ground. She tried to resist but he held her with one hand while he removed her slacks and panties with the other, took off his pants, and had intercourse with her. After the act was completed she was very frightened and did not know how she was going to get away. She got up from the ground, put on her clothing, and started to walk up the path. Defendant then offered to drive her to her bus station. Because they were far up in the mountains she got back in the car. On the way down the mountain appellant asked her if she liked to dance. Thinking that she could entrap him, she said that she did like to dance, and arranged to meet him the next Saturday night at the drugstore at Hollywood and Vine. When they came to Vermont Avenue and Sunset she asked to be let out of the car, and appellant stopped. She jumped out, ran over to a restaurant, and immediately telephoned the police. When the police arrived she told them of the rape and about the arrangements made for the next Saturday night. At the suggestion of the police she kept the date as she had arranged, but appellant did not appear.

Regarding the rape and kidnapping of E. Helen Shelton, the record provided in *California v. Darryl Thomas Kemp* (1961) provides the following details:

Mrs. Shelton, who was also a nurse, testified that about 5:20 p.m. on July 15, 1959, she was driving through Griffith Park in an isolated area when defendant passed her in a green jeep truck and forced her to stop. Appellant, whom the witness positively identified, approached Mrs. Shelton's car, identified himself as a park attendant, told her that the road was closed and that she would have to turn around. While saying this he approached her car. Both doors were locked, but the window on the driver's side was down. Appellant reached in and opened the door. He grabbed her by her hair and threw her down in the street. He then beat her head on the street and said: "I am going to kill you; you are going to die." He beat her until she went limp. Appellant then dragged her to a secluded area and threw her down and kicked her. He ripped off one of her stockings and tried to put it around her neck. He then said: "Oh, damn, it is too short, there is not enough." He then ripped off part of her clothing and told her, in unmistakable language, that he was going to rape her. He kept beating her and threatening to kill her. Just before she lost consciousness she heard him say: "I am going to murder you, I am going to murder you like I did the Hipperson woman." Appellant then hit the witness with a rock and choked her until she lost consciousness. She was not conscious when the rape was actually perpetrated. When she regained consciousness she had severe pains in her vaginal area and defendant was gone. She crawled up the path.

. . .

The police testified that she was bruised and bleeding when they arrived, and that she told them she had been raped. They took her to the receiving hospital. There smears were taken and an examination made. She had undoubtedly been raped. There was semen and spermatozoa in the vaginal area. She had suffered a severe and brutal beating. She was in the hospital for a week.

This case was solved because Mrs. Shelton gave a good description of the pickup truck used by her attacker to the police, and they acted on it. Later that same night, a Los Angeles police officer saw a vehicle matching that description, chased it for 3 blocks, and finally got it to pull over. The truck, driven by Mr. Kemp, was loaded with his personal belongings, including a shirt and a pair of overalls similar to those described by Mrs. Shelton as being worn by her attacker. The officer arrested Mr. Kemp on the spot. He was ultimately identified by each of the victims, and via his fingerprints, which he had left at the scene of the murder.

Two court-appointed "alienists" (forensic psychiatrists) determined that Mr. Kemp was a sexual psychopath. However, they also determined that he was legally sane, both when he committed the offenses and when they examined him (*California v. Darryl Thomas Kemp*, 1961).

This case involves *anger-retaliatory* offense behaviors that involve an incredibly dangerous M.O. and signature. First, the M.O. involves the use of a ligature to control the victim. This method of control is by itself very dangerous and can easily kill the victim if too much force is applied. Second, the signature behavior involves overkill, that is to say, the use of more force than is necessary to commit the crime, as evidenced by the severe beating suffered by each victim. Combine the need for overkill and the use of a ligature, and it is a surprise that more victims didn't die. This is not to say that Mr. Kemp intended to kill his first victim. The fact that he didn't kill subsequent victims supports the opposite conclusion, as well as the fact that he began raping victims in the outdoors and stopped using a gag. The facts do not support the conclusion that Mr. Kemp intended to kill a living witness.

Terrance Bolds: Serial Rape and Burglary

Terrance Bolds was tried and ultimately convicted of burglary, sodomy, and forcible rape charges relating to attacks on four different victims, including a pregnant mother, all of which took place during the summer of 1997.

Regarding the rape of P.M., the record in *Missouri v. Terrance Bolds* (2000) provides the following details:

> [On August 21, 1997, around 6:20 a.m., Mr. Bolds] entered P.M.'s house with a revolver. P.M., who was two months pregnant at the time of the incident, lived with her three-year-old son. Defendant instructed P.M. not to scream and directed her to the living room. Defendant forced the victim to undress and perform oral sex on him, while pointing the gun at her. Before leaving, defendant told victim, "You better not call the police or I will come back and kill you and your son." Afterwards, defendant took P.M.'s television, car keys, a

diskette with her son's photo on it, Rolodex, ATM card, credit card and a receipt from a doctor's visit.

Regarding the rape of J.J. on August 23, 1997, the record in *Missouri v. Terrance Bolds* (2000) provides the following details:

> [Mr. Bolds] entered J.J.'s apartment through a window in her four-year-old son's bedroom around 4:00 a.m. Defendant forced the victim, under gunpoint, to undress and to put on a compact disc and dance for him. Shortly after that, defendant forced the victim to perform oral sex on him. Defendant raped her vaginally and anally, had her perform oral sex on him again and raped her vaginally and anally a second time. Afterwards, defendant tied J.J. up in the bathtub, bound her wrists together, placed her facedown in the tub, and bound her ankles to her wrists. A while later, defendant put an egg in J.J.'s mouth, gagged her with a pair of her "biker pants," and left. Defendant also took J.J.'s Illinois identification card, a Victoria's Secret bag, an Adidas bag, and a Dooney-Burke bag.

Regarding the rape of W.T. on August 26, 1997, the record provided in *Missouri v. Terrance Bolds* (2000) provides the following details:

> [Mr. Bolds] assaulted W.T. Inside the house, defendant took two rings from W.T.'s fingers at gunpoint. Defendant raped her several times, vaginally and anally. He also forced her to perform oral sex on him. Throughout the assault, defendant held a gun to W.T.'s head.

Regarding the rape of R.F. on August 29, 1997, the record provided in *Missouri v. Terrance Bolds* (2000) provides the following details:

> Around 5:00 a.m. defendant [Mr. Bolds] R.F. Defendant entered R.F.'s bedroom with a gun in his right hand and wanted her to perform oral sex on him. When the victim did not cooperate, defendant forced his penis into her mouth. After defendant switched the gun from his right hand to the left hand, R.F. attempted to take the pistol from the defendant. A struggle ensued and defendant told her "Bitch, you are going to die now," and repeatedly hit and bit R.F. R.F. pulled off the defendant's ski mask and got the pistol away from him. She tried to shoot defendant with the gun but the gun would not fire. Defendant took the pistol and told R.F. to turn around, that he was going to shoot her. The gun would not fire and he ran out of the house.

> During the struggle, R.F. heard her ten-year-old son moving around and yelled at him to call the police because a stranger was in the house. Unfortunately, her son's phone was not working. After defendant ran out of the house, she called the police. While she was trying to call the police, defendant came back and tried to open her bedroom door. When he could not open the door, he

fired two shots through the door. Bullet fragments hit R.F.'s thigh. She also had scratches on her face and hands and bite marks in five different places. Her car keys, water pitcher, and CDs were missing and the children's bedroom window was broken.

At trial, Mr. Bolds' former girlfriend testified that she left him because (*Missouri v. Terrance Bolds*, 2000)

> he used to hit me before and he did—basically he scared me. He would threaten me. I was pregnant when I left. I was about a month pregnant and his behavior was getting more and more violent whereas, you know, I had to leave because he would, you know, want to have sex all the time. And he also would leave, you know, late at night and then come back in the morning, by the time it was time to go to work. And sometimes he would come in the middle of the night and want to have sex and he'd leave and come back in the morning and he would take my car, you know, and he would have my car and he would leave at night.

This case involves *power-assertive* and *profit-oriented* offense behaviors that were meant to satisfy Mr. Bolds' need to sexually control and possess his victims through physical and verbal degradation, as well as terror. The M.O. indicates planning via numerous precautionary acts, as well as reflecting a history of burglary offenses. These rapes were not, however, sadistic in nature.

Steven Sera: Serial Rape and Rohypnol

Steven Sera, the 39-year-old owner of the Chandler Lumber Company of Dallas, Texas, was tried for multiple rape and kidnapping charges relating to sexual attacks on two victims in Arkansas. A peculiar feature of this case was use of the drug *Rohypnol* (**as shown in Figure 13-1**) to render victims unconscious so that Mr. Sera could videotape the sexual attacks without the victims' knowledge.

Mr. Sera claimed that these relationships were actually consensual, and that he was guilty only of bad judgment for taping his sexual encounters with Melanie Hataway, a 32-year-old Colleyville, Texas, woman; Jackie Haygood, a 26-year-old Arkansas woman; and Patty Coleman, 18, his sister-in-law, then a college freshman. He testified that they consented to be videotaped. The victims in turn agreed that while there were preexisting relationships with Mr. Sera, some of which were sexual, they did not consent to the sexual attacks that had been videotaped while they were unconscious. They each testified that they must have been drugged and then raped. Similar testimony from two additional victims was allowed during this trial.

This case was brought to light when Mr. Sera's wife, Nancy Sera, found the videotape that he had made, showing him committing sexual acts with unconscious naked women, at their home. According to police, the tape showed Mr. Sera having sex

Figure 13-1

Examples of 2-mg tablets of the drug Rohypnol. Rohypnol produces sedative–hypnotic effects including muscle relaxation and amnesia. It can also produce dependence and may be lethal when mixed with alcohol or other depressants. Rohypnol is not approved for use in the United States, and its importation is banned.

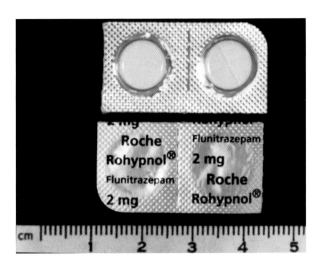

with women from several different states, including Texas and Arkansas. Nancy Sera reported that she and Mr. Sera were married 8 1/2 years earlier, and that she was pregnant with their second child when he was arrested.

According to the record provided in *Arkansas v. Steven Anthony Sera* (2000):

> Nancy testified that until mid-1996, she believed she and Sera had a strong marriage, and she became pregnant with the couple's second child in July, 1996. She testified that Sera was "thrilled" with the news. But, by early 1997 she suspected Sera was having an affair, and confirmed this during the Hataway incident. According to Nancy, in December 1996, a man came to the door, and Sera pretended to be his own brother, Tony, when he spoke to the man. She identified the person at the door as Fred Daugherty. Daugherty later became the private investigator for Nancy's divorce attorney. According to Nancy, she found the videotape sometime in mid-June 1997 after she and Sera had separated. Sera's testimony contradicted her and he contended that Nancy found the tape much earlier. Nancy explained that she had gone to their house (she was living in an apartment at the time) to get the video camera Sera had purchased to record an upcoming family event. Nancy still had a key and thus access to the home. After returning to her apartment, she checked the videotape in the camera and saw the videotaped incidents of Sera with three women including her own younger sister, Patty Coleman. Nancy called her divorce attorney who told her to give the tape to Daugherty who in turn gave it to the police after having copies made. Daugherty had it copied onto some VHS tapes at a video store where he took many of his work projects.

Nancy also testified that once when she cleaned out Sera's suitcase after a trip, she found a bottle labeled "Rohypnol," and she hid the bottle with several pills in it. When Sera looked for his pills, he became very upset when he could not find them, according to Nancy. Nancy eventually gave this bottle to Daugherty in the course of his investigation.

When Nancy confronted Sera about the tape and told him that she had taken it to the police, he told her that if she didn't get the tape back, he would go to jail. He then took their daughter Chandler and left town for several days. Nancy and Daugherty returned to the house some time later, and Daugherty searched the house and took packets of medicine from Sera's shaving kit.

At the trial, Mr. Sera testified that there were actually several sexual encounters with Patty Coleman, and that they had mutually agreed to videotape these episodes. He also claimed that he and Patty Coleman had taken still photographs of each another, and that Nancy had found them and burned them in the fireplace. He asserted that Nancy, his wife, was aware of his relationship with her sister.

In terms of his character, everything about Mr. Sera suggests a pattern of psychopathic behavior, from the manipulation and grooming of his victims, to the web of deceit woven for the benefit of his wife to conceal his numerous affairs with other women. As discussed in Wrolstad (1997):

> Dozens of interviews and court documents indicate that he was an alternately charming and arrogant salesman whose success hid a succession of firings; whose vanity about weight and age led him to pursue a second round of liposuction and plastic surgery between his rape arrests; whose schemes were so bold that while allegedly carrying a fourth victim into an inn, he was unknowingly interrupted by a former girlfriend.

An expert from Hoffman-LaRoche, the manufacturer of Rohypnol, testified at trial as to the pharmacological effects of the drug. He testified that Rohypnol is in the class of drugs called benzodiazepines, a class which includes Valium, and that the effects of the drug on the human body can include hypnosis, sleep, total muscle relaxation, and loss of memory. He also described the test he developed to detect the presence of Rohypnol metabolites in urine samples to determine if and when someone had ingested the drug. He found those metabolites in Jackie Haygood's urine. He further testified that, after watching the videotape of Mr. Sera having sex with several unconscious victims, he believed it was possible that these women were under the influence of Rohypnol; however, he could not rule out the presence of other drugs.

The jury ultimately did not believe Mr. Sera's version of events, and he was convicted of multiple rape and kidnapping charges relating to the sexual attacks on the two victims in Arkansas. This conviction withstood Mr. Sera's appeal. As of this writing there are charges pending in other states relating to the other two victims.

Steven Gordon: Recidivism, Rape, and Abduction

Steven Gordon of Nashua, New Hampshire, was first convicted of raping a teacher at New Hampshire Technical College in 1992. He was placed on probation after serving less than 4 years of a 6-to-15-year prison sentence. A year later, in 1998, he started raping again. According to published reports, he stalked and then raped a real estate agent (Ramer, 1998):

> On July 7 [1998] . . . [Gordon] raped [a Manchester] real estate agent while posing as a homebuyer, then used a gun to force the 47-year-old woman to drive him to Nashua.

> Later that evening, he is suspected of robbing a D'Angelo's sandwich shop in Stoughton, Mass. Shortly after midnight on July 8, a man fitting Gordon's description robbed a store in Burlington, the Holiday Inn Express store in Lexington, and a Cumberland Farms in Chelmsford.

Then, according to the record, he abducted two Irish women on a summer work-exchange program into a rental car at gunpoint, drove them to a cemetery (*New Hampshire v. Steven Gordon*, 2002):

> On July 18, 1998, the two victims, Young and Griffith, left a party in Hampton Beach at around 1:45 a.m. They were walking along the beach when the defendant ordered them into his car at gunpoint. He drove to a wooded area in Portsmouth and stopped the car. The defendant screamed at the women, ordering them to take their clothes off. The defendant ordered Young at gunpoint to engage in oral sex with Griffith, then forced her to have oral sex with him. He anally raped Young and then vaginally raped Griffith while pointing the gun at Young. He then ordered the women to get out of the car and lay face down on the ground. He told them he would shoot them if they looked at the car or the license plate. The defendant said he would throw their clothes out of the car after he left.

> The car drove off, then stopped, and the women heard a man shouting. Afraid the defendant was coming back, they ran in opposite directions. Young hid in some nettles and bushes. After quite a while she decided to get up because the nettles hurt and she was covered with flies. She could hear Griffith calling her over and over but she didn't answer because she was afraid the defendant had captured Griffith and was forcing her to call to lure Young. Eventually, as it was getting light, the women found each other by following the sounds of their voices. Both women were naked, covered with scratches, and lost. They found their way to a house and knocked on the door.

> . . .

> The women were taken to Portsmouth Regional Hospital where they were interviewed and treated by medical personnel. They were crying and frightened. Griffith refused to let the doctor examine her. She told the

physician, Dr. Gilston, they had been abducted and raped at gunpoint. Griffith was given medications to prevent and treat sexually transmitted diseases and to prevent pregnancy. Young also told the doctor that they had been abducted at gunpoint. Young was examined by the doctor who found that she was covered with abrasions and scratches and suffered a fresh, acute tear on her anus. Young was given a tetanus shot, medications to prevent and treat sexually transmitted diseases and an HIV test.

Gordon was almost immediately linked to the attack on the Irish women by investigators who traced him through rental car records. Unfortunately, he had fled the United States to Amsterdam by the time the connection was made. Within a short period of time, he turned himself in and was extradited back for trial (*New Hampshire v. Steven Gordon*, 2002):

> On July 23, 1998, the defendant's probation officer received a collect call from the defendant who was in Belgium. The defendant admitted that he assaulted the victims. On July 20, 1998, the Portsmouth Police Department issued a warrant for the defendant's arrest. An extradition request was sent to Belgium. The defendant was extradited to the United States and arraigned in the Portsmouth District Court on February 24, 1999.

On September 22, 1999, two hours after a jury found Gordon guilty of five counts of aggravated felonious sexual assault and two counts of kidnapping, he made a failed attempt to escape police custody by kicking out the back window of a prison van while handcuffed (Maddocks, 1999). Officers with OC pepper spray immediately subdued Gordon.

Randy Comeaux—Serial Rapist with a Badge

In January of 1999, 37-year-old Ernest "Randy" Comeaux **(shown in Figure 13-2),** a 20-year veteran investigator in the juvenile division of the Lafayette Parish Sheriff's Department, Louisiana, confessed to committing more than six rapes in Lafayette and Acadia (he is suspected of at least eight more). He would attack his victims while they were home alone at night. Wearing a ski mask and using a gun, he would threaten to harm them if they reported the rape. He also took money from some of the victims and gave advice on how they could avoid being victimized in the future (Woolhouse, January 20, 1999).

Mr. Comeaux was linked to the rapes by epithelial cells extracted from saliva left on cigarette butts that police found at the various crime scenes. At first, he pled not guilty by reason of insanity. He later pled guilty to all six counts of aggravated rape, detailed as follows by District Attorney Keith Stutes (Woolhouse, March 16, 1999):

Figure 13-2

Former Lafayette Parish Sheriff's Deputy and convicted serial rapist Randy Comeaux.

At 4:30 a.m. on Nov. 2, 1986, a Lafayette woman awoke to find a hand over her mouth, he said. When the woman's 9-year-old daughter walked in the room, he ordered the child to lie down on the floor. Then he ordered the girl's mother to disrobe, exposed himself and asked the victim for "sexy panties" before raping her in her living room.

On Oct. 18, 1987, a Lafayette woman was awakened early in the morning. Comeaux ordered her to hold up a phone cord so he could cut it. He searched the house for cash, Stutes said, raped her at gunpoint, and later hit her in the head with his flashlight.

On Nov. 16, 1992, a Lafayette woman awoke after being hit in the head with the barrel of a gun. Comeaux asked for her purse, Stutes said, and Comeaux raped her in her bed.

In October of 1994, a Lafayette woman awoke with a hand over her mouth. Armed with a gun, Comeaux told the woman he wouldn't hesitate to kill her and raped her at gunpoint.

On Oct. 31, 1995, a Lafayette woman awoke with a hand over her mouth. Comeaux brandished a gun and told her to shut up, Stutes said. He then forced her to have sex.

A sixth rape occurred in Acadia Parish during the daylight hours of Sept. 30, 1993. Comeaux brandished a gun and raped the woman as she came back in her home after hanging out laundry.

Mr. Comeaux was sentenced to three life terms. The sentence cannot be appealed.

Of particular interest is Mr. Comeaux's own alleged search for meaning during his 15-year career as a rapist. At one point, he read *Men Who Rape* (Groth, 1979). This issue was discussed by various experts, including Dr. Groth, as follows (Woolhouse, March 19, 1999):

> After Randy Comeaux pleaded guilty to a string of rapes Monday, he told the court that he knew his victims wanted to know why. Why would a 20-year-veteran law enforcement officer who helped countless people by day rape women at gunpoint at night?
>
> Comeaux said he wanted to know why, too. In the early 1990s, he sought help at different counseling centers in Alexandria and Lafayette. He even read a clinical textbook on the subject, titled "Men Who Rape: The Psychology of the Offender."
>
> According to psychologists and forensic experts, there are no easy answers. Genetic and social factors, anger and other issues may combine to create a rapist, experts say. There are few avenues for treatment for serial rapists and sex offenders and differing opinions on how much treatment they deserve.
>
> Dr. A. Nicholas Groth, who wrote the book "Men Who Rape," said he believes society needs to study these men to understand and prevent them from striking again.
>
> "Sadly, this man caused a lot of suffering," said Groth. "The victims, their families, his family. A lot of people have been hurt. Had there been more help, had we been a more enlightened society, maybe we could have spared some pain."
>
> Groth, a psychologist who has worked with hundreds of convicted rapists in prisons in Massachusetts and Connecticut, said that there are typically three general types of rape: anger rape, power rape and sadistic rape. Police say that Comeaux fits the description of a power rapist.
>
> "In these assaults, it is not the offender's desire to harm his victim but to possess her sexually," Groth wrote. "Sexuality becomes a means of compensating for underlying feelings of inadequacy and serves to express issues of mastery, strength, control, authority, identity and capability. His goal is sexual conquest, and he uses only the amount of force necessary to accomplish this objective."
>
> Groth said often such offenders may have obsessive fantasies in which the victim initially resists his sexual advances, he overpowers her, and unable to resist his sexual prowess, she becomes receptive.

Groth stressed that this is deviant behavior by men who have blurred the boundaries between fantasy and reality. The need to rape is a test of the offender's competency, he said, and the rapist feels a mixture of excitement, anxiety, anticipated pleasure and fear. Most rapists of this type find little sexual satisfaction in the rape because it never lives up to the fantasy.

That is why he must find another victim, Groth said. In his work with rapists, he found that most rapists had experienced sexual trauma during their formative years and had no one to go to for help. The trauma may be in the form of direct sexual abuse, but it could be the product of witnessing sexual abuse. Groth used the example of a son knowing his father was molesting his sister.

. . .

Fred Berlin, founder of the Johns Hopkins Sexual Disorders Clinic in Baltimore, said it's important to remember that rape is about eroticized power.

"It's not just liking to push somebody around," he said. "It's the erotic power tied into a biological drive that makes them dangerous."

About 40 percent of rapists report drinking before an intended rape. Groth said many do this as a way of blocking out their constant sexual thoughts, yet the alcohol only lessens their inhibitions.

While Groth said the fact that Comeaux was reading to understand his compulsion showed "something of a conscience," others say it wasn't enough. He only stopped because he was caught, a victim said.

Brent E. Turvey, a forensic scientist and criminal profiler . . . speculated that Comeaux may have been an officer who, after dealing with so many victims as a sheriff's detective each day, began to think there are "no victims, only volunteers."

Comeaux typically entered homes through unlocked doors and windows. Once he told a rape victim that she should have locked her back window.

"The offender may rationalize . . . that he is not abnormal and is entitled to rape," Turvey said.

Such rapists have a psychopathic inability to empathize with their victims' suffering and a serious inability to take responsibility for their behavior.

He also said Comeaux may have gotten a secondary satisfaction or thrill from the fact that his fiancée worked at the Rape Crisis Center.

He said the fact that Comeaux occasionally wore women's underwear during a rape and other times stole underwear from the women he was raping is a fetish, probably rooted in something in his childhood or adolescence.

Both Groth and Turvey said that typically such rapes do not escalate to murder.

. . .

Comeaux committed depraved acts of violence, Groth said, but he is also the same person who did good work in his career in law enforcement.

Turvey warned against too much sympathy.

"Now his entire secret little life has been exposed," Turvey said. "Now he gets to play the victim."

Whether this was for his job as an investigator, to understand his victims better, or to understand himself better, we may never know. What we do know is that whatever remorse he showed during his trial, he did not stop raping women until he was caught and confronted with irrefutable physical evidence. He may even have rationalized that he was doing his victims a favor by exposing the weaknesses in their personal security.

REFERENCES

Arkansas v. Steven Anthony Sera (2000) No. CR 98-1222, May 25, 2000 (2000 WL 675546 (Ark.)).

California v. Darryl Thomas Kemp (1961) Cr. 6632, March 29, 1961 (11 Cal.Rptr. 361).

Gombu, P. Jane Doe gets apology. *Toronto Star*, July 10, 1998, p. 1.

Griffiths, J. (1999) Review of the investigation of sexual assaults, Toronto Police Service. *City Auditor, Toronto Audit Services*, October.

Gross, H. (1924) *Criminal Investigation*, 3rd ed. London: Sweet and Maxwell.

Groth, A. N. (1979) *Men Who Rape: The Psychology of the Offender*. New York: Plenum Press.

Kidwell, D., and Carral, O. "Police, lab trade charges over delay in DNA tests: Serial attacker could have been confirmed many months earlier," *Miami Herald*, June 13, 2003.

Kirk, P. (1974) *Crime Investigation*, 2nd ed. New York: John Wiley & Sons.

Maddocks, D. Gordon found guilty of rape. *Portsmouth Herald*, September 23, 1999.

Missouri v. Terrance Bolds (2000) No. ED 75483, Feb. 7, 2000 (11 S.W.3d 633).

New Hampshire v. Steven Gordon (2002) No. 99-802, The Supreme Court of New Hampshire, December 18, 2002.

Ramer, H. Rape suspect surrenders to police in Belgium. Associated Press, July 26, 1998.

Simon, L. (1997) The myth of sex offender specialization: An empirical analysis. Symposium: The Treatment of Sex Offenders, *New England Journal on Criminal and Civil Confinement*, Summer.

Svensson, A., and Wendel, O. (1965) *Crime Scene Investigation*, 2nd ed. New York: American Elsevier.

Turvey, B. (2002) *Criminal Profiling: An Introduction to Behavioral Evidence Analysis*, 2nd ed. London: Academic Press.

Woolhouse, M. Saliva on cigarette links deputy to several rapes. *Baton Rouge Advocate*, January 20, 1999.

Woolhouse, M. Ex-deputy pleads guilty to rape, gets 3 life terms. *Baton Rouge Advocate*, March 16, 1999.

Woolhouse, M. Experts: No easy answers in rape case. *Baton Rouge Advocate*, March 19, 1999.

Wrolstad, M. Wife's discovery of sex tapes leads to serial rape case. *The Dallas Morning News*, November 16, 1997, p. A-29.

CHAPTER 14

RAPE AND SEXUAL ASSAULT ON TRIAL

John O. Savino and Brent E. Turvey, MS

It is little wonder that rape is one of the least-reported crimes. Perhaps it is the only crime in which the victim becomes the accused and, in reality, it is she who must prove her good reputation, her mental soundness, and her impeccable propriety.

Freda Adler, *Sisters in Crime,* **Chapter 9 (1975)**

Investigators compile the initial case against an accused rapist and make the resulting arrest. However, a state prosecutor is ultimately responsible for deciding whether or not actual criminal charges will be filed, and must present the case against the accused rapist in a court of law. It is therefore important for sex-crime investigators to remember that their responsibility does not end with an arrest; an arrest is just the beginning. The goal of the investigator and prosecutor in the long run is the same: the successful prosecution of the right offender for the crime that they committed, to the fullest extent of the law. To accomplish this, the investigator needs to think of the prosecution mechanism as soon as they are assigned to a case. Every decision, every delay, every word can and will be questioned by a defense attorney at the trial.

Police make arrests based on *probable cause.* Typically it is held that probable cause exists when the known facts and circumstances, of a reasonably trustworthy nature, are sufficient to justify a person of reasonable caution or prudence in the belief that a crime has been or is being committed by the person being arrested. This definition can vary between different jurisdictions.

Prosecutors win cases not on probable cause, but based on *proof beyond a reasonable doubt.* There is a great deal of confusion around this concept. A reasonable doubt is a legitimate doubt based on reason and common sense, and not just the possibility of innocence. A reasonable doubt is the kind of doubt that causes a reasonable person to hesitate. Proof beyond a reasonable doubt must be so convincing that a reasonable person would not hesitate to believe it and act on it. A reasonable doubt is not proof beyond all possible doubt.

To meet these burdens competently, the prosecutor may be needed to assist the investigator with pre-arrest victim interviews, pre-arrest search warrants, and any related subpoenas. This requires that the sex-crime investigator have a good working relationship with the prosecutors, more so than in any other type of case.

State prosecutors have many options available to them when investigators present them with their case. These include, but are not limited to, one of the following:

- Criminal prosecution for rape or sexual assault
- Criminal prosecution for lesser related offenses
- Further investigation required
- Decline prosecution (DP)

To help make their decision, prosecutors will evaluate a number of factors, including the nature of the rape, victim cooperation, the victim's effectiveness as a potential witness, the nature and quality of the physical evidence, the character of the accused, and the public interest in seeing a prosecution. Most of these factors are dependent on the extent and quality of the police investigation that has occurred to that point.

If, after considering these and other factors, the prosecutor believes that there is a low probability of obtaining a conviction, the prosecutor may DP the case despite the very best efforts of everyone involved. Cases have been dropped, for example, as a result of factors related to the victim's mental condition. A victim may have a history of mental illness, or a learning disorder, and consequently may be unable to give coherent or consistent testimony at a trial.

Case Example:

A young woman's ex-boyfriend was in town to see a baseball playoff game, and after the game she invited him to use her apartment to spend the night because it ran late. They had not seen each other in about 6 months. A pullout bed had been set up for the ex-boyfriend to sleep on.

The ex-boyfriend arrived shortly after 2:00 A.M. and brought a bottle of wine. After one glass of wine and talking about old times, the victim felt dizzy and sick and decided to go to bed. She went into her bedroom and fell asleep. She came to about an hour later, groggy and barely able to move. The ex-boyfriend had removed her clothing while she was passed out and was now on top of her, raping her. She attempted to push him off and tell him to stop, but she did not have the strength and the words would not come out.

When she came to in the morning, they were now both on the pullout bed. She had no memory of other events or how she got to the couch. Embarrassed and not knowing what to do, she did not immediately report the crime. Three days later after talking with friends and parents, the woman went to a hospital and reported the incident. An evidence collection kit was collected along with blood and urine specimens. Fortunately, she had also saved the unfinished wine bottle and the two glasses they drank from. Test results eventually showed no evidence of any type of date rape drugs in her system or in the wine or glasses.

There was also no evidence discovered in the rape kit, and attempts to interview the suspect resulted in him contacting an attorney.

The prosecutor's office decided not to prosecute this case because the probability of a conviction was low, and the trial may have done more harm to the victim. It would have been her word against his, with him as an invited guest, and no physical evidence.

The logic behind this kind of decision-making involves weighing future victim anguish resulting from a trial, and finite prosecutorial resources, against the possibility of an acquittal. As expressed by one prosecutor (Wood, 2001):

> "There's nothing worse than going through the trial and having him be acquitted" and smile at the victim as he leaves the courtroom, [Assistant Commonwealth's Attorney Jon R.] Zug said, adding that he has seen it occur. Everything that has happened during the trial to help the victim heal "can be erased."

Prosecuting a rapist is not always easy, and without a competent investigation as a platform from which to work it is impossible.

In many sexual assault cases the only evidence a prosecutor may have is the oral testimony of the victim herself. There may not be a lot of physical evidence to work with. Despite good victim recall and heroic efforts by detectives, crime-scene personnel, and the crime lab, today's rapists are evidence conscious and do think about what they might leave behind during their crimes. It is not uncommon for a rapist to wear a condom, a hat, a mask, or gloves. They may even go so far as make their victims bathe before leaving the scene, to wash away potential transfer evidence. In such a case, unless there is a confession, the prosecutor may be unwilling to carry it forward.

Case Example:
In May of 2000, a young woman entered her mid-town apartment. She was nervous and cautious because only a week before, the apartment had been burglarized. As she entered her bedroom, a male came out of the closet; he was wearing a mask and forced her into a bathroom. He blindfolded and tied her hands behind her back. He sexually assaulted the woman, ejaculated on her body, and then fled her apartment.

There were no other similar cases until December of 2001, in another part of the city. As a young woman was sleeping, a masked man entered her apartment. She was blindfolded with her hands bound behind her back, and then sexually assaulted. This time, however, the male forced the victim into the bathroom and forced her to shower while he stood nearby. He instructed her to wash her vaginal area, and took the washcloth and towel she used with him when he fled the scene.

DNA was recovered from this victim, however, and was matched to the biological evidence collected in the prior rape back in May of 2000.

With the past and current proliferation of fictional and documentary television shows featuring the many advantages of forensic evidence, showing real and contrived forensic collection techniques, it is not that hard for even inexperienced offenders to learn how to take precautions. Additionally, as offenders have more contact with the justice system (arrest, conviction, jail time, etc.), they will certainly learn more and have the opportunity to become more aware of what they may leave behind. Some offenders act on this information while others can always be counted on to ignore it entirely.

In the second place, the offender myths discussed in the first chapter can influence the perceptions and decisions of the judge and the jury. They may expect that all rapists are seething antisocial monsters, with devilish eyes and a perverse, easily discernible grin. In point of fact, many rapists clean up well and appear affable, leaving behind a good first impression. What may show up in court may appear to be a clean-shaven family man with a long history of going to church and coaching girls' basketball at the high school. In other words, the accused may be someone who lives an apparently normal life and does not look like they "need to rape."

In the third place, the victim myths discussed in the first chapter can also influence the perceptions and decisions of the judge and the jury. They may expect to see a complete innocent who has been brutally attacked and suffered all manner of injury. What may be brought to court is a homeless drug addict who was raped in a shelter, or a prostitute who was raped at gunpoint by an offender posing at first as a customer.

The total impact of these perceptions is summed up in Baker (1997):

> Stereotypical constructions of rape have made rape convictions particularly hard to secure because the men on trial often do not appear to be weird, perverted, or different, and the women victims often fail to reflect the pure (and white) image that jurors feel the need to protect.

It is therefore the responsibility of investigators to make certain that, before they hand their case over to the prosecutor, and before they make an arrest, they have prepared their case from top to bottom. Every fact should be established to the best of their ability, and every detail should be investigated until it is an exhausted possibility. For the sex-crimes investigator, this must be a matter of routine practice, a matter of civic conscience, and a matter of professional pride.

The test of a good case comes when it is confronted by the defense strategy of the accused. Investigators should be thinking of this long before thinking about how they are going to enjoy putting the handcuffs on them.

THE DEFENSE

A defendant who stands accused of rape or sexual assault typically has only one of three defenses: they can argue that no sexual penetration of any kind occurred, let alone rape; they can argue that it's a case of mistaken identity; or they can argue that sexual activity happened, but it wasn't rape. To the defendant's advantage is the fact that in most cases of rape or sexual assault, there are only two witnesses who know what really happened: the victim and the accused.

NO SEXUAL PENETRATION

In these cases, the accused may admit to knowing or being with or being around the victim. They may even admit to kissing or other forms of sexual contact with them. They will not, however, admit to any sexual penetration. Such a defense may arise when there is no biological transfer evidence, such as sperm or semen recovered from the victim or their clothing. This in combination with a lack of victim injury can make a strong case for the defense. In such a case, it becomes the word of the victim against the word of the accused.

In these types of cases, and in the case of a drug-facilitated sexual assault, a case can be made stronger with the aid of a "pretext" phone call to the suspect, where legal. Some states require court authorization before recording a phone call. This call is placed by the victim to the suspect under the supervision and direction of the investigator. The call is recorded and used to solicit statements or admissions from the suspect to be used against him at a later time. The statements obtained can be used by investigators during questioning or can be powerful evidence when introduced at a trial.

This is also the kind of case that the *pre-scene interview* discussed at the end of Chapter 2 is designed to preserve. By establishing the actions of the offender during the attack and afterward, the lead investigator and forensic personnel can direct their efforts to help corroborate the victim's version of events. If the victim tells the investigator that the attacker lifted her shirt and licked her breasts or any other part of her body, a DNA swab should be taken of that area. If the victim claims that she injured her attacker, that should also be investigated, established, and documented. The more that the forensic evidence can corroborate, the less the case becomes the word of the victim against the word of the accused.

MISTAKEN IDENTITY

There are two kinds of mistaken identity cases—those involving biological evidence and those involving eyewitness identification.

The advent of DNA testing, with the various advances in DNA collection and technology discussed in this text, has all but eliminated the suggestion of mistaken identity when biological evidence is present. If it associates the victim and the accused, and more specifically associates the accused with some form of sexual contact, this argument becomes all but untenable. This is true in cases where the biological evidence has provided an individuating result, such as a complete STR DNA profile.

The only alternative the accused has when confronted with such powerful evidence, aside from a plea bargain, is to suggest that the evidence was tainted or planted. To accomplish this, the accused must convince the judge and jury that at least one of the following circumstances is plausible:

1. That the character of the officers charged with maintaining the chain of evidence (who presumably refute any allegation that the evidence was planted) is suspect or corrupted
2. That the *chain of evidence* was weak or nonexistent at the point in time when and where the evidence was planted[1]
3. That the forensic lab personnel responsible for testing the biological evidence were biased, incompetent, and/or prone to error

Law enforcement officers and investigators are commonly accused of bias, incompetence, and corruption in court. Sometimes it is the only area of attack by a defense attorney. The idea is to make the investigative work appear sloppy, rushed, and mistake-ridden, and then any work they do is suspect. This happens often enough that seasoned investigators expect it, are prepared for it, do not

---

[1] As discussed in Chapter 4, the *chain of custody* is the record of everyone who has controlled, taken custody of, or had contact with a particular item of evidence from the beginning of this process to the current day's activities. It includes the investigator's notes and reports, the crime-scene security log, the evidence log, chain-of-custody forms, and the photographic record. Anyone coming to court without such a record for their physical evidence can be made to look at best incompetent, and at worst deceptive.

take it personally, and can easily dissuade others of its basis in fact. It is simply part of the job.

However, if bias and corruption can be proven, or allegations can be combined with any of the other two circumstances, juries have been known to respond by voting for an acquittal. The days of police officers and forensic scientists being taken at their word in court have long since passed. In today's courtroom, a chain of custody must be demonstrated for all evidence, and the character of those presenting it must be above reproach.

For the lead investigator, this all comes back to *knowing your people* and *knowing your crime lab*, as discussed in Chapter 2. If there are problems with either, they should be uncovered and dealt with well before the accused is fashioning their defense. When legitimate concerns have been raised, the solution may be to use a private forensic lab to corroborate findings.

In cases where there is no biological evidence, and the identification of the accused rests solely on eyewitness identification, commonly from the victim, this will be the focus of the defense case. Depending on the victim's lifestyle, background, and circumstances, the defense may avoid questioning their identification and attack eyewitness ID in general as flawed. This is not an illegitimate line of doubt to pursue, as even the most certain eyewitness identifications have been known to fail spectacularly in the face of DNA technology, which may not have been available at the time of an original investigation and subsequent conviction.

In such cases, it is the duty of the investigator to establish the reliability of the witness and his or her subsequent identification of any suspects. If the witness is unsure, go back and start over. Investigators can also interview alibi witnesses, family of the suspect, and any other leads that could help with placing the suspect at the scene. Don't push witnesses toward an ID that could crumble in court or convict the innocent. According to the Innocence Project, which maintains their findings online at http://www.innocenceproject.org, incorrect eyewitness identification is the number one cause of wrongful convictions, occurring in 61 of the first 70 DNA exonerations. It is a mechanism of identification that is commonly flawed for a variety of reasons.

Investigators must work to prevent incorrect eyewitness identification, or even the perception of it. Accuracy and reliability begins with the suspect lineups and photo spreads that are shown to eyewitnesses when a suspect has been found. Green (2003) writes:

> Dr. Ronald P. Fisher, a psychology professor at Florida International University, said, "There should either be a homogenous appearance of the photographs, or at least enough variation across all of the photographs, so that the suspect's photo does not stand out."

Fisher has studied eyewitness identification and the methods police use for photo spreads.

Also, experts say it is difficult to identify a stranger one just has met under the best of circumstances. It is easy for an eyewitness, particularly one caught in the emotional fog and trauma of a violent crime, to err when identifying a suspect.

Identifications of a member of one race by a member of another are particularly difficult.

Once the mistake has been made, however, the witness, who now believes the incorrectly identified person is the assailant, rarely has a change of mind.

To guard against incorrect eyewitness identification, the research suggest that the following steps be taken (Wells, *et al.*, 1998):

1. Use a double-blind line-up or photo spread. The person showing the eyewitness the suspects should not know anything about the case and should be unable to purposefully or accidentally leak pertinent information, or signal approval or disapproval regarding the identification.
2. The eyewitness should be forewarned that the suspect might not be present, and that they are under no obligation to make an identification.
3. Distracters should be selected based on the eyewitness's verbal description of the offender. In other words, if the eyewitness said that the assailant had a beard, put a guy in there with a beard who is known to be innocent.
4. Eyewitness confidence should be assessed and recorded at the time of the identification.

These steps and others have been further developed and approved by the Technical Working Group for Eyewitness Evidence (TWGEYEE, 1999):

Photo Lineup: In composing a photo lineup, the investigator should:

1. Include only one suspect in each identification procedure.
2. Select fillers who generally fit the witness' description of the perpetrator. When there is a limited/inadequate description of the perpetrator provided by the witness, or when the description of the perpetrator differs significantly from the appearance of the suspect, fillers should resemble the suspect in significant features.
3. If multiple photos of the suspect are reasonably available to the investigator, select a photo that resembles the suspect description or appearance at the time of the incident.

4. Include a *minimum* of five fillers (nonsuspects) per identification procedure.

5. Consider that complete uniformity of features is not required. Avoid using fillers who so closely resemble the suspect that a person familiar with the suspect might find it difficult to distinguish the suspect from the fillers.

6. Create a consistent appearance between the suspect and fillers with respect to any unique or unusual feature (e.g., scars, tattoos) used to describe the perpetrator by artificially adding or concealing that feature.

7. Consider placing suspects in different positions in each lineup, both across cases and with multiple witnesses in the same case. Position the suspect randomly in the lineup.

8. When showing a new suspect, avoid reusing fillers in lineups shown to the same witness.

9. Ensure that no writings or information concerning previous arrest(s) will be visible to the witness.

10. View the spread, once completed, to ensure that the suspect does not unduly stand out.

11. Preserve the presentation order of the photo lineup. In addition, the photos themselves should be preserved in their original condition.

Live Lineup: In composing a live lineup, the investigator should:

1. Include only one suspect in each identification procedure.

2. Select fillers who generally fit the witness' description of the perpetrator. When there is a limited/inadequate description of the perpetrator provided by the witness, or when the description of the perpetrator differs significantly from the appearance of the suspect, fillers should resemble the suspect in significant features.

3. Consider placing suspects in different positions in each lineup, both across cases and with multiple witnesses in the same case. Position the suspect randomly unless, where local practice allows, the suspect or the suspect's attorney requests a particular position.

4. Include a *minimum* of four fillers (nonsuspects) per identification procedure.

5. When showing a new suspect, avoid reusing fillers in lineups shown to the same witness.

6. Consider that complete uniformity of features is not required. Avoid using fillers who so closely resemble the suspect that a person familiar with the suspect might find it difficult to distinguish the suspect from the fillers.

7. Create a consistent appearance between the suspect and fillers with respect to any unique or unusual feature (e.g., scars, tattoos) used to describe the perpetrator by artificially adding or concealing that feature.

Summary: The above procedures will result in a photo or live lineup in which the suspect does not unduly stand out. An identification obtained through a lineup composed in this manner may have stronger evidentiary value than one obtained without these procedures.

There is nothing inherently problematic or onerous about following these simple suggestions, each of which adds a layer of reliability and accountability. Furthermore, the research has shown that jurors overwhelmingly respond to eyewitness confidence in such cases (Wells *et al.*, 1998). The more confident the eyewitness, the more convincing he or she is to a jury; the less confident, the less convincing. This is important information for the prosecutor to have if the decision is made to use eyewitness identification at trial.

Consider the case of Mark Allan Parr, where mistaken identity was used as his defense against charges of forcible oral copulation and assault with the intent to commit rape. Taken entirely from *California v. Mark Allan Parr* (2003):

In the early morning hours of August 8, 1997, a nude Caucasian man wearing only a pair of tan construction boots and a sheer nylon stocking over his head, entered the home of Michelle H. without her permission. The man climbed into Michelle's bed, held a 12-inch knife to her throat, covered her mouth with his other hand, and told her that he intended to rape her. He told her not to scream or he would harm her and her four-year-old daughter, who was asleep on the floor directly beside her mother's bed. He touched Michelle's breasts over and under her nightgown and her vaginal area on the outside of her panties. He grabbed her hair, pushed her head to his penis, and commanded her to orally copulate him. Michelle repeatedly refused, while keeping her mouth closed and pulling her head away. Eventually, the man forced Michelle's mouth onto his penis. However, he failed to achieve an erection and did not ejaculate.

In apparent frustration, the man forced Michelle out of bed and into the living room, where he put on underwear. He threatened to hurt Michelle and her daughter if she called the police. He grabbed "a pile of stuff" beside the front door and left the apartment. Unbeknownst to Michelle, her purse was included in the collection of articles her assailant removed from her home.

Michelle immediately telephoned a girlfriend. She and her friend talked about the incident for approximately two hours. Michelle told her friend a man of "big build" and clad only in construction boots entered her apartment and "jumped on her." Michelle remembered the man had a stocking over his head, but said it looked like he had a mustache. She also described the man as having a lot of body hair. He was carrying a knife wrapped with a towel and forced her to orally copulate him. He also told her she had left her front door open, and asked Michelle why she was always alone. The man then forced her into the living room at knife-point, and he left the apartment wearing underwear and boots. Michelle later discovered he had also taken her purse.

Later that morning, Michelle called to cancel various credit cards and reported the theft to police. Her girlfriend persuaded her to report the sexual assault to police that afternoon. To the desk officer, Michelle described her assailant as a muscular, "medium race" man, who was larger in size than herself and had a lot of body hair. He also smelled of cologne, or body odor and cologne. The officer noted that Michelle was uncertain whether or not the assailant had facial hair, but she thought he was right handed. In a telephone interview three days later, Michelle stated "she was pretty sure he had a mustache."

Around 10:00 A.M. the following day, a Riverside County Deputy Sheriff arrested defendant and searched his car. The officer discovered Michelle's cell phone, credit cards and other documents that had been in her purse, a pair of tan construction boots, and two small knives. At the time, defendant had "kind of long" shaggy hair and a mustache.

Sometime before August 12, 1997, defendant was charged with possession of stolen property in Riverside County. Michelle was subpoenaed to appear for the preliminary hearing. As she waited to testify, she saw about 15 prisoners, including defendant, brought into court. Michelle recognized defendant and became so upset she was forced to leave the courtroom. In October, defendant pleaded guilty to the charge of possession of stolen property.

In 1998, charges were filed in Orange County. Michelle identified defendant as her attacker at the Orange County preliminary examination. At trial, Michelle testified that her attacker had a small penis, facial hair, and a lot of body hair. The prosecution introduced, over defense objection, a photograph of defendant, standing nude and facing the camera. The court ordered the photo displayed with a Post-it note to cover his face. Michelle identified the man in the picture as her attacker.

Defendant did not testify at trial. His mother and stepfather testified as character witnesses to his calm, nonviolent demeanor, and his mother claimed he was left-handed. His mother also provided an alibi. She testified defendant lived with her in August 1997. On August 7, the day before the incident, she worked her usual 4:00 to 10:30 P.M. shift. Defendant was asleep in his bedroom when she arrived home at approximately 10:45 P.M. Defendant came out of his bedroom at approximately 6:30 A.M. the following morning. Later in the day, defendant accompanied his mother and sister on a trip to Moreno Valley for his sister's medical appointment. An Orange County construction project manager testified defendant's boots were of a type commonly worn by construction workers. A forensic psychologist testified as an expert in eyewitness identification. He opined that eyewitness identification of strangers is "extremely unreliable under the very best of circumstances."

Despite the absence of biological evidence and a facial identification from the victim, Mr. Parr was convicted. This conviction was achieved on the recognition of Mr. Parr's naked body by the victim, and his possession of her stolen property. The method used to obtain the ID was poor, involving a single nude photo of the defendant. The weakness of this conviction is evident, and makes it the kind of case that would be a candidate for DNA testing should such evidence be uncovered in the future. This is not to say that Mr. Parr is obviously innocent; it is to say that prosecutors have met a very low threshold of reliability in achieving this conviction.

Consider the following cases, taken from many contemporary examples.

Herman Atkins

In 1988, Herman Atkins was convicted of two counts of forcible rape, two counts of forcible oral copulation, and robbery as the result of incorrect eyewitness identification. His case is profiled on the Innocence Project Web site (http://www.innocenceproject.org), which provides the following summary:

Herman Atkins was convicted by a jury in 1988 of robbery, rape, forcible oral copulation, and for using a handgun in the commission of these crimes. The victim was raped in a shoe store in Lake Elsinore, California, in 1986. Atkins was sentenced to over forty-five years in prison.

On April 8, 1986, the victim was working at the shoe store when, sometime between 11:30AM and 12:00PM, she was raped and robbed at gunpoint. During the rape, the assailant ejaculated and wiped the semen from his genitals onto her sweater. The victim called the police and was taken to the hospital where vaginal swabs were collected. Her clothing, including the pink sweater with the semen stains, was collected and marked for identification. She then went to the police station and was shown Elsinore High School yearbooks but was unable to find her assailant. She did not identify Atkins as her assailant until after she was taken to a police station briefing room, where she saw a wanted poster for him on unrelated charges. After seeing the wanted poster, she was shown a photo lineup and identified Atkins as her assailant. A witness who worked at the store next to where the rape occurred was shown the wanted poster with Atkins's picture and identified him as a man who had been in her store earlier that day.

Atkins's defense was mistaken eyewitness identification. He presented an alibi witness and testified on his own behalf. In addition to the eyewitness identifications, the prosecution proffered testimony from a criminalist with the State of California's Riverside Laboratory. The criminalist testified that the semen found on vaginal swabs was deposited by someone with blood type A and PGM 2+1+. This typing was consistent with both the victim and Atkins. The criminalist also testified that the semen stain recovered from victim's sweater revealed the presence of a type A secretor and that about 25.9% of the black population have type A blood, and 80% of the population are secretors. Further, he testified that approximately 21.4% of the population (both caucasian and black) have PGM Type 2+1+. He concluded that, based on these numbers, Atkins was included in a population of approximately 4.4% of people who could have committed this rape. The prosecutor argued during summation that this evidence was "evidence [which] can't be used to say this is exactly [the defendant], but it excludes a large percentage of the people, and does not exclude him, and that's corroboration."

Atkins's case was accepted by the Innocence Project in 1993. After locating the sweater and vaginal swabs in 1995, the Innocence Project began trying to gain access to the evidence for DNA testing. The prosecution refused to allow access to the evidence. In 1999, the Innocence Project filed a motion to compel the prosecutor to relinquish control of the evidence and send it to a laboratory for the purposes of DNA testing. The motion was granted and the evidence was sent to Forensic Science Associates.

After receiving the specimens, which consisted of biological evidence used at trial, FSA performed STR based DNA testing on the semen stains found on the victim's sweater. The vaginal swabs were consumed by the serological testing conducted at the time of trial and thus not amenable to DNA testing. Testing was conducted on three separate areas of the sweater. In all three areas, the results were consistent. The spermatozoa found were determined to be from someone other than Atkins. Based on the test results, Herman Atkins was released from prison in February 2000, after spending twelve years in prison for a crime he did not commit.

As stated, Mr. Atkins served almost 12 years in prison until he was exonerated by DNA evidence in early 2000.

Larry Johnson

Forty-seven-year-old Larry Johnson of St. Louis, MO, was sentenced in September 1984 on charges that he had kidnapped, raped, sodomized, and robbed a 20-year-old Saint Louis University student in her car 8 months earlier.

Mr. Johnson's case is profiled on the Innocence Project Web site (http://www.innocenceproject.org), which provides the following summary:

The victim was attacked in her car in the early morning. The attacker, whose face was masked by a sweatshirt and scarf, forced his way into her car and threatened her with a knife. She was then driven to an alley where she was raped and sodomized for two hours. After the attack, the victim drove home and contacted the police and was taken to a hospital for the purposes of collecting a rape kit.

The victim described the assailant as a clean shaven black man. She helped the police produce a composite sketch and later identified Larry Johnson's picture from a photo array, despite the fact that he had a mustache. After his arrest, the victim picked Johnson from a lineup.

At trial, the defense was barred from asking about identification of the spermatozoa that had been recovered from the vaginal slide, the victim's panties, and a swatch from her sweater. The court relied on previous decisions that had addressed the issue of inclusion statistics on saliva tests. No fingerprints were found in the victim's car. Based largely on the victim's cross racial identification, Johnson was convicted in August 1984.

Johnson's appeals failed. He contacted the Innocence Project in 1995 seeking assistance with gaining access to the biological evidence for DNA testing. He and the Project would face considerable resistance to these efforts.

Various Innocence Project students, beginning in 1996, attempted to verify the existence of the evidence. They were told that there was a record of the evidence existing but that the police department would not physically check absent a court order. The Circuit Attorney's Office offered similar resistance to finding the evidence. In 1998, all other government offices were instructed to refrain from helping the Innocence Project confirm the existence or destruction of the evidence.

In 2000, the Innocence Project filed a civil rights suit seeking injunctive relief in the form of access to the biological evidence. Again, the prosecution would not release the evidence. Their office began a review of the Johnson case and several other Innocence Project cases in Missouri in December 2000.

In February 2001, the Supreme Court of Missouri adopted a rule, effective September 1, 2001, that allowed for the filing of motions seeking postconviction DNA testing. The Project perfected a motion on Johnson's behalf and filed in November 2001.

The following January, the Court ordered the Circuit Attorney's Office to respond to the motion. Finally, in March 2002, the Circuit Attorney's Office replied indicating that it would not oppose Johnson's motion. According to the protocol adopted, both parties would receive the results from testing simultaneously.

Testing began at the state crime laboratory in July 2002. On July 26, 2002, the Innocence Project was informed by the Associated Press that the Circuit Attorney had scheduled a press conference for the same day to announce that DNA testing had excluded Larry Johnson as the perpetrator.

Johnson was exonerated and released on July 30, 2002.

Mr. Johnson spent almost 18 years in prison for a rape he didn't commit, and was freed in 2002 after DNA tests exonerated him.

Eyewitness identification has problems under even the best circumstances. However, there are some easy steps that investigators can take to mitigate these problems and increase or even test eyewitness reliability. The regular employment of less reliable tactics ensures that police and prosecutors will convict the innocent in a percentage of cases, resulting in future liability.

THE CONSENT CASE

Unless it can be proven that the victim and the accused are complete strangers with no reason whatsoever for their paths to cross, this is perhaps the hardest defense to beat at trial. The accused claims that the victim consented, or at least did not outwardly object, to the sexual activity that occurred. Consequently, from the point of view of the accused, the alleged victim gave their consent to the sexual activity that followed.

The laws regarding consent are often ambiguous and complicated. In some states, the victim must essentially prove that they did not give consent during their attack, and even the hint of reticence is enough to cloud the waters. In other states, it has been found that a man may be convicted of rape if his sexual partner first consents but later changes her mind during a sexual act and asks him to stop.

In any case, if the investigation has been thorough it will be less onerous for the prosecutor to navigate and evaluate where the case actually fits in terms of the law. The prosecutor must consider many elements in such a case: not just the evidence and the witnesses, but the potential jury as well. According to Assistant Commonwealth's Attorney Jon R. Zug of Virginia (Wood, 2001):

> "I've never won an acquaintance rape jury trial," he said, often because of skeptical jurists. Women jurors aged 35 and older are the toughest demographic in rape cases, Zug said. "I went a long time trying to pack cases with women [jurors]—until I started talking to them." At that point he realized older women could be tough judges of victims; in cases where the victim had something to drink (and was drunk or not), older women jurors feel that "she was putting herself in that position" while they excuse the defendant's drinking.

In such cases, a major issue is the presence or absence of victim resistance in the form of injury. Research in the area victim injury has shown again and again that the following is true (Bowyer and Dalton, 1997; Slaughter, Brown, Crowley, and Peck, 1997; Sawyer-Sommers, Schafer, Zink, Hutson, and Hillard, 2001)[2]:

- In crimes of rape, only some of the victims who are examined show evidence of injury. Depending on the study, this percentage was sometimes a majority and sometimes a minority.
- The absence of injury does not exclude the possibility of rape.
- A small percentage of the women examined as part of a consensual-sex control group reported injury.

In any event, if there is no evidence of victim resistance in a particular case, investigators should already know the explanation, whether it includes the attacker's use of a weapon, their physical size, or the personality of the victim. Not all rape results in injury, and there are reasons why. In many cases, just the threat of violence or harm is enough to overcome a victim's resistance. Whatever the reason, the failure to establish it in a given case is a weakness that the defense will exploit.

Unfortunately, largely as a result of television and movies, much of the public has a preconceived notion of how a sexual assault victim should present (i.e., black eyes, bloody face, torn and messy hair, crying hysterically, etc.). As a result, it is common for jurors to succumb to the misperception that if someone was forced to have sex there will be resulting vaginal injuries. In fact, it is almost completely opposite; many victims are in a state of shock during the attack and are unable to fight back. At trial, this can be explained by qualified medical personnel.

Consider the case of Abdiel Ariza, where consent was used as his defense against charges of rape in concert by force or violence, rape by force or fear, and sodomy in concert by force or fear. Taken entirely from *California v. Abdiel Ariza* (2002):

---

[2] In one study of 801 forensic examinations of victims of alleged sexual assault, there was evidence of trauma in 202 (57%) of the examinations, and spermatozoa were found at the time of the forensic examination in 110 (31%) of the cases in which a suspect was identified (Gray-Eurom, Seaberg, and Wears, 2002). In another study, genital trauma occurred in 35.7% of the cases of the first group (victims examined in emergency within 72 hours after the last sexual assault), and in 19.5% of the cases of the second group (examined after 72 hours). Additionally, hymenal, vulvo-vaginal, and anal lesions were found in 11%, 20%, and 7% of the cases, respectively, examined in emergency (Grossin *et al.*, 2003).

On August 6, 1999, Charisse A. threw a birthday party for herself and Mike Alcazar at a Long Beach bar where she was employed. Alcazar was Charisse A.'s brother-in-law, the husband of her sister, Tamala. Charisse A. invited several friends; Alcazar came with appellant, his stepbrother. Tamala wanted to come to the party but she could not find a babysitter.

. . .

Charisse A. drank beer and mixed drinks during the party, but she did not get drunk. Charisse A. had the "capacity of her senses"; she did not fall down, get sick or pass out. At the party, appellant did not drink alcoholic beverages.

At the party, Charisse A. played pool and sang karaoke with her friends. She did not flirt with appellant; she never kissed him or had her arm around him.

The bar closed at 2:00 a.m. and Charisse A. prepared to leave. She could not find her car key. Alcazar and appellant offered to give Charisse A. a ride home. She invited the men to sleep on her living room couch. She was concerned that Alcazar avoid driving home after drinking. Alcazar and Tamala lived about 45 minutes away in Placentia and had previously stayed at Charisse A.'s apartment with their children.

Charisse A. entered her apartment alone while the men were parking the car. She began to get ready for bed by changing into sweatpants, a long t-shirt and socks. She placed pillows and blankets on the living room couch for Alcazar and appellant, in case they decided to stay over.

Tamala called Charisse A.'s apartment twice to speak to Alcazar. He and appellant were there when Tamala telephoned the second time. Tamala was upset because her husband had not come home. Charisse A. went to bed and fell asleep, while Alcazar was speaking to his wife on the telephone.

Charisse A. was suddenly awakened by appellant. He had entered her bedroom and began touching her bottom and pelvic area. Charisse A. resisted, telling appellant to go to bed. He continued fondling her and he began to remove her clothing. Charisse A. struggled with him; she was crying and telling him to stop. Appellant pulled on her shirt and stretched it while she tried to keep her shirt on.

At some point, Alcazar appeared in the bedroom. He and appellant simultaneously and forcibly sexually assaulted Charisse A. Appellant "penetrated her vagina" with his penis. Alcazar simultaneously sodomized her. Charisse A. "felt [the men] holding her down," as she lay on her right side. She could not get away. Charisse A. cried and felt "a lot of pain, pressure, and force." She begged them to stop. The assault seemed to last "forever."

Charisse A. pleaded to go to the bathroom and the men released her. She grabbed her bathrobe, and ran from the apartment. Charisse A. knocked on the doors of two of her neighbors. They heard her, but they did not respond. She ran to the apartment of a friend. Charisse A. was crying and assumed a fetal position on his kitchen floor. She screamed she had been raped. The friend telephoned police and Charisse A. spoke to a 911 operator.

The police arrived at Charisse A.'s apartment. Appellant and Alcazar were no longer there. Charisse A. was taken to the hospital. Jan Hare, a forensic nurse specialist and registered nurse examined her and determined that Charisse A. had suffered blunt trauma to the vagina and anus. Her multiple injuries were inconsistent with consensual sex.

Gregory Wong, a Senior Criminalist for the Los Angeles Crime Law examined the rape kit. He found no semen in the vaginal sample, but he did find semen in the rectal sample. The sample was too small to conduct a DNA test.

Immediately after the assault, Charisse A. was hysterical and in extreme pain. She no longer wanted to live in her apartment and moved out days later. Weeks later, the injuries to her anus had not completely healed. At that point, Charisse A. was tearful, upset and had trouble sleeping. She also suffered long-term trauma. In court, Charisse A. had difficulty testifying without crying. Her friends testified that her demeanor had changed as a result of the assault. Previously, Charisse A. was happy and easy going. After the assault, she was reclusive and emotional.

. . .

[Ariza]'s overall theme is Charisse A., as well as the other prosecution witnesses, had consumed alcohol to the point where their perceptions and/or memories of events were too unreliable to substantiate the occurrence of forcible sexual assault in concert. It also appears appellant claims the record shows he engaged in sexual activity with Charisse A. under a reasonable and good faith but mistaken belief she had consented.

In presenting his defense, Mr. Ariza attacked the credibility of the witnesses, noted the consumption of alcohol, and picked apart numerous inconsistencies in the victim's statements. He also claimed that the victim's socks lying on her dresser, and her sweatpants lying on top of her panties, do not supporting a finding of forcible sexual assault; the victim had taken the time to stack her clothing in a pile. He admitted to having sex with her, but claimed it wasn't rape.

According to the court, the defense issues were inconsequential owing to the following (*California v. Abdiel Ariza*, 2002):

> Charisse A.'s testimony was not shaken by cross-examination or substantially impeached as to the forcible sexual assault. Her demeanor while testifying and conduct during and after the forcible rape and sodomy in concert corroborated her testimony. The medical examiner's testimony essentially corroborated the forcible sexual assaults occurred as claimed by Charisse A. Moreover, a neighbor, who was not at the birthday party, testified she heard Charisse A. "crying and wailing" at the time of forcible sexual assault and "yelling and fighting with a man."

So, despite the claims of consent by the accused, the absence of confirming biological evidence, the association of alcohol with the crime, and inconsistencies with the victim's version of events, a solid case was put together that dealt with each of these issues. Key issues included the overwhelming evidence of victim injury and the victim's confidence at trial.

LEAD INVESTIGATOR'S COURT-READY CASE CHECKLIST

It is the lead investigator's responsibility to strive to make his or her case as courtroom ready as possible before handing it up to the prosecutor's office to refer charges. The following is a checklist of basics to consider:

1. *Know your victim.* Be the first to uncover and discuss any inconsistencies in their statement, or any circumstances that may give rise to doubt about their truthfulness or reliability. Hide nothing from anyone. If the victim is not telling the truth about something, be the first to uncover it, not the last. If the victim is not certain about something, document it. Go over the case with the victim until you are certain that every doubt and inconsistency is out in the open and fully appreciated.
2. *Organization is everything.* Sometimes departments have a policy about how to organize their case files; sometimes not. If not, sit down with your prosecutor and your supervisor and work one out. A case file means very little if others cannot navigate it easily. Document every investigative step and effort; leave nothing to chance. Remember—if it is not documented, you did not do it; the record of your investigation must be clear and concise.
3. *Put together a solid case.* There's no point in bringing a case to a prosecutor that hasn't been put together very well. Put it together right the first time or give it to somebody who can. Experienced or competent prosecutors will DP a poorly assembled case; an inexperienced or incompetent prosecutor will take it forward and make fools of his office and the police department both. Until you know which your prosecutor is, don't trust his or her judgment to protect your cases and your credibility.

4. *Have your chain of custody carefully locked in.* For each item of evidence, account for every step that it made along the way. Be prepared to explain any potential breaks or weaknesses. You must be responsible for your evidence; it is your case and you must make sure evidence is properly handled and tested.

5. *Know the evidence and where it fits.* If you feel that you don't understand your evidence with full confidence, discuss it with your crime lab personnel or your sexual assault nurse examiner until you feel that you do. This is not a bother to anyone and can save you from potential errors and confusion.

6. *Explain the legal process to your victim and keep them involved.* Stay in regular contact with your victim. They are important and need to hear that. Let them know what they are in for, how long the process will take, how often they may have to tell their story. Eliminate, to the degree possible, the element of surprise. Be the first person to tell her what's going to happen and maintain their trust through professionalism, integrity, and reliability. The security that comes from reliability is the big one here, because this is one of the things that has been damaged or taken by the attack—the sense of security.

7. *Know your case.* Be able to discuss your case from all angles by the time you are ready for trial. Having that organized binder of files is going to help. Nothing substitutes for the hard files. If you have followed the guidelines outlined in this text, then you are better prepared than most.

If sex-crime investigators follow even some of the guidelines provided in this text, all of which are born out of years of trial and error by the authors and their colleagues, then they will have a better chance of increasing their clearance rates, of increasing their rate of prosecutable cases, and of protecting the community that they serve. They will know their cases to well and can hold their heads high when it comes time to refer a case to the prosecutor's office. They can also look victims in the eye, without shame, and assure them that everything that can be done has been done.

As discussed at the beginning of this work, sex crimes investigation is not something that just anyone can do. It requires a commitment to thoroughness and to justly establishing the facts no matter what the climate. In this way, victims and rapists will receive justice, and communities will be safer for everyone. It is the hope of the authors of this work that the information we have provided will help sex-crimes investigators to serve these ends.

REFERENCES

Baker, K. (1997) Once a rapist? Motivational evidence and relevancy in rape law. *Harvard Law Review*, January.

Bowyer, L., and Dalton, M. E. (1997) Female victims of rape and their genital injuries. *British Journal of Obstetrics and Gynaecology* 104(5), pp. 617–620.

California v. Abdiel Ariza (2002) No. B154362. (Super.Ct.No. NA041838) Oct. 23, 2002 (2002 WL 31379941 (Cal.App. 2 Dist.)).

California v. Mark Allan Parr (2003) No. G028623 (Super.Ct.No. 98NF1795) March 27, 2003.

Gray-Eurom, K., Seaberg, D. C., and Wears, R. L. (2002) The prosecution of sexual assault cases: correlation with forensic evidence. *Annals of Emergency Medicine* 39(1), pp. 39–46.

Green, F. Eyewitness ID fallibility shown. *Richmond Times-Dispatch*, March 16, 2003.

Grossin, C., Sibille, I., Lorin, de la Grandmaison, G., Banasr, A., Brion, F., and Durigon, M. (2003) Analysis of 418 cases of sexual assault. *Forensic Science International* 131(2–3), pp. 125–130.

Sawyer-Sommers, M., Schafer, J., Zink, T., Hutson, L., and Hillard, P. (2001) Injury patterns in women resulting from sexual assault. *Trauma, Violence, and Abuse* 2(3), pp. 240–258.

Slaughter, L., Brown, C.R., Crowley, S., and Peck, R. (1997) Patterns of genital injury in female sexual assault victims. *American Journal of Obstetrics and Gynecology* 176(3), pp. 609–616.

TWGEYEE (1999) Eyewitness evidence: A guide for law enforcement. U.S. Department of Justice, National Institute of Justice, NCJ 178240, October.

Wells, G. L., Small, M., Penrod, S. J., Malpass, R. S., Fulero, S. M., and Brimacombe, C. A. E. (1998) Eyewitness identification procedures: Recommendations for lineups and photospreads. *Law and Human Behavior*, Vol. 22, pp. 603–647.

Wood, M. (2001) City attorney shares reality of prosecuting sexual assault cases. University of Virginia School of Law, *News and Events*, March.

State of California
Governor's Office of Criminal Justice Planning

FORENSIC MEDICAL REPORT:
ACUTE (<72 HOURS)
ADULT/ADOLESCENT SEXUAL ASSAULT
EXAMINATION

OCJP 923 INSTRUCTIONS

For more information or assistance in completing the OCJP 923 please contact
University of California, Davis California Medical Training Center at:
(916) 734-4141

This form is available on the following Web site:
www.ocjp.ca.gov

OCJP 923
Forensic Medical Report: Acute (<72 hours)
Adult/Adolescent Sexual Assault Examination

REQUIRED USE OF STANDARD STATE FORM:

Penal Code Section 13823.5(c) requires that every health care practitioner, who conducts a medical examination of a sexual assault or a child sexual abuse victim for evidence of sexual assault or sexual abuse, must use a standard form to record findings. This form is intended to document forensic findings and, as such, is not a complete medical treatment record.

SUGGESTED USE OF THE STANDARD STATE FORMS: FOLLOW LOCAL POLICY.

OCJP 923	• History of **acute sexual assault** (<72 hours) • Examination of adults (age 18 and over) and adolescents (ages 12-17)
OCJP 925	• History of **nonacute sexual abuse** (>72 hours) • Examination of children and adolescents under age 18
OCJP 930	• History of **acute sexual abuse or assault** (<72 hours) • Examination of children under age 12
OCJP 930	• History of **chronic sexual abuse (incest) and recent incident** (<72 hours) • Examination of children and adolescents under age 18
OCJP 950	• Examination of person(s) suspected of sexual assault or sexual abuse

Key terms for Sexual Assault or Sexual Abuse Exams	
Acute	Less than 72 hours have passed since the incident (<72 hours)
Nonacute	More than 72 hours have passed since the incident (>72 hours)

These terms are used to describe timeframes, not rigid standards. This is not to suggest that after 72 hours a complete exam should not be done. It is not unusual to detect injuries or possible trace and biological evidence after 72 hours.

INSTRUCTIONS FOR OCJP 923

These instructions contain the recommended methods for meeting the minimum legal standards established by Penal Code Section 13823.11 for performing evidential examinations.

LIABILITY AND RELEASE OF INFORMATION:

This medical report is subject to the confidentiality requirements of the Medical Information Act (Civil Code Sec. 56 et seq.), the Physician-Patient Privilege (Ev. Code Sec. 990), and the Official Information Privilege (Ev. Code Sec.1040). It can only be released to those involved in the investigation and prosecution of the case: a law enforcement officer, district attorney, city attorney, crime laboratory, county licensing agency, and coroner. Records may be released to the defense counsel only through discovery of documents in the possession of a prosecuting agency <u>or</u> after the appropriate court process (i.e., judicial review and a court order).

Complete this report in its entirety. Use N/A (not applicable) when appropriate to show that the examiner attended to the question.	Patient identification: This space is provided for hospitals and clinics using plastic plates for stamping identification information.

A. **GENERAL INFORMATION: Print or type the name of the facility where the examination was conducted.**
1. **Enter the patient's name and identification number (if applicable).**
2. **Enter the patient's address and telephone number <u>only if required by requesting agency</u>.**
   • This information is confidential. Every effort must be made to protect the privacy and safety of the patient.
3. **Enter the patient's age, date of birth (DOB), gender, and ethnicity; date/time of arrival; and date/time of discharge.**

B. **REPORTING AND AUTHORIZATION: Indicate jurisdiction where the incident(s) occurred.**
1. **If a telephone report was made to a law enforcement agency, enter the name, agency, identification and telephone number of the officer who took the report, the name of person making the report, and the date and time.**
2. **If the patient was accompanied by a law enforcement officer or a patrol officer responded to your facility, enter the officer's name, agency, identification number, and the telephone number of the agency.**
3. **Obtain the signature and identification number of the law enforcement officer to authorize payment for the evidential examination at public expense, the name of the agency, telephone number, date, time, and case number. If telephone authorization was obtained, enter the name of the authorizing party, identification number, and the date and time in the Telephone Authorization box.**
4. **Medical facilities with contracts and memorandums of understanding may not require separate patient authorization.**

C. **PATIENT INFORMATION**
   • Ask the patient (or the patient's parent or guardian, if appropriate) to read the items and initial.
   • **For patients requesting examination and treatment only:** Penal Code Sections 11160-11161 require health care practitioners and health care facilities to notify a law enforcement agency by telephone and in writing if treatment is sought for injuries inflicted in violation of any state penal law. If the patient consents to treatment only, complete Part A to record the patient's name and address, Part H to record the type and extent of injuries, and mail this form to the local law enforcement agency.

D. **PATIENT CONSENT**
   • Ask the patient (or the patient's parent or guardian, if appropriate) to read the items, initial, and sign on the line below.
   • Family Code Section 6927 permits minors (12-17 years of age) to consent to medical examination, treatment, and evidence collection related to a sexual assault without parental consent. Family Code Section 6928 requires health care professionals to attempt to contact the minor's parent or legal guardian and to note in the minor's treatment record the date and time the attempted contact was made, including whether the attempt was successful or unsuccessful. This provision **is not applicable** when the health professional reasonably believes the parent(s) or guardian committed the sexual assault on the minor.

E. PATIENT HISTORY

Allow the patient or other person providing the history to describe the incident(s) to the extent possible. Determine and use terms familiar to the patient. Follow-up questions may be necessary to ensure that all items are covered. This information is necessary to guide the medical/legal examination and for interpretation of crime laboratory results. A careful patient history must be taken as some patients may be reluctant to describe all the acts committed, particularly anal penetration.

1. **Record the name of the person providing the patient history, the relationship to the patient, date and time.**
2. **Obtain pertinent medical history.**
    - Record the date of the last menstrual period. This information is used to determine whether the patient was menstruating at the time of the examination and to evaluate the possibility of pregnancy and postcoital options.
    - Obtain recent (past 60 days) information on any anal-genital injuries, surgeries, diagnostic procedures, or medical treatment that may affect the interpretation of current physical findings. This information is requested to avoid confusing preexisting lesions with injuries or findings related to the alleged assault.
    - Describe any other pertinent medical conditions that may affect the interpretation of current physical findings.
    - Describe any pre-existing physical injuries.
3. **Obtain pertinent pre- and post-assault related history.**
    - Ask whether the patient has had other anal or vaginal intercourse within the past 5 days.
    - Ask whether the patient has had other oral copulation within the past 24 hours.
    - If yes, ask when. If yes, ask whether ejaculation occurred, and where. If yes, ask if a condom was used.

    > This information is required by the crime laboratory to properly interpret the findings.
    > **Do not record any other information regarding sexual history on this form.**

    - Record whether there was any voluntary drug/alcohol use prior to the alleged assault and any drug/alcohol use since the assault. If yes, describe.
    - This information is relevant for accurate interpretation of blood alcohol and toxicology results and for issues pertaining to consent and non-consent.
    - If the answers to the drug/alcohol questions are yes, collection of toxicology samples is recommended according to local policy.
4. **Record post-assault hygiene activity if the incident occurred within 72 hours of the examination.**
    - This information is relevant because it can affect the interpretation of findings.
    - If the patient has bathed, showered, or douched, the examiner should still collect samples from the appropriate body areas to attempt to preserve any biological or trace evidence.
    - Ask the patient if tissue, wipes, or clothing were used to cleanse the mouth, genitals, and/or body. If yes, collect these items, if available. Air dry, package, label, and seal. If not available, notify law enforcement so these items can be collected.
5. **Obtain assault-related history.**
    - If any of the boxes are marked "yes", use the space provided to describe.
    - The loss of memory and lapse of consciousness questions help assess whether drugs may have been used to subdue the patient. If yes, collection of toxicology samples is recommended according to local policy.
    - The pain and bleeding questions direct the health care professional to look for injury and evidence not readily visible.

F. ASSAULT HISTORY

1. **Enter date and time of the assault(s)**
    If the assault took place over an extended period, the most important time sensitive information is when injuries occurred and whether ejaculation took place.
2. **Describe the pertinent physical surroundings that may have come in contact with the patient.**
    - During the physical examination, look for pattern injuries associated with the physical surroundings and/or for trace evidence (e.g., grass, sand) transferred from the scene to the patient.
3. **Record the identify of the alleged assailant(s) by name or nickname, approximate age, gender, ethnicity, relationship to the patient, and whether the assailant(s) are known or unknown to the patient.**
    - Use a numbering system to identify multiple assailants by name, if known, or a brief description such as the "big guy". This numbering system can be used to relate the assailant to the acts described on the next page.
4. **Describe the methods employed by the assailant(s)**
    - Complete this section by checking "yes" or "no" in the appropriate boxes.
    - Describe what happened using the patient's own words, and place quotation marks around the patient's comments.
    - The drug/alcohol questions help assess whether samples should be collected for toxicology analysis. The presence of alcohol and/or drugs in the blood or urine may have clinical and legal implications. The assailant may have used drugs to subdue the patient; or, the patient may have lost the ability to make rational decisions or may have lost consciousness.
    - If the patient reports ingestion of drugs, describes symptoms, or shows signs of drug ingestion (e.g., lapse of consciousness, memory loss, abnormal vital signs, confusion, etc.), collection of toxicology samples is recommended according to local policy. Vomiting can also be a possible indicator.
    - Some drugs may be detected in urine up to 96 hours after ingestion. Alcohol is not usually detected past 24 hours post ingestion.
      - For blood alcohol analysis, collect 5cc of blood in a gray stoppered evacuated blood collection vial.
      - For ingestion of drugs, collect 100cc of urine in a clean container. It is important to collect the first available sample.
5. **Ask whether injuries were inflicted by the patient upon the assailant(s) during the assault**
    Complete this section by checking "yes" or "no" in the appropriate boxes. If the box is marked "yes", use the space provided to describe the injuries, possible locations on the body, and how they were inflicted. Identify the assailant(s) by number.

G. ACTS DESCRIBED BY PATIENT

Identify all acts. Each act may lead to evidence of a chargeable crime and evidence related to the acts must be sent to the crime laboratory. Any penetration, however slight, of the labia or rectum by the penis or any penetration of a genital or anal opening by an object or body part constitutes an act. Oral copulation requires only contact. **Identify and distinguish acts performed by multiple assailants using the numbering system started on page 2.**

1. **Penetration of vagina**

   Mark the appropriate box for each method of penetration of the vagina. Mark "attempted" if it is reasonably clear, based upon the patient's statement, that the assailant(s) intended an act but was thwarted by the patient, an intervening occurrence, or was unable to accomplish the act. If either "attempted" or "unsure" is checked, provide a description in the adjacent space. If more than one assailant was involved, identify each one by number on the lines adjacent to the boxes. If an object was used, describe it.

2. **Penetration of anus**

   Mark the appropriate box for each method of penetration of the anus/rectum. Mark "attempted" if it is reasonably clear, based upon the patient's statement, that the assailant(s) intended an act but was thwarted by the patient, an intervening occurrence, or was unable to accomplish the act. If either "attempted" or "unsure" is checked, provide a description in the adjacent space. If more than one assailant was involved, identify each one by number on the lines adjacent to the boxes. If an object was used, describe it.

3. **Oral copulation of genitals**

   Mark the appropriate box. Mark "attempted" if it is reasonably clear, based upon the patient's statement, that the assailant(s) intended an act but was thwarted by the patient, an intervening occurrence, or was unable to accomplish the act. If either "attempted" or "unsure" is checked, provide a description in the adjacent space. If more than one assailant was involved, identify each one by number on the lines adjacent to the boxes.

4. **Oral copulation of anus**

   Mark the appropriate box. Mark "attempted" if it is reasonably clear, based upon the patient's statement, that the assailant(s) intended an act but was thwarted by the patient, an intervening occurrence, or was unable to accomplish the act. If either "attempted" or "unsure" is checked, provide a description in the adjacent space. If more than one assailant was involved, identify each one by number on the lines adjacent to the boxes.

5. **Non-genital act(s)**

   Mark the appropriate box. If yes, describe the act and note where it occurred on the adjacent line. Mark "attempted" if it is reasonably clear, based upon the patient's statement, that the assailant(s) intended an act but was thwarted by the patient, an intervening occurrence, or was unable to accomplish the act. If either "attempted" or "unsure" is checked, provide a description in the adjacent space. If more than one assailant was involved, identify each one by number on the lines adjacent to the boxes.
   - **Note: Identify bites and alert law enforcement about their existence.** Bites can provide very specific evidence and they fade very quickly. Bites should be swabbed for saliva, measured, and photographed. Contact a forensic odontologist or law enforcement to evaluate the need for impressions.
   - **Note:** The term suction injury means "hickey".

6. **Record any other act(s).**

7. **Did ejaculation occur?**

   Mark the appropriate box. For body surfaces, note location(s) on the diagrams. For clothing, bedding, or other surface(s), describe in the space provided. If more than one assailant ejaculated, identify each one by number on the lines adjacent to the boxes. If "unsure" is checked, provide a description in the adjacent space.

8. **Contraceptive or lubricant products**

   Note whether a contraceptive or a lubricant product was used. If yes, record the type or brand used, if known.

H. GENERAL PHYSICAL EXAMINATION: COLLECT AND PRESERVE EVIDENCE. RECORD FINDINGS.

1. **Record vital signs.**
2. **Record the date and time the examination was started and completed.**
3. **Describe the patient's general physical appearance.**
4. **Describe the patient's general demeanor.**
   - Describe behaviors such as crying, wringing of hands, willingness or ability to cooperate, responsiveness, ability to give history, etc. The issue of non-cooperativeness can cause exam delays and impair the examiner's ability to collect evidence. Avoid the use of vague, subjective, or judgmental descriptors such as "hysterical", "strange", "spacey", etc.
   - Documenting helps the examiner recall the patient's behavior and response during the examination for future reference.
5. **Describe the condition of clothing upon arrival (rips, tears, presence of foreign materials).**
6. **Collect outer and under clothing worn during or immediately after the incident.**
   - Coordinate with the law enforcement officer regarding clothing to be collected.
   - Wear gloves while collecting clothing.
   - Have patient disrobe on two sheets of paper placed one on top of the other on the floor. Have patient remove shoes before stepping on the paper. Shoes may be collected, if indicated, and packaged separately.
   - Package each garment in an individual paper bag, label, and seal.
   - Carefully fold the top sheet of paper into a bindle, label, and seal. Discard the bottom sheet. Place this large bindle and all individually bagged garments into a large paper bag(s) with a chain of custody form, label, and seal.
   - Wet stains or other wet evidence require special handling. Consult local policy.
   - Give special focus to items that are close to the genital structures or otherwise have the highest potential to contain seminal fluid according to the assault history. According to local policy, these items may be placed in the evidence kit.
7. **Conduct a general physical examination and record all findings.**

> **Physical Findings:** A physical finding includes observable or palpable tissue injuries, physiologic changes, or foreign material (e.g. grass, sand, stains, dried or moist secretions, or positive fluorescence). If none of the above are present, mark "No Findings".

   - Be observant for erythema (redness), abrasions, bruises, swelling, lacerations, fractures, bites, and burns.
   - Note areas of tenderness or induration.

DOCUMENTATION OF INJURIES AND FINDINGS USING DIAGRAMS AND LEGEND
   - Record size and appearance of injuries and other findings using the diagrams, the legend, and a consecutive numbering system.
   - Bruises: describe shape, size, and color.
   - Use the legend to list and describe the injury/finding drawn on the diagram. Show the diagram letter followed by the finding number. Use the abbreviations in the legend to describe the type of finding. Example: A 1, EC 2x3cm red/purple indicates that the first finding on Diagram A is an ecchymosis (bruise) that is red/purple in color and 2x3 centimeters in size. See example below.

Locator #	Type	Description
A-1	EC	2x3 cm red/purple
A-2	DS	Dried secretion
A-3	CS	Control swab

   - **Photograph injuries and other findings according to local policy.**
   - **Use proper forensic photographic techniques.**
     - Use an appropriate light source and a scale near the finding.
     - Note: The plane of the film must be parallel to the plane of the finding.
8. **Collect dried and moist secretions, stains (including semen, bloodstains, saliva from bites, suction injury [hickey], licking, and kissing), and foreign materials from the body.**
   - **Scan** the entire body with a Wood's Lamp (long wavelength ultraviolet light) or other alternate light source. Note fluorescent area(s) on the diagrams and record in legend as WL⊕.
   - **Swab moist secretions** with a dry swab to avoid dilution. Label and air dry before packaging.
   - **Swab dried stains and/or Wood's Lamp positive area(s)** with a swab (or multiple swabs for large stains) moistened with sterile, deionized, or distilled water. Label and air dry the evidence swab(s) before packaging. Make a control swab by swabbing an unstained area <u>adjacent</u> to the stain (when possible). Label, air dry, and package the control swab separately from the evidence sample.
   - **Collect** foreign materials such as fibers, sand, hair, grass, soil, and vegetation. Place in bindles and/or envelopes as appropriate for each location on the body. Label and seal.
   - **Record** all findings on the diagrams and the legend as shown above.
     - Use the legend locator number to label evidence collection envelopes.
     - Record the locations of swab collection sites and control swabs.
9. **Collect fingernail scrapings or cuttings according to local policy.**
   - Use clean toothpicks or manicure sticks to collect scrapings from under the fingernails. Place scrapings from **each** hand into separate containers or bindles, then place into envelopes. Label (indicating right or left hand) and seal; **OR,**
   - Use a clean fingernail cutter or scissors to cut the fingernails, and place the cuttings from **each** hand into separate containers or bindles. Package and label as above.

I. HEAD, NECK, AND ORAL EXAMINATION
1. **Examine the face, head, hair, scalp, and neck for injury and foreign materials.**
    - Give special focus to the lips, perioral region, and nares in the examination.
    - Record injuries and other findings using the diagrams and legend.
    - Photograph injuries and other findings according to local policy. A colposcope may be used.
2. **Collect dried and moist secretions, stains and foreign materials from the face, head, hair, scalp, and neck.**
    - **Swab moist secretions** with a dry swab to avoid dilution. Label and air dry before packaging.
    - **Swab dried stains and/or Wood's Lamp positive area(s)** with a swab (or multiple swabs for large stains) moistened with sterile, deionized, or distilled water. Label and air dry the evidence swab(s) before packaging. Make a control swab by swabbing an unstained area <u>adjacent</u> to the stain (when possible). Label, air dry, and package the control swab separately from the evidence sample.
    - **Collect** foreign materials such as fibers, sand, hair, grass, soil, and vegetation. Place in bindles and/or envelopes as appropriate for each location on the body. Label and seal.
    - **Cut** matted head or facial hairs (for males) bearing crusted material and place in a bindle. Package, label, and seal.
    - **Record** all findings on the diagrams and legend.
    - Use the legend locator number to label evidence collection envelopes.
    - Record the locations of swab collection sites and control swabs.
3. **Examine the oral cavity for injury and foreign materials (if indicated by the assault history).**
    - Give special focus to frenulums, buccal surfaces, gums, and soft palate.
    - Record injuries, foreign materials, and other findings using the diagrams and legend.
    - Photograph injuries and other findings according to local policy. A colposcope may be used.
    - Collect foreign materials found in the oral cavity, e.g. hair. Package, label, and seal.
4. **Collect 2 swabs from the oral cavity for seminal fluid up to 12 hours post assault and prepare one dry mount slide from one of the swabs.**
    - Swab the gum to the tonsillar fossae, the upper first and second molars, behind the incisors, and the fold of the cheek (buccal space).
    - Label and air dry swabs and slide. Code the swab to enable the crime laboratory to determine which swab was used to make the slide. Package, label, and seal.
5. **Collect head hair reference samples according to local policy.**
    - According to local policy, pull (or have patient pull) 20-30 hairs representative of variations of length and color from different areas of the head; **OR**, cut the hairs, <u>close to the skin.</u> Package, label, and seal.

J. GENITAL EXAMINATION - FEMALES

> **Advisory:** Record observations, take colposcopic photographs, and collect swabs before using the visualization enhancement Toluidine Blue Dye.

1. **Examine the inner thighs, external genitalia, and the perineal area for injury, foreign materials, and other findings. Check the appropriate boxes if there are assault related findings.**
   - Use a colposcope, if available, or employ other means of magnification.
   - Record size and appearance of injuries, foreign materials, and other findings using the diagrams, the legend, and a consecutive numbering system. Note swelling and areas of tenderness and induration.
   - Use the legend to help identify and describe the findings drawn on the diagrams. Example: D-5 LA 1.5 centimeter means Diagram D finding #5 is a laceration 1.5 centimeters long.
   - Photograph injuries and other findings according to local policy.
2. **Collect dried and moist secretions, stains and foreign materials.**
   - **Scan** the area with a Wood's Lamp (long wavelength ultraviolet light) or other alternate light source. Note fluorescent area(s) on the diagrams and record in legend as WL⊕.
   - **Swab moist secretions** with a dry swab to avoid dilution. Label and air dry before packaging.
   - **Swab dried stains and/or Wood's Lamp positive areas** with a swab (or multiple swabs for large stains) moistened with sterile, deionized, or distilled water. Label and air dry the evidence swab(s) before packaging. Make a control swab by swabbing an unstained area <u>adjacent</u> to the stain (when possible). Label, air dry, and package the control swab separately from the evidence sample.
   - **Collect** foreign materials such as fibers, sand, hair, grass, soil, and vegetation. Place in bindles and/or envelopes as appropriate for each location on the body. Label and seal.
   - **Cut** matted pubic hairs bearing crusted material and place in a bindle. Package, label, and seal.
   - **Record** all findings on the diagrams and legend.
   - Use the legend locator number to label evidence collection envelopes.
   - Record the locations of swab collection sites and control swabs.
3. **Collect pubic hair combing or brushing.**
   - Place a paper sheet under the patient's buttocks. Comb the pubic hair downward to remove any loose hairs or foreign materials. Collect and fold the paper with the comb or brush inside. Package, label, and seal.
4. **Collect pubic hair reference samples according to local policy**.
   - According to local policy, pull (or have patient pull) 20-30 hairs representative of variations in length and color from different areas of the pubic region; **OR**, cut the hairs <u>close to the skin</u>. Package, label, and seal.

VAGINAL AND CERVICAL EXAMINATION

> Vaginal samples: Be certain that the question regarding other intercourse (page 2) has been answered so that the analytical results can be interpreted.

5. **Examine the vagina and cervix for injury, foreign materials, foreign bodies (tampon, condom, etc.) and other findings. Check the appropriate boxes if there are assault related findings. Record findings using the legend and diagrams.**
   - Collect foreign materials and foreign bodies. Allow foreign bodies to dry for at least one hour. If any item is still wet, package and handle as "wet evidence". Consult local policy.
   - Use a non-lubricated warm speculum moistened with water.
   - Use a colposcope, if available, or employ other means of magnification.
6. **Collect 4 swabs from the vaginal pool**.
   - Hold the swabs together as a unit and insert them into the vaginal pool at the same time. Rotate the swabs as a unit in the vaginal vault to ensure uniform sampling. Allow adequate time for saturation of the swabs. Separate the swabs before drying.
   - Prepare a wet mount slide from one swab using normal saline or a buffered nutrient medium. Examine immediately for motile or non-motile sperm. A phase contrast or other optically staining microscope facilitates this exam. Label the swab and slide as "wet mount". Air dry the slide with cover slip in place. Package, label, and seal.
   - Prepare one dry mount slide from one of the other swabs. Package, label, and seal.
   - Code the swab(s) used to make the wet mount and dry mount slides to enable the crime laboratory to determine which swab was used to make each slide. Air dry all swabs and slides. Package, label, and seal.
   Note: Aspirates or washings may be collected for the detection of spermatozoa. Consult local policy.
7. **If 48 hours or more post assault, also collect two cervical swabs.**
   - Label the swabs so it is clear that these are cervical, not vaginal swabs. Air dry, package, label, and seal.

ANAL AND RECTAL EXAMINATION (Conduct exam if indicated by assault history.)

8. **Examine the buttocks, perianal skin, and the anal folds for injury, foreign materials, and other findings. Check the appropriate boxes if there are assault related findings. Record findings using the legend and diagrams.**
   - Use a colposcope, if available, or employ other means of magnification.
   - Photograph injuries and other findings according to local policy.
9. **Collect dried and moist secretions, stains, and foreign materials. Foreign materials may include lubricants.**
   Collect samples and record findings using the techniques described under #2 above.
10. **Collect 2 anal and/or rectal swabs and prepare one dry mount slide**.
    - To avoid contaminating anal/rectal swabs with vaginal drainage, clean the perianal area thoroughly. This should only be done after the vaginal samples, external secretions, and foreign materials have been collected.
    - An anal speculum or anoscope moistened with warm water may be used for this exam. Obtain the samples under direct visualization from above the tip of the instrument.
    - Label and air dry the swabs and slide. Code the swab to enable the crime laboratory to determine which swab was used to make the slide. Package, label, and seal.
11. **Conduct an anoscopic exam if rectal injury is suspected or if there is any sign of rectal bleeding.**
    - Check the box if there is rectal bleeding and describe findings.
12. **Record exam position used to ensure proper orientation and location of findings on the photographs.**

K. GENITAL EXAMINATION - MALES

Advisory: Record observations, take colposcopic photographs, and collect swabs before using the visualization enhancement Toluidine Blue Dye.

1. **Examine the inner thighs, external genitalia, and perineal area for injury, foreign materials, and other findings. Check the appropriate box(es) if there are assault related findings.**
    - Use a colposcope, if available, or employ other means of magnification.
    - Record size and appearance of injuries, foreign materials, and other findings using the diagrams, the legend, and a consecutive numbering system. Note swelling and areas of tenderness and induration.
    - Use the legend to help identify and describe the findings drawn on the diagrams. Example: H-7 LA 1.5 centimeters means Diagram H finding #7 is a laceration 1.5 centimeters long.
    - Photograph injuries and other findings according to local policy.
2. **Record whether circumcised or not.**
3. **Collect dried and moist secretions, stains, and foreign materials.**
    - **Scan** the area with a Wood's Lamp (long wavelength ultraviolet light) or other alternate light source. Note fluorescent area(s) on the diagrams and record in legend as WL⊕.
    - **Swab moist secretions** with a dry swab to avoid dilution. Label and air dry before packaging.
    - **Swab dried stains and Wood's Lamp positive areas** with a swab (or multiple swabs for large stains) moistened with sterile, deionized, or distilled water. Label and air dry the evidence swab(s) before packaging. Make a control swab by swabbing an unstained area <u>adjacent</u> to the stain (when possible). Label, air dry, and package separately from the evidence sample.
    - **Collect** foreign materials such as fibers, sand, hair, grass, soil, and vegetation. Place in bindles and/or envelopes as appropriate for each location on the body. Label and seal.
    - **Cut** matted pubic hairs bearing crusted material and place in a bindle. Package, label, and seal.
    - **Record** all findings on the diagrams and legend.
    - Use the legend locator number to label evidence collection envelopes.
    - Record the locations of swab collection sites and control swabs.
4. **Collect pubic hair combing or brushing.**
    - Place a paper sheet under the patient's buttocks. Comb the pubic hair downward to remove any loose hairs or foreign materials. Collect and fold the paper under the buttocks with the comb or brush inside. Package, label, and seal.
5. **Collect pubic hair reference samples according to local policy.**
    - According to local policy, pull (or have patient pull) 20-30 hairs representative of variations in length and color from different areas of the pubic region; **OR**, cut the hairs <u>close to the skin</u>. Package, label and seal.
6. **Collect 2 penile swabs, if indicated by the assault history, e.g., if the suspect orally copulated the male victim.**
    - Hold the swabs together as a unit and swab the glans, shaft, and base of the penis with a rotating motion to ensure uniform sampling. Avoid swabbing the urethral meatus. Use swabs moistened with sterile, deionized, or distilled water for these swabbings. Air dry, package, label, and seal.
7. **Collect 2 scrotal swabs, if indicated by the assault history, e.g. if the suspect orally copulated the victim.**
    - Hold the swabs together as a unit and swab the scrotum in a rotating motion, focusing on the area that is in closest proximity to the penis. Use swabs moistened with sterile, deionized, or distilled water. Air dry, package, label, and seal.

ANAL AND RECTAL EXAMINATION   (Conduct exam if indicated by assault history.)

8. **Examine the buttocks, perianal skin, and the anal folds for injury, foreign materials, and other findings. Check the appropriate boxes if there are assault related findings. Record findings using the legend and diagrams.**
    - Use a colposcope, if available, or employ other means of magnification.
    - Photograph injuries and other findings according to local policy.
9. **Collect dried and moist secretions, stains, and foreign materials. Foreign materials may include lubricants.**
    Collect samples and record findings using the techniques described under **#3** above.
10. **Collect 2 anal and/or rectal swabs and prepare one dry mount slide.**
    - To avoid contaminating anal/rectal swabs, clean the perianal area thoroughly. This should be done after the external secretions and foreign materials have been collected.
    - An anal speculum or anoscope moistened with warm water may be used for this exam. Obtain the samples under direct visualization from above the tip of the instrument.
    - Label and air dry the swabs and slide. Code the swab to enable the crime laboratory to determine which swab was used to make the slide. Package, label, and seal.
11. **Conduct an anoscopic exam if rectal injury is suspected or if there is any sign of rectal bleeding.**
    - Check the box if there is rectal bleeding and describe findings.
12. **Record exam position used to ensure proper orientation and location of findings on the photographs.**

All swabs and slides must be air dried prior to packaging (Penal Code Section 13823.11). Air dry in a stream of cool air for 60 minutes. Only place samples from one patient at a time in the swab drying box. Wipe or spray the swab drying box with 10% bleach before each use.

Labeling requirements: Swabs, slides, bindles, and small containers must be individually labeled with the patient's name and sample source. Code swabs and slides to show which slides were prepared from which swabs. Containers for these individual items must be labeled with the name of the patient, date of collection, description of the evidence including location from which it was taken, and signature or initials of the person who collected the evidence. Include the legend locator number, if the legend was used to document the location from which the evidence was collected. Package containers in a Sexual Assault Evidence Collection Kit and record the chain of custody.

L. RECORD ALL EVIDENCE COLLECTED AND SUBMITTED TO THE CRIME LABORATORY
1. **Record all items of clothing collected.**
2. **Record all foreign materials collected and the name of the person who collected them.**
   - **Note:** An intravaginal foreign body may include a tampon, diaphragm, condom, etc.
   - Consult the local crime laboratory for packaging recommendations for foreign bodies.
3. **Record information about the oral/genital/anal/rectal samples.**
   - Record the number of swabs and slides collected, the time collected, and the person who took the samples.
4. **Record information about the vaginal wet mount slide.**
   - Record whether the wet mount slide was prepared and whether or not motile or non-motile sperm were observed.
   - Record the time the slide was prepared, observed, the person who prepared it, and the person who examined it.

M. TOXICOLOGY SAMPLES
- Collect samples for blood alcohol/toxicology at the discretion of the examiner and/or law enforcement officer in accordance with local policy.
- Cleanse the arm with a non-alcoholic solution and collect 5cc of blood in a gray stoppered evacuated vial. Label vial and envelope and seal.
- Up to 96 hours after suspected ingestion of drugs, collect a urine specimen (100cc) in a clean container. It is important to collect the first available sample.

N. REFERENCE SAMPLES: Policies pertaining to whether reference samples are collected at the time of the exam or later vary by jurisdiction. If collected at the time of the exam, ALWAYS collect after the evidence samples. For those jurisdictions not performing conventional serology, a buccal swab can be taken in place of the blood reference sample. Consult your local crime laboratory.

Blood:
- Collect blood sample in lavender and/or yellow stoppered evacuated vials as specified by local policy.
- A blood card is optional in some jurisdictions.
- Label vial(s) and envelope(s) and seal.

Buccal (inner cheek) swabs:
- Collect as a DNA reference sample.
- Rub two swabs gently but firmly along the inside of the cheek in a rotating motion to ensure even sampling.
- Air dry, package, label, and seal.

Saliva:
- **Note:** If a saliva reference sample is required by the local crime laboratory, collect it whether or not an oral assault occurred.
- Collect sample by placing two swabs in the mouth and allowing them to saturate.
- Air dry, package, label, and seal.

Head hair:
- According to local policy, pull (or have patient pull) 20-30 hairs representative of variations in length and color from different areas of the scalp; **OR**, cut the hairs close to the skin.
- Package, label, and seal.

Pubic hair:
- According to local policy, pull (or have patient pull) 20-30 hairs representative of variations in length and color from different areas of the pubic region; **OR**, cut the hairs close to the skin.
- Package, label, and seal.

O. RECORD PHOTO DOCUMENTATION METHODS
- Document photographic methods used and areas which were photographed. Documentation must clearly link the patient's identity to the specific photographs of injuries and/or findings. For example, include a picture of the patient identification on the roll or use a databack camera which can be programmed with the patient's identification number.

P. RECORD EXAM METHODS USED.

Q. RECORD EXAM FINDINGS.

R. RECORD ASSESSMENT OF FINDINGS.

S. SUMMARIZE FINDINGS.

T. PRINT NAMES OF PERSONNEL INVOLVED. OBTAIN SIGNATURE AND LICENSE NUMBER OF EXAMINER.

U. EVIDENCE DISTRIBUTION: List to whom the evidence was given.

V. OBTAIN SIGNATURE OF OFFICER RECEIVING EVIDENCE.

State of California
Governor's Office of Criminal Justice Planning

FORENSIC MEDICAL REPORT: SEXUAL ASSAULT SUSPECT EXAMINATION

OCJP 950 INSTRUCTIONS

For more information or assistance in completing the OCJP 950 please contact
University of California, Davis California Medical Training Center at:
(916) 734-4141

This form is available on the following Web site:
www.ocjp.ca.gov

OCJP 950
Forensic Medical Report: Sexual Assault Suspect Examination

INSTRUCTIONS FOR OCJP 950

These instructions contain the recommended methods for performing sexual assault suspect evidential examinations. This form is recommended for examination documentation, however, it is not required by state law. Follow local policy.

Liability and Release of Information:

This medical report is subject to the confidentiality requirements of the Medical Information Act (Civil Code Sec. 56 et seq.), the Physician-Patient Privilege (Ev. Code Sec. 990), and the Official Information Privilege (Ev. Code Sec.1040). It can only be released to those involved in the investigation and prosecution of the case: a law enforcement officer, district attorney, city attorney, crime laboratory, county licensing agency, and coroner. Records may be released to the defense counsel only through discovery of documents in the possession of a prosecuting agency or after the appropriate court process (i.e., judicial review and a court order).

Complete this report in its entirety. Use N/A (not applicable) when appropriate to show that the examiner attended to the question.	Patient identification: This space is provided for hospitals and clinics using plastic plates for stamping identification information.

GENERAL GUIDELINES FOR CONDUCTING SEXUAL ASSAULT SUSPECT EXAMINATIONS

- Examinations of suspects will yield more useful information if conducted within hours of the alleged assault.
- In most circumstances, a general guideline for conducting suspect exams is within 72 hours of the assault. Injuries such as lacerations, bruises, and bites, however, can be observed after a longer period of time.
- The longevity of most evidence is dependent upon activities of the suspect after the assault such as bathing, changing clothes, etc.
- For these reasons, 72 hours should not be viewed as a rigid cut-off. Professional judgment should be used.

A. GENERAL INFORMATION: Print or type the name of the facility where the examination was conducted.
1. Enter the patient's name and identification number (if applicable).
2. Enter the patient's address and telephone number.
3. Enter the patient's age, date of birth (DOB), gender, and ethnicity; date/time of arrival; and date/time of discharge.

B. AUTHORIZATION: Indicate jurisdiction where the incident(s) occurred.
1. Enter the law enforcement officer's name, agency, identification number, and the telephone number of the agency.
2. Obtain the signature of the law enforcement officer to authorize payment for the evidential examination at public expense, date, time, and case number.

C. MEDICAL HISTORY
1. Obtain recent (past 60 days) information on any anal-genital injuries, surgeries, diagnostic procedures, or medical treatment that may affect the interpretation of current physical findings. This information is requested to avoid confusing pre-existing lesions with injuries or findings related to the alleged assault.
2. Describe any other pertinent medical conditions that may affect the interpretation of current physical findings.
3. Describe any pre-existing physical injuries.

D. RECENT HYGIENE INFORMATION
Record hygiene activity if the alleged incident occurred within 72 hours of the examination. This information is relevant because it can affect the interpretation of findings. If the patient has bathed or showered, the examiner should still collect samples from the appropriate body areas to attempt to preserve any biological or trace evidence.

E. GENERAL PHYSICAL EXAMINATION: COLLECT AND PRESERVE EVIDENCE. RECORD FINDINGS.
1. Record vital signs.
2. Record the date and time the examination was started and completed.
3. Record height, weight, hair and eye color, and indicate whether the patient is right or left-handed.
4. Describe the patient's general physical appearance.
5. Describe the patient's general demeanor.
    - Describe behaviors such as cooperative, agitated, etc.
6. Describe the condition of clothing upon arrival (rips, tears, presence of foreign materials).
7. Collect outer and under clothing worn during or immediately after the incident.
    - Coordinate with the law enforcement officer regarding clothing to be collected.
    - Wear gloves while collecting clothing.
    - Have patient disrobe on two sheets of paper placed one on top of the other on the floor. Have patient remove shoes before stepping on the paper. Shoes may be collected, if indicated, and packaged separately.
    - Package each garment in an individual paper bag, label, and seal.
    - Carefully fold the top sheet of paper into a bindle, label, and seal. Discard the bottom sheet. Place this large bindle and all individually bagged garments into a large paper bag(s) with a chain of custody form, label, and seal.
    - Wet stains or other wet evidence require special handling. Consult local policy.
    - Give special focus to items that are close to the genital structures or otherwise have the highest potential to contain biological evidence from the victim according to the assault history. According to local policy, these items may be placed in the evidence kit.

E.   GENERAL PHYSICAL EXAMINATION
8.   **Conduct a general physical examination and record all findings.**

> **Physical Findings:** A physical finding includes observable or palpable tissue injuries, physiological changes, or foreign material (e.g. grass, sand, stains, dried or moist secretions, or positive fluorescence). If none of the above are present, mark "No Findings".

- Record findings relevant to identification, e.g. tattoos, scars, body piercing, chronic skin lesions, distinguishing physical features, etc.
- Be observant for erythema (redness), abrasions, bruises, swelling, lacerations, fractures, bites, and scratches.
- Note areas of tenderness or induration.

DOCUMENTATION OF INJURIES AND FINDINGS USING DIAGRAMS AND LEGEND
- Record size and appearance of injuries and other findings using the diagrams, the legend, and a consecutive numbering system.
- Bruises: describe shape, size, and color.
- Use the legend to list and describe the injury/finding drawn on the diagram. Show the diagram letter followed by the finding number.
- Use the abbreviations in the legend to describe the type of finding. Example: A-1, EC 2x3cm red/purple indicates that the first finding on Diagram A is an ecchymosis (bruise) that is red/purple in color and 2x3 centimeters in size. See example below.

Locator #	Type	Description
A-1	EC	2x3 cm red/purple
A-2	DS	Dried secretion
A-3	CS	Control swab

- **Photograph injuries and other findings according to local policy.**
- **Use proper forensic photographic techniques.**
  - Use an appropriate light source and a scale near the finding.
  - Note: The plane of the film must be parallel to the plane of the finding.

9.   **Collect dried and moist secretions, stains (including semen, bloodstains, and saliva from bites), and foreign materials from the body.**
- **Scan** the entire body with a Wood's Lamp (long wavelength ultraviolet light) or other alternate light source. Note fluorescent area(s) on the diagrams and record in legend as WL⊕.
- **Swab moist secretions** with a dry swab to avoid dilution. Label and air dry before packaging.
- **Swab dried stains and/or Wood's Lamp positive area(s)** with a swab (or multiple swabs for large stains) moistened with sterile, deionized, or distilled water. Label and air dry the evidence swab(s) before packaging. Make a control swab by swabbing an unstained area adjacent to the stain (when possible). Label, air dry, and package the control swab separately from the evidence sample.
- **Collect** foreign materials such as fibers, sand, hair, grass, soil, and vegetation. Place in bindles and/or envelopes as appropriate for each location on the body. Label and seal.
- **Record** all findings on the diagrams and the legend as shown above.
  - Use the legend locator number to label evidence collection envelopes.
  - Record the locations of swab collection sites and control swabs.

10.   **Collect fingernail scrapings or cuttings according to local policy.**
- Use clean toothpicks or manicure sticks to collect scrapings from under the fingernails. Place scrapings from **each** hand into separate containers or bindles, then place into envelopes. Label (indicating right or left hand) and seal; **OR**,
- Use a clean fingernail cutter or scissors to cut the fingernails, and place the cuttings from **each** hand into separate containers or bindles. Package and label as above.

11.   **Collect chest hair reference samples according to local policy.**
- According to local policy, pull (or have patient pull) 20-30 hairs representative of variations in length and color from different areas of the chest; **OR**, cut the hairs close to the skin. Package, label, and seal.

F. HEAD, NECK, AND ORAL EXAMINATION

1. **Examine the face, head, hair, scalp, and neck for injury and foreign materials.**
    - Give special focus to the lips, perioral region, and nares in the examination.
    - Record injuries and other findings using the diagrams and legend.
    - Photograph injuries and other findings according to local policy. A colposcope may be used.
2. **Collect dried and moist secretions, stains and foreign materials from the face, head, hair, scalp, and neck.**
    - **Swab moist secretions** with a dry swab to avoid dilution. Label and air dry before packaging.
    - **Swab dried stains and/or Wood's Lamp positive area(s)** with a swab (or multiple swabs for large stains) moistened with sterile, deionized, or distilled water. Label and air dry the evidence swab(s) before packaging. Make a control swab by swabbing an unstained area <u>adjacent</u> to the stain (when possible). Label, air dry, and package the control swab separately from the evidence sample.
    - **Collect** foreign materials such as fibers, sand, hair, grass, soil, and vegetation. Place in bindles and/or envelopes as appropriate for each location on the body. Label and seal.
    - **Cut** matted head or facial hairs bearing crusted material and place in a bindle. Package, label, and seal.
    - **Record** all findings on the diagrams and legend.
        - Use the legend locator number to label evidence collection envelopes.
        - Record the locations of swab collection sites and control swabs.
3. **Examine the oral cavity for injury and foreign materials (if indicated by the assault history, e.g., ejaculation by a male victim).**
    - Give special focus to frenulums, buccal surfaces, gums, and soft palate.
    - Record injuries, foreign materials, and other findings using the diagrams and legend.
    - Photograph injuries and other findings according to local policy. A colposcope may be used.
    - Collect foreign materials found in the oral cavity, e.g. hair. Package, label, and seal.
4. **Collect 2 swabs from the oral cavity for seminal fluid up to 12 hours post assault and prepare one dry mount slide from one of the swabs.**
    - Swab the gum to the tonsillar fossae, the upper first and second molars, behind the incisors, and the fold of the cheek (buccal space).
    - Label and air dry swabs and slide. Code the swab to enable the crime laboratory to determine which swab was used to make the slide. Package, label, and seal.
5. **Collect head and facial hair reference samples according to local policy.**
    - According to local policy, pull (or have patient pull) 20-30 hairs representative of variations in length and color from different areas of the head and face (if patient has a beard); **OR**, cut the hairs <u>close to the skin</u>. Package, label, and seal

G. GENITAL EXAMINATION

1. **Examine the inner thighs, external genitalia, and perineal area for injury, foreign materials, and other findings. Check the appropriate box(es) if there are assault related findings.**
    *   Use a colposcope, if available, or employ other means of magnification.
    *   Record size and appearance of injuries, foreign materials, and other findings using the diagrams, legend, and a consecutive numbering system. Note swelling and areas of tenderness and induration.
    *   Record findings relevant to identification, e.g. tattoos, scars, body piercing, chronic skin lesions, etc.
    *   Use the legend to help identify and describe the findings drawn on the diagram. Example: H-7 LA 1.5 centimeters means Diagram H finding #7 is a laceration 1.5 centimeters long.
    *   Photograph injuries and other findings according to local policy.

2. **Record whether circumcised or not.**

3. **Collect dried and moist secretions, stains, and foreign materials.**
    *   **Scan** the area with a Wood's Lamp (long wavelength ultraviolet light) or other alternate light source. Note fluorescent area(s) on the diagrams and record in legend as WL⊕.
    *   **Swab moist secretions** with a dry swab to avoid dilution. Label and air dry before packaging.
    *   **Swab dried stains and Wood's Lamp positive areas** with a swab (or multiple swabs for large stains) moistened with sterile, deionized, or distilled water. Label and air dry the evidence swab(s) before packaging. Make a control swab by swabbing an unstained area adjacent to the stain (when possible). Label, air dry, and package separately from the evidence sample.
    *   **Collect** foreign materials such as fibers, sand, hair, grass, soil, and vegetation. Place in bindles and/or envelopes as appropriate for each location on the body. Label and seal.
    *   **Cut** matted pubic hairs bearing crusted material and place in a bindle. Package, label, and seal.
    *   **Record** all findings on the diagrams and legend.
        *   Use the legend locator number to label evidence collection envelopes.
        *   Record the locations of swab collection sites and control swabs.

4. **Collect pubic hair combing or brushing.**
    *   Place a paper sheet under the patient's buttocks. Comb the pubic hair downward to remove any loose hairs or foreign materials. Collect and fold the paper under the buttocks with the comb or brush inside. Package, label, and seal.

5. **Collect pubic hair reference samples according to local policy.**
    *   According to local policy, pull (or have patient pull) 20-30 hairs representative of variations in length and color from different areas of the pubic region; **OR**, cut the hairs close to the skin. Package, label and seal.

6. **Collect 2 penile swabs, if indicated by the assault history.**
    *   Hold the swabs together as a unit and swab the glans, shaft, and base of the penis with a rotating motion to ensure uniform sampling. Avoid swabbing the urethral meatus. Use swabs moistened with sterile, deionized, or distilled water for these swabbings. Air dry, package, label, and seal.

7. **Collect 2 scrotal swabs, if indicated by the assault history.**
    *   Collection of scrotal swabs is recommended because secretions from the victim may also be transferred to this area.
    *   Hold the swabs together as a unit and swab the scrotum in a rotating motion, focusing on the area that is in closest proximity to the penis. Use swabs moistened with sterile, deionized, or distilled water. Air dry, package, label, and seal.

8. **Record other findings per history.**

All swabs and slides must be air dried prior to packaging (Penal Code Section 13823.11). Air dry in a stream of cool air for 60 minutes. Only place samples from one patient at a time in the swab drying box. Wipe or spray the swab drying box with 10% bleach before each use.

Labeling requirements: Swabs, slides, bindles, and small containers must be individually labeled with the patient's name and sample source. Code swabs and slides to show which slides were prepared from which swabs. Containers for these individual items must be labeled with the name of the patient, date of collection, description of the evidence including location from which it was taken, and signature or initials of the person who collected the evidence. Include the legend locator number, if the legend was used to document the location from which the evidence was collected. Package containers in a Sexual Assault Evidence Collection Kit and record the chain of custody.

H. RECORD ALL EVIDENCE COLLECTED AND SUBMITTED TO THE CRIME LABORATORY
  1. **Record all items of clothing collected.**
  2. **Record all foreign materials collected and the name of the person who collected them.**
  3. **Record information about the oral/genital samples.**
     - Record the number of swabs and slides collected, the time collected, and the person who took the samples.

I. TOXICOLOGY SAMPLES
  - Collect samples for blood alcohol/toxicology at the discretion of the examiner and/or law enforcement officer in accordance with local policy.
  - Cleanse the arm with a non-alcoholic solution and collect 5cc of blood in a gray stoppered evacuated vial. Label vial and envelope, and seal.
  - Up to 96 hours after suspected ingestion of drugs, collect a urine specimen (100cc) in a clean container. It is important to collect the first available sample.

J. REFERENCE SAMPLES: Policies pertaining to collection of reference samples and the time and manner of collection vary by jurisdiction. If collected at the time of the exam, ALWAYS collect after the evidence samples. For those jurisdictions not performing conventional serology, a buccal swab can be taken in place of the blood reference sample. Consult your local crime laboratory.

  Blood:
  - Collect blood sample in lavender and/or yellow stoppered evacuated vials as specified by local policy.
  - A blood card is an option in some jurisdictions.
  - Label vial(s) and envelope(s) and seal.
  Buccal (inner cheek) swabs:
  - Collect as a DNA reference sample.
  - Rub two swabs gently but firmly along the inside of the cheek in a rotating motion to ensure even sampling.
  - Air dry, package, label, and seal.
  Saliva:
  - **Note:** If a saliva reference sample is required by the crime laboratory, collect it whether or not an oral assault occurred.
  - Collect sample by placing two swabs in the mouth and allowing them to saturate.
  - Air dry, package, label, and seal.
  Chest and facial hair:
  - According to local policy, pull (or have patient pull) 20-30 hairs representative of variations in length and color from different areas of the face or chest; **OR**, cut the hairs close to the skin.
  - Package, label, and seal.
  Head hair:
  - According to local policy, pull (or have patient pull) 20-30 hairs representative of variations in length and color from different areas of the scalp: **OR**, cut the hairs close to the skin.
  - Package, label, and seal.
  Pubic hair:
  - According to local policy, pull (or have patient pull) 20-30 hairs representative of variations in length and color from different areas of the pubic region; **OR**, cut the hairs close to the skin.
  - Package, label, and seal.

K. RECORD PHOTO DOCUMENTATION METHODS
  - Document photographic methods used and areas which were photographed. Documentation must clearly link the patient's identity to the specific photographs of injuries and/or findings. For example, include a picture of the patient identification on the roll or use a databack camera, which can be programmed with the patient's identification number.
L. RECORD EXAM METHODS USED.
M. RECORD EXAM FINDINGS.
N. SUMMARIZE FINDINGS.
O. PRINT NAMES OF PERSONNEL INVOLVED. OBTAIN SIGNATURE AND LICENSE NUMBER OF EXAMINER.
P. EVIDENCE DISTRIBUTION: List to whom the evidence was given.
Q. OBTAIN SIGNATURE OF OFFICER RECEIVING EVIDENCE.

PEOPLE V. OLIVER JOVANOVIC: FROM CYBERSEX TO SEXUAL ASSAULT ALLEGATIONS

Michael McGrath, MD

On a Monday in late November 1996, the mother of a Barnard College student called the director of Barnard College's security department to report that her daughter had been sexually assaulted over the weekend at the apartment of a Columbia graduate student. The case was notable for the publicity and media attention it garnered due to the sadomasochistic features of the alleged assault and, possibly more importantly, the fact that it was one of the first Internet related sexual assault cases. Oliver Jovanovic was convicted at trial of the assault[1] and sentenced to 15 years to life in prison. His conviction was overturned on appeal, after he had served 20 months in prison, related to the trial judge inappropriately using the so-called Rape Shield Law to keep information related to email traffic between Jovanovic and the victim, as well as other evidence favorable to the defense, out of the jury's reach. Eventually the Manhattan District Attorney's office declined to retry Mr. Jovanovic due to the unwillingness of the victim to testify at a second trial (Fritsch and Finkelstein, 2001), and also probably due to questions raised about her credibility, including reports from close family members that she had made false accusations in the past (Finnegan, 2000).

Aside from the material facts of the case, the appellate brief filed by Jovanovic's lawyers also addresses what appears to have been an overzealous prosecution. It was reported in the media that after the conviction was overturned a plea bargain was offered that would have settled for time served, but Mr. Jovanovic refused to plead (Hentoff, 2001), maintaining that the sexual activity that occurred between him and the victim was consensual and nonviolent. The purpose of this appendix is not to declare with certainty whether or not a sexual assault occurred, but rather to examine this case from the point of view (or what should have been the point of view) of the investigating police and prosecutors in reaching a decision as to whether to proceed to trial.

---

[1] Kidnapping in the first degree, three counts of Sexual Abuse in the first degree, Assault in the second degree, and Assault in the third degree.

The evidence available to them will be assessed as to whether there were sufficient credibility issues or red flags that should have alerted the police and the Manhattan DA's office to consider the possibility that the report as filed by the victim was a false allegation. It should be noted that the victim has never recanted.

WHAT HAPPENED?

The complainant, JR, had struck up an online conversation with Oliver Jovanovic in the spring of 1996 while a student at Barnard College.[2] She went home for the summer and, after returning to college in the fall, contacted him again online. They had several email conversations covering different subjects, one of which was sadomasochism. JR revealed to Jovanovic that she was engaged in a sadomasochistic relationship and liked it, at least as portrayed in the emails. JR had begun a relationship with Luke, who played in a band, in early November 1996. The relationship included sadomasochistic behavior by JR's report. Luke had ended a relationship with another woman, KK, when he began seeing JR several weeks before.

On November 15, 1996, KK called JR and asked her to come over to her apartment where she informed JR that she thought she may have been raped the night before. KK recounted how she met a student in a bar and brought him back to her apartment. She advised the student that she was not ready for sex (having recently broken up with Luke). The two spent time together with consensual physical contact. KK reported she was under the influence of alcohol, as was the male student. At some point they engaged in sexual intercourse. It was only later, after talking to JR, that KK consolidated the belief that she had been raped. JR urged her to report the rape, called college security, and accompanied KK to the hospital for an examination. KK advised hospital personnel that she did not want to report the alleged rape. About a month later KK reported the event to police as a rape. The investigation of this report failed to lead to an arrest, and, in fact, the detective investigating the allegation documented that it was his opinion that no rape had taken place. Describing this event on November 18 in an email to Jovanovic, JR opined that this had been a false allegation by Luke's ex-girlfriend, designed to get attention from him.

Over the next few days Jovanovic and JR emailed each other and JR sent her telephone number. On November 22, at about 3 A.M., Jovanovic called and they had a telephone conversation that lasted almost 5 hours. At the end of the

---

[2] The events as relayed are taken from police reports, the defendant-appellant brief filed by Mr. Jovanovic's attorney's filed September 1998, and the NY State Supreme Court, Appellate Division ruling of February 1999.

conversation Jovanovic invited JR to a movie that night and she gave him the address of her college dorm. JR slept for a few hours, then went to baby-sit for several hours and later went to a French class that ended at 7 P.M. that Friday evening. Jovanovic picked up JR at 8:30 P.M. in front of her dorm at 116th Street, and they went to the Lemon Grass Grill for dinner. Dinner ended around 10:15 P.M. and Jovanovic suggested they go to his apartment to watch a movie. The couple arrived at his Washington Heights apartment at about 11:30 P.M.

JR was served tea, which she later claimed had a metallic taste. They looked at a book that had photographs of corpses and watched a movie in which Muppet-like characters portray violent and/or sexual activity. Jovanovic reportedly told JR to remove her sweater, then her pants and then tied her arms and legs to the frame of a futon they had been sitting on. According to JR, Jovanovic went and got molten wax from a candle and poured it on her. After that he poured hot wax on her external genitalia and thighs. At this point JR reported that she was screaming from the pain of the hot wax and begged Jovanovic to stop. He then allegedly gagged her and blindfolded her. After that he reportedly bit her nipples and collarbone. Over the course of the next few hours Jovanovic allegedly struck her thighs with a club or baton, and then inserted it[3] into her rectum, causing great pain.

JR stated she eventually passed out and woke at some time on Saturday, November 23, still hog-tied. Later that night, JR managed to loosen her bindings and was able to stand up and, despite Jovanovic's reported attempts to stop her, ran around the apartment, picking up pieces of clothing as she ran and putting them on and escaping out the apartment door. JR reported taking the subway home, arriving some time after 10 P.M. None of her roommates were home. She called her boyfriend, Luke, and left him a message. She then went to the bathroom to urinate, something she stated she had not done since going to Jovanovic's apartment, a period of at least 20 hours. JR reported noticing blood on the inside seam of her pants and after wiping her urethra and anus, saw blood covering the tissue. She placed her pants, her sweater, her bra and one sock in her closet. JR showered, felt dizzy, went to bed and fell asleep. When she awoke she showered again and reported noticing her legs were red from where she had been struck by the baton and she had bruises on her breasts, her shoulder, and between the shoulder and breasts.

At 1 A.M., Sunday, November 24, Luke returned JR's phone call. She went by herself to Luke's 114th Street apartment and arrived appearing upset. JR told Luke she had spent Friday night with Jovanovic and that she had been tied up and assaulted with a club, sodomized, and burned with wax. JR slept in

---

[3] Or possibly his penis. JR was not sure which.

Luke's bed and he slept on the couch. Later that Sunday JR woke and went back to her dorm. She called her mother in Long Island and told her she had been hit with a club and sodomized by someone she had met. The mother told JR to report it to the police and to seek medical attention. She offered to come to New York City, but JR declined. Later, after taking a shower JR told a roommate she had had a "bad date" and had been sodomized with a police baton. Sometime that Sunday night JR spoke again with Luke by phone.

Around 11 P.M., Sunday the 24th of November, JR went to Columbia's Butler Library and retrieved an email from Jovanovic sent at 10:35 P.M. the night before, about a half hour after JR had escaped from his apartment. The email advised that JR had left a gold chain at his apartment and he could mail it to her, or bring it over in person if it was valuable. Jovanovic's email also referred to the time spent in his apartment and that he did not think she had learned much, but also that he hoped she had gotten home okay. JR's response to the email was to say (in referring to sadomasochism) she had learned a lot, was "bruised mentally and physically, but never so happy to be alive." She quoted William Burroughs: ". . . the taste is so overpoweringly delicious, and at the same time, quite nauseating." Several subsequent emails passed between JR and Jovanovic.

On Monday, November 25, JR told the woman she baby-sat for that she had been tortured and sodomized over the weekend. Tuesday, the 26th, Jovanovic answered JR's last email to him. His post questioned her wisdom in going to the apartment of someone she did not really know, whether she knew much about sexually transmitted diseases, whose needs were met by the interaction between them, etc. Sometime on that Tuesday JR's mother called the security department at Barnard College and reported the alleged sexual assault. The head of security, Mr. O'Connor, called JR and she went to speak to him. He arranged for a medical evaluation at the college health services where JR was examined, apparently by a nurse. JR did not go to an emergency room and she did not report the assault to the New York City Police Department. Mr. O'Connor offered to call the police, but JR said she was tired. The next day Wednesday, November 27, Mr. O'Connor called the NYPD to report the allegation.

JR was examined that day by an OB-GYN at Barnard Health Services. The MD found no vaginal or rectal bleeding, either on visual inspection or testing for microscopic blood in the stool.[4] No bruises were found on JR's thighs. No burn marks or teeth marks were found on her nipples. There were several bruises on JR's upper body and a bruise on the areola.[5] During the recto-vaginal examination JR complained of tenderness and soreness. A yeast

---

[4] Hemoccult test.
[5] Pigmented area of the breast around the nipple.

infection was diagnosed and antifungal cream was prescribed. That evening JR met with two detectives from the Manhattan Special Victims Unit and wrote out a statement for them. On December 5, 1996, Jovanovic was arrested at his apartment.

On December 10, JR turned over to police the pants she had worn in Jovanovic's apartment,[6] as well as a pink sock. On December 11 a detective picked up a sweater and bra from JR's dorm room, where they had been in a closet since the assault. On December 16, JR gave the police the panties she said she wore at the time of the assault. She had found the underwear in the ruffle skirt around her bed. JR had told the detective previously that the panties had been left in Jovanovic's apartment. On December 16, 24 days after the alleged assault, the prosecution sent JR to another OB-GYN. This physician found a small labial laceration. JR told the physician that she had been penetrated anally and vaginally with a hard plastic object.

ASSESSING THE ALLEGATION

When faced with an allegation of sexual assault the investigator at times walks a fine line between being supportive of a victim and trying to determine if the allegation of sexual assault is a false report. Sex crimes investigators are fully aware that false allegations of sexual assault are quite common. There are several collections of red flags for false allegations. (For example, see Baeza, 2000; McDowell and Hibler, 1987). These flags must be used in a measured manner as a truthful person can easily raise some red flags. It is important to keep in mind that the complainant may be telling the complete truth, or may be either holding information back or misrepresenting parts of their report. Simply because one has determined that a complainant has lied in one area, does not necessarily mean that they have lied in all areas, or that an assault did not take place. For example, a victim could report a rape and when the investigators go to the alleged crime scene they might determine that the report is not corroborated by the condition or evidence at that scene. It may be that the report is unfounded, but it could also be that the victim (for whatever reason) is reluctant to place themselves at the true crime scene. It is important to sort out inconsistencies early in the investigation to either identify a false report, or to salvage a prosecution.

This author suggests taking a three-pronged approach (McGrath, 2000) consisting of assessing behavioral, linguistic, and physical evidence in an attempt to determine the credibility of the victim–witness.[7] Behavioral red flags would

---

[6] JR claimed they had blood on the inside seam. Forensic testing of the pants found that whatever was there was consistent with normal vaginal secretions.

[7] It should be kept in mind that determining the credibility of a witness (which is what the complainant may eventually be) should be an important step in any criminal investigation.

include the presentation of the victim and how cooperative she or he was, among other things. Some examples (McGrath, 2000) are:

- Any behavior that functions to interfere with the investigation
- Initiation of report, or pressure to report, by someone other than the victim, unless the victim is unable to report or is too young to represent themselves
- Complainant unable to say where assault occurred (unless some aspect of the crime would preclude knowing where it occurred)
- Vague description of assailant when descriptions of other facets of crime are more detailed
- Interest of complainant more directed to a goal other than report of the crime (e.g., change in housing, disability payments, attention, lawsuit)
- Report of rape serves to provide an alibi

Linguistic assessment would be related to any statements made by the victim and/or suspects that can be examined to help determine credibility and identify areas that warrant further exploration. In this author's opinion, properly performed statement analysis can be more helpful than a polygraph examination.[8] It should be noted that statement analysis is actually a form of behavioral analysis. Since there are multiple ways of saying the same thing, choosing how to say or write something is a behavior that can be analyzed.

Physical evidence is often overlooked in investigations on two levels: first, as far as collecting it, and, second, as far as ensuring that the description of a crime (either by a victim, or as a result of a confession) matches to a reasonable extent the evidence found at the crime scene or as a result of forensic testing. Examples of issues related to physical evidence that should raise concern are (McGrath, 2000):

- Crime-scene reconstruction is at odds with story of victim.
- Injuries sustained by victim are consistent with known patterns of self-inflicted injuries and/or there is a lack of defensive wounds when a significant struggle is reported.
- Damage to clothing is not consistent with either the account of the assault ("He grabbed my collar and yanked me toward him," yet shirt or blouse is neatly ironed) or wounds.
- Lack of injury to victim when account implies significant force was used.

Faced with the allegations of JR, how should the sex crimes detectives and the DA's office have proceeded? It is this author's opinion that this case should

---

[8] It should be noted the author is not endorsing the polygraph, just commenting on it, as polygraph exams are often used in investigations.

not have proceeded to trial. From an investigative standpoint the witness lacked credibility on several levels. In reading the following assessment, the reader may feel that something presented under one category belongs in a different category, or even something presented under a category is better described separately, etc., under that category. Many of the issues discussed here could be arranged differently than presented here and it would not materially affect the analysis.

BEHAVIORAL ANALYSIS

- *Delay in reporting:* JR waited from about 10 P.M. Saturday, the 23rd of November, 1996, when she left Jovanovic's apartment, to about 7 P.M. on Wednesday the 27th to file an official police complaint, a period just 3 hours short of 4 days. Delayed reporting of sexual assault is, in this author's opinion, not the major red flag that it has historically been viewed as. There are many reasons why a victim may not immediately go to the police (from shame and feelings of guilt, to fear of the offender and/or police) that are not related to false reporting. Delayed reporting often takes on an aura it does not deserve.

- *Initial report to authorities made by someone other than the victim:* Unless the victim is a minor or lacks competency to fend for themselves, this is a significant red flag. JR's mother is the one who called Barnard College security to report the alleged sexual assault. It appears that, but for the mother's intervention, this allegation would never have been made. Barnard Security contacted JR to ask about the crime, not the other way around. Also, it was the head of security who, the next day (Wednesday the 27th of November), called NYPD to report the allegation, not the victim. This red flag becomes even more important when seen in light of JR's intervention with Luke's ex-girlfriend, KK. The fact that KK's allegation of rape was unfounded is actually not the issue, nor is it that JR influenced KK to go to the hospital to be examined. The point to note is that JR was fully aware of the resources available to a rape victim and appeared not to have any qualms in urging another to report a questionable sexual assault, yet she chose not to report what, by her account, was a very vicious sexual assault and torture that went on for 20 hours. Also, when the head of security at Barnard offered to call NYPD while JR was in his office, she declined, advising that she was too tired. A victim of a sexual assault who is "too tired" to talk to investigators has raised a crimson flag.

- *Story of victim lacks credibility:* The description of JR's escape from Jovanovic's apartment defies logic. Jovanovic, a martial arts instructor, reportedly untied JR's hands then saw JR stand (she had just managed to wriggle her legs free from being hogtied) and run around the apartment for close to 20 minutes[9] while not only was Jovanovic chasing her, but she was picking up pieces of clothing as she ran around, putting them on while running and upon reaching the door, unlocked it and ran out of the apartment before her captor was able to catch up with her. Much of JR's description of being hogtied for hours does not ring true. Also, this would have been expected to cause ligature injuries, which were never noted or even claimed. JR claimed to be confused or surprised by Jovanovic's sadomasochistic activities in his apartment, when in fact emails not allowed at trial (but available to detectives and prosecutors) between JR and Jovanovic (both before and after the alleged assault) would seem to belie this claim. Even if JR exaggerated her interest in S&M, the evidence clearly shows an awareness of and an interest in discussing such behaviors, not only with Jovanovic, but with others. In fact, her relationship with her boyfriend at the time was described as having sadomasochistic qualities. It is certainly possible that any injuries ascribed to Jovanovic could just as well have been attributed to sexual activity between JR and her boyfriend.

According to JR there were multiple times during her imprisonment and torture when she screamed loudly. The apartment was fairly small. She had reported that the apartment was hot and two windows were open from 6 inches to a foot, yet no one at the time heard the screams,[10] either in the same building or outside. It is hard to believe this did not raise at least some doubt on JR's story in the eyes of the police investigators.[11] It would be easy enough to use a sound level meter and ask JR to scream as loud as she did on the night in question. The decibel range could be recorded and then a policewoman could go into Jovanovic's locked apartment in the early morning and scream several times, attempting to stay in the decibel range reached by JR. It could then be assessed crudely by hearing and more accurately by sound level meter how likely it would be that female screams would have elicited a response from neighbors from the hallway, adjacent apartments, outside the windows of the apartment, etc.

- *Misleading investigators/examiners:* JR reported to the Barnard Health examiner that she had not had sexual relations (aside from events at Jovanovic's

---

[9] Per her trial testimony. The NYPD detectives and DA's office must have spoken with her about this prior to trial, so they must have known how incredible this sounded. The apartment was essentially a studio apartment. Jovanovic must have had at least one opportunity to grab JR during her 20-minute run.

[10] Later a witness reported hearing something, but review of this report is not impressive. The report was vague and not consistent with the time that JR was allegedly screaming. In any event, no one heard anything that led to a 911 call during the time that JR was in Mr. Jovanovic's apartment.

[11] Even JR testified at trial that she heard snoring coming from an adjacent apartment.

apartment) since August 1996, when she had been sexually active with her boyfriend in November 1996.

- *The allegation of sexual assault provides an alibi:* JR's boyfriend, Luke, was playing in a band at a club the Friday night of the alleged assault. JR might have been expected to be there to watch, but did not show. After the alleged assault JR was not seen by anyone between the time she left Jovanovic's apartment at 10 P.M. and when she arrived at her boyfriend's apartment at 1 A.M. Despite allegedly reporting the 20-hour imprisonment, torture, and penetration with a baton to the boyfriend, the response is to go to sleep—she in Luke's bed, he on the couch. It is not clear if any conversation occurred as to whether the police should be called. When JR left Luke's apartment somewhere between 6 and 7 A.M., he was half asleep on the couch and they did not talk. This would indicate that they did not even say goodbye, a strange occurrence in this author's view.

LINGUISTIC ANALYSIS

JR wrote out a several-page statement for the Manhattan sex-crimes detectives who met with her. They left her by herself to write out her version of what happened. This is a good thing to do with a victim, witness, or suspect. But one must review the statement to determine the level of credibility of the complainant. Also, questions raised in reviewing the statement can be helpful in indicating not only whether a person is lying, but also if they are telling the truth. And any issues identified in the statement can help develop leads in a truthful statement.

- *Time gap:* There are huge time gaps in the story of the assault. The statement opens with the time: "7:30 Dinner." (Also note this is not a sentence. From the opening of the statement the writer is having difficulty committing to the statement.) The fourth line opens with 10ish. The "ish" also telegraphs lack of commitment to the time she is giving. The eleventh line begins: "12ish." Again, there is a lack of commitment to the times given. This is the last time mentioned in a statement that is 267 lines long and covering at least 20 hours. This would indicate that time was not important in this statement.
- *Social introductions:* How people are introduced in a statement is important. Mr. Jovanovic is introduced in the second line with "we." The actual beginning of the statement is:

> 7:30 Dinner
> We decided to go to his residence to watch a film since we were
> late for the film we had planned on seeing

It should be noted that JR had corresponded over a period of months with Mr. Jovanovic and spoke with him for hours prior to their dinner date, as well as during dinner and the events leading up to the alleged sexual assault. She knew his name. The introduction starts with "we" indicating that they were acting in concert. This is not unexpected and would be significant if used after the assault began. (It was later used around where the assault was beginning, but crossed-out and changed. That, in and of itself, should have signaled to the detectives that this statement was suspect. See later discussion.) But, it would be expected that she would have introduced him with something like: "Oliver and I decided to go to his apartment . . ." or "Oliver, the guy I met on the Internet . . ." By not using his name JR has not identified him. This is very important, as during the rest of the statement she never once says who "he" is. This should have raised a red flag as to her actual commitment to accusing Mr. Jovanovic of a sexual assault.

The only other specific person introduced (aside from Jeffrey Dahmer) is near the end of the statement, after JR has escaped from Jovanovic's apartment and arrived at her dorm apartment, when she writes: "So I called a friend and stayed at their house." Who was this "friend"? It was JR's boyfriend. Why would she not identify him in the statement? Why would she feel the need to distance herself from her boyfriend? In later testimony it was determined that when JR went to her boyfriend's apartment he slept on the couch and she slept on his bed. This is interesting, as it does not imply that the relationship was going well. Allegedly she confided in the boyfriend that she had been tortured and kept captive for 20 hours. And his response is to go to sleep on the couch? It may place things in a more understandable context if the reader is reminded that the boyfriend expected JR to come and see him play in his band the night before. Also, note that "there" was crossed out and replaced with "their." The "friend" was singular, the "their" is plural. This is further linguistic evidence that JR was attempting (perhaps unconsciously) to disguise who the friend was.

- *I don't know:* When writing down a statement of what happened, declarations of "I don't know," "I don't remember," "I didn't know what was happening" are problematic. They indicate missing information that the writer has chosen not to give us. Note, in the following lines, JR tells us that she does not know: "So again he got a gag and put it in my mouth and tied something around my head—covering my mouth so that it would stay in place. And also—blind folded me. Then he put me on my stomach and I don't know— because I couldn't see being on my back and blindfolded, But I know that he put something inside me vaginally and anally".

But notice that after she tells us she does not know, she stops and does not actually tell us what it is she does not know. (Aside from this, how would one know that they did not know something?) After thinking a moment (the dash), she explains that she does not know (but we still do not know what it is she does not know) because she is on her back and blindfolded. We are left to assume she did not know what was being inserted into her, Jovanovic's penis or the baton. But she never says this. Only later does she add that she knows he put something inside her. Why does she not know? If she is on her back and hogtied, how does Mr. Jovanovic penetrate her with his penis?[12] If she were penetrated by a plastic baton, would not the temperature be different from the penis of a living person?[13] In any event, JR feels the need to explain why she was unable to tell whether she was penetrated by a penis or a baton. The explanation, though, is revealing. The main reason is that she was allegedly blindfolded. But note she says the reason she was unable to identify the instrument of rape was that "I couldn't see." The reason would be that she was blindfolded. But that is not what she tells us: "I couldn't see being on my back. . . ." Only after that does she add ". . . and blindfolded." The order of things in a statement is important. So, we must assume that being blindfolded was less of a reason for not knowing than being on her back. But reading the sentence only leads to more questions, as JR tells us that she is on her stomach, not her back. So the conditions of not knowing do not appear to actually hold.

- *Unimportant information:* In an open statement the writer tells what happened. Any explanations or other unimportant information is extraneous from the perspective of telling the story. But from the perspective of the writer such information can be very important, as it can either fill in for missing information or attempt to influence the mindset of the reader. For example, in the following there is nothing that furthers our being told *what* was happening, only what JR was thinking: "I thought if I went to his apartment the events that would occur would be similar in consistency to how we acted before— we discussed film, philosophy, intellectual things. I did not think that by joking along with him would hurt me."

The entire statement contains 2206 words. When one counts up the "unimportant" sections, one gets a word count of 1096, or essentially half the statement. This alone would raise a significant question of whether this statement should be accepted as truthful. In other words, in a handwritten statement of what happened during a prolonged torture and sexual assault, half of the statement is off task.

---

[12] This certainly would be an area that the sex-crimes detectives would ask about, but it is not clear if any such conversation took place.

[13] It is certainly possible for a traumatized rape victim to not be sure what they were penetrated with, but they would clearly state that. The paragraph must be seen in its entirety.

- *Cross-outs:* There are multiple cross-outs in the handwritten statement. This is clear evidence that JR edited what she was saying (writing). The detectives should have told JR (perhaps they did) that if she made a mistake she should draw a single line through the "error." Most of her cross-outs obliterated what was underneath, making it impossible to determine what was changed. Why the need to do this? In one example, in the second line of the statement, the word "decide" is crossed out to change "We decide to go to his residence . . ." to "We decided to go to his residence. . . ." This is noteworthy, as the use of present tense in such a statement is a sign (not proof) that the writer is making that part of the account up, i.e., not drawing on memory.

  Later, in describing becoming alarmed at Jovanovic's behavior (per the statement, he had just tied her limbs to the frame of a futon) there is much crossing out and writing over. This signifies a problem with her rendition of this part of the story. Per JR: "I was getting scared at this point a [illegible cross-out] little—I thought it was a bit dangerous and that I should go. . . ." The change from "we" to "I" implies retrospective falsification. It is logical to assume that after writing "we," which implies acting in concert (i.e., the behaviors described were consensual), JR felt the need to distance the behavior from herself. In other words, for the story to be presented as an assault, it is necessary that she should want to go, not the two of them. But that is, in fact, what she started to say.

  Further on in the statement JR writes: "He just kept biting and pouring wax on me." The first two letters of the word "pouring" were actually a "d" and an "r" that were overwritten by a "p" and an "o". The inference this examiner draws from this is that JR had begun to write "dripping" or "dropping." Why make such a change? It is this examiner's opinion that very likely Mr. Jovanovic and JR were involved in consensual dripping of wax onto her body. When describing the alleged assault though, JR starts to describe what actually happened, but then edits it to make it sound more violent. "Pouring" wax on someone sounds worse than "dripping" wax on someone.

  At the point in the narrative that defines the sexual assault, JR writes: "But I know that he put something inside me vaginally and anally." But, there are several completely crossed-out and unreadable words following "inside me" and inserted over the obliterated words is "vaginally and anally." So, at potentially the most important (emotionally and legally) part of the statement, the complainant has to edit and redo her statement, and does so in a manner that renders it impossible to determine what she first wrote. This statement begs for a reinterview of the witness as well as a request for a second written statement prior to that interview.

- *Insertion of information:* On the first page of the statement there is an insertion (i.e., addition) that is telling. "I thought it was a bit dangerous and that

I should go because of what was happening . . ." becomes "I thought it was a bit dangerous and that I should go *home* because of what was happening . . . ." The word "home" was inserted. One might argue, what is the problem? The issue is that JR is writing down what happened. After writing that she should go, she has a need to go back and add "home," obviously assuming the reader needs to know that. But why would the reader need to know she would go home? Why not somewhere else? Luke's apartment, for example? It is possible that there was consideration of JR and Mr. Jovanovic leaving his apartment and going somewhere else. If so, "we" could be changed to "I" and "home" inserted to conceal this.

- *Pointing out the negative:* When writing a statement describing what happened, there is no reason for the writer to document what did not happen or what was not present. When such statements are present they telegraph sensitivity over that issue. For example, after being tied to the futon JR says: "I still had no reason not to trust this person." Why would she have the need to include this, especially in a tortured double negative? Later, ". . . I didn't think I was in any real danger." Again, this "unimportant" information is likely included to influence the reader. Note: She does not go further to explain why she is not in danger, only that she thought she was not, apparently explaining why she had gone to the apartment of a man she did not know well and allowed him to tie her to a futon frame. Later in the statement, after describing being struck by a baton on her legs, JR wrote: ". . . and he told me to spread my legs. And I didn't—I mean who would let some guy hit the most sensitive area of their body with a club?" Here JR is telling us that she resisted opening her legs. But rather than simply stating this, she feels the need to explain why she would not open her legs. There is no need for this, unless, of course, the writer assumes the reader will need an explanation.

- *Explanations:* In a narrative one writes down what happened. Explanations of why things happened are outside the area of answering: "Write down for me what happened." Therefore if one explains why something occurred, this is significant as the writer feels the need to be sure the reader has the understanding that the writer wants to convey, not some understanding that the reader might deduce on his/her own. Again, regarding the command to spread her legs: "So he hit me on my thighs and between my thighs—I was on my back with my ankles tied to my wrists and he told me to spread my legs. And I didn't—I mean who would let some guy hit the most sensitive area of their body with a club?" There is no need for the explanation of why JR resisted opening her legs. One is tempted to opine that JR protests too much.

- *Use of language:* In the opening of the statement, JR refers to Mr. Jovanovic's apartment as "his residence." This is an odd way to refer to where he lived.

As the opening sentence of a statement is very important, it appears JR was distancing herself from the location, as "residence" is much too formal for a graduate student's one-room apartment. One might argue that emotionally it was difficult for JR to write the statement and distancing herself from the site of the assault was emotionally necessary to describe the assault. But later in the statement she refers to Mr. Jovanovic's residence as "his apartment." Also, further on in the statement JR uses the phrase "his apartment"[14] in relation to where Jeffrey Dahmer killed his victims. One might argue that linguistically JR is equating Jovanovic's living quarters with Jeffrey Dahmer's, a place where people were killed and dismembered. That might be a convincing argument if she had used a different term[15] to link Jovanovic's and Dahmer's apartments together. What sticks out is the initial use of residence, not the subsequent expected use of apartment.

Another interesting use of language was in using "events" to stand for the assault and torture that JR allegedly endured. "I thought if I went to his apartment the events that would occur would be similar in consistency to how we acted before. . . ." Here "events" is presented in a foretelling sense (which is still off task) and arguably not reflective of a label for the upcoming torture and sexual assault, but an expectation that nothing untoward would happen. But later "events" is used as a label for the torture and assault. There seems to be little emotional attachment to what went on in the apartment, despite JR's description of herself as terrified and in fear of her life in several places. The reader should keep in mind that Mr. Jovanovic and JR had never been together before that night. So what could she be referring to when saying "to how we acted before"? Their telephone conversations? Or the email correspondence (likely reflective of what they talked about on the phone), in which there is clear evidence of sadomasochistic interest on JR's part? One might infer, then, that JR is actually revealing telling a truth here: that what occurred in the apartment between them was consistent with what they had "acted" (or talked about) before. Also notice the use of "similar in consistency." Does anyone actually talk (write) like this? Later in the statement: "Also throughout the events on the futon (where we had watched the movie) he kept telling me 'Stop screaming or I'll punish you.'" Again, rather than describing or specifically referring to the assaultive behaviors, the reader is offered the sterile term "events." Still later, after the sexual assault: "This argument is what he told me during the course of events; maybe to make me more afraid or something." Again, a multihour torture and sexual assault is reduced to "the course of events." The inference this examiner draws from

[14] In the statement there is a section describing a discussion about Jeffrey Dahmer.
[15] Different, that is, from the expected term "apartment" used to describe one of many residential units in an apartment building.

the use of the term "events," for the sexual assault and torture that JR endured, is that there is a lack of commitment by the writer of this statement to the events that occurred in Mr. Jovanovic's apartment being a sexual assault.

- *Lack of commitment to the statement:* It was noted previously that there are areas where JR showed a lack of commitment to her statement. There are other linguistic cues to lack of commitment. Use of words such as *think* or *guess* signals lack of commitment. JR used such words several times in her statement. Some examples: (a) "So *thinking* he wasn't attracted to me" is given as a reason for feeling safe in the apartment. Since JR has not committed to this, we should not accept it; (b) "So I played along *thinking* all was well and safe. And continuing with this joke he tied my legs to the fouton {sic}" is given as a reason why JR allowed herself to be tied to the frame of the futon. Since JR has not committed to this, we should not accept it. (c) "I *thought* it was a bit dangerous and that I should go home because of what was happening, that what was now playful could led {sic} to bad circumstance." Since JR has not committed to this, we should not accept it. (d) "I have no idea where this source of strength murged {sic} from—fear for my life I *guess*. . . ." Since JR does not commit to this (being afraid for her life) we should not accept it either.

A portion of the statement is as follows:

> So he hit me on my thighs and between my thighs—I was on my back with my ankles tied to my wrists and he told me to spread my legs. And I didn't—I mean who would let some guy hit the most sensitive area of their body with a club? So he bit my nipple and breast again—the other most sensitive area (now even more sensitive since all the trauma of biting + wax). So I spread my legs apart and screamed and cried. So again he got a gag and put it in my mouth and tied something around my head—covering my mouth so that it would stay in place. And also—blind folded me. Then he put me on my stomach and I don't know—because I couldn't see being on my back and blindfolded, But I know that he put something inside me vaginally and anally I was just terrified at this point That I was going to die and be dismembered so I just wanted him to be happy.

The reader should visualize the position JR is in. She is hogtied and on her back. She later claims not to know if she were violated by the baton or by Mr. Jovanovic's penis. It is hard to imagine how he penetrated her with his penis while she was hogtied and on her stomach. Also, the paragraph contains unnecessary explanations of why she did or did not do something, or why she did not know something. Also, although one would expect a victim to experience terror, etc., in a truthful statement such exclamations tend to come near the end of the statement, after the situation is over, not at what would seem logical points in the narrative. The reader should note the final clause of the paragraph. JR is saying that she "just wanted him to be happy." This appears to be presented in the context that keeping the assailant happy will possibly keep her alive. But that is not actually what JR has said (written). The reader must draw the inference that the reason JR wants the assailant to be happy is to save her life.

PHYSICAL EVIDENCE ANALYSIS

- *Claims of injuries without marks:* JR claimed to have been burned with candle wax that caused her to scream in pain. Candle wax is not hot enough to burn the skin, let alone cause significant pain. JR reported that Jovanovic used ice to keep the wax from causing burns. Although it is possible that ice and candle wax were used to assault JR, there is no need to use anything to prevent burns from candle wax.

- *Can an injury be self-inflicted or a result of something other than the alleged assault:* When examined by an OB-GYN at Barnard Health Services two days after JR left Jovanovic's apartment there were no findings supportive of violent insertion of a baton into JR's rectum or vagina. When examined 24 days after the alleged assault, however, a labial laceration was noted by the examiner. This was not present during the earlier examination.

- *Panties:* Once JR found the panties in the skirt ruffle of her bed, they were turned over to the police. A hair was found on them. This hair did not match Jovanovic or JR. These panties were reportedly worn by JR during the period when Jovanovic was supposed to be pouring wax on her, after pulling down the top of the panties so her external genitalia were exposed. The panties were tested for the presence of wax. As the results of the testing were never introduced at trial, one can safely assume no wax was found. In fact, no evidence of wax was found on the futon or anywhere in the apartment.

- *Hogtied for hours:* No contusions, abrasions, or other possible ligature marks were noted on JR's wrists or ankles when she was examined at Barnard Health Services.

- *Baton:* There was no medical evidence to support JR's claim that she had been struck repeatedly on the thighs with a baton. There was no medical evidence to support violent anal and vaginal penetration with a baton-like instrument.

- *Bleeding:* There was no medical evidence to support JR's claim that she had been bleeding for days from her vagina and rectum following her stay with Jovanovic. JR had claimed that she was bleeding from one of her nipples (due to Jovanovic allegedly biting her), but there was no blood transfer to her bra or sweater.

- *Bruises:* Bruises were noted on JR's upper body and areola during examination at Barnard Health Services. No bite marks were observed. The OB-GYN examiner estimated the bruises were a week old,[16] which would have been several days before JR's date with Jovanovic. It is possible Jovanovic caused these bruises during forced sexual activity. It is also possible that he caused them during consensual sadomasochistic sex, and it is possible Luke or someone else caused them.

SUMMARY

Review of the available information in regard to the complaint by JR that she was tortured and sexually assaulted by Mr. Oliver Jovanovic reveals many areas of concern. There are clear problems with her story as presented by her, evidenced by the issues highlighted earlier in the areas of behavioral, linguistic, and physical evidence. That this case was allowed to go to trial is troubling. At the very least, investigators should have approached JR from the point of view of a potential false report and asked her to help clarify the troubling issues.

REFERENCES

Baeza, J. (2000) Baeza false report index. Available online at http://www.anusha.com/jov-deci.htm

Finnegan, M. Accuser kin aids cybersex suspect. *New York Daily News,* final edition, p. 6, January 10, 2000.

Fritsch, J., and Finkelstein, K. Charges dismissed in Columbia sexual torture case. *The New York Times,* late edition, final, section D, page 1, column 2, November 2, 2001.

Hentoff, N. Will Morgenthau do justice? The first trial judge was over his head. *The Village Voice,* October 26, 2001. Available online at http://www.cybercase.org/.

McDowell, C., and Hibler, N. (1987) False allegations, in Hazelwood, R., and Burgess, A. (eds.), *Practical Aspects of Rape Investigation: A Multidisciplinary Approach.* New York: Elsevier. Reprinted in Aiken, M. M., Burgess, A. W., and Hazelwood, R. R. (1995) False rape allegations, in Hazelwood, R. R., and Burgess, A. W. (eds.), *Practical Aspects of Rape Investigation: A Multidisciplinary Approach,* 2nd ed. pp. 229–238. Boca Raton, FL: CRC Press.

McGrath, Michael (2000) False allegations of rape and the criminal profiler. *The Journal of Behavioral Profiling,* Vol. 1, No. 3.

---

[16] Aging of bruises is difficult and not always reliable.

People v. Jovanovic (1999) NYS Supreme Court, Appellate Division, 1st, M 513, 12/21/1999.

Supreme Court of the State of New York, Appellate Division, First Department: Brief of Defendant-Appellant in People v. Jovanovic, NY County Indictment No. 10938-96, filed by Attorneys for Oliver Jovanovic on September 1st, 1998.

TASK FORCE MANAGEMENT

Det. John J. Baeza

A *task force* is a team of individuals assembled for the purposes of investigative information gathering, information organization, and information sharing in a major case or series of related cases. The primary goals of a task force include the streamlined development of investigative leads and strategy, the coordination of investigative efforts and resources, and the identification and investigation of suspects.

When the public and those outside of law enforcement hear the term "task force," many automatically think of a "lean, mean, investigative machine," that leaves no stone unturned, no lead unfollowed, and no possibility unchecked.

However, those of us who have participated on task forces know all too well how disorganized, political, and chaotic they can be. We hear the term "task force," and, sadly, we immediately envision bureaucratic or supervisory incompetence leading to a great deal of frustration for task force members.

This is hardly what we want, or need, but we must be honest with ourselves and identify these problems before we can engage effective solutions. A major case task force does not have to be a chaotic venture, but it often is. This brings us to the identification of the very first problem faced by those forming a major case task force: *no plan!*

Any agency's task force protocols should be in place prior to the start of an investigation. This means starting today, while there is no investigative pressure bearing down on us, and establishing our own guidelines and protocols that will be there for us when we need them. In that spirit, we offer the following guidelines and insights to aid investigators and supervisors when they undertake to plan for, or form, a major case task force. They are intended to provide a basic overview of some of the common problem areas related to task force formation and operation. However, these guidelines are by no means an exhaustive list. In fact, it is hoped that others will find ways to improve upon

This chapter was originally published in Baeza, J. (1999) Task force management, in Turvey, B. (ed.), *Criminal Profiling: An Introduction to Behavioral Evidence Analysis*. London: Academic Press.

the quality of these suggestions, and that they will come up with their own innovative ideas that address their specific situation and utilize their particular agency's resources and associations.

It is also intended that this will provoke others to think more critically about the organization and function of their existing task forces.

FORMATION OF A TASK FORCE

Task forces are formed for a variety of reasons. Typically, it is because a series of often violent crimes is somehow linked, and the need for a task force becomes evident because of the large amount of information that needs to be investigated. These crimes can include sexual assaults, homicides, robberies, bombings, arsons, kidnappings, and the investigation of organized crime, just to name a few examples.

The litmus test for whether or not an agency needs to form a task force to address a crime or a series of related crimes consists of three basic qualifiers:

1. The case involves multiple victims or multiple jurisdictions
2. The investigation of the case requires more resources than the investigating agency has on its own
3. The case involves a serious, immediate threat to public safety

The existence of any of these criteria may be sufficient for a department to form a task force. If more than two of the qualifiers exist in a given case, then task force formation is almost mandatory.

Time is critical, once the need for the formation of a task force has been identified. Unfortunately, what happens all too often is that a task force is formed too late. The investigators then have to go back, sometimes years, and work on cases that have gone cold. Victims and witnesses may not be around for them to interview. Crucial evidence may be lost. All of this can be averted if a task force is formed as soon as possible after a series of crimes is linked.

When crimes are committed in different jurisdictions, the formation of a task force may be even more difficult. "Turf wars," rivalries, and egos may all contribute to losing precious investigative time. Even if one agency forms a task force, another agency that is involved may not cooperate or wish to share information. Decisions regarding who will lead the task force, how responsibilities will be delegated, financial considerations, etc., need to be made as swiftly as possible.

The resolution requires teamwork, a plan for action, and setting aside all personal issues to encourage a streamlined, competent investigation.

HOW MANY INVESTIGATORS SHOULD BE ASSIGNED?

The answer to this question requires the consideration of many factors, the least of which should be the following:

- The amount of evidence and other case-related materials (reports, documentation, tips and leads) that need investigating
- The number of cases being investigated
- The resources, including manpower and budget, of the investigating agency (a department with 600 detectives can likely contribute less manpower than a department with 6000)

WHO SHOULD BE ASSIGNED?

Supervisors need to look for investigators who are critical thinkers as well as hard workers. Investigators who work methodically and have an open mind can be a great asset to a task force.

Regarding experience—although having the appropriate level of experience can be an important consideration, it should not be the only requirement for assignment to a task force. An experienced investigator can still be a poor investigator. Experience means nothing if an investigator has performed poorly for 20 years.

If the case encompasses a crime, or a particular type of criminal behavior, that would ordinarily be investigated by a specialty unit (sex crime, robbery, homicide, bomb squad, juvenile crimes, etc.), then a representative from one of those units should be assigned to the task force. These investigators bring with them specialized insight and experience in their particular field.

When the crime is a sexual homicide, then homicide and sex-crime investigators should work side by side. Sex-crime investigators may not have much experience working homicides and dealing with crimes in which the victim is dead and, likewise, homicide detectives may not have much experience dealing with the dynamics of sexual assault and motives of sexual offenders. We get a more effective investigation when we pool individual talents.

LEAD INVESTIGATORS

There can be only one leader. Ideally, the lead investigator should have the most knowledge about the case, a strong background in working with the criminal behaviors involved in the case, and a good relationship with the victims or witnesses. A good relationship with a victim or witness can be invaluable when it comes time to show photos, conduct line-ups, or go to trial. And there is no one better suited to advise the supervisor in charge of the case than the most knowledgeable investigator. The investigator who has this knowledge and relationship with the victim or witness does no good sitting on the sidelines.

TASK FORCE MEETINGS

An initial task force meeting should be held as soon as possible after all assigned detectives are gathered together. This meeting should be run by a supervisory officer who has full knowledge of all the details of the case up until this point. This supervisor can give an overview of the incident(s) and all investigative work done to date. Detectives who have completed some of the investigative duties can explain to everyone in the task force what has been done in the case; this brings everyone up to speed. The crime-scene photographs should be made available to all assigned detectives so they can familiarize themselves with the scene details. This is a crucial point because it gives all task force members the knowledge they need when interviewing potential suspects and witnesses in the field. All assignments can be disseminated during this initial meeting (as well as at following meetings).

The initial meeting may be the most important gathering of assigned detectives. It is at this meeting that everyone is put on the same page as far as the investigation goes.

Follow-up meetings should be held at least twice daily. This allows detectives working different shifts to update each other on the progress of the investigation. When possible, each detective assigned should speak about what actions he or she has taken during the shift. The supervisor who conducts these meetings should discuss any questions or comments that the detectives have and clear up any misunderstandings or problems.

Charts and graphs can be used effectively to inform investigators about important information. A timeline of the victim's last 24 hours as well as victim and witness statements related to this 24-hour period should be charted and displayed for all assigned investigators. An evidence chart tracking all evidence related to the case can be very valuable to investigators. First, it gives everyone a clear picture of what was collected at the scene or scenes. Second, it helps investigators and supervisors keep track of all evidence and is especially useful at the time of trial. A chart showing a synopsis of each case being investigated should be displayed. This chart can include things such as day, date, time, and location of incident, as well as victim pedigree, offender description, weapon used, words spoken, sex acts committed, and a breakdown of the details of the crime. These charts and graphs will help keep everyone involved informed and up to date. Information sharing is the main concern here.

All of these actions promote information sharing and teamwork. The teamwork concept is a very important aspect regarding the success of a task force. Anything that degrades teamwork, or bottlenecks information, should be avoided. For example, all too often a clique of investigators who know everything about the investigation will develop. They may withhold information, intentionally or not, leaving investigators on the outside who have scant information about the investigation. Utilizing the methods described earlier can help eliminate these cliques by treating everyone involved as an important part of the team.

PITFALLS

This section will detail some of the major pitfalls in task force management. This is by no means an all-inclusive list and is largely a product of the experiences of this detective:

1. Very often there are "*too many chiefs and not enough Indians.*" These multiple "chiefs" may attempt to micromanage a task force or investigative effort. This is cited time and time again by investigators as the **number one pitfall** of a major case investigation.
2. *Supervisors with no organizational skills* who find themselves sinking rapidly amid a pile of information. Supervisors in charge of the task force investigation must be well educated in the management of a major case task force. Ideally, an experienced supervisor will head the task force from the start to eliminate any problems caused by information overload. An experienced supervisor, however, is not always the answer to the problem.
3. *Supervisor apathy.* The task force supervisor should maintain his own interest in the case and encourage his investigators to do the same. If the supervisor in charge has lost interest in the case, then ultimately, so will his subordinates. This can be avoided by holding regular meetings as well as simply talking with individual investigators about the case. Leadership, charisma, and the ability to instill investigators with the confidence that what they are doing is valued are key.
4. *The need for a quick fix.* Not all task forces result in immediate fixes. Sometimes these investigations can take months and even years. Investigative confidence can deteriorate. Task force members and supervisors need to understand that most major cases are solved by a combination of luck and sound police work.

   For example: A composite sketch is prepared at the investigator's request. A citizen sees the composite printed in the newspaper, realizes it looks like an acquaintance, and calls the information in to the hotline. A suspect is developed and arrested. All well and good.

But what about the cases where nothing has worked? Sound police work has been employed but luck is not forthcoming. This is where the problems start. Some investigators, and supervisors, will now wait around for that lucky break. The investigation stalls and disinterest follows. Investigators assigned to prolonged investigations must realize that stubborn cases can be solved, even after many years. What it takes is endurance, constancy, deliberation, and hard work.

What it may also take is willingness on the part of investigators to try innovative investigative tools and methods, such as those described later in this appendix.

TIPS AND LEADS

Here are some of the common tip and lead sources.

LAW ENFORCEMENT

Many times fellow law enforcement officers, both local and from outside agencies, will call in with information about prior cases, current cases, persons they have arrested in the past, and so on.

THE PUBLIC

The nature and reliability of tips from the public vary widely. They can range from a caller who saw a lookalike of the suspect 2 years ago on a bus traveling downtown, to a caller who states that the suspect is her brother. Callers who state that the offender is their brother, sister, relative, or significant other should be given priority. Detectives need to use their judgement here and prioritize.

PSYCHICS

Quite often psychics will call to offer investigators assistance. Their motivations can vary from self-promotion to a heartfelt belief that they can help. Some will give specific information about the suspect's whereabouts, name, and past. Some will ask to visit the crime scene prior to providing information.

The use of a psychic to aid the investigation will most often lead to a wild goose chase and a waste of valuable investigative resources and time. If a psychic demonstrates knowledge of a case that was not obtained through the media or through casual conversation with investigators (watch out for this—they can be very tricky), then they should be investigated for relationships with potential suspects and as potential suspects themselves. All psychics should be viewed with suspicion by investigators.

THE MEDIA

This is another source of information where the motivations can vary from the quest for a good story to a real desire to assist the police. There are times when the media will provide "witnesses" for the police to interview as a smokescreen to get inside details of the investigation. This does not happen often, but investigators should be aware that it occurs. Investigators usually know which reporters are honest and mean well, and information received from those individuals should be given priority.

In any case, the task force should determine whether it wants to develop a healthy relationship with the media or no relationship at all. Sometimes the most effective task force is the one that is not made public. Task forces that are merely a public relations venture should not be ventured into at all.

This is just an overview of the types of tips and leads that may be channeled into an investigation. Since it is not always possible to follow up on all tips and leads the moment they are received, investigators must be able to prioritize them and decide which can wait and which need to be investigated immediately. Developing competent mechanisms for prioritizing information is important, but do not forget that *all* tips and leads should be investigated to their conclusion.

Often, there is a desire to fit incoming tips and leads into case theories developed by investigators. This can cause tips and leads that do not fit those theories to be given less priority than others, or to be completely disregarded. Investigators must remain objective throughout the investigation and treat nothing as trivial.

PROCESSING TIPS AND LEADS

A vast number of leads can come in at one time, and the task force can be overloaded with information. The ideal answer to this problem is a computerized case management system that can process all tips and leads and cross reference other databases such as those that include motor vehicles witnessed in the area of the crime, persons stopped and questioned, and criminal record files. This can enable investigators to ascertain which suspects turn up on more than one database and allow them to prioritize these suspects. The system can also allow tracking of tips and leads by keeping a record of which investigators are assigned and what work they have done. There are several computer programs available that are custom-made to manage major case information.

Although a computerized major case management system is a great asset to an investigation, there are other ways to manage information without one. Simple database programs are available that have the capability to search for entered information. The only drawback with such a system is that many times there is no cross-reference capability.

The reality of the situation is that many departments still handle incoming information without the aid of computer technology. Tips can be entered on tip/lead sheets and assigned unique identifying numbers (usually sequential) so that they can be logged and tracked. If this is the case, then one person, preferably a supervisor, should be in charge of all incoming tips and leads. This supervisor should have the responsibility for assigning the tips and leads and for making sure that all of these are followed up on and investigated fully. It is best to have every investigator informed of every tip and lead, but realistically this may not be possible. The supervisor in charge of tips and leads will have knowledge of all incoming tips and leads and can determine the priority of these prior to assigning them.

The task force should have a separate telephone line assigned solely for incoming tips. This telephone number can be distributed to the public through the media as well as informational posters and fliers. A member of the task force should be assigned to man this telephone at all times. If the telephone will be unmanned during the night, then an answering machine should be in place to record any messages left during this period. If the hotline telephone number is changed for any reason, then call forwarding from the old number should be arranged. Investigators assigned to this telephone should be advised to take the information first and then worry about the caller's name, address, and phone number. Callers may be leery about giving personal information and may hang up if this is the first thing they are asked. Preprinted tip/lead forms should include space for all pertinent information about the incoming tip and the caller. This preprinted form will ensure that investigators get all of the important information necessary.

THE MEDIA

Used properly, the media can assist the task force in getting important information to the public. This can include airing the case on a "most wanted" type show or featuring the case in the local newspaper. However, there should always be certain important facts that are withheld from the media. These include the fact that biological evidence containing DNA was recovered, signature elements of the offender, and the exact nature of items taken from the victim (as well as a host of other detailed facts). It is the duty of the task force supervisor to ensure that these facts are withheld from the media. When these details leak out to the media, major problems should be expected. An offender may change his modus operandi, start using a condom if he was not using one before, cover his face, or destroy evidence such as souvenirs and trophies taken from the victims.

COMPOSITE SKETCHES

The use of composite sketches in major investigations has become commonplace. In most cases, if a victim or witness has observed the suspect, then a sketch is prepared. This happens even when the witness's recollection may be poor. A task force must use good judgement when deciding whether to have a sketch prepared, because a poor sketch can steer an investigation off course. There have been many cases where the composite sketch looked nothing like the offender. The public, investigators, and patrol officers usually put a lot of emphasis on the composite sketch of an offender. If the sketch looks nothing like the offender, then all of them end up chasing a "red herring."

Sketch artists work in different ways. Some may show a victim photographs of faces and ask the victim to pick out facial features that are similar to those of the attacker. This method can severely distort and taint fragile recall. Others do not use photographs but use memory enhancement interviewing techniques.

It is best to use the services of a forensic artist who is schooled in memory, perception, and *posttraumatic stress disorder (PTSD)*. These artists, sometimes called facial identification specialists, do not use mug shots or facial catalogs, but instead rely on interviewing techniques that draw from the eyewitness's actual recall without implanting new information. Memory can be influenced and distorted very easily. For this reason, having the victim view numerous mug shots is discouraged by these artists. This may mean limiting victim viewing to 6 or 12 photographs and then only when a good suspect is developed. This may be difficult for many investigators who are hounded by supervisors to show as many photos as possible. It may also be difficult because investigators and supervisors still do not understand the importance of what these forensic identification specialists are speaking about here. The "old school" still prevails when it comes to composite sketches and mug shot viewing. We need to change this by educating investigators and supervisors.

CRIME-SCENE PERSONNEL

The task force must maintain a good working relationship with the crime-scene and crime-lab personnel. This provides the task force with two-way information roads regarding how available evidence is being documented, collected, and tested, and the results of any analysis. The same should be true of the ME/coroner's office. To create these information roads, a member of both the ME/coroner's office and the crime lab should be assigned to the case and to the task force. That way one person in each agency can be relied upon by the task force to act as both an information conduit and a diplomat.

PATROL OFFICERS

Patrol officers often play an important role in the apprehension of the suspects sought by a task force, by virtue of performing routine stops and being familiar with the MOs of criminals operating in the area. They work in the neighborhoods and on the streets where these crimes are committed. They know the people who live and work there. They also know the people who commit crimes there. Patrol officers often have a wealth of information to share, and investigators would be wise to develop a working relationship with them.

At the very least, a representative of the task force should address the officers at roll call every day. The shift addressed will depend on the time the crimes are being committed. Keep the officers updated about the case and answer any questions they may have. Make them feel that they are part of the team. Advise them about what they should say and what they should not say to suspects. Give them the task force's telephone number in case they develop information that might relate to the case.

The task force may also wish to consider creating *daily confidential bulletins* (DCBs) for patrol officers, with suspect information, relevant photos, and pertinent case developments. Basically, the DCB gives patrol officers something in-hand to reference when out on their patrol, making them a valuable part of the task force's arsenal.

THE DISTRICT ATTORNEY

The task force investigators must always keep in mind that a case is not over after an arrest is effected. Investigators are responsible for assisting in the prosecution of the offender.

Working closely with the district attorney's office allows investigators easy access to legal advice to ensure that nothing the task force does jeopardizes the case at trial. This type of relationship with the district attorney can act as a sort of early warning system. The district attorney's office can also assist in the preparation of search warrants when the time comes. This suggestion in no way implies that the district attorney's office will take over the investigation or direct it in any way. The district attorney's role here is to assist with the investigation, not to usurp law enforcement's role as the lead agency.

It is not advised that the district attorney's office have hands-on control of the task force's day-to-day activities (to prevent micromanaging). It is recommended that their office assign someone to the task force as an advisor from the very beginning, to offer educated counsel, advice, and support when necessary.

THE COMMUNITY

Community groups may become more active when a major crime or crimes has been committed in their neighborhood. Most of these groups mean well, but if left undirected they can cause damage to an investigation. If these groups feel law enforcement is not responsive to their needs (whether this is real or imagined) then they may start using the media to attack law enforcement. This takes the focus off the offender and puts it on the task force.

This problem can be addressed by developing a relationship with these community groups. They should be contacted by the task force and reassured that a full-scale investigation is being conducted. These community groups, when given direction, can assist a task force immensely. They can distribute informational fliers and composite sketches, arrange to hold public meetings where the case is discussed, focus the media on the case, and offer a reward for the apprehension and conviction of the offender. Innovative investigators will think of many other ways to include these community groups in the investigation.

THE VICTIM

When task force detectives are dispatched to a fresh crime scene in which there is a living victim, a task force investigator (preferably the lead investigator) should interview the victim as soon as possible. This is not to say that patrol officers should not get the vital information that they need to dispatch to the other officers on the streets (such as an offender description, direction of travel, weapons used), but that the detailed interview should be conducted by a task force investigator.

There is no need for a supervisor of any rank to interview the victim. From time to time supervisors, sometimes of high rank, try to get involved in an investigation by interviewing the victim. Most have good intentions, but all are misdirected. This is an example of micromanagement at its worst.

If a victim complains about a specific investigator, then it would be prudent for the supervisor to interview the victim about that complaint. But that is not what we are talking about here. We are talking about supervisors who get in the way at the scene by attempting to interview victims. The worst part is that many of these supervisors have not had much experience doing detailed interviews of victims. The bottom line is that a good supervisor does what they are supposed to do—supervise.

Investigators who are dealing with living victims have many responsibilities. A wise investigator once said that a victim is like a glass of water; every time you show photos, conduct line-ups, reinterview, or utilize the victim in some manner, you take a drop of water out of that glass. A good investigator will temper his use of the victim so the glass will not end up empty at the time of trial.

One or two investigators—preferably the lead investigator(s)—should be assigned as a contact person for the victim. The same investigator should contact the victim when the need arises. Victims tend to react negatively when a barrage of different investigators contacts them.

Imagine how you or one of your loved ones would feel if you were contacted by a different investigator every time the police needed your assistance. A strange voice (and face) can be disturbing to a victim who was violently assaulted—even if it is a police investigator. The same goes for a deceased victim's family, or a witness.

Victims should be notified, when possible, of all planned media events surrounding the case. Victims can feel "left out" of the investigation when they are not updated and have to rely on the media for information.

Investigators should schedule contacts with the victim or victims. A task force is a team, and the living victim is the most important part of that team. It is imperative that victims be kept updated as to the progress of the investigation. This can be done weekly at the start of the investigation and then extended to monthly or longer if the investigation becomes very lengthy. The investigators should confer with the victim and ascertain how often they would like to be contacted. This contact plan does not imply that investigators must divulge every detail to the victim. Obviously, there are details that the victim cannot know about for legal purposes (i.e., taint identification, trial testimony, etc.), and if the investigator has any questions about this they should contact the district attorney's office representative assigned to prosecute the case.

THE BEHAVIORAL-ORIENTED INTERVIEW

A task force responsible for investigating a sexual assault case should ensure that every victim is asked the 14 questions contained in the *Behavioral-Oriented Interview*. Retired FBI Supervisory Special Agent Roy Hazelwood developed these questions as a way to ascertain the offender's motivations and thereby make it easier to accurately profile the offender. They also assist in linking cases through behavior. The answers to these questions can be invaluable to an investigation and will assist in the preparation of both a criminal and a geographic profile. It is recommended that the Behavioral-Oriented Interview be mandatory for all stranger sexual assault cases whether part of a major case or not.

Victim interviews conducted by police officers and investigators can range from the highly detailed account to the one-paragraph narrative that says nothing. The Behavioral-Oriented Interview gives structure to an interview and allows the victim to answer some very important questions. If the victim has not been asked the behavioral-oriented questions, it might be a good idea to give them a written copy so they can answer them at their own pace in private. All sex-crime investigators are urged to incorporate the behavioral-oriented questions in their victim interviews. This way when cases are linked and a task force is formed, investigators will not have to go back and ask these questions at a time when the victim's memories may have faded.

UTILIZING PSYCHOLOGICAL AND GEOGRAPHIC PROFILES

Psychological and geographic profiles may be a very useful tool for a task force when utilized properly.

Before employing any type of profiler, investigators should ask these important questions:

- Is the profiler familiar with or does he have experience with the type of case being investigated?
- What is the exact method he uses to come to his conclusions?
- What case materials are required?
- Will he visit the crime scene or scenes (if a crime scene exists)?
- Will investigative suggestions be included in the profile?

Be very wary of any profiler:

- Who is uninterested in or unfamiliar with the importance of using physical evidence to establish offender behavior (who will just take the task force's word for it, or who offers a complete profile based on things read in the newspaper)
- Who shows no interest in visiting the crime scenes
- Whose profile seems to be taken directly from Organized/Disorganized, or one of the typologies
- Who refuses to write his profile down
- Whose profile is less than two pages long

- Whose geographical profile is not based on a sound psychological profile prepared by a competent psychological profiler (many geo-profilers will attempt, inappropriately, to construct one themselves)
- Whose sole purpose in soliciting a profile appears to be for profit, or personal gain and recognition

In any case, it is imperative that the profile, whether psychological or geographical, be prepared as a written report that can be perused by task force members.

> "Casual, verbal advice appears to make little impact and to be easily forgotten."
> —Det. Chief Inspector Gary Copson, London Metro Police, 1995.

Another important component of any profile is investigative suggestions. A good profile will include investigative suggestions for the task force to follow up on. This may include areas to recanvass, persons to reinterview, and types of crimes to focus on, as well as many other suggestions. The important thing to remember here is that these suggestions should be followed up and investigated to the fullest.

When a profile is prepared, the task force should be prepared to meet with the profiler. At this meeting any and all questions and concerns of the detectives can be addressed. It is common for detectives to have many questions about psychological and geographic profiling, and if these questions go unanswered it could pose a danger of hindering an investigation—hence the meeting with the profiler. Investigators should never be hesitant about questioning a profile itself, or a profiler regarding their methods or conclusions.

The results of a psychological and geographic profile should be treated as a tool that the task force can use to develop investigative strategies to solve the crime. The results are not written in stone, and suspects should not be eliminated, or accused for that matter, based on a psychological or geographic profile alone. In the same respect, suspects and tips can be prioritized based on the profile. Prioritization can be very useful when tips are inundating the task force.

SUBJECT INDEX

NAME INDEX

Marchbanks, P.J., 135, 144

Markovchick, V., 135, 136, 145

Marshall, W.L., 17, 21, 22

Martin, L.D., 98

Mayer, J., 150, 151, 164

Mazur, Mary Ann, 237

McAuslan, P., 150, 163

McClintock, T., 177, 208

McCormick, Professor, 271

McCoy, C., xi, xii, xvii

McDowell, C., 257, 258, 373, 385

McDowell, Charles P., 239, 240, 241, 242

McGrath, Michael, xxxiv, 32, 148, 164, 369, 373, 374, 385

McGrath, R.J., 106, 118

McHugh, Dennis, 249

Melnikoff, Arnold, 32, 33

Melville, Herman, 65

Mendelsohn, Benjamin, 217

Mercy, J.A., 135, 144

Miller, B., 249, 257

Miller, Henry, 23

Miller, J.V., 131, 144

Mills, Stanley, 216

Mobly, Timothy, 212, 213

Monegan, Walt, xiii

Monteleone, J., 227

Montez, Michael, 297, 298

Moore, C.M., 133, 145

Moore, M., 34, 40

Moore, Michael, 53

Moran, Robin, xi, xvii, 8

Motro, U., 82, 91

Mozani, A., 144

Murphy, W., 129, 145

Murrin, M., 14, 22

N

Nam, Jennifer, 289, 290

Nash, Ogden, 147

Negrusz, A., 133, 145, 150, 151, 164

Negruz, A., 159, 163, 164

Netzel, L., 131, 144

Newman, Beth, 54

Nickel, J., 176, 208

Nickel, Lesley, 254

Nickel, Lisa, 254

Norris, Natasha, 56

Novoselski, Y., 82, 91

O

O'Brien, C., 125, 145

O'Connell, J., 45, 63, 65, 91, 111, 118, 227, 234, 261, 300

Ofshe, Richard, 103, 104, 118

O'Gorman, E., 135, 143

O'Hara, C., 275, 299

O'Hara, Charles E., 65, 71, 75, 91, 111, 118

Olshaker, M., 152, 163

Orwell, George, 1

Ota, Seiichi, 9

Ove, T., 253, 258

Owen, D., 176, 208

Oz, C., 82, 91

P

Palaparthy, R., 133, 145

Palenek, S., 40

Palmer, C., 8, 13, 22, 235, 244, 258

Paolinetti, L., 132, 144

Park, John J., 288, 289, 290, 292, 294, 299

Parr, Mark Allan, 340, 342, 351

Pasqualone, G.A., 134, 145

Pate, Jude, 56

Peck, R., 137, 145, 244, 257, 346, 351

Pehote, Jackie, 214, 215, 216

Penrod, S.J., 338, 340, 351

Petrak, J., 135, 145

Pex, J., 78, 91

Pharm, B., 133

Pitchfork, Colin, 176

Pitsch, M., 32, 40

Pittel, Stephen M., xxxiv, 147

Poiser, K.R., 133, 145

Poklis, A., 150, 151, 164

Prentsky, R.A., 276, 300

Q

Quickenden, T.I., 90